Women, Knowledge,
and Reality

Women, Knowledge, and Reality:

Explorations in Feminist Philosophy

Ann Garry

Marilyn Pearsall

Boston
UNWIN HYMAN
London   Sydney   Wellington

Unwin Hyman, Inc.
8 Winchester Place, Winchester, Mass. 01890, USA

Published by the Academic Division of
Unwin Hyman Ltd
15/17 Broadwick Street, London W1V 1FP, UK

Allen & Unwin (Australia) Ltd,
8 Napier Street, North Sydney, NSW 2060, Australia

Allen & Unwin (New Zealand) Ltd in association with the
Port Nicholson Press Ltd,
Compusales Building, 75 Ghuznee Street, Wellington 1, New Zealand

First published in 1989.
Second impression 1990

Library of Congress Cataloging-in-Publication Data

Women, knowledge, and reality:
Ann Garry, Marilyn Pearsall.
  p.   cm.
Includes bibliographies and index.
ISBN 0–04–445221–7. — ISBN 0–04–445222–5 (pbk.)
1. Feminism—Philosophy. 2. Philosophy. 3. Knowledge, Theory of.
I. Garry, Ann. II. Pearsall, Marilyn.
HQ1154.W88384   1989
305.4'2'01—dc 19   89–5456
                                                               CIP

British Library Cataloguing in Publication Data

Women, knowledge and reality:
1. Feminism. Philosophical perspectives
I. Garry, Ann   II. Pearsall, Marilyn
305.4'2
ISBN 0–04–445221–7
ISBN 0–04–445222–5 pbk

Typeset in 10 on 12 point Palatino by Nene Phototypesetters Ltd,
and printed in Great Britain by the University Press, Cambridge

Cover art: Copyright © 1984 by The Metropolitan Museum of Art.
L'Arlesienne by Vincent Van Gogh. The Metropolitan Museum
of Art, Bequest of Sam A. Lewisohn, 1951. (51.112.3)

For our sons
as well as our daughters.

Contents

Preface   page   ix

Introduction   xi

Part I   Methodology   1

1   A Paradigm of Philosophy: The Adversary Method
    Janice Moulton   5
2   Philosophical Methodology and Feminist Methodology:
    Are They Compatible?   *Susan Sherwin*   21
3   Women Who Beget Women Must Thwart Major Sophisms
    Jeffner Allen   37

Part II   Metaphysics   47

4   A Different Reality: Feminist Ontology   *Caroline Whitbeck*   51
5   To See and Be Seen: The Politics of Reality   *Marilyn Frye*   77
6   A Feminist Aspect Theory of the Self   *Ann Ferguson*   93

Part III   Theory of Knowledge   109

7   The Man of Reason   *Genevieve Lloyd*   111
8   Love and Knowledge: Emotion in Feminist Epistemology
    Alison M. Jaggar   129
9   Experience, Knowledge, and Responsibility   *Lorraine Code*   157

Part IV   Philosophy of Science   173

10   Feminism and Science   *Evelyn Fox Keller*   175
11   Feminist Justificatory Strategies   *Sandra Harding*   189
12   Can There Be a Feminist Science?   *Helen E. Longino*   203

Part V   Philosophy of Language   page 217

13   The Myth of the Neutral "Man"   *Janice Moulton*   219
14   The Voice of the Serpent: French Feminism and Philosophy
     of Language   *Andrea Nye*   233

Part VI   Philosophy of Mind   251

15   Gendering the Body: Beauvoir's Philosophical Contribution
     Judith Butler   253
16   Anger and Insubordination   *Elizabeth V. Spelman*   263
17   Playfulness, "World"-Traveling, and Loving Perception
     María Lugones   275

Part VII   Philosophy of Religion   291

18   Liberating Philosophy: An End to the Dichotomy of Spirit
     and Matter   *Hilde Hein*   293
19   While Love is Unfashionable: Ethical Implications of Black
     Spirituality and Sexuality   *Toinette M. Eugene*   313
20   Anarchic Thinking: Breaking the Hold of Monotheistic
     Ideology on Feminist Philosophy   *Gail Stenstad*   331

     List of Contributors   341

     Index   345

Preface

We hope that this collection will be useful to students and instructors in philosophy and women's studies as well as to members of the larger community who wonder what on earth feminist metaphysics and theory of knowledge could be. We have included a range of articles suitable for both introductory courses in philosophy and upper-division courses in philosophy and in feminist theory.

The scope of the papers is limited to Western philosophical traditions, focusing on contemporary issues. Although many of the authors use historical figures in their discussions, only Lloyd's piece on Descartes has an historical focus. We have organized the collection into parts titled by traditional fields of philosophy: methodology, metaphysics, theory of knowledge, philosophy of science, philosophy of language, philosophy of mind, and philosophy of religion. There might be feminists who find it strange that we have used traditional names for philosophical fields—names that have been used at times to separate questions that should be integrated, names that bias a field toward male-identified questions. We agree that these are serious problems. We retained the traditional names as signposts to help beginners find a connection between feminist thinking and traditional philosophy and to be able to see how feminist philosophers are revolutionizing the fields of philosophy themselves.

We have excluded papers that focus primarily on ethics, social and political philosophy, and other fields of value theory because most other collections of feminist philosophy tend to emphasize questions of values (including co-editor Pearsall's *Women and Values*). We see a need for an up-to-date collection that recognizes the value component that underlies all feminist philosophy, yet puts the major emphasis on questions in metaphysics and theory of knowledge. Many of the authors explicitly relate their subject matter to ethics and other value questions (for example, Whitbeck, Ferguson, Lloyd, Jaggar, Code, Spelman, Lugones, and Eugene). Instructors whose courses include topics in ethics might consider assigning some of these papers.

In addition to the brief general introduction, each part of the book contains an introduction relating feminist philosophy to traditional

philosophical questions in that field. We placed the field-specific
introductions at the beginning of each part with the hope of catching
students' attention. However, at the risk of sounding like professors on
the first day of class, we strongly urge you to read through all the
introductions at once for an overview of the book and of these fields of
feminist philosophy.

A few words for those philosophy instructors integrating feminist
philosophy into their traditional upper-division courses. It will come as
no surprise that there are many more articles on metaphysics than have
been placed in the chapter with that title. In particular, the authors in
the chapters on philosophy of mind and religion discuss metaphysical
questions. Similarly, all the authors in philosophy of science are writing
on epistemological issues, as are Lugones in philosophy of mind,
Stenstad in philosophy of religion, and so on.

Instructors organizing courses around topics or themes, whether
in women's studies or philosophy, might consider the following
examples: Nye, Lugones and Stenstad on women's voice; Frye, Allen
and Code on women's experience; Butler and Eugene on sexuality and
the body; Jaggar and Spelman on emotions; Nye, Allen and Stenstad on
French feminism; Sherwin, Allen and Harding on feminist method;
Nye, Allen and Harding on postmodernism. (Note that there are
introductory comments on postmodernism in the chapter on methodology.)

Thanks go to many people for their suggestions or support for our
collective project. Lisa Freeman, our editor at Unwin Hyman, Lauren
Osborne, editorial assistant, and Peggy McMahon, production coordi-
nator, Jeffner Allen, Sharon Bishop, Susan Bordo, Ricardo Gómez,
Sandra Harding, Rosemarie Tong, Terry Winant, and our families. We
especially want to thank the authors who were willing to revise their
papers for this volume.

Introduction

Feminist philosophy has two sources—the feminist movement and traditional academic philosophy. The feminist movement has opened our eyes to the deep and varied ways in which the ideals and institutions of our culture oppress women. In addition to providing a devastating critique of male-dominated society, feminists have affirmed the positive value of women's experience. Academic feminist philosophers build upon and contribute to the insights and work of the women's movement. Feminist philosophers examine and criticize the assumptions and presuppositions of the ideals and institutions of our culture. We write about a wide range of topics, from the most overtly political issues such as job discrimination, rape, and the use of sexist language, to the subtle underlying metaphysical and epistemological assumptions of our culture and our philosophical traditions.

Feminist philosophy, especially in its academic forms, also has its roots in traditional philosophy. Although traditional philosophy has been shaped by men who have taken their experiences, their values, and their views of the world as the standard for all human beings, it is in the philosophical traditions of these men that academic feminist philosophers were educated. Even today the philosophical methods we are taught to practice and the subject matter we are taught to consider appropriate for philosophy are by and large not feminist; they are the traditional male methods, fields, and topics of philosophy.

As feminist philosophers incorporated insights from our political practice into our academic work, we became aware that the androcentric character of traditional philosophy made it limited, biased, and liable to oppressive use. This is true of theories not only in social and political philosophy and ethics, but also in metaphysics and theory of knowledge, the fields some consider the core of the western philosophical tradition. Although there is too much diversity in philosophy to permit easy generalization, we can say that feminist philosophers call attention to the themes pervading the various strands of western male thought that have led to distortion and bias in philosophy itself and have lent themselves readily to the oppression of women and other subordinate groups.

For example, consider two philosophical themes that have been linked to attempts to justify the oppression of women: "value-hierarchical" thinking and "normative dualism."[1] When philosophers routinely perceive mere difference or diversity as ordered in a hierarchical way, they are using "value-hierarchical" thinking. They give greater value to what is seen as higher (for example, men, culture, minds, or reason) and lesser value to what is seen as lower (for example, women, nature, bodies, or emotion). This valuation lends itself readily to what Karen Warren calls the "logic of domination"—an attempt to justify the subordination of the group of "lower value" by the dominant group of "higher value."

Like value-hierarchical thinking, "normative dualism" also is exhibited when philosophers look at mind/body, reason/emotion, man/woman, and so on. Philosophers inclined to normative dualism will interpret things that may be complementary or even inseparable in terms of exclusive disjunctions (either/or, but not both). For example, something mental may be categorized under "reason" or "emotion" but not under both. They then value one disjunct more highly than the other, for example, reason over emotion, or mind over body. The thing of lesser value is excluded from the thing of higher value. As in the case of value-hierarchical thinking, such a valuation lends itself to an attempt to justify domination of what is less valued.

The feminist critique of traditional philosophy is an important ongoing project. The papers in this collection illustrate the ways in which feminist philosophers spell out and analyze the limitations, biases, or misogyny of particular traditions, philosophers, or fields of philosophy. The authors detail the ways in which traditional philosophers have specifically undermined women's values, made our experiences invisible, and weakened philosophy. As one can see by the examples in the preceding two paragraphs, feminist criticism of philosophy is no mere tinkering around the edges; it goes to the heart of philosophy—the central presuppositions and key concepts of the discipline.

There is more to feminist philosophy than the continuing critique and analysis of what has gone wrong. Feminist philosophers are trying in many diverse ways to reconstruct philosophy. We want to redefine the methods and subject matter of philosophy in ways that value women's experiences and enable women to move from the position of object to positions of subject, of knower, and of agent. We want to redeem philosophy, to "get philosophy right," recognizing the difficulty in even thinking about what standards, if any, there are for doing it "right."

In trying to reconstruct philosophy, one of the hardest questions is what can be salvaged from traditional philosophy and what should be rejected. While it would be foolish to disregard valuable insights of male philosophers, one cannot determine quickly what, if anything, is free from androcentric assumptions. This is an ongoing process that requires feminist philosophers to build upon each other's contributions, for what appears to be gender neutral one year may look obviously androcentric the next. Feminist philosophers realize that reconstructing or "re-visioning" philosophy is a very large, open-ended project.

Although feminist philosophers take a variety of positions on the best approach to problems, there is much we share. First of all, we are feminists. As feminists we seek to understand and explain women's experiences and women's practices; we see women's subordination as systemic and structural; we work toward the liberation of women. Because feminist philosophy is a philosophy of liberation we seek to find commonalities with others at home and around the world working toward liberation, for example, from racial or class oppression.

Feminist philosophers also participate in a larger interdisciplinary community of feminist scholars. This community is usually called women's studies, or less frequently gender studies or feminist studies. Feminist philosophers along with feminists from other backgrounds are making important contributions to women's studies by thinking about fundamental questions in feminist theory.

Recognizing that feminist philosophers share the joint heritage of feminism and philosophy and are at the same time individuals with diverse points of view, what can one expect to find when reading feminist philosophy? To answer this question it is best merely to describe some of the characteristic features of feminist philosophy, for it would be contrary to the spirit of feminist inquiry to try to delineate rigid boundaries of, or criteria for, feminist philosophy.

To start with, feminist philosophers are saying in a multiplicity of ways that gender matters—even in very abstract theories in which one might not suspect that it would. Because gender matters, we are prone to resist easy moves to speak in a "neutral," nongendered voice. We are also likely to focus on the ways in which values underlie and permeate theories; again, this is not just in fields one might expect, such as political philosophy, but also in the most fundamental questions of metaphysics and theory of knowledge.

Feminist philosophers also strive to connect theories to everyday experience. We ask fundamental philosophical questions about life, meaning, value, and being. Yet we try to ensure that our answers are not merely about some abstract "meaning of life," but are informed by the meaning of real lives and experiences. We place high value on differing experiences of diverse women, whether diverse in class, race, ethnicity, sexual orientation, age, or able-bodiedness. We try to be especially attentive to the ways in which the oppressions associated with these categories, e.g., racism or class oppression, intersect with sexism. The diversity among women has led to interesting controversies about the possibility of speaking in a "woman's voice" or a "feminist voice."

In addition, feminist philosophers often seek to integrate what is valuable to their work from different disciplines, from several traditions within a discipline, or from different fields of study within a discipline. For example, a feminist philosopher writing about the self might draw on anthropologists and poets as well as philosophers from more than one tradition; she might also call attention to the ways in which questions of value cannot be separated from metaphysical theories of the self. She might find that traditional styles of writing philosophy are too limiting; her style might be more personal or otherwise different from those of traditional philosophers.

This collection of papers represents some of the feminist philosophers writing in the areas that traditional philosophy has categorized as methodology, metaphysics, and theory of knowledge, as well as their subgroups: philosophy of science, philosophy of language, philosophy of mind, and philosophy of religion. The authors address a wide variety of topics within these fields and have diverse philosophical training, styles, backgrounds, and personal lives. The presentation of these essays helps to balance the absence of feminist perspectives in the philosophical literature. Taken together the essays exhibit some of the collective strength of feminist philosophy as well as an indication of its rich possibilities.

NOTE

1. Although a number of feminist philosophers have made similar points, our discussion of hierarchical thinking and normative dualism draws heavily on Karen J. Warren, "Critical Thinking and Feminism," *Informal Logic* 10, 1 (Winter 1988).

Part I

Methodology

One cannot speak about philosophical method as if all philosophers agree that there is one and only one method that is correct. There have been serious disagreements about the best or proper way to do philosophy throughout its history. There are both longstanding and recent philosophical traditions that have deeply ingrained methodological assumptions and practices. No tradition is immune from the probing of feminist philosophers. Among the fundamental questions feminist philosophers raise about philosophical method are (1) the extent to which the methods of philosophy presuppose or mesh with the dominant political ideology of the culture of its practitioners; (2) the extent to which philosophical methods ignore, obscure or deny the experiences of women; (3) whether or to what extent the methods of philosophy are compatible with the methods of feminist theory and feminism.

Feminist philosophers deny that a philosophical method can be completely free from ideological connection. For example, analytic philosophers often believe that their method is "neutral," "impartial," "objective," or free from ideology because they are merely analyzing language. Yet they have overlooked the important fact that our language itself is sexist; it embodies the concepts and conceptual schemes of the male-dominated ideology of its time. Feminist philosophers point out that to do philosophical analysis of language that raises no question about this male bias is not to be objective, neutral, or impartial, but is instead to affirm the male biased view of the world that is embodied in the language. Analogous feminist critiques can be made of other philosophical methods.

Some traditional philosophers also use their own particular preferred methods to exclude other approaches as not "real philosophy." One of the many harmful consequences of this exclusionary practice is that philosophy has lost the rich experiences of women. By ignoring feminist philosophy and more broadly feminist theory, traditional philosophers overlook the very theorists who are trying to understand and explain women's experiences and to show their relevance to previous theories.

Some particular styles of doing philosophy may be more problematic than others. Janice Moulton focuses on a style she calls the "adversary paradigm." In this paradigm opposing adversaries try to defend their positions against counterexamples produced by their opponent. Moulton points out some of the serious limitations and biases of this paradigm if it is considered the best (or only) way to do philosophy. She also links the adversary paradigm to the views of aggression and success commonly held in our culture.

Susan Sherwin directs our attention to a fundamental question: are feminist theoretical methods, which grow from feminist consciousness-raising, compatible with traditional philosophy at all? She argues that the two methods can be compatible, but only with significant efforts both from feminists and from traditional philosophers.

The final essay in this part concerns a feminist response to "postmodernism." The current controversy in philosophy and feminist theory over postmodernism is very sophisticated, for it presupposes an understanding of traditional philosophy and its postmodernist critics as well as of previous feminist philosophy. It is also difficult because the language and style of writing are often unfamiliar. Postmodernists reject much of traditional philosophy, for example, the quest for truth, rationality, objectivity, and essences, and the belief in stable self-identity. The postmodern project of "deconstruction" erodes claims of universality, replacing them with multiple historically rooted, fragmented, flexible, and diverse discourses.

Feminist philosophers share with postmodernists a deeply critical stance toward traditional philosophy. However, there is a tension within feminism about postmodernism. On the one hand, feminist philosophers concur with the postmodernists' rejection of the white male "grand narratives" of traditional philosophy; these are the very theories that have overlooked or denigrated women and have put women in the margins. On the other hand, postmodernism seems to undermine some important aspects of feminist theory as well. For, insofar as feminist theory is making universal claims about reality or about right and wrong, it, too, is in line for postmodernist deconstruction. In addition, postmodernists call into question the possibility of a gendered, stable subject—the self—which is a key feature of feminist theory and practice.

Feminist philosophers meet the challenge of postmodernism in diverse ways.[1] Some adopt a postmodernist stance themselves, some argue against it and many others struggle within their own thinking to resolve their mixed reactions to it. Jeffner Allen is in the last group. In her essay, she asks whether or not she can or would wish to enter the postmodern discourse. She responds by offering stories, tales. The first is metaphysical, the second is postmodern; they deal with the "difference" ascribed to women at the beginning of the modern era and at the beginning of the postmodern era. Finally, she tells her own tale of visiting the modernist and postmodernist worlds and of finding ways in which women can position themselves freely.

NOTE

1. See Linda Nicholson, ed., *Feminism/Postmodernism* (New York: Methuen/Routledge and Kegan Paul, 1989).

Chapter 1

A Paradigm of Philosophy: The Adversary Method

Janice Moulton

THE UNHAPPY CONFLATION OF AGGRESSION WITH SUCCESS

*I*t is frequently thought that there are attributes, or kinds of behavior, that it is good for one sex to have and bad for the other sex to have. Aggression is a particularly interesting example of such an attribute. This paper investigates and criticizes a model of philosophic methodology that accepts a positive view of aggressive behavior and uses it as a paradigm of philosophic reasoning. But before I turn to this paradigm, I want to challenge the broader view of aggression that permits it positive connotations.

Defined as "an offensive action or procedure, especially a culpable unprovoked overt hostile attack," aggression normally has well-deserved negative connotations. Perhaps a standard image of aggression is that of an animal in the wild trying to take over some other animal's territory or attacking it to eat it. In human contexts, aggression often invokes anger, uncontrolled rage, and belligerence.

However, this negative concept, when it is specifically connected to males *qua* males or to workers in certain professions (sales, management, law, philosophy, politics) often takes on positive associations. In a civilized society, physical aggression is likely to land one in a jail or a mental institution. But males and workers in certain professions are not required to physically attack or eat their customers and co-workers to be considered aggressive. In these contexts, aggression is thought to be related to more positive concepts such as power, activity, ambition, authority, competence, and effectiveness—concepts that are related to success in these professions. And exhibition of these positive concepts

Source: From *Discovering Reality*, ed. Sandra Harding and Merrill B. Hintikka (Dordrecht: Reidel, 1983), 149–164. Copyright © 1983 by Janice Moulton. Reprinted by permission of the author and of Kluwer Academic Publishers.

is considered evidence that one is, or has been, aggressive.

Aggression may have no causal bearing on competence, superiority, power, etc., but if many people believe aggressive behavior is a sign of these properties, then one may have to learn to behave aggressively in order to appear competent, to seem superior, and to gain or maintain power. This poses a dilemma for anyone who wants to have those positive qualities, but does not wish to engage in "culpable unprovoked overt hostile attacks."

Of reluctant aggressors, males have an advantage over females. For as members of the masculine gender, their aggression is thought to be "natural." Even if they do not engage in aggressive behavior, they can still be perceived as possessing that trait, inherently, as a disposition. And if they do behave aggressively, their behavior can be excused—after all, it's natural. Since women are not perceived as being dispositionally aggressive, it looks like they would have to behave aggressively in order to be thought aggressive. On the other hand, since women are not expected to be aggressive, we are much more likely to notice the slightest aggressive behavior on the part of a woman while ignoring more blatant examples by men just because they are not thought unusual. But when done by a female, it may be considered all the more unpleasant because it seems unnatural. Alternatively, it may be that a woman who exhibits competence, energy, ambition, etc. may be thought aggressive and therefore unnatural even without behaving aggressively. Since, as I shall argue, aggressive behavior is unlikely to win friends and influence people in the way that one would like, this presents a special problem for women.

Some feminists dismiss the sex distinction that views aggression in a female as a negative quality and then encourage females to behave aggressively in order to further their careers. I am going to, instead, question the assumption that aggression deserves association with more positive qualities. I think it is a mistake to suppose that an aggressive person is more likely to be energetic, effective, competent, powerful or successful and also a mistake to suppose that an energetic, effective, etc. person is therefore aggressive.

Even those who object to sex-roles stereotyping seldom balk specifically at the assumption that more aggressive people are better suited to "be the breadwinners and play the active role in the production of commodities of society," but only at the assumption that aggression is more natural to one sex than the other.[1] Robin Lakoff assumes that more aggressive speech is both more effective and typical of males, and objects to the socialization that forbids direct questions and assertions, devoid of polite phrases, in women's speech.[2] Lakoff recognizes that the speech she characterizes as women's speech is frequently used by male academics, but she still assumes that aggressive speech is more powerful and more effective. She does not see that polite, nonabrupt speech, full of hesitations and qualifiers can be a sign of great power and very effective in giving the impression of great thought and deliberation, or in getting one's listeners on one's side. Although polite, nonabrupt speech can be more effective and have more power than aggressive speech, the conceptual conflation of aggression with positive concepts has made this hard to remember.

Consider some professional occasions where aggression might be thought an asset. Aggression is often equated with energy, but one can be energetic and work hard without being hostile. It may seem that aggression is essential where there is competition, but people who just try to do their best, without deliberately trying to do in the other guy may do equally well or even better. Feelings of hostility may be distracting, and a goal of defeating another may sidetrack one to the advantage of a third party. Even those who think it is a dog-eat-dog world can see that there is a difference between acting to defeat or undermine competition and acting aggressively towards that competition. Especially if one's success depends on other parties, it is likely to be far wiser to *appear* friendly than to engage in aggressive behavior. And in professions where mobility is a sign of success, today's competitors may be tomorrow's colleagues. So if aggression is likely to make enemies, as it seems designed to do, it is a bad strategy in these professions. What about other professional activities? A friendly, warm, nonadversarial manner surely does not interfere with persuading customers to buy, getting employees to carry out directions conscientiously, convincing juries, teaching students, getting help and cooperation from coworkers, and promotions from the boss. An aggressive manner is more likely to be a hindrance in these activities.

If these considerations make us more able to distinguish aggression from professional competence, then they will have served as a useful introduction to the main object of this essay: an inquiry into a paradigm of philosophy that, perhaps tricked by the conflation of aggression and competence, incorporates aggression into its methodology.

Scientific Reasoning

Once upon a time it was thought that scientific claims were, or ought to be, objective and value-free; that expressions of value were distinguishable from expressions of fact, and that science ought to confine itself to the latter. This view was forsaken, reluctantly by some, when it was recognized that theories incorporate values, because they advocate one way of describing the world over others, and that even observations of facts are made from some viewpoint or theory about the world already presupposed.[3]

Still devoted to a fact-value distinction, Popper recognized that scientific *statements* invoked values, but believed that the *reasoning* in science was objective and value-free.[4] Popper argued that the primary reasoning in science is deductive. Theories in science propose laws of the form "All *A*'s are *B*'s" and the job of scientific research is to find, or set up, instances of *A* and see if they fail to produce or correlate with instances of *B*. The test of a theory was that it could withstand attempts to falsify it. A good theory encouraged such attempts by making unexpected and broad claims rather than narrow and expected claims. If instances of *B* failed to occur given instances of *A*, then the theory was falsified. A new theory that could account for the failure of *B* to occur in the same deductive manner would replace the old theory. The reasoning used to discover theories, the way a theory related to physical or mathematical models or other beliefs, was not considered essential to the scientific enterprise. On this view, only the thinking that was exact and certain, objective and value-free was essential to science.

However, Kuhn then argued that even the reasoning used in science is not value-free or certain.[5] Science involves more than a set of independent generalizations about the world waiting to be falsified by a single counter-instance. It involves a system, or paradigm, of not only generalizations and concepts, but beliefs about the methodology and evaluation of research: about what are good questions to ask, what are proper developments of the theory, what are acceptable research methods. One theory replaces another, not because it functions successfully as a major premise in a greater number of deductions, but because it answers some questions that the other theory does not—even though it may not answer some questions the other theory does. Theory changes occur because one theory is more *satisfying* than the other, because the questions it answers are considered more *important*. Research under a paradigm is not done to falsify the theory, but to fill in and develop the knowledge that the paradigm provides a framework for. The reasoning involved in developing or replacing a paradigm is not simply deductive, and there is probably no adequate single characterization of how it proceeds. This does not mean that it is irrational or not worth studying, but that there is no simple universal characterization of good scientific reasoning.

This view of science, or one like it, is widely held by philosophers now. It has been suggested that philosophy too is governed by paradigms.

PHILOSOPHY REASONING—THE ADVERSARY PARADIGM

I am going to criticise a paradigm or part of a paradigm in philosophy.[6] It is the view that applies the now-rejected view of value-free reasoning in science to reasoning in philosophy. On this view all philosophic reasoning is, or ought to be, deductive. General claims are made and the job of philosophic research is to find counterexamples to the claims. And most important, the philosophic enterprise is seen as an unimpassioned debate between *adversaries* who try to defend their own views against counterexamples and produce counterexamples to opposing views. The reasoning used to discover the claims, and the way the claims relate to other beliefs and systems of ideas are not considered relevant to philosophic reasoning if they are not deductive. I will call this the Adversary Paradigm.

Under the Adversary Paradigm, it is assumed that the only, or at any rate, the best, way of evaluating work in philosophy is to subject it to the strongest or most extreme opposition. And it is assumed that the best way of presenting work in philosophy is to address it to an imagined opponent and muster all the evidence one can to support it. The justification for this method is that a position ought to be defended from, and subjected to, the criticism of the strongest opposition; that this method is the only way to get the best of both sides; that a thesis that survives this method of evaluation is more likely to be correct than one that does not; and that a thesis subjected to the Adversary Method will have passed an "objective" test, the most extreme test possible, whereas any weaker criticism or evaluation will, by comparison, give an advantage to the claim to be evaluated and therefore not be as objective as it could be. Of course, it will be admitted that the Adversary Method does not *guarantee* that all and only sound philosophical claims will survive, but that is only because even an adversary does not always think of all the things that ought to be criticized about a position, and even a proponent does not always think of all the possible responses to criticism. However, since there is no way to determine with certainty what is good and what is bad philosophy, the Adversary Method is the best there is. If one wants philosophy to be objective, one should prefer the Adversary Method to other, more subjective, forms of evaluation that would give preferential treatment to some claims by not submitting them to extreme adversarial tests. Philosophers who accept the Adversary Paradigm in philosophy may recognize that scientific reasoning is different, but think "So much the worse for science. At least philosophy can be objective and value-free."

I am going to criticize this paradigm in philosophy. My objection to the Adversary Method is to its role as a paradigm. If it were merely *one* procedure among many for philosophers to employ, there might be nothing worth objecting to except that conditions of hostility are not likely to elicit the best reasoning. But when it dominates the methodology and evaluation of philosophy, it restricts and misrepresents what philosophic reasoning is.

It has been said about science that criticism of a paradigm, however warranted, will not be successful unless there is an alternative paradigm available to replace it.[7] But the situation in philosophy is different. It is not that we have to wait for an alternative form of reasoning to be developed. Nonadversarial reasoning exists both outside and within philosophy but our present paradigm does not recognize it.

DEFECTS OF THE ADVERSARY PARADIGM

The defense of the Adversary Method identified adversary criticism with severe evaluation. If the evaluation is not adversarial it is assumed it must be weaker and less effective. I am going to argue that this picture is mistaken.

As far back as Plato it was recognized that in order for a debate or discussion to take place, assumptions must be shared by the parties involved.[8] A debate is not possible among people who disagree about everything. Not only must they agree about what counts as a good argument, what will be acceptable as relevant data, and how to decide on the winner, but they must share some premises in order for the debate to get started.

The Adversary Method works best if the disagreements are isolated ones, about a particular claim or argument. But claims and arguments about particular things rarely exist in isolation. They are usually part of an interrelated system of ideas. Under the Adversary Paradigm we find ourselves trying to disagree with a system of ideas by taking each claim or argument, one at a time. Premises which might otherwise be rejected must be accepted, if only temporarily, for the sake of the argument. We have to fight our opponents on their terms. And in order to criticize each claim individually, one at a time, we would have to provisionally accept most of the ideas we disagree with most of the time. Such a method can distort the presentation of an opponent's position, and produce an artificially slow development of thought.

Moreover, when a whole system of ideas is involved, as it frequently is, a debate that ends in defeat for one argument, without changing the whole system of ideas of which that argument was a part, will only provoke stronger support for other arguments with the same conclusion, or inspire attempts to amend the argument to avoid the objections. Even if the entire system of ideas is challenged, it is unlikely to be abandoned without an alternative system to take its place. A conclusion that is supported by the argument in question may remain undaunted by the defeat of that argument. In order to alter a *conclusion*, it could be more effective to ignore confrontation on the particular points, not provide counterexamples, however easy they may be to find, and instead show how other premises and other data support an alternative system of ideas. If we are restricted to the Adversary Method we may have to withhold evaluation for a system of ideas in order to find a common ground for debate. And the adversarial criticism of some arguments may merely strengthen support for other ideas in the system, or inspire makeshift revisions and adjustments.

Moreover, the Adversary Paradigm allows exemption from criticism of claims in philosophy that are not well worked out, that are "programmatic." Now any thesis in philosophy worth its salt will be programmatic in that there will be implications which go beyond the thesis itself. But the claims that have become popular in philosophy are particularly sketchy, and secure their immunity from criticism under the Adversary Paradigm *because* their details are not worked out. A programmatic claim will offer a few examples that fit the claim along with a prediction that, with some modification (of course), a theory can be developed along these lines to cover all cases. Counterexamples cannot refute these claims because objections will be routinely dismissed as merely things to be considered later, when all the details are worked out. Programmatic claims have burgeoned in philosophy, particular in epistemology and philosophy of language. It has become a pattern for many philosophy papers to spend most of the paper explaining and arguing against other claims and then to offer a programmatic claim or conjecture of one's own as an alternative at the end without any support or elaboration. (Perhaps this is the beginning of a new paradigm that is growing out of a shortcoming in the evaluation procedures of the Adversary Paradigm.) Some programmatic claims that were once quite popular are now in disrepute, such as sense-data theories, but not because they were disproved, perhaps more because they failed to succeed—no one ever worked out the details and/or people gave up hope of ever doing so. The Adversary Method allows programmatic claims to remain viable in philosophy, however sketchy or implausible, as long as they are unrefuted.

MISINTERPRETING THE HISTORY OF PHILOSOPHY

Under any paradigm we are likely to reinterpret history and recast the positions of earlier philosophers. With the Adversary Paradigm we understand earlier philosophers as if they were addressing adversaries instead of trying to build a foundation for scientific reasoning or to explain human nature. Philosophers who cannot be recast into an adversarial mold are likely to be ignored.[9] But our reinterpretations may be misinterpretations and our choice of great philosophers may be based not so much on what they said as on how we think they said it.

One victim of the Adversary Paradigm is usually thought to be a model of adversarial reasoning: The Socratic Method. The Socratic Method is frequently identified with the *elenchus*, a method of discussion designed to lead the other person into admitting that her/his views were wrong, to get them to feel what is sometimes translated as "shame" and sometimes as "humility." *Elenchus* is usually translated as "refutation," but this is misleading because its success depends on convincing the other person, not on showing their views to be wrong to others. Unlike the Adversary Method, the justification of the elenchus is not that it subjects claims to the most extreme opposition, but that it shakes people up about their cherished convictions so they can begin philosophical inquiries with a more open mind. The aim of the Adversary Method, in contrast, is to show that the other party is wrong, challenging them on any possible point, regardless of whether the other person agrees. In fact, many contemporary philosophers avoid considerations of how to convince, supposing it to be related to trickery and bad reasoning.

In general the inability to win a public debate is not a good reason for giving up a belief. One can usually attribute the loss to one's own performance instead of to inadequacies in one's thesis. A public loss may even make one feel more strongly toward the position that wasn't done justice by the opposition. Thus the Adversary Method is not a good way to convince someone who does not agree with you.

The *elenchus*, on the other hand, is designed just for that purpose. One looks for premises that the other person will accept and that will show that the original belief was false. The discussion requires an acceptance by both parties of premises and reasoning.

Of course, one could use the *elenchus* in the service of the Adversary Paradigm, to win a point rather than convince. And it has been assumed by many that that is what Socrates was doing, that his style was insincere and ironic,[10] that his criticisms were harsh and his praise sarcastic. But in fact Socrates's method is contrasted with that of an antagonist or hostile questioner in the dialogues.[11] Socrates jokes frequently at the beginning of a dialogue or when the other party is resisting the discussion, and the jokes encourage the discussion, which would not be the case if they were made at the expense of the speaker.[12] Any refusals and angry responses Socrates received occurred when cherished ideas were shaken and not as a result of any adversary treatment by Socrates.[13] Socrates avoided giving an opinion in opposition to the one being discussed lest it be accepted too easily without proper examination. His aim is not to rebut, it is to show people how to think for themselves.

We have taken the *elenchus* to be a duel, a debate between adversaries, but this interpretation is not consistent with the evidence in the dialogues. I suspect that the reason we have taken Socrates's method to be the Adversary Method, and consequently misunderstood his tone to be that of an ironic and insincere debater instead of that of a playful and helpful teacher, is that under the influence of the Adversary Paradigm we have not been able to conceive of philosophy being done any other way.

RESTRICTIONS OF PHILOSOPHICAL ISSUES

The Adversary Paradigm affects the kinds of questions asked and determines the answers that are thought to be acceptable. This is evident in nearly every area of philosophy. The only problems recognized are those between opponents, and the only kind of reasoning considered is the certainty of deduction, directed to opposition. The paradigm has a strong and obvious influence on the way problems are addressed.

For example in philosophy of language, the properties investigated are analyzed when possible in terms of properties that can be subjected to deductive reasoning. Semantic theory has detoured questions of meaning into questions of truth. Meaning is discussed in terms of the deductive consequences of sentences. We ask not what a sentence says, but what it guarantees, what we can deduce from it. Relations among ideas that affect the meaning are either assimilated to the deductive model or ignored.[14]

In philosophy of science, the claim that scientific reasoning is not essentially deductive has led to "charges of irrationality, relativism, and the defense of mob rule."[15] Nondeductive reasoning is thought to be no reasoning at all. It is thought that any reasons that are good reasons must be deductive and certain.

In ethics, a consequence of this paradigm is that it has been assumed that there must be a single supreme moral principle. Because moral reasoning may be the result of different moral principles that may make conflicting claims about the right thing to do, a supreme moral principle is needed to "adjudicate rationally [that is, deductively] among different competing moralities."[16] The relation between moral principles and moral decision is thought to be deductive. A supreme moral principle allows one to deduce, by plugging in the relevant factors, what is right or wrong. More than one principle would allow, as is possible if one starts from different premises, conflicting judgments to be deduced. The possibilities that one could adjudicate between conflicting moral precepts without using deduction, that there might be moral problems that are not the result of conflicts in moral principles, and that there might be moral dilemmas for which there are no guaranteed solutions, are not considered.

There is a standard "refutation" of egoism that claims that egoism does not count as an ethical theory and therefore is not worthy of philosophical consideration because an egoist would not advocate egoism to others (would not want others to be egoists too). It is assumed that only systems of ideas that can be openly proclaimed and debated are to count as theories, or as philosophy. Again this is the Adversary Paradigm at work, allowing only systems of ideas that can be advocated and defended, and denying that philosophy might examine a system of ideas for its own sake, or for its connections with other systems.[17]

There are assumptions in metaphysics and epistemology that language is necessary for thinking, for reasoning, for any system of ideas. It is denied that creatures without language might have thoughts, might be able to figure out some things, because the only kind of reasoning that is recognized is adversarial reasoning and for that one must have language.[18]

With the Adversary Paradigm we do not try to assess positions or theories on their plausibility or worthiness or even popularity. Instead we are expected to consider, and therefore honor, positions that are most *un*like our own in order to show that we can meet their objections. So we find moral theories addressed to egoists,[19] theories of knowledge aimed at skeptics. Since the most extreme opposition may be a denial of the existence of something, much philosophic energy is expended arguing for the existence of some things, and no theory about the nature of those things ever gets formulated. We find an abundance of arguments trying to prove that determinism is false because free will exists, but no positive accounts giving an explanation, in terms of chance and indeterminism, of what free will would be. Philosophers debate and revive old arguments about whether God exists, but leave all current discussions about what the nature of God would be to divinity schools and religious orders.

Philosophy, by attention to extreme positions because they are extreme, presents a distorted picture about what sorts of positions are worthy of attention, giving undo attention and publicity to positions merely because they are those of a hypothetical adversary's and possibly ignoring positions that make more valuable or interesting claims.

THE PARADIGM LEADS TO BAD REASONING

It has mistakenly been assumed that whatever reasoning an adversary would accept would be adequate reasoning for all other circumstances as well.[20] The Adversary Paradigm accepts only the kind of reasoning whose goal is to convince an opponent, and ignores reasoning that might be used in other circumstances: To figure something out for oneself, to discuss something with like-minded thinkers, to convince the indifferent or the uncommitted. The relations of ideas used to arrive at a conclusion might very well be different from the relations of ideas needed to defend it to an adversary. And it is not just less reasoning, or fewer steps in the argument that distinguishes the relations of ideas, but that they must be, in some cases, quite different lines of thought.

In illustration, let us consider the counterexample reasoning that is so effective in defending one's conclusions against an adversary. When an adversary focuses on certain features of a problem, one can use those features to construct a counterexample. To construct a counterexample, one needs to abstract the essential features of the problem and find another example, an analogy, that has those features but that is different enough and clear enough to be considered dispassionately apart from the issue in question. The analogy must be able to show that the alleged effect of the essential features does not follow.

But in order to reach a conclusion about moral issues or scientific theories or aesthetic judgments, one may have to consider *all* the important features and their interactions. And to construct an analogy with all the features and their interactions, which is *not* part of the issue in question, may well be impossible. Any example with all the features that are important may just be another example of the problem at issue. If we construct an analogy using only some of the important features, or ignoring their interactions, a decision based on this could be bad reasoning. It would ignore imporant aspects of the problem.

Consider a work in the Adversary Paradigm, Judith Thomson's excellent "A Defense of Abortion."[21] Thomson says: All right, let's give the "right-to-lifers" all their premises. Let's suppose, for the sake of argument, that a fetus is a person, and even that it is a talented person. And then she shows by counterexample that it does not follow that the fetus has a right to life. Suppose that you woke up one morning and found that you were connected to a talented violinist (because he had a rare kidney disease and only you had the right blood type) and the Music Lover's Society had plugged you together. When you protested, they said, "Don't worry, it's only for nine months, and then he'll be cured. And you can't unplug him because now that the connection has been made, he will die if you do." Now, Thomson says to the right-to-lifers, surely you have the *right* to unplug yourself. If the time were shorter than nine months, say only nine minutes, you might be an awful person if you did not stay plugged in, but even then you have the *right* to do what you want with your body.

The violinist analogy makes the main point, and Thomson explains it by comparing the right to one's own body to the right to property (a right that the right-to-lifers are unlikely to deny). One's right to property does not stop because some other person needs it, even if they need it to stay alive.

The argument using a counterexample is as effective against adversaries as any argument could be, and therefore a good method for arguing within the adversary tradition. One uses the premises the adversary would accept—property rights, the fetus as a person—and shows that the conclusion—that "unplugging" yourself from the fetus is wrong—does not follow. In general, in order to handle adversaries one may abstract the features they claim to be important, and construct a counterexample which has those same features but in which the conclusion they claim does not hold.

All Thomson tried to show was that abortion would not be wrong just because the fetus was a person.[22] She did not show that abortion would, or would not, be wrong. There are many features beside personhood that are important to the people making a decision about abortion: That it is the result of sexual intercourse so that guilt, atonement or loyalty about the consequences may be appropriate; that the effects only occur to women, helping to keep a power-minority in a powerless position; that the developing embryo may be genetically like others who are loved; that the product would be a helpless infant brought into an unmanageable situation; that such a birth would bring shame or hardship to others. There are many questions connected to whole systems of ideas that need answers when abortion is a personal issue: What responsibility does one have to prevent shame and hardship to others—parents, friends, other children, future friends and future children? When do duties toward friends override duties of other sorts? How is being a decent person related to avoiding morally intolerable situations—dependence, hate, resentment, lying? There is a lot of very serious moral reasoning that goes on when an individual has to make a decision about abortion, and the decisions made are enormously varied. But this moral reasoning has largely been ignored by philosophers because it is different from the reasoning used to address an adversary and it is too complex and interrelated to be evaluated by counterexamples.

A good counterexample is one that illustrates a general problem about some principle or general claim. Counterexample reasoning can be used to rule out certain alternatives, or at least to show that the current arguments supporting them are inadequate, but not to construct alternatives or to figure out what principles *do* apply in certain situations. Counterexamples can show that particular arguments do not support the conclusion, but they do not provide any positive reason for accepting a conclusion, nor can they show how a conclusion is related to other ideas.

If counterexample reasoning is not a good way to reach conclusions about complex issues, and it is a good way to construct arguments to defeat adversaries, then we should be careful when we do philosophy to bear this in mind. Instead, most of the time we present adversary arguments as if they were the only way to reason. The Adversary Paradigm prevents us from seeing that systems of ideas that are *not* directed to an adversary may be worth studying and developing, and that adversarial reasoning may be incorrect for nonadversarial contexts.

How would discarding the Adversary Paradigm affect philosophy? Any paradigm in philosophy will restrict the way reasoning is evaluated. I have argued that the Adversary Paradigm not only ignores some forms of good reasoning, but fails to evaluate and even encourages some forms of bad reasoning. However, criticism of the Adversary Paradigm is not enough; we need alternatives.

One of the problems with a paradigm that becomes really entrenched is that it is hard to conceive of how the field would operate without it. What other method of evaluating philosophy is there but the Adversary Method?

An alternative way of evaluating reasoning, already used in the history of philosophy and history of science, is to consider how the reasoning relates to a larger system of ideas. The questions to be asked are not just "Must the argument as it stands now be accepted as valid?" but also "What are the most plausible premises that would make this argument a good one?" "Why is this argument important?" "How do its form and its conclusion fit in with other beliefs and patterns of reasoning?" For example, one can consider not only whether Descartes's proofs of the existence of God are valid, but what good reasons there are for proving the existence of God; how Descartes's concept of God is related to his concept of causation and of matter. One can examine the influence of methodology and instrumentation in one scientific field on the development of a related field.[23] With such an approach relations of ideas that are not deductive can also be evaluated. We can look at how world views relate to different philosophical positions about free will and determinism, about rationality and ethical val. values, about distinctions claimed between mind and body, self and other, order and chaos.

A second way of treating systems of ideas involves a greater shift from the Adversary Paradigm. It may even require a shift in our concept of reasoning for it to be accepted. It is that experience may be a necessary element in certain reasoning processes. While many philosophers recognize that different factual beliefs, and hence basic premises, may arise from different experiences, it is believed that philosophical discussions ought to proceed as if experience plays no essential role in the philosophical positions one holds. Experience may be necessary to resolve factual disputes but aside from errors about the facts, any differences in experience that might account for differences in philosophical beliefs are ignored or denied. It is thought that all genuine philosophical differences can be resolved through language. This belief supports the Adversary Paradigm, for adversarial arguments could be pointless if it was experience rather than argument that determined philosophical beliefs. Yet might it not be possible, for example, that belief in a supreme deity is correlated with perceived ability to control one's future? When there is little control, when one is largely powerless to organize one's environment, then belief in a deity helps one to understand, to be motivated to go on, to keep in good spirits. When one feels effective in coping with the world, then belief in a supreme being does not contribute to a satisfactory outlook. Belief in a deity would benefit, would be rational for the very young, the very old, the poor and the helpless. But for others, with the experience of being able to control their own lives and surroundings, the difference in experience would give rise to a different belief.

I am not arguing for this account, but suggesting it as an illustration for how different experiences could determine different philosophical positions that are not resolvable by argument. A similar case might be made for differences in the free will/determinism issue.

These alternatives to the Adversary Paradigm may be objected to by philosophers who are under the delusion that philosophy is different from science, that unlike science, its evaluation procedures are exact and value-free. But for those who accept that what philosophers have said about science (that scientific evaluation is not free from uncertainty and values, because it is dependent on paradigms) is also true of philosophy, other means of evaluation besides the Adversary Method will not be so objectionable.

I have been criticizing the use of the Adversary Method as a paradigm. And I think one of the best ways to reduce its paradigm status is to point out that it *is* a paradigm, that there are other ways of evaluating, reasoning about and discussing philosophy.

NOTES

1. Ann Ferguson, "Androgyny as an Ideal for Human Development," in *Feminism and Philosophy*, ed. M. Vetterling-Braggin, F. Elliston and J. English (Totowa, New Jersey: Littlefield, Adams and Co., 1977), 47.

2. Robin Lakoff, *Language and Woman's Place* (New York: Harper & Row, 1975).

3. Logical positivism.

4. Sir Karl Popper, *The Logic of Scientific Discovery* (New York: Harper & Row, 1958).

5. Thomas Kuhn, *The Structure of Scientific Revolutions*, 2nd edition (Chicago: University of Chicago Press, 1962).

6. It may be that the Adversary Method is only part of the larger paradigm that distinguishes reason from emotion, and segregates philosophy from literature, aligning it with science (dichotomies that Martha Nussbaum [*Philosophy and Literature* 1, 1978] attributes to Plato). Believing that emotions ought not to affect reasoning, it may seem to follow that who one addresses and why, ought not to affect the reasoning either. I consciously employ the kinship philosophy claims with science in this paper, arguing that truths we have learned about scientific reasoning ought to hold for philosophic reasoning as well.

7. Thomas Kuhn, "Reflections on My Critics," in *Criticism and the Growth of Knowledge*, ed. Imre Lakatos and Alan Musgrave (Cambridge: Cambridge University Press, 1970), 231–278.

8. See the *Meno*, 75d–e

9. Perhaps this is why Emerson, Carlyle and others are discussed only as part of English literature, and their views are not studied much by philosophers. They are not addressing adversaries, but merely presenting a system of ideas.

10. See Richard Robinson, *Plato's Earlier Dialectic* (Oxford: Clarendon Press, 1953) for this view of Socrates's style. I don't mean to single out Robinson for what seems to be the usual interpretation of Socrates. Robinson at least thought irony and insincerity objectionable. The term "irony" covers a variety of styles including feigned ignorance to upset an opponent, vicious sarcasm and good natured teasing. It is only the latter that would be justifiably attributed to Socrates from the evidence in the dialogues.

11. See *Euthydemus* 227d, 288d, 295d, where Socrates's method is contrasted with Euthydemus's jeering and belligerent style, and *Meno* 75c–d where Socrates contrasts the present friendly conversation with that of a disputatious and quarrelsome kind. Socrates disapproved of ridicule (*Laches* 1959, *Gorgias* 473d–e, *Euthydemus* 278d, and *Protagorus* 333e).

12. Socrates teases Polus to get him to change his style (*Gorgias* 461c–462a) and responds to Callicles's insults with praise to get him to agree to a dialogue. Socrates flirts with Meno when he resists questioning (*Meno*, 76b–c) and draws out Lysis by getting him to laugh at his questions (*Lysis*, 207c and ff.).

13. *Euthydemus* 288b, 259d, 277d.

14. For example, Donald Davidson, "Truth and Meaning," *Synthese* 17 (1967): 304–323.

15. T. Kuhn, "Reflections on My Critics," 234. See Feyerabend, Watkins, etc. in that volume and Dudley Shapere's review of *Structure of Scientific Revolutions*, in *Philosophical Review*.

16. For example, Alan Gewirth, *Reason and Morality* (Chicago: University of Chicago Press, 1978).

17. See particularly Brian Medlin, "Ultimate Principles and Ethical Egoism," *Australasian Journal of Philosophy* 39 (1957), 111–18.

18. See, for example, Ludwig Wittgenstein, *Notebooks, 1914–1916*, ed. G. E. M. Anscombe and G. H. von Wright, translated by G. E. M. Anscombe (Oxford: Basil Blackwell, 1961), 82, 12 September 1916. "Now it is becoming clear why I thought that thinking and language were the same. For thinking is a kind of language."

19. Many people disagree with the universal beneficence and supremacy of moral considerations advocated by current ethical theories and think that they, and many others, by putting their own interests first, are thereby egoists. But their limited beneficence, which Hume thought was the foundation of morality, is very different from the egoism headlined by philosophers. A philosopher's egoist has *no* moral beliefs and not only thinks "me first" but does not care who comes second, third, or last. A philosopher's egoist has no loyalties to ideals or people and is quite indifferent about the survival and well being of any particular individual or thing.

20. See John Rawls, *A Theory of Justice* (Cambridge, MA: Belknap Press, 1971), 191, where he says: "Nothing would have been gained by attributing benevolence to the parties in the original position" rather than egoism because there would be some disagreements even with benevolence. But surely the reasoning needed for people who care about others will be different than for people who do not care about others at all.

21. Judith Jarvis Thomson, "A Defense of Abortion." *Philosophy and Public Affairs* 1, no. 1, 1971.

22. Thomson, in general, makes it very clear that she is addressing an adversary. Nevertheless, she does claim to reach some conclusion about the morality of abortion, although the central issues for people making the decision are barely discussed—the consequences. See her section 8.

23. Lindley Darden and Nancy Maul, "Interfield Theories," *Philosophy of Science* 44 (1977): 43–64.

Chapter 2 ―――――――――――――――――――――――――――――――――

Philosophical Methodology and Feminist Methodology: Are They Compatible?[1]

Susan Sherwin

*B*oth "philosophy" and "feminism" are broad terms covering a variety of activities and subject matter. Each identifies an area of central concern to me: I frequently tend, in fact, to define myself in terms of them (I do philosophy; I am a feminist—though, curiously, I seldom say I am a philosopher; never I do feminism). But, more and more, I find myself wondering just how compatible these two interests are. They often seem to present different, and conflicting, demands.

The tension I experience revolves around the question of method. This is a particularly serious issue, since some philosophers recommend that we make method the defining characteristic of philosophy. Jay Rosenberg, for instance, says in *The Practice of Philosophy*, "Philosophy as a discipline is perhaps thought of most fruitfully as being distinguished by its method rather than by a subject matter."[2] The question then naturally arises of what that methodology is, and, whether it is compatible with the methodology of feminism.

In "Feminism, Marxism, Method, and the State," Catharine A. MacKinnon defines feminist methodology as consciousness-raising: "consciousness-raising is the major technique of analysis, structure of organization, method of practice, and theory of social change of the women's movement."[3] We must ask, then, whether this methodology of consciousness-raising falls within the scope of acceptable philosophical methodology.

Immediately, we are confronted by the problem of which methodology to use to examine the question of the compatability of philosophical and feminist method without distortion. Reflecting my deep ambivalence on this matter, I have chosen to consider the various aspects of the

Source: From *Feminist Perspectives: Philosophical Essays on Method and Morals,* ed. Lorraine Code, Christine Overall, and Sheila Mullet (Toronto: University of Toronto Press, 1988), Copyright © 1988 by University of Toronto Press. Reprinted by permission of the author and of University of Toronto Press.

21

question alternately from each perspective to see what insight I can derive as to whether I may keep both hats, only one, or, perish the thought, none. (Hence, as some critics have noticed, this paper rather schizophrenically reflects virtues and vices of each approach at various points. I see no way to avoid that dilemma in this particular case.)

This is not a disinterested or purely academic question. This paper is motivated by a particular personal experience. Hence, following feminist methodology, I shall begin by describing and interpreting that experience. Here we come quickly to the first point of departure from philosophy, for there is no comparable beginning from a philosophical orientation. Philosophy does not encourage focusing on particular personal experiences such as this.

> THE EXPERIENCE: A paper I submitted to the Canadian Philosophical Association (CPA) in 1984, entitled "Ethics: A Feminist Approach", was rejected by the CPA; it was, however, accepted by the Canadian Society for Women in Philosophy (C-SWIP) and enthusiastically received at the C-SWIP session of those same meetings. An earlier draft was also read at the annual meeting of the Canadian Research Institute for the Advancement of Women (CRIAW) meeting, where it received a great deal of encouragement (and two requests for publication).[4]

Among the referees' comments from the CPA were the following remarks:

> REFEREE 1:   "The discussion at the bottom on p. 4 implies that there is 'a common experience of being female' that women generally share, that is distinctive of the sex and that is morally significant so that a correct moral theory must take it into account. What is this 'common experience' and what is the evidence for its prevelance? Also, why is it morally relevant?" [These questions are precisely the ones addressed by the paper.]
>
> REFEREE 2:   "This essay is . . . not up to the standards we should expect for CPA philosophy papers. . . . The author's thesis is likely false. Much of contemporary feminism is individualistic in ways criticized by the author. . . ."
>
> REFEREE 3: "Exactly what thesis does the paper profess? Is it a philosophical thesis? (To put the question differently, does the paper seek to prescribe a morality different from those it identifies as dominant or traditional? Or does it seek to produce a moral theory which describes morality more accurately than the disfavoured theories?) If (as it seems to this reader) the paper seeks to do the first, what is its relevance to a philosophical congress?" [In fact, it was a first step toward developing a feminist approach to a normative theory; I continue to consider such a project relevant to a philosophical congress.]

The experience of receiving such scathing reviews is painful. Like many women, I am inclined to accept deprecating judgements of my limited philosophical ability. I've certainly made similar judgements myself often enough. But, under my feminist hat, I know that I am obliged to look more deeply. The personal may just be political even here.

I consider it significant that I continue to run into nonfeminist philosophers who insist that what I do is "not philosophy." The viciousness with which feminist work is dismissed by such philosophers is a frequent source of concern. It is helpful, though, to note that this hostility is not directed exclusively at me; other feminist philosophers have experienced similar sorts of attack from the pens and word-processors of mainstream (malestream) philosophers. The target of this rage is often difficult to determine, for the objectors usually insist that they have no problem with the feminist content of the work per se; they are always very eager to make clear their tolerance for radical thought. Rather, they say, the problem is with the sloppiness, the ignorance, the incompetence of the author qua philosopher. If they were to write feminist philosophy, they suggest, they would do a far more "professional" job of it. I believe they might, but would it be equally good by feminist standards?

I imagine they would produce work something like the books on feminist themes that have been published over the last few years by writers who are clear about their philosophical identity, and who are prepared to use unquestioningly their certified philosophic expertise to provide helpful guides for feminists, generously showing them how philosophy can clarify their thinking; I have in mind such works as *Women's Choices* by Mary Midgley and Judith Hughes, and *Women, Reason, and Nature* by Carol McMillan.[5] Implicit in their promise to bring the clear light of philosophy to feminist thought is a patronizing attitude—recognizable by the third person references to feminism by which they dissociate themselves from most feminist thought; the distancing, patronizing tone limits the value of their work to feminist thinking. Janet Radcliffe Richards provides a borderline case in *The Secptical Feminist*, for she oscillates between including herself in and distancing herself from feminist thinkers.[6] There is a striking contrast in tone and content between these books and others by explicitly self-identified feminist philosophers, such as Marilyn Frye, Alison Jaggar, or the collection edited by Sandra Harding and Merrill Hintikka.[7] The latter books, produced by self-proclaimed feminist philosophers, expand and deepen feminist thought, rather than constrain and reduce it. There are important differences in approach that reflect the divergent paradigms of the two models.

Feminist methodology directs us to look for the political significance of personal experience. What is the political message underlying the scorn with which our individual work is frequently received within the profession? Clearly, the work of feminist philosophers generally is not of lower quality than the norm for mainstream philosophical meetings, so it is puzzling that a paper welcomed at feminist forums is not even worthy of a hearing at "regular" philosophical association meetings. Hence, we are left to wonder whether the feminist content is so threatening that the males who dominate the standards of scholarship in philosophy cannot bear to allow it a hearing, or whether there are different methodological criteria operating in the different forums.

The question is partly empirical, and in that sense, it is already suspect by purely philosophical standards. Philosophy assumes that there exist objective criteria by virtue of which any paper, whatever its political orientation, could be evaluated. A suspicion of political resistance on the part of referees is a claim most philosophers would find profoundly offensive.

It may just be, though, that there is no way to do genuinely feminist research and have it thoroughly respected by one's nonfeminist colleagues. Feminism, after all, is ultimately extremely radical, challenging the status quo in thought as well as in practice. Feminist philosophy does not just offer new truths, or new perspectives on truth, nor is it simply another point of view in these relativist philosophic times. I believe that feminism demands a distinct way of doing philosophy and challenges the very practice most philosophers pride themselves on having mastered. Hence, I shall proceed to explore this intuition—which, qua philosopher, I find disturbing—to see whether or not it is possible to discuss feminism in a way that is "philosophically respectable."

What, then, are the methods that characterize philosophy, and are they compatible with feminist methodology? As with most things, philosophers tend to disagree about the method. Throughout this paper, I will be referring to the style of philosophy that is characteristic of the Anglo-American approach, a method that has its roots in analytic philosophy and prizes a "scientific" approach to thought. This is the tradition dominant in philosophy departments throughout the English-speaking world and is the approach to philosophy in which I was trained and continue to function. I readily acknowledge that other approaches to philosophy differ in many significant respects, and some of my specific comments may not be applicable to other styles of philosophy. Although I suspect there are other specific barriers between modern feminist methodology and the various other styles of philosophy, I shall not attempt to review them here.

Even within the Anglo-American style of philosophy, there are differences about what constitutes appropriate methodology.

Rosenberg (in *The Practice of Philosophy*) characterizes the method of philosophy as "the application of reason to its own operations, the rational study of rational practices" (p. 6). He considers philosophy to be primarily a "second-order" activity occupied with abstract "radical generalizations." He recommends that we appeal to the history of philosophy as a major methodological tool, seeing it as our common *"medium"* of inquiry. "It provides philosophers with a common expository idiom, a shared vocabulary of *concepts*, and a set of paradigms of philosophical reasoning, which can serve as shared starting points for contemporary reexplorations of central philosophical concerns" (p. 11). In other words, we do philosophy by learning the traditions the masters have handed down to us and carrying on in a similar vein; philosophy is defined by what philosophers have done.

If we take Rosenberg's advice seriously and look to the history of philosophy for the common assumptions of method and concepts, feminists are bound to have some concerns. The first thing feminists are sure to notice is that there are seldom any women listed among the philosophic greats, and, as Genevieve Lloyd puts it, the female philosophers we find in the history of philosophy "have been philosophers despite, rather than because of, their femaleness; there has been no input of femaleness into the formation of ideals of Reason."[8] The tradition, it would seem, has long been biased against the perspective of women.

The next thing feminists observe is that the work of the leading historical figures is embarrassingly filled with powerful misogynist statements. Apart from Plato, Augustine, and Mill, it is difficult to find a major historical figure who had a good word to say about women; and the claims of equality from these three are so qualified as to be almost as offensive as their less generous colleagues to some feminists. Most contemporary philosophers are more careful in their discussions of gender than the historical figures were; they tend to be "liberal" on such matters, and generally excuse their predecessors as naively misguided by the culture of their times when it came to the question of women. It is commonly accepted that we can simply excise the offensive empirical claims from their philosophy and maintain the pure intellectual core. Feminist historians are far less certain about the externality and peripheral character of an author's views on women. Many recent papers have argued that the misogyny runs right through to the core of most major philosophers.[9] Again quoting Lloyd, "It is clear that what we have in the history of philosophical thought is no mere succession of surface misogynist attitudes, which can now be shed, while leaving intact the deeper structures of our ideals of Reason. . . . women cannot easily be accommodated into a cultural ideal which has defined itself in opposition to the feminine" (pp. 103–104).

If we look to the method recommended by history we find that although philosophers disagree about the best method of doing philosophy, the debates tend to include agreement about certain principles that psychologists have identified as male-oriented. Descartes, for instance, urged a method that he expressly claimed would be suitable "even for women." It was the method of pure thought, moving privately from general universals to particulars by the pure activity of the mind uncontaminated by the influence of the body. Being more generous than many other philosophers, he assumed that women had minds as well as bodies; hence, apparently, he genuinely believed that women, too, were capable of truth. Unfortunately, he did not take into account his further claims that such activity required a concentration that necessitates freedom from concern with practical demands. It is still common to think that philosophic activity demands total concentration; for example, "The real philosopher, it might be said, exhibits a full, intense commitment to his work, as Socrates did. . . . The 'real' philosopher, it might be argued, spends most of *his* time doing philosophy" (italics mine).[10] Yet, as Virginia Woolf observed in *A Room of One's Own*, such a luxury was/is available only to men, for the culture provides that women will see to the demands of practical living, leaving men free for the "important work." Given our socialization and the real demands on our time for nontheoretical tasks, it is hardly surprising that few women are perceived as engaged in "real philosophy." In contrast, we should note, within feminist circles, practical work is an important component of one's contribution to theory.

Moreover, in our society at least, men are inclined towards abstract general thought, and tend to find universals clearer and more comfortable than particulars, just as Descartes imagined. Women, however, seem to think most readily in terms of particulars. Universal, abstract ideas are things they can think towards, but seldom are they the place where thought begins for women.[11] In this sense, perhaps the Socratic model of reasoning from the particular to the general is more suitable for women. If so, it is unfortunate that it passed out of philosophic style for so many centuries.

Turning now to feminism, several important differences in norms are apparent. The methodology of consciousness-raising is very much a "first-order" methodology, where we begin by focusing on the concrete and the specific, and delay abstraction and generalization to a later stage. Consciousness-raising involves "collective critical reconstitution of the meaning of women's social experience, as women live through it."[12] Thus, where philosophers are encouraged to seek abstract generalization, feminists try to learn to uncover the personal. So while philosophers seek objective truth, defined as truth valid from any possible viewpoint, feminists consider it important to look to the actual point of view of the individual speaking. Philosophers tend to believe that emotion and personal feeling are impediments to truth, since they can seldom be generalized objectively, but feminists, who consider direct, personal experience an important component of truth, pay particular attention to the emotional content of claims. The quest for abstract universality is reflected in the fascination philosophers have with hypothetical counter-examples. Feminists, however, tend to concentrate on the texture of a complex range of different but related real experiences.

Psychologists have observed that women tend to prefer social, interactive processes, unlike men who long for the isolation of completely private thought.[13] In this sense, then, the methodology of feminism is the methodology of women's thought: consciousness-raising begins with personal experience, focusing on the details of experience, and then collectively moves to a broader analysis. Generalizations come after a number of particulars are presented. This is an interactive activity, and not the sort of private process Descartes envisioned.

Feminists do not assume that the truth is readily accessible if only we concentrate hard enough. Recognizing that what has been claimed to be objective and universal is in reality the male point of view, feminists seek to concentrate on women's own experience and explicitly avoid any claims of being "objective, abstract or universal."[14] Feminists acknowledge that their perspective is not universal or unpremised, recognizing that women's perspective may in fact be different in a different world. After all, women's experience is experience within patriarchy, and "the male perspective is systematic and hegemonic."[15] Philosophers, in contrast, continue to hope to find the pure, general, universal point of view. Thus, feminists readily admit to "bias" in our perspective, embracing it as a virtue, while other philosophers continue to assume bias should, and can be, avoided. This is, then, a point of serious conflict between the two approaches.

Another area of difference is that feminist scholarship is explicitly interdisciplinary. Feminist scholars have argued that they are constrained in their work by limits connected with the established frameworks of existing disciplines. Such constraint has been cited as constituting one of the most insidious barriers to development of feminist thought,[16] and it is of as much concern to those with a background in philosophy as it is to those from other disciplines. Hence, by definition, feminists will rely on an eclectic methodology, having its roots in various disciplines, and will not restrict themselves entirely to any single disciplinary approach, neither that of philosophy, nor any other. Although there is a sense in which philosophy is also interdisciplinary, it views its relation to other disciplines in metatheoretic terms, and so it is not interdisciplinary in the methodological sense of involving genuine collective cross-disciplinary thought. It maintains its own sense of method and sees its task as criticially examining the presuppositions of other disciplines, but not specifically adopting the methods of the disciplines it examines (though, in fact, scientific methodology has been highly attractive to modern philosophers.)

Another area of apparent difference is found in the definition of the criteria of acceptability and criticism within each field. In philosophy, the emphasis on universality makes positive claims virtually impossible to prove and renders counterexamples potentially devastating, hence commenting on a philosopher's thought is often taken to require a furious search for the decisive counterexample, however hypothetical it may be. Negative theses, disproving the analysis someone else has offered, is the most natural route for a critical philosopher to take. The logic of the argument is the most important feature of a philosophic position, far more important than the plausibility of the claims or the usefulness of the insight to other questions. In commenting on a philosophic thesis, one may identify a logical flaw, challenge the underlying assumptions, or note the inadequacy of its explanatory power. It is taken for granted that the task of colleagues discussing this work is to test the thesis along these logical dimensions, seeking to demolish it to make room for their own clever innovations.

In feminist scholarship, logic is also important—as Richards et al. take delight in pointing out—and theories that are logically flawed, or clearly false, or lacking in explanatory power are subject to criticism among feminists as well. But feminists have political as well as intellectual aims, which they are quite willing to admit to. (Feminists have provided powerful arguments to show that historically, philosophers commonly have political agendas, as well,[17] and suspect their contemporary philosophic colleagues of also having political aims, but, apart from Marxists and feminists, few philosophers will admit to politics shaping their work.) What this means in practice is that a theoretical claim in feminism must be consistent with overall feminist values, and, in fact, it should further the pursuit of those values. The effect, as well as the logic, of a theory is significant. A theory that did not contribute to political change is of only limited interest. In other words, feminists view political effects as one measure of acceptability, though certainly not the only measure. Philosophers tend to be appalled by such frank admissions of bias.

Moreover, it is commonly accepted among feminists that theory alone is not sufficient—that the theorist should also be directly involved in social activism. In this way, we guard against the danger of ungrounded theory. So, where philosophers are deeply suspicious of explicit political concerns shaping one's intellectual exploration, feminists are suspicious of theoretic arguments that deny any political implications. Philosophers, for the most part, now recognize that value-free reasoning is an impossible goal in science, yet they continue to aspire to it within their own discipline.

Feminists are also unlikely to tolerate a theory that rejects or denies personal experience. Many philosophers, for their part, seem to take a perverse delight in shocking others by providing an analysis that appears to fly in the face of experience. And where feminists consider it important to fit their ideas into the broader picture of developing feminist thought, philosophers are often most pleased if they can turn existing philosophic thought on its head and present some radically original position that brings much prior work into question.

This difference in standards of acceptability and grounds of criticism leads to differences in style of interaction within the area of study. Janice Moulton has provided a clear feminist critique of the standard model of interaction among modern philosophers. As she argued in "A Paradigm of Philosophy: The Adversary Method"[18] (Chapter One of this volume), the model of philosophic debate is that of a contest of adversaries, where aggression is at least as important as truth is to the outcome. Aggression, however, is not an attractive or desirable model for anyone to pursue in professional debates, and it is particularly alien and dangerous for women, let alone feminists. There are clear defects in such an approach as a means of arriving at the goal of philosophic activity, truth. By making debating skill a chief criterion of success, the profession of philosophy rewards traits such as aggression and competitiveness; but feminists reject the view that these traits are desirable, for they see them to be central to patriarchy. By making truth an all or nothing affair, and encouraging us to seek any hole in a colleague's argument by which her/his position might be demolished, we foster a rather frightening model of the pursuit of truth. More than one clever philosopher has abandoned the profession because she lacks the taste for the combative search for truth. Moreover, it is a difficult tool to use in the pursuit of truth. Recognizing that the truth is complex and elusive, philosophers nonetheless expect one another to pursue it at all stages with air-tight arguments and supreme confidence. It often is the case, though, that one's first attempts in a new direction are tentative and exploratory, and not best pursued by subjecting them, alone and unassisted, to the strongest opponent.

Feminist scholarship, in contrast, holds onto an ideal of cooperative, collective work. Scholarship in pursuit of a shared goal is to be undertaken as a collective enterprise where different people do piece work on different aspects of the problem. Ideas are shared as part of this collective enterprise, and, as long as they contribute to the overall goals of feminist activity and are not thoroughly false, the goal of criticism is to help develop those ideas further in the direction begun. Assumptions are shared and, hence, one can get immediately to the business at hand of furthering the argument, rather than reviewing it yet again. Each contribution is related to the larger system of ideas, the larger project, and not offered as a private theory to then bear one's name. (It is a feminist view of justice we seek, not a Kantian, Marxist, Rawlsian, or Nozikian one—or even a Fryian, Jaggarian, or Hardingist theory.)

This, of course, is an idealized description of feminist work. There are different approaches to feminism, and the disputes among various interpretations can be significant. Certainly many feminist scholars have felt shocked and betrayed to find their work (and often themselves) under attack by other feminists. The reason for the shock, however, is that it really is a violation of feminist values and norms to attack destructively (rather than criticize in some constructive way) another's work. It happens, but, unlike the widely held philosophic norm, it is not an explicit ideal of the discipline to view debate as a pitched battle. Feminists consciously aim at cooperative solutions and seek to avoid personally devastating attacks.

My philosophy colleagues sometimes express puzzlement on how to criticize feminist work if the adversary system is not acceptable. One approach is to try to understand how the paper at issue fits into the larger picture of feminist goals, and the broad view of social and political or ethical (or epistemological, metaphysical, etc.) thought. Feminists begin with a spirit of charity in trying to decipher the thrust of a colleague's work. For feminists, the nit-picking inherent in the current Anglo-American approaches to philosophy comes after a general consideration of the plausibility of the problem. In fairness, I must add that it does seem true, lately, that many nonfeminist philosophers are recognizing the limits of the adversary method; more and more sessions at conferences seem to eschew that approach and see the task at hand as a collective search for the truth. (I think, in fact, feminist philosophers can take some of the credit for this shift in style. We really do offer a more attractive paradigm.)

Consider now another aspect of academic activity, namely teaching, from both perspectives. Here, too, there is a different ideal envisioned in philosophy classes from that in feminist studies. In academic contexts, feminist teaching does not proceed by the Socratic method where the wise but humble teacher skillfully directs the unreflective student to the truth he/she has overlooked; rather it involves a cooperative exploration of perceptions and experience toward a new understanding for all members of the class. Feminist teaching incorporates feminist values. Hence, feminist classrooms are noted for "an acceptance of, and even emphasis on, the personal/affective element in learning; and a warm human relationship among persons in the class, students and teachers."[19] As Marilyn Webb notes, feminist teachers are conscious of the politics of the classroom:

> When we teach about sexual politics, it's a class hierarchy we are attacking. If we recreate this class division within our teaching, our analysis is "devoid of form." That's why as feminist teachers, it's just as important for us to look at how we teach as to look at what we teach.[20]

More precisely, Webb goes on to sketch the methods of achieving these ideals, including: the attempt to teach without imposing authoritarian structures; the attempt to build a "consciousness of an alternative, e.g., collective learning and action" rather than individual isolation and competition; an attempt to incorporate "actual experience of what we are talking about in our teaching"; and a general commitment to an emphasis on the experiential (p. 417). These aspects of feminist teaching are not explicitly rejected in general philosophic pedagogy, but they are certainly not accepted as central to the enterprise either. In fact, in philosophy, as in other disciplines, feminist pedagogy tends to contradict mainstream methods, creating hostility and rejection of our approach within the model of other academic classes.[21]

It seems, then, that there are many important differences in the approach I see taken by philosophers and feminists. Nonetheless, there are many of us who believe ourselves to be both feminists and philosophers, and much high quality work has been produced that seems to satisfy the norms of both disciplines. There must, then, be room for overlap. Hence, what I am really seeking here is a way of characterizing that area of overlap, of identifying some method of feminist philosophy which is acceptable from both perspectives.

One aspect I can perceive of shared approach is the important fact that both are committed to a strong and general skepticism about authoritative pronouncements of the truth. Both disciplines train initiates not to accept statements of fact without question. It is not really such a surprise that some philosophers are pursuing radical feminist alternatives to the standard problems of philosophy. Philosophy has always tolerated, and perhaps from time to time has even encouraged, radical rethinking of its underlying assumptions. It is not unreasonable for feminists to align themselves with this time-honored philosophic tradition.

Moreover, philosophers have never actually agreed on any single method. While individual philosophers and schools have identified particular methods as paradigm, other philosophers have always challenged such restrictions and introduced different approaches as legitimate. (And some, like Rorty, seem to deny that there is any proper philosophic method—as it is now conceived by Anglo-American philosophers—at all.)[22] There is no single authorized method, wholly original and unique to the discipline, which does not have counterparts and inspiration in other disciplines. So, too, for feminism, where there is a great diversity of opinion on the best approach. In fact, both philosophy and feminism have always involved rather an eclectic variety of methods. Thus, there is no single, accepted method by which philosophers can reject feminist methodology out of hand.

Perhaps more importantly, it would be a violation of feminist principles to reject philosophic methods. Feminism relies on whatever morally and epistemologically acceptable methods[23] are available and can contribute toward its overall ends, and surely philosophy can help in that enterprise. Those feminists who have expressed skepticism over the rational methods of philosophy are recording a well-deserved distrust of methods and ideas which have been used to limit women's freedom and imagination. But, as philosophers never tire of pointing out, feminists can only express their case by use of such rational methods themselves, and in most cases the difficulty they have with rationality can be attributed in part to their unexamined—and mistaken—assumptions about what rationality involves. What is seen by some feminists as a methodological barrier is actually the result of abuses of a rational approach by misogynist philosophers.

One of the dangers that feminists have pointed to within traditional methodologies is the hazard of accepting dichotomies. Dichotomous thinking forces ideas, persons, roles, and disciplines into rigid polarities. It reduces richness and complexity in the interest of logical neatness, and, in doing so, it distorts truth. Moreover, the creation and use of dichotomies seem to be important elements in the very structure of patriarchy; the institution of patriarchy involves power relations that rest on the assumption of fundamental and unbridgeable differences between the sexes reflected in multiple forms of polarity. Hence, I believe that it is important for feminists to resist the temptation to pursue dichotomies from our own perspective; i.e., we should take care not to define philosophic methodology as inherently opposed to feminist thought or imagine the differences in approach to involve a schism that cannot be forded.

I cannot, therefore, conclude that feminist and philosophic methodologies are incompatible. They are, however, made compatible only with significant effort from each end. Many standard approaches and assumptions in philosophy are not acceptable from a feminist point of view, so it is not all of philosophy that can be seen as compatible with feminism. Philosophers, from their perspective, must make some noticeable effort to understand the feminist enterprise before dismissing it as not meeting the usual professional norms. They must recognize that feminists have much ground to cover in rethinking the philosophic activity of the past 2500 years, and they should be prepared to tolerate a bit of sketchiness and hand-waving as feminists explore the ways in which ethics, epistemology, and metaphysics may have to be revised when we change their underlying political assumptions. Perhaps the greatest challenge comes from the need to pay attention to the genuine criticisms of their discipline which feminists have to offer. Philosophers should consider whether the particular approaches feminists take to philosophic questions can in fact serve philosophic ends. I seem still to believe that feminism can enrich philosophy and that it behooves philosophers to learn to be open to feminist style and commitments.[24]

For our part as feminists, in order to help philosophers make such modifications in their usual methods of evaluation, we should continue to try to put our thoughts into a language they can understand and relate our analysis to familiar issues when possible. In doing so, though, I believe we must remain conscious of the risks involved. It is important to be able to rely on one another for the support necessary when philosophers fail to notice the significant differences involved in adopting a feminist perspective. We should never forget that philo- sophic gatherings and journals are still predominantly hostile environ- ments for feminists, and we ought not to venture far into such terrain without adequate support from one another.

POSTSCRIPT. I noticed as I concluded this paper that I experienced a familiar sense of unease that the ideas seem tentative and lacking in drama and surprise. Writing this paper was a valuable cathartic exercise for me, for I now realize that this deja vu feeling of dissatisfaction is in fact yet another symptom of my ambivalence about appropriate stan- dards. Under my philosopher's hat, the ideal is to come up with the decisive conclusion, settling the question once and for all; I feel as if I ought now to be prepared to defend my view against all comers. On that criterion, this paper, like the earlier one so disliked by the referees, is flawed.

But as a feminist paper, the agenda is different. Under my feminist hat, I see my task to be an exploration of my views and feelings on this broadly abstract and deeply personal question. Having done that, I am quite comfortable to pass the issue on to others who will share the responsibility of following these ideas through, taking them in direc- tions I cannot clearly foresee. From that perspective, it is acceptable to be reflective about a matter that troubles me without presuming to have entirely settled it. Clearly, this dilemma is a piece of a greater puzzle, and it is open to modification in light of the experience and insight of others who approach it constructively. Or, in other words, this is a paper that is best read at a conference for feminist philosophers.

NOTES

1. This paper was originally written for the meeting of the Canadian Society for Women in Philosophy, Vancouver, B.C., October, 1985. I am very grateful for the encouragement and helpful feedback received there, and for the thoughtful editorial suggestions offered by Ann Garry.

2. Jay Rosenberg, *The Practice of Philosophy*, second edition (Englewood Cliffs: Prentice Hall, 1984), 6.

3. Catharine MacKinnon, "Feminism, Marxism, Method, and the State," in *Feminist Theory*, ed. Nannerl O. Keohane, Michelle Z. Rosaldo, Barbara C. Gelpi (Brighton: The Harvester Press, 1982), 5.

4. The paper, called "From Feminism to a New Conception of Ethics," was published in a collection of selected papers from the proceedings of that CRIAW meeting, called *Knowledge Reconsidered: A Feminist Overview* (CRIAW, 1984). An abridged version, called "Ethics: Towards a Feminist Approach," was published in *Canadian Women's Studies* 6.2 (Spring 1985). I have since developed these ideas further and they have appeared as "A Feminist Approach to Ethics," *The Dalhousie Review* 64.4 (Winter, 1984–5) and reprinted in the special philosophy issue of *Resources for Feminist Research/Documentation sur la Recherche Feministe* 16.3 (September 1987): 25–28.

5. Mary Midgley and Judith Hughes, *Women's Choices: Philosophical Problems Facing Feminism* (London: Weidenfeld and Nicolson, 1983). Carol McMillan, *Women, Reason and Nature* (Oxford: Basil Blackwell, 1982).

6. Janet Radcliffe Richards, *The Sceptical Feminist: A Philosophical Enquiry* (Markham, Ont.: Penguin Books, 1980).

7. Marilyn Frye, *The Politics of Reality: Essays in Feminist Theory* (Trumansburg, N.Y.: The Crossing Press, 1983). Alison M. Jaggar, *Feminist Politics and Human Nature* (Totowa, N.J.: Rowman and Allanheld, 1983). Sandra Harding and Merrill Hintikka, eds. *Discovering Reality: New Perspectives on Women and Philosophy* (Dordrecht: Reidel, 1983).

8. Genevieve Lloyd, *The Man of Reason: "Male" and "Female" in Western Culture* (Minneapolis: University of Minnesota Press, 1984), 108.

9. See, for instance, the historical papers in Harding and Hintikka, eds., *Discovering Reality* and in Lorene M. G. Clark and Lynda Lange, eds., *The Sexism of Social and Political Theory* (Toronto: University of Toronto Press, 1979).

10. "Introduction: Some Approaches to Philosophy," *The Owl of Minerva*, ed. Charles J. Bontempo and S. Jack Odell (New York: McGraw-Hill Paperbacks, 1975), 27.

11. Some of this evidence is provided by Carol Gilligan in *In a Different Voice: Psychological Theory and Women's Development* (Cambridge, Mass.: Harvard University Press, 1982), and, more recently in Mary Field Belenky, Blythe McVicker Clinchy, Nancy Rule Goldberger, and Jill Mattuck Tarule, *Women's Ways of Knowing: The Development of Self, Voice and Mind* (New York:

Basic Books, Inc., 1986). To see how it applies specifically to the philosophic context, see Annette Baier, "What Do Women Want in a Moral Theory?" *Nous*, XIX, 1 (March 1985).

12. MacKinnon, "Feminism, Marxism" (1982), 29.

13. Gilligan, *In a Different Voice*.

14. Catharine MacKinnon, "Feminism, Marxism, Method, and the State: Toward Feminist Jurisprudence," *Signs*, 8.4 (1983), 636.

15. Ibid.

16. Toni Laidlaw and Gisele Thibault, "Women and Schooling: The Importance of a Multi-disciplinary Approach," unpublished paper presented at the Learned Societies Meeting, Vancouver, 1983.

17. See the historical essays in Harding and Hintikka, eds., *Discovering Reality*, Clark and Lange, eds., *The Sexism of Social and Political Theory*, and Lloyd, *The Man of Reason*.

18. Janice Moulton, "A Paradigm of Philosophy: The Adversary Method," in Harding and Hintikka, eds., *Discovering Reality*. (Reprinted as Chapter One of this volume.)

19. Sheila Tobias, ed., *Issues in Feminism: A First Course in Women's Studies* (Boston: Houghton Mifflin, 1980), 15.

20. Marilyn Webb, "Feminist Studies: Frill or Necessity?" in *And Jill Came Tumbling After*, ed. Judith Stacey et al. (New York: Dell Publishing, 1974), 412.

21. Gisele Thibault, "The Dissenting Academy: A History of the Barriers to Feminist Scholarship" (unpublished Ph.D. diss., Dalhousie University, 1985), 29–139.

22. Richard Rorty, *Philosophy and the Mirror of Nature* (Princeton, New Jersey: Princeton University Press, 1979).

23. Feminists may, however, appeal to different criteria of moral and epistemological acceptability than those embraced by mainstream philosophers.

24. I believe that a feminist approach does result in different analyses of philosophic questions. Such a contention is best evaluated by reviewing the evidence. Most essays in this anthology would serve as providing such evidence. My own work arguing concretely for the significance of the different perspective feminism offers is developed in two recent papers: Susan Sherwin, "Feminism and Theoretical Perspectives on Peace," *Atlantis*, 12.1 (Fall 1986) and Susan Sherwin, "Feminist Ethics and In Vitro Fertilization," *Canadian Journal of Philosophy* 17.3 (September 1987).

Chapter 3

Women Who Beget Women Must Thwart Major Sophisms

Jeffner Allen

*H*ow do I enter into a discourse from which I, a feminist, am banished? How do I enter into the discourse of postmodernism when, largely and for the most part, the disciplinary practices of postmodernity dismiss feminist politics?*

Yet, perhaps I do not wish to enter *into* postmodern discourse. I will restate my opening question. How do I, a feminist, locate myselves, among which is a philosophical self, when postmodernism has become a dominant discourse of western philosophy in the twentieth century?

Source: First published in *Philosophy and Social Criticism* 13, 4 (1988): 315–326. Copyright © 1988 by Jeffner Allen. Reprinted by permission of the author.

* Postmodernism designates a shift in how western culture understands itself, a shift in how it understands cultural formations such as theory and art, knowledge and power. Postmodernism is a growing movement in the twentieth century that takes issue with modernism, that worldview that establishes and maintains dominance through its demand for unity, hierarchy, and conformity to norms, or essences, which it posits as natural. The European voyages of conquest, which sought to bring the "New World" under European control economically and ideologically, are an instance of the modern worldview.

In practice, modern and postmodern perspectives sometimes are separate and readily distinguishable, and sometimes overlap. Nevertheless, for feminists, postmodernism offers a promise. In contrast to modernism, a salient characteristic of postmodernism is its claim to affirm multiplicity and difference and to attribute to these characteristics the power to undermine what it calls "phallogocentrism," the masculist and rationalist tradition of western culture. Because postmodernism rejects the notion that language and writing are mere tools that represent what is real, and instead considers reality to be inseparable from interpretation, it holds that the language and writing of multiplicity and difference are radically transformative. The promise of postmodernism is, however, deceptive, and as I will show, its sophistry is ironically present in postmodern discussions of women and feminism.

Yet, if I can neither return to modernism nor reform postmodernism, both of which deny my existence, how do I understand the times that I live, times that do not coincide with, and often are independent of, those perspectives? I desire not a linear narrative whose claim to authority might reinforce abstract rationality, might offer answers rather than recognize open spaces, might render a reader receptive rather than creative. Rather, in this cycle of stories and more stories, I hope to touch some of the conditions for my survival.

This question presents not only an ethical quandary, though that in itself is no slight matter, but an epistemological and ontological dilemma that is inseparable from politics. While feminist politics has always been far from receiving institutional sanction, this question announces itself somewhat urgently, and with uneasiness, for one who is a feminist and a philosopher teaching postmodernism in an educational institution.

I would like to tell the "Tale of the Amazons," and the "Tale of the Feminine and the Feminist," stories I did not invent, while recounting at the same time a tale of my own. If the article "the" appears somewhat disconcertingly in the titles of these tales, I can say only that the narrators from whom I first heard them were neither *an* amazon, *a* feminine creature, or *a* feminist, but had positioned themselves seemingly outside the narrative, at a distance. With luck, I will tell my own story with a certain intensity and feeling, for as one amazon, feminine creature and feminist among many, I wish to explore the ways in which these tales are intimately connected with my life.

TALE OF THE AMAZON

The "Tale of the Amazon" and the "Tale of the Feminine and the Feminist" are stories of the difference that was ascribed to woman at the beginning of modernity and at the end of modernity, that is, the beginning of the postmodern era. They are two distinct stories of the positioning of woman as difference, and yet, they also are possibly but one story, the same. If the first is an exploration of difference at the edges of the world, the second, taken from the age of "world" as discourse, may be considered an exploration of difference at the edges of the text.

Many were the stories told by the western European conquerors as they ventured to the new world revealed by the epochal voyages of Columbus, but the story perhaps most persistently told and retold was the legend of the amazons.[1] *Eager to learn of these amazons I listen to the story, but by what right?*

Columbus's report of amazons on islands past which he had cruised and of their alleged proximity to earthly paradise opened new and likely possibilities for locating the amazons at last. Adventurers, Nuño de Guzmán, Francisco Orellana, Francisco Cortés, soon told of a new hemisphere where amazons and wealth were inseparable. Califia and other amazons emerged in description as inhabitants of a craggy island, "California," celebrated for its abundance of gold and the amazons' man-eating griffons. Pigafetta, eyewitness and chronicler of Magellan's circumnavigation of the globe in 1523, recounts that after touching Java, "our oldest pilot told us that there is an island called Acoloro which lies below Java Major where there are not persons but women, and that the latter become mothers by the wind."[2] *Must I tell this story as it has been told? Why ask?*

What relation do I have to this tale of the conquerors who, after all, sought the amazons as a romantic proposition and for gold, to fulfill a business agreement? A standard clause in the expedition contracts was: Find the amazons.

Although the voyages of discovery showed that old conceptions of the earth were mistaken, they might have remained in place if the new world could have been fit within the old. And one way to do that was to incorporate latent and volatile manifestations of the new world into the old world commerce. Hence the unstated terms of the contract: if the amazons are at the edges of the earth, find that virtual otherworldliness, appropriate otherness.

The amazons, however, remained elusive and inaccessible. The amazons of whom Columbus spoke lived in caves on some of the islands of the Caribbean where strong winds prevented his approach. The amazons described by Juan Díaz, chronicler of Diego Velásquez's voyage to the Yucatan in 1517, were said to inhabit a beautiful tower on a point along the coast of a shore where the expedition did not land. Amazons of great wealth were always further away, in lands not yet explored. The new world did not reveal the marvels for which the conquerors had hoped. *But why this story, is there no other?*

What does it mean that a contract might never be fulfilled, might in principle preclude closure? Did the metaphysical distance established by the contract grant, albeit inadvertently, a space where amazons might never be found by conquerors and difference might never be tamed? Slipping stealthily through spaces left by metaphysical distance, amazons might, then, have set foot on earth and led everyday lives, lives infinitely more interesting than amassing gold and awaiting battle.

Or might not amazons have been among the cultures from which conquerors extracted gold and labor? The metaphysical quest, which posited amazons as otherworldly, could not have recognized amazons living in the moment, amazons surviving while subjected to the tangibility of western European violence.

Which is not to say that amazons did not exist and did not have their own stories—perhaps told in amazon caves at the basin of the Amazon, at Santarem and the island of Martajo—but only that I can learn nothing of amazons by telling and retelling this metaphysical tale. *Is there another way to begin?*

TALE OF THE FEMININE AND THE FEMINIST

Why one tale and not another is a question for which there may be no definite answer.

I am drawn to this postmodern tale of woman, to its anti-metaphysical stance, its concern for language, its promise of another beginning. Yet I have learned that women's histories and the history of ideas may not be synchronous. The renaissance, that beginning of modernity when many men in western Europe experienced an unfolding of opportunity and knowledge, was a time when almost all women in western Europe were subject to greater restraints and restrictions than they had experienced during earlier centuries.[3] I am wary of this postmodern tale, lest its promise not be intended for me, lest its beginnings not be mine.

I decide to set aside the question of whether women might be better off in modern or postmodern tales. Gayatri Chakravorty Spivak, "French Feminism in an International Frame," Teresa de Lauretis, "Feminist Studies/Critical Studies: Issues, Terms, and Contexts," and Rosa Lee, "Resisting Amnesia: Feminist Painting and Postmodernism," have each developed theories that show that feminism and postmodernism are distinct and often at cross-purposes.[4] I am but the teller of a story of how one spirited being endeavors to situate herself in relation to a modern and a postmodern tale of difference. My primary concern is not a matter of modernism vs. postmodernism, but a speculative matter of spirit.

The "Tale of the Feminine and the Feminist" is a postmodern tale in which the amazon, a transcendent ideal of modernity, is split and recast. The "Tale of the Amazon" is displaced by this new romance of the margins, a romance that entails a twofold discipline of woman as difference: the domestication of different, represented as "the feminine," and the outright dismissal of difference that takes the form of "the feminist," she who, by her autonomy, would defy the postmodern power of representation.[5] Out of an intimate concern for how a free spirit might survive such a tale, I will tell this story one more time.

Eager, so eager, I read one postmodern text after another, each as soon as it appears, so eager am I for philosophical discussion of women and for philosophical texts by women writers. I believe I might inhabit a postmodern textuality. Yet I find that textuality constructs me in ways I do not understand. When I come to understand the construction, I find no way in which I might hold it of myself.[6] Unable to find a way I can enter into that construction, I place myself beside the text and listen to its story.

The "Tale of the Feminine and the Feminist" is a postmodern tale of difference: that difference *is*, what difference is and is not, that woman, if she will be, must be *as* difference. *Can I be as difference?*

Glowing accounts abound of the romance of the margin that approaches the center, a center once said to be everywhere, but now said to be nowhere, or at least in a state of dissolution. No conquerors are on this scene.

Difference approaches freely. She comes from off the page onto the text, of her own accord. The old metaphysical conceptions of subjectivity, knowledge, truth, now found to be mistaken, might be dislodged, if a new world could displace the old. Difference, unselfish, by her own good virtue, saves the logocentric western tradition from itself. While working miracles untold, difference brings with her a new dawn.

What is difference—the feminine, feminine writing, women's bodies, mothers and daughters, oranges and eggs, the forgotten air and water? *Why should difference engage herself in this manner?* Had difference the power to bring to an end the institutions of the West, would not she have exercised that power long ago?

Postmodern cartographers write multifarious encounters with difference. Derrida tells of the polylogue, "A jumble of voices, an indeterminate number, of which some seem masculine, others feminine, and which is marked at times in the grammar of the phrase."[7] Yet Derrida's choreographic texts with polysexual signatures urge the indifferentiation of gender and warn feminists to avoid putting energy into describing a specifically female subject. Foucault, proponent of the multiplication of local narratives that, by their very existence, challenge the claim to hegemony of universalizing systems of knowledge and power, also ignores differences in context when he states, "Whether one punches his fist in someone's face, or his penis in the sexual organ makes no difference . . . it is nothing but an assault, and nothing more."[8]

Does difference enter the scene only to vanish in a time when women perform two-thirds of the world's work, receive five percent of the world income, own less than one percent of the world land; when in the United States every seven minutes a woman is raped, every eighteen seconds a woman is battered; when women and children in female-

headed households are estimated to comprise almost all of the population in poverty by the year 2000?[9] *Does the promised inclusion of
difference in the transformation of the text place difference at risk of the loss
of her own writing and life experience? What has happened to difference?*

The postmodern tale turns from the amazon, a transcendent ideal,
to the feminine, a fictive existence for which any reference outside the
text is indeterminate. Whereas the metaphysical tale is a romance that
precludes fulfillment (the amazon and her gold are sought and cannot
be found), the postmodern tale is a romance fulfilled, even if momen-
tarily, and at great risk to its object. The feminine appears upon the
postmodern scene where, as a mere reflection of its theory, she is
elevated to the rank of highest value, denied reference to specificities of
her life experience, eclipsed. The postmodern critique of reference as
metaphysical and essentialist sets the conditions for a romance in
which difference, a harbinger of postmodernity, vanishes in the indifference of the text.

If the postmodern critique of reference as the product of a naive
metaphysics is perilous for those who would claim reference apart from
the text, it is, nonetheless, limited in scope: just as reference need not be
essentializing, neither need reference be indeterminate. The compass of
postmodern cartographies assumes the privilege of indifference when,
by precluding reference, it rises above difference and sets the course for
navigation of the text. However, unless a narrative recognizes women
as individuals who inhabit distinctive histories, unless a narrative
moves with a certain intimacy and proximity to tangible events, unless
a narrative questions the privilege of its own discursive requirements,
that narrative may make little difference for women's lives.

A great silence accompanies the tale of the feminine, a silence that
is itself a story, a story with far too many words to tell them all. The
romance of the margins is at once silent and full of words for that which
has chosen to move apart from its spell: feminist politics.

"Shrill," "hysterical," "angry," "one finds that weak, naive, and
ugly," "like a man," "a reversal," "coming to the same bad end," say
postmodernists Julia Kristeva, Hélène Cixous, Luce Irigaray, Jacques
Lacan, Roland Barthes, and Jacques Derrida, of feminist politics and
writing.[10] No political movement in the twentieth century, or at any
time in history, is criticized by postmodernists as frequently, or with
such vehemence, as is the feminist movement, or more aptly, feminist
movements, of the last two decades. The postmodernists cited above
make such remarks, moreover, without publishing a single interpretation of a feminist text written by a writer who calls herself a feminist. (*A
prominent feature of disciplinary practices is that one cannot explain why*

one form of discipline is imposed, rather than another, or why discipline is deemed necessary at all.) "Down with feminism," a sign carried by members of the collective *Politique et Psychanalyse*, including Irigaray, during a march in the streets of Paris on International Women's Day, is emblematic of the antipathy many postmodernists have evinced toward feminism.

The tale of the feminist, in most French postmodern writing,[11] would disrupt by its silences and by its outbursts women's most carefully conceived efforts to position ourselves apart from the prescription that females be feminine, or be not at all. The disciplinary act of cancellation exercised by this postmodern tale would strike out any attempt that women make to position ourselves freely.

Women, and feminisms, do not merely transgress postmodern cartographies of woman, as a son might transgress the law of the father. Women, and feminisms, are not so much illegal within postmodernism as we are, often in our daily lives and our writings, outside postmodernism from the very start. I cannot translate into the postmodern discourse of difference, for instance, the new *mestiza* who, in Gloria Anzaldúa's tale of *Borderlands/La Frontera*, learns to juggle ambiguity and contradictions: "She has a plural personality, she operates in a pluralistic mode—nothing is thrust out, the good the bad and the ugly, nothing rejected, nothing abandoned. Not only does she sustain contradictions, she turns the ambivalence into something else."[12] The new *mestiza* is not an echo of postmodern theory. She is an individual who is her own, felt, life movement and histories.

Feminists, including myself, who have attempted to utilize some postmodern tools, often have focused on one of the few debates concerning "woman" that coincides with the debate of modernism and postmodernism, humanism and antihumanism: the discussion of woman as essence and woman as social construction. Such discussion frequently has not questioned the extent to which postmodern theory and feminist reflection on women's lives are synchronous, and has accepted as determinate postmodern prioritization of critical reflection on dualities sprung from a Cartesian inheritance. Not surprisingly, to the extent that these discussions have not questioned sufficiently their discursive presuppositions, they have been unduly constrained in terms of what they might offer a female subject who wishes to understand herselves.

I do not understand myself well as a social construction: that which is built by society (by what society, or societies, seldom is specified) piece by piece over time. Nor do I understand myself well as essential difference: the fixed product of nature, or of a naturalizing process (echo of the masculist tradition that would label the offspring of nature, when she conceives without the aid of humans, "uncultured," "not fully human," "inert"). I cannot classify as essentialist or constructionist, for instance, the well-known passage by Cherríe Moraga, "I am a white girl gone brown to the blood color of my mother / speaking to her through the unnamed part of my mouth / the wide-arched muzzle of brown women."[13] Teresa de Lauretis writes, "Merely to say that sexual difference is 'cultural' allows no greater understanding of female subjectivity, and of women's actual and real differences, than to believe it to be 'natural.'"[14] Or, I would suggest, even feminist debates on woman as essence and woman as social construct, including the discussion in this paper, may leave women no better off than we were before in terms of understanding ourselves. Such debate may offer a parenthesis, a space for women's existence between modern and postmodern cartographies of difference, but it is not likely to offer writings that live intimately with the realities, the struggles, the pains, and the joys, of women's lives.

MY OWN TALE (CONTINUING)

Ever so many tales might be told of woman positioned as difference at the edges of the world, of woman positioned as difference at the edges of the text. My own tale, however, moves around, through, and apart from these two tales, tales I have told not with indifference, objectivity, or distance, but with the hope of hearing something of women, that is, from a position of interest.

My tale addresses actual implications of the "Tale of the Feminine and the Feminist." In academia, during the past decade, postmodernists have tended to define feminist theory more and more restrictively, as the texts, criticism, and interpretation that are produced almost exclusively by writers in educational institutions. In course titles and descriptions in college catalogues, and in numerous academic publications, there is a tacit and sometimes explicit assumption that feminist theory offers highly developed skills especially well-suited to thinking about women, but that feminism, women acting and speaking openly from a position of interest and with a sense of urgency, women who may or may not work and publish in an academic setting, does not. I question, in my tale, this distinction between feminist theory and feminism, especially its tendency to favor apparent neutrality over committed positionality, generality over individuality, and abstract rationality over emotions grounded in daily life, may lead to the dismissal of valuable feminist reflection and may limit feminist theorizing.

I read the overlapping cartographies of modernism and postmodernism, a feminist familiar with the languages of both. I do not live on these maps, but I visit them from time to time, hoping that, as one map overlays another, as the maps shift back and forth, something unexpected and new might be found.

I must decide, as I read these maps, Will I tell their tales as they have been told? Will I tell their tales and make additions? Will I tell their tales at all? *By what right do I listen to these tales? . . . What relation do I have to this tale of the conqueror? . . . Can I be as difference?* Clamorous questions, one by one, encircle, cross, move outside the tales of discipline. Solitary questions become ongoing conversations, resisting, refusing discipline, domestication, dismissal. I decide that I will tell everything that I can.

In the din of these voices I become oblivious to the romance of the margins, the tales of woman as difference. By an assertion of epistemological and ontological autonomy, I thwart major sophisms. No longer caught between modernism and postmodernity, I discover spaces in which women beget women.[15] To beget is not to assure the continuity of theory, textual authority, tradition. To beget is to move into a proximity with life; a spirited conception of tales so imbued with life that there is no place for discipline.

A tale, once heard differently, can be retold.

On the verge of uncovering the sophistry of my own tale, and telling an unending story, I suggest that women who beget women might explore with cartographies that inhabit worlds, rather than cartographies that proscribe and position. Explorations with cartographies thát inhabit might enjoy an intimate understanding, which arises in the interplay of tales that touch, and are touched by, each other; a listening and a telling that resist translation and that are, therefore, without assimilation or loss; a delight in reference, such that experiences written off the text might seep onto the page; the friendship of women with ourselves. While to beget by such a tale telling might seem an unfathomable leap into the blue, it is a skill that we have already when, listening to old stories, we cultivate tales that spring anew from spaces of survival.

NOTES

1. Pierre Samuel, *Amazones, guerriéres et gaillardes* (Brussels: Editions complexe/Presses universitaires de Grenoble, 1975), 22–33; Irving A. Leonard, *Books of the Brave: Being an Account of Books and of Men in the Spanish Conquest and Settlement of the Sixteenth Century New World* (Cambridge: Harvard University Press, 1949), 39–64.

2. Ibid., 38

3. Joan Kelly-Gadol, "Did Women Have a Renaissance," in Renate

Bridenthal and Claudia Koonz, *Becoming Visible: Women in European History* (Boston: Houghton Mifflin, 1977), 137–164.

4. Gayatri Chakravorty Spivak, "French Feminism in an International Frame," *Yale French Studies* 62 (1981): 154–184; Teresa de Lauretis, "Feminist Studies/Critical Studies: Issues, Terms, and Contexts," in *Feminist Studies/ Critical Studies*, ed. Lauretis (Berkeley: University of California Press, 1987), 1–19; Rosa Lee, "Resisting Amnesia: Feminist Painting and PostModernism," *Feminist Review* 26 (Summer 1987): 6–26.

5. "The feminine" and "the feminist" are considered here as representations of postmodernist ideology. Certainly femininity need not be linked with the domestication of women and feminists do not always defy postmodernism.

6. I would like to thank María Lugones, "Playfulness, 'World'–Travelling, and Loving Perception," *Hypatia: Journal of Feminist Philosophy* 2.2 (1987): 3–20, for suggesting concepts with which I have come to understand some of the complexities of world travel. (This article reprinted as Chapter Seventeen of this volume.)

7. Jacques Derrida, *Feu de cendre* (Paris: des femmes, 1987), 56, 57.

8. Monique Plaza, "Our Damages and their Compensation, Rape: The Will not to Know of Michel Foucault," *Feminist Issues* 1.3 (1981): 25–36, cites Foucault's comments on rape, which were published by the Collectif Change in *La Folie encerclée* (October 1977).

9. *Women's International Network News*, ed. Fran P. Hosken, 8 (Autumn 1982): 1, and 6 (Autumn 1980): 20.

10. I cite here only a few of the many references for comments of this type: Julia Kristeva, "From Ithaca to New York," *Polylogue* (Paris: Seuil, 1977), 495–515; Hélène Cixous, "Interview with Hélène Cixous," *Sub-Stance* 13 (1976): 27, and "voice i . . . ," *Boundary 2* 12.2 (1984): 67; Luce Irigaray, *This Sex Which Is Not One* (Ithaca: Cornell University Press, 1985), 160–162; Roland Barthes, *The Grain of the Voice* (New York: Hill and Wang, 1985), 315; Jacques Derrida, "Choreographies," *diacritics* (Summer 1982): 66–77. On Foucault see Monique Plaza, *Our Damages*, noted above, and on Lacan and Psychoanalysis see Monique Plaza, "Psychoanalysis: Subtleties and Other Obfuscations," *Feminist Issues* 4.2 (1984): 51–58.

11. Monique Wittig and Nicole Brossard are writers who are sometimes considered postmodern, and who are exceptions to the discussion in this paragraph.

12. Gloria Anzaldúa, *Borderlands/La Frontera: The New Mestiza* (San Francisco: Spinsters/Aunt Lute, 1987), 79.

13. Cherríe Moraga, "For the Color of My Mother," *Loving in the War Years* (Boston: South End Press, 1983), 60.

14. Teresa de Lauretis, "Feminist Studies/Critical Studies: Issues, Terms, and Contexts," in *Feminist Studies/Critical Studies*, ed. Lauretis (Berkeley: University of California Press, 1987), 12.

15. Michèle Causse, *seven portraits* (Paris: Le Nouveau commerce, 1980), 20, suggests the title for this paper. Also relevant to this discussion is Michèle Causse, (   ), (Montreal: Editions Trois, 1987), 119, 143.

Part II ─────────────────────────
Metaphysics

▬▬▬▬▬▬▬▬▬▬▬▬▬▬▬▬▬▬▬▬▬▬▬▬▬▬▬▬

Metaphysics is both one of the oldest and one of the more controversial areas of philosophy. This field, also called ontology by some philosophers, deals with the theory of reality. The subject matter and methods of metaphysics have been the source of heated arguments through generations of philosophers. Characterizations of metaphysics by traditional philosophers have ranged from "first philosophy" or "the queen of the sciences" to outright "nonsense."

In spite of this controversy, traditional metaphysicians have often sought to provide answers to broad questions such as, "What are the fundamental categories and structures of reality?," "What is the nature of things?," "What is being as such?," and "What is existence (or what does it mean to exist)?" In addition to these very broad questions, contemporary philosophers include in metaphysics topics such as whether human beings have free will, the nature of persons and of the self, and the nature of space and time.

In what respect might one say that such metaphysics is male or male-centered? Its practitioners are men, usually men of privilege; they are the products of androcentric cultures who have had little reason to question the limitations their cultures imposed on their viewpoint. In their metaphysical theories they examine the presuppositions of, try to account for, and attempt to systematize *their* gendered experience. The fact that it is male experience that is reflected on in metaphysics should not surprise us. For it is a customary part of the privilege of the dominant group to be in the position to define reality for themselves and for their subordinates. Naming and defining reality are among the ways in which the dominant group takes and keeps possession of its world.

Simone de Beauvoir believes that women have had the world mediated for them by men; she means that men have told women what the nature of things is. Women have not been expected to "trouble our heads about" questions such as, "What is reality?" or "Of what is the world constituted?"

Now feminists are challenging this allocation of philosophical concerns. Feminist philosophers address questions that spring from women's experience, pertain to women's ways of being, and help us see the ways in which some women's very existence has simply been denied. Such topics are part of the growing field of feminist theory of reality. For example, feminist thinkers are challenging the dualism that underlies and pervades much traditional ontological (metaphysical) theory. Feminist philosophers are carefully scrutinizing the dichotomies of self-other, spirit-matter, mind-body, and active-passive, for these dichotomies reflect the fundamental opposition of male-female, dominant-subordinate, and valued-devalued beings.

Critiquing this dualism so characteristic of male-centered metaphysical theory, Caroline Whitbeck proposes what she terms "a feminist ontology." She calls for the rejection of the model of dualistic opposition; she posits instead a model based on the relation of differentiation, not of opposition. The self-other opposition is replaced by a self-other relationship that is grounded in analogies or similarities between the two beings. She describes this way of being in the world as one of "mutual realization." She sees the mother-child relationship as the paradigm that would be central to this kind of nondualistic women's ontology. Whitbeck's interactive model of self-other is central to her feminist vision of reality and to the project of constructing a feminist ontology.

In discussing what she terms "the politics of reality," Marilyn Frye refashions the traditional male way of dealing with the question "What is reality?" Frye shows us how women have been erased by the patriarchal concept of reality. Reality is what is seen to be, and what is not seen is not real. Women who are not seen (or are not visible to men) are thereby not real; they do not exist. Lesbians, especially, are not visible to men because lesbians are women-centered and do not focus on males' projects; so lesbians do not exist. Frye details this erasure and calls for its end.

Ann Ferguson focuses on theories of the self in a way that weaves together metaphysics with ethics. She asks how women can develop a strong sense of self. Comparing three theories of the self, she rejects the

Rational Maximizer view that sees both men and women as acting out of self-interest, and the Difference Theory that sees women, unlike men, acting in an incorporative mode. Both contain important insights, but are static and essentialist. She posits instead an Aspect Theory that sees an ongoing process of conscious selfhood, with many parts including rationality and incorporative elements. Since the self is developed by participating in social practices, we can empower a women's self by degendering these practices.

Chapter 4

A Different Reality: Feminist Ontology

Caroline Whitbeck

INTRODUCTION

*I*n this chapter I outline a feminist ontology or metaphysics, and argue for its adequacy. This ontology has at its core a conception of the self-other *relation* that is significantly different from the self-other *opposition* that underlines much of so-called "western thought." Dualistic ontologies based on the opposition of self and other generate two related views of the person and of ethics: the patriarchal view and that of individualism. The proponents of individualism or of patriarchy often argue for their view by attacking the other view, as though the only possibilities were variants of these two masculist viewpoints. The feminist ontology outlined here is based on a conception of the relation of self and other(s) that is neither oppositional nor dyadic, and engenders a view of the person and of ethics that is significantly different from both those of individualism and of patriarchy.

The self-other opposition is at the heart of other dualistic oppositions, such as theory-practice, culture-nature, spirit-matter, mind-body, human-divine, political-personal, public-private (or productive-reproductive), knower-known, theory-practice, lover-beloved, that figure prominently in "western thought."[1] The feminist ontology outlined here yields a distinctive, nonoppositional, and nondualistic conception of these subjects, as well as a new view of the person and of ethics. Furthermore, because the relation of self to other is not taken to be represented by gender difference, gender is neither taken to be, nor to be symbolic of, an important ontological difference. Because differentiation does not depend on opposition, the differentiation of the proposed ontology from dualistic ontologies does not require that it be interpreted as the opposite view, or even the only alternative to dualism.

Source: From *Beyond Domination: New Perspectives on Women and Philosophy*, ed. Carol Gould (Totowa, N.J.: Rowman & Allanheld, 1984), 64–88. Copyright © 1984 by Rowman & Allanheld. Reprinted by permission of the author and of the publisher.

The ontology presented here must be understood in relation to a certain general type of practice. By practice I mean a coherent form of cooperative activity, or joint action, as Carol Gould calls it, that not only aims at certain ends but creates certain ways of living and develops certain characteristics (virtues) in those who participate and try to achieve the standards of excellence peculiar to that practice.[2] The practice that I consider to be the core practice is that of the (mutual) realization of people. I take this practice to have a variety of particular forms, most, if not all, of which are regarded as women's work and are therefore largely ignored by the dominant culture. Among these are the rearing of children, the education of children and adolescents, care of the dying, nursing of the sick and injured, and a variety of spiritual practices related to daily life.

These practices are sometimes described as nurturing. Although this language has the advantage of being familiar, it has often been used to evoke a sentimental picture of a woman doing a variety of mindless tasks in response to the demands of other, and for that reason I am reluctant to use it.[3] The creativity and reponsibility of all parties in the conduct of the practice in its full, liberated form is inconsistent with the sentimental picture of women's self-sacrifice. These points will be illustrated in the discussion of the practices of family life, below, and will be discussed further in the section on the ontology of the person.

A characterization of the core practice that would be adequate to represent it in its major forms and in a variety of cultural contexts will require discussion of the forms of that practice from a variety of individual and cultural perspectives. It may only be from a few cultural perspectives that it seems plausible to work out the associated ontology, or at least to describe it as ontology.

The vision of society that fits the ontology outlined in this paper is that of society organized around the practices of mutual realization, practices which by and large have been "women's work." This is close, if not identical, to the vision of society that Barbara Ehrenreich and Deirdre English point to at the end of their book, *For Her Own Good: 150 Years of the Expert's Advice to Women* (p. 292). The views that they characterize as romantic and as rationalist are the exemplifications in recent Anglo-American culture of the views that I term patriarchal and individualistic, respectively. (Unfortunately they call the feminist view to be developed a "synthesis" of the replaced views. This use of Marxian-Hegelian jargon obscures the point that, as their book documents, *neither* the romantic nor rationalist alternative attends to women's experience, as contrasted with men's representations of women. A literal synthesis of two views rooted in dualism would only yield another dualistic view.)

Since the liberation of women's practices is central to this vision, it must be developed by articulating the experience of those engaged in the practices. Although this is a task that can be assisted and midwifed by academics and other theoreticians, I think that little can be contributed by dissociating ourselves from what have been women's practices, and the women engaged in them, since we will then either ignore those practices or inadvertently perpetuate the false account that masculist culture gives of them.

In the second section I summarize some earlier research that uses influential psychological theories to expose the dualistic ontology presupposed by "western thought." This is followed by an examination of the views of the person and of ethics that derive from the patriarchal and from the individualist variants of dualism. The project of constructing a feminist ontology, and the heuristic function of feminist psychology for that philosophical project, are considered in the fourth section. The main features of the ontology are next presented: reality is understood in terms of the interactions among multiple factors that are often analogous, rather than in terms of dualistic oppositions. The sixth section contains the account of the person that flows from the feminist ontology presented in the preceding section. I argue that the person is a relational and historical being whose creativity and moral integrity are both developed and realized in and through relationships and practices. The correlative ethical viewpoint outlined in the seventh section takes the notion of the moral responsibilities that go with relationships as the fundamental moral notion. Moral rights, including human rights, have their ultimate warrant as the moral claims on others and on social institutions that safeguard a person's ability to fulfill the responsibilities of relationships that person has formed or may form. A summary of the ontology is given in the final section.

THE USE OF PSYCHOLOGICAL THEORY TO REVEAL MASCULIST ONTOLOGY

Several years ago, I documented a remarkable constancy over 3,000 years in the themes or motifs embodied in the theories proposed by philosophers and scientists to identify and explain sex differences (Whitbeck 1973–74). I shall briefly summarize that research since it reveals some major features of masculist ontology. Three themes repeatedly occur:

1. woman is an incomplete man;
2. there are two opposing or complementary principles, masculine and feminine, that are constitutive of reality; and

3. the strengths or virtues proper to women are defined by male
   needs.

In some cases a single theory exemplifies two or more of these themes.
The recurrence of these themes is all the more notable when one
considers that our views about nature, scientific method, and the like
have undergone profound changes in that period of time. Each theme
shows an androcentric bias; that is, the male, or the male experience, is
taken as the norm.

Although the theories of Freud and the Jungians exemplify the first
and second themes and are incoherent in their treatment of *female*
development, their theories of male development give major clues as to
how the three recurrent themes arise in the thoughts and fantasies of
little boys. In particular, the view that the masculine and feminine are
opposite principles that symbolize other major oppositions, especially
an opposition of self and other, is one that the Jungians trace to the
(male) infant's differentiation of his masculine self from the feminine
primordial nurturer. It is this second theme, which dates at least from
Pythagoras, that is central to masculist ontology. (It turns up even in
influential theories, such as those of Aristotle and Freud, that for the
most part view woman as an incomplete man.) The masculine principle
is taken to have whatever attributes the culture sees as appropriate to
the conscious and rational self. The characteristics that are viewed as
opposite are attributed to the second, the feminine principle. Although
the two principles are frequently held to be complementary, the
association of the masculine principle with rationality leads to a
hierarchical interpretation of the relationship between the principles,
so that the masculine is viewed as superior and the feminine as
inferior.[4]

Norman O. Brown echoes the same ontological dualism based on
sexual opposition when he says, "Dual organization is sexual organization. The structural principle is the union of opposites. . . . The *agon*, the
contest between winter and summer, night and day is coitus" (Brown
1966, pp. 22–23). (Brown's statement accurately reflects a crucial ambiguity or confusion in the dualistic thought concerning the nature of the
relation of the self to the other. On the one hand, the relation is
represented as attraction; on the other, it is represented as one of
conflict that gives rise to a struggle for dominance. The confusion
between attraction and aggression is evident in the view that rape is a
normal expression of male sexuality.)[5]

Standing outside the ontology based on dualistic oppositions, one
can easily recognize what is odd about the attempt to represent cyclical
changes as an alternation between opposing states. If we consider the
seasons, for example, we find there is nothing about those cycles that

dictates what two points should be taken as the supposed extremes of the cycle. One might select extremes of temperature, or of duration of daylight, or any number of other pairs of points.

It is important to distinguish clearly between dualistic ontology and the ontology proposed in my fifth section. Too often the project of constructing a feminist view is confused with the project of simply affirming the goodness or the primacy of the characteristics associated with what masculist dualistic thought views as the feminine principle, or appropriate to the feminine gender, or arising from female biology. The latter tendency, which is common in the writing of Jungians and some feminists, was prefigured in the defense of Mother-Right and the Dionysian (as opposed to Father-Right and the Apollonian) in the writings of Nietzsche and Bachofen.[6]

TWO VERSIONS OF DUALIST ONTOLOGY: PATRIARCHY AND INDIVIDUALISM

Masculist dualist ontology has been developed along two related lines. The first, and older, line of development generates patriarchy in the strict sense—the rule of the fathers, with its hierarchal organization of political life modeled on the organization of the patriarchal family. This view is followed, and to some extent is replaced by individualism, with what may be called "the rule of the sons." The resulting view of family, political, and psychic life, however, presupposes the preceding patriarchal view.

The sisters are rarely mentioned in the theories of liberation associated with the rebellion of the sons against the father. Brothers would be brothers to sisters as well as to one another. The absence of any reference to the sisters symbolizes a key feature of individualism; that is, individualism reflects the concerns of a certain group of men, those whose primary experience of domination was at the hands of a father or a monarch, and provides the basis for an ideological justification for their rebellion against that oppression. It retains the same opposition of self to other. It is therefore hardly surprising that individualism leaves untouched forms of domination other than domination of the sons by the father and of propertied citizens by the monarch. (In Locke's original scheme the right to vote did not extend even to those free men who did not own property. In early America property was widely available, so the distinction between those men who had property and those who did not was not of major significance in creating societal divisions. The denial of the civil and human rights of slaves on the basis that they themselves were property shows the strength of the idea of property rights in early America, however [see

Lodge 1977, chapter 4].) The same dualism underlies Hegel's version of patriarchy and the individualism of Sartre's *Being and Nothingness*. (An illuminating account of the central place of sexual dualism in Sartre's discussion of the dualistic opposition between the for-itself and the in-itself has been given by Margery Collins and Christine Pierce [1973–74].) Indeed, these philosophical frameworks exhibit the features of dualism even more explicitly than do Hobbesian-Lockean individualism and Aristotelian patriarchy, to which I shall give more attention. For example, in Hegel's *Phenomenology of Spirit*, the presupposition of an opposition between self and other is underscored by the statement that "the relation of the two self-conscious individuals is such that they prove themselves and each other through a life and death struggle" (Hegel 1977, pp. 113–14). Indeed, Hegel starts by taking the self-other relation to be a master-slave relation. Some philosophers desire to interpret the notion of dialectic in Hegel in a way that replaces the notion of opposition with something more congenial to the notion of historical development that is also in Hegel; however, the difficulty is in Hegel—opposition is where Hegel starts.[7] If a mother saw the emerging person who is her child in the way that Hegel describes, human beings would not exist. The failure of Hegel's scheme to apply to the mother's experience in the primordial mother-child relation is a significant failure. An understanding of differentiation that does not depend on opposition and a life and death struggle is essential to the ontology outlined here.

From the dualistic perspective the other is taken to be opposite to the self. Therefore, if one takes existence itself as a predicate, solipsism becomes a plausible ontological viewpoint; that is, one can ask, "If I am, can anything else even exist?" Indeed, in view of the potential threat to the self of an other assumed to be opposite, solipsism may even be an attractive position. If one is willing to grant the existence of others, their character becomes a question.

Dualism runs through Aristotle's thought, from his early thinking recorded in the *Physics* to his late work in *Generation of Animals*. Aristotle took the dualistic opposition between male and female as his *starting point*, and he used it as the model for the relation of form to matter, which is at the core of his entire ontology (*Physics*: Book Alpha, 192a). Form is rational and active; matter is irrational and passive. Thus, far from being a quaint aberration in Aristotle's thought, his construal of the relation between male and female as dualistic opposition is crucial to his ontology.

According to Aristotle, only the free adult male (in fact only the Athenian citizen) qualifies as a full person, because only he has fully functioning and authoritative rational capacity (*Politics* Book 1). Aristotle says explicitly, and repeatedly, that to be born female is the most common kind of deformity (*Generation of Animals* 728a, 18 and 766b, 20). Because only the free male adult (Athenian citizen) has full and authoritative rational powers, his relation to others, i.e., to female non-slaves, to slaves, and to children (presumed free and male), is largely determined by his obligation to reason for them.

In view of Aristotle's analogy between the relation of male to female and the relation of form to matter, it is not surprising that in the *Politics* he needs explicitly to disclaim the view that the relation of a man to a woman is necessarily that of a master to a slave. (This is a view that he attributes to the "barbarians" in a handy bit of projection.) Aristotle argues that wives, for example, are to be managed, whereas slaves and children are to be ruled as a monarch rules his subjects. According to Aristotle, the female is naturally attracted to the male (although not the reverse), and so the wife, unlike the slave or barbarian, willingly accepts management by the husband.

Aristotle's scheme is more egalitarian than those in which only the eldest son eventually matured to take on the full status of a patriarch. This is not surprising since we know the limited democracy in which Aristotle lived. In Aristotle's thought we find some of the seeds of the individualism that was to follow, and his thought gives important clues as to how individualism develops out of patriarchy. (Just as some elements of individualism were prefigured in some patriarchal systems, so elements of the patriarchal view are to be found in the thinking and legal systems of our contemporary individualistic society.)[8]

Let us return to the story of development: if, or to the extent that, children do not identify with their care givers and do not take the skills appropriate to mutual realization as appropriate to the self, then the relation to siblings must be constituted as one of competition for the attentions of the primordial nurturer(s). In what follows, I shall call the adult counterparts of such children "the peers."[9]

The notion of an "equal" or "peer" assumes a hierarchic ranking in which people are identified as superiors, inferiors, and equals. The notion of equality also reflects those peculiar concerns with measurement that seem to enter into men's relations with each other. For example, men "take each other's measure" and speak of the need to "measure up." In contrast to the relationship that exists among the sisters (and brothers) who acquire, and aspire to, the skills and virtues necessary for eliciting the strengths of others, the sons' relationships to one another are, at best, enforceable contracts that function to keep competition within bounds, or alliance against some common enemy, like a domineering father or monarch. In view of the centrality of the theme of competition in defining their relationships and the practices in which they are engaged (competitive sports, wars of rebellion, class war, or wars of national interest), alliance against a common enemy, rather than friendship, is the basis for cooperation among the peers. The moral aspects of the relationships among the peers are specified in terms of rights that generate moral requirements that vary only with changes of contract.

According to individualism the self is assumed to be a peer, that is, only the perspective of the peers is taken into account.[10] Furthermore, only such peers are regarded as full persons, in the sense that the only decisions that are regarded as significant are the decisions of peers. The person is regarded as an atom, in the sense that individualism ignores both the interdependence of people and their historical character. The denial of interdependence is a consequence of confining attention to the peers or later to all men.[11] Restriction of the concept of a person so that it extends only to peers—and ignores the women, children, and (for a period) enslaved men and laborers—ignores the agency of the latter groups and the dependency of the peers on them. In particular, the practices regarded as women's work are ignored.[12]

The model of people offered in individualism is adequate to model only the transactions among the peers (in a certain type of market society; see Hartsock 1981). What happens, even to the peers, when they are too young or old or sick to compete and contract with other peers is largely ignored and unrepresentable in terms of the atomic model of persons. Just as it ignores all areas of human vulnerability, so the individualistic model ignores human development. In this respect individualism is less adequate than patriarchy, notwithstanding the extension of full personhood to a larger group—the peers rather than just the patriarchs.

The atomistic representation of persons is implicit not merely in the work of those thinkers from Hobbes and Locke through Nozick, who emphasize the individual's right to pursue self-interest, but also in the work of those from Rousseau through Rawls, who assume they can found the notion of a just society on an agreement among ideal individuals who are construed as existing apart from the history of their relationships and, therefore, apart from their own cultural and intellectual history.

THE PROJECT OF CREATING FEMINIST ONTOLOGY

The very idea of a feminist ontology is not likely to sit well in some circles. Those who balk at the idea of a feminist ontology are, nonetheless, usually able to envision the possibility that there is a pattern of psychological development typical for women that is alternative to that typical for men. Furthermore, although constructing reality in a certain way is not reducible to having undergone a certain pattern of psychological development, feminist theories of women's development do serve a heuristic function for the construction of a feminist's ontology.

Freud (and others) tell us that the male infant's differentiation from a Nurturer (who is viewed as opposite) leads to a preoccupation with the possession of the Nurturer, and with the issue of competing with others with similar designs (Rawlinson 1982). These masculist theories of development have an androcentric (not to mention ethnocentric) bias that make them inapplicable to the development of the girl. First, as I have argued, the mother-son relation has itself been read by men in terms of their own (culturally mediated) adult relation to women so that, for example, the attachment of the infant to the mother is interpreted on the model of a man's sexual attraction to a woman (Whitbeck 1983b). It is possible that this has lead to a misreading of the attachment of infants to their mothers. It is certainly an error to interpret the *mother's* attachment to her daughter (and even to her son) as sexual in the narrow sense (although as I have argued it is both sensual and erotic [Whitbeck 1975]), because of the comparative rarity of mother-child incest as compared with father-child, and brother-sister, incest.

The arguments of feminist psychologists may not be read as ontology, however. First, it may be necessary to free the psychological account of any terminology that presupposes the received, masculist ontology. (I would argue that much of the terminology of ego psychology, as well as that of Freudian, Jungian, and Lacanian psychoanalytic theory, assumes masculist self-other distinction.[13] Therefore, in spite of the importance of the insights to be gained from reading works by feminist psychologists like Juliet Mitchell and Nancy Chodorow, who employ the technical terminology of psychoanalytic theory and ego psychology, it is important to recognize that concepts such as that of "object relations" presuppose the masculist opposition of self and other. It does so in postulating an either/or investment of libidinal energy, that is, in postulating that energy is *either* directed toward the self *or* directed toward an other in a way that makes it impossible to represent caring about the-self-in-relation-to-others.)

Some feminist philosophers in the last five years have discussed feminine development in a way that relies heavily on dualist categories taken from psychoanalytic theory and object relations theory, and in ways that do not provide a heuristic for a feminist ontology. For example, Sandra Harding says the "feminine personality develops through the struggle to separate and individuate from a kind of person whom she will in fact nevertheless become—a devalued woman" (Harding 1981, p. 315). Such a reading is an account of the perpetuation of women's oppression. If that reading were formative for a woman's own self-understanding, it would lead either to despair or to the attempt to dissociate oneself from women and women's practices.

Even where the psychological theory dispenses with masculist categories (or makes as little use as is possible for a contemporary speaker of English, Spanish, etc.), it is necessary to distinguish, at least provisionally, those features of women's thinking and practice that are the results of women's oppression. Finally, even where feminist psychologists write without recourse to masculist categories, and explicitly address the issue of distinguishing the results of oppression from other features of women's psychology (as do Jean Baker Miller in *Toward A New Psychology of Women*, and Janet L. Surrey in "The Relational Self in Women"), there still remains the philosophical project of extracting the view of reality and of ethics implicit in women's liberated practice.

I read the girl's development as follows: girls form their self-concepts in large part through identification with their first significant other(s) who share the same socially defined possibilities of a female body. As a result, the self-other distinction is neither symbolized by a distinction between the sexes, nor does it involve the assumption that the self and other possess opposing characteristics. Therefore, I disagree with the view expressed by Chodorow and Harding that mothers internalize the representation of gender difference as a dualistic opposition, and then recreate or pass on this dualistic understanding to their sons (Chodorow 1978, p. 166; Harding 1981, p. 315). I think Chodorow and Harding have missed the crucial distinction between seeing another as an opposite, and seeing the other as distinct and different in some respect.[14] A girl's (socially reinforced) identification with her nurturers also often leads to an identification with the virtues and skills necessary for the practices of mutual development.[15] Furthermore, since sisters, grandmothers, and aunts commonly care for children in many cultures, the girl is typically involved in a multiagent network of mutual realization.

The heuristic function of the foregoing arguments should not be forgotten: I do not claim that it is *only* by undergoing a particular course of early development that one can come to the ontological position described here. Although a certain history of relationships may incline a person to seek out other relationships and practices that embody a similar ontological outlook, people may become convinced of the superiority of a particular ontology and seek the relationships and practices consistent with that view. (Theory may guide practice!) I agree with Sara Ruddick that "although some men do, and more generally men should, acquire maternal thinking [or, more generally, self-others thinking], their ways of acquisition are necessarily different from ours" (Ruddick 1980, p. 346). I maintain that the extent of that difference is determined by differences in relationships and practices in which a man has participated. (Notable in my experience of mother-reared men who have internalized self-others thinking and practice are men who have internalized the practice of Friends—Quakers.) People who have little familiarity with the practices and relationships that embody self-others thinking seem to need to give and receive arguments to the effect that "no man is an island."

It is not easy to make clear an ontological proposal when basic concepts are involved. The difficulty is that the terminology in which the new ontology is to be articulated is automatically interpreted in terms of the accepted ontology, so that one is always at the risk of having one's statements construed either as nonsense, or as a quaint phrasing of what are familiar truths according to the old ontology. For example, although we can *now* express the changes in our concepts of space and time brought about by the special theory of relativity by saying that "space and time form a single continuum," or by referring to the "relativity of non-accelerated motion," those phrases would have been of little use to Einstein in *introducing* his theory. Such statements would probably have been misconstrued to state what were taken to be truths according to the Newtonian view. If, on the other hand, Einstein had said that simultaneity or, more generally, that the time elapsed between two events, is relative to the observer's state of motion, the statement would have seemed nonsensical. (Einstein actually tried to make his point by describing information gained by the sending of light signals. The predictable result was that his central claim about the nature of space-time was confused with claims about the speed of light and about conventionality of simultaneity for a *given* observer [Whitbeck 1969].)

Today, one of the easiest ways to introduce the concepts of space-time to students who have a background in mathematics is to use the Minkowski graphic representation. It is instructive to recall that not only was this representation no part of Einstein's original thinking, but that when it was presented to him, he did not initially recognize it as expressing what he wanted to say.

This illustrates an important feature of ontological proposals: further articulation of an ontological position is not separable from the proposal of an ontology, and therefore any significant ontological proposal is unlikely to be the work of a single individual. In particular, the ontology outlined here depends on a deeper understanding of the practices of mutual realization for its development, since to the extent that these relationships and practices have been represented in the dominant culture, they have been misrepresented (Ehrenreich and English 1978). Mother-children relationships and the practice of mothering and/or family living are paradigmatic examples. Nursing and caring for the sick, disabled, and elderly, teaching psychotherapy and counseling, and various forms of spiritual practice are others. (For some feminist representations of these and related relationships and practices, see McBride 1972; Freire 1973, 1974; Miller 1976; Rich 1976; Boulding 1978; Christ and Plaskow 1979; Ruddick 1980; Gilligan 1982; Lindemann and Oliver 1982; Whitbeck 1975, 1981a and b, 1982, 1983b; Joan Ringelheim's research on the women of the Holocaust—1983; Addelson, unpublished; and the references in each.)

FEMINIST ONTOLOGY: AFTER DUALISM, OR, NONE OF THE ABOVE

At the core of the ontology that I am proposing is a self-other relation that is assumed to be a relation between beings who are in some respects analogous, and the scope and limits of that analogy (what Mary Hesse calls points of "negative and positive analogy" [Hesse 1965]) are something to be explored in each case. This starting point is quite different from that which arises from the opposition of self and other, namely, that the burden of proof is on anyone who claims that the other is in any way like the self. A recurrent tendency that results from the opposition of self and other is to deny the existence of the other to a greater or lesser degree or to make any existing other into the self. In the extreme this results in solipsism or in various forms of patriarchy that represent the patriarch or the state as the decision-maker for the family, clan, or nation. (Elsewhere I have argued that this assumption of dualism lies behind the so-called "problem of other minds" in philosophy. In addition to assuming mind-body dualism, this supposed problem assumes that the burden is to show that the other is like the self in "having" a mind [Whitbeck 1983b].)

The question for those who hold the ontology based on a self-other relation is, what are the scope and limits of the analogy between the self and an other? Since an other is not taken to be opposite to the self, the character of the self does not uniquely define the character of the other by opposition to it: others may be similar or dissimilar in an unlimited variety of ways. Even to make the relation a dyadic relation distorts the ontological position I am outlining here. The relation is not fundamentally dyadic at all, and is better expressed as a self-others relation, because relationships, past and present, realized and sought, are constitutive of the self, and so the actions of a person reflect the more-or less-successful attempt to respond to the whole configuration of relationships.

Since the relations of the self to others are relations among analo-gous beings, and the scope and limits of that analogy are to be discovered or, if the other is another person, to be mutually created and transformed, relationships between people are understood as developing through identification and differentiation, through listening and speaking, with *each other*, rather than through struggles to dominate or annihilate the other. That the images associated with transformation are nonviolent should not be taken to suggest that the transformations are less profound, or more gradual, or easy, but only that the process of change is more complex than that which can be represented in terms of successive dualistic oppositions. Birth is hardly trivial or gradual, and may be painful or difficult. (Mary Condren argues on the basis of a great deal of textual evidence that whereas women's creativity is expressed in relation to the giving and sustaining of life, men's creativity takes place in relation to death and death-defying activities [Condren 1982].)

In place of an ontology characterized by dualistic oppositions, of self-other, egoism-altruism, theory-practice, culture-nature, mind-body, knower-known, male-female (and therefore, straight-gay), public-private (or productive-reproductive), human-divine, political-personal, spiritual-material, etc., the self-others relation generates a multifactorial interactive model of most, if not all, aspects of reality. Because the content of each related term is not defined by opposition to the content of the term with which it is paired, these terms no longer mean what they meant in masculist theory.

Thus, for example, theory aims at the clarification of practice, rather than the discovery or creation of some sort of Popperian or Platonic World of Ideas, itself immune from decay and death, that might confer an immortality of sorts upon its creators; culture does not aim at the pornographic objectification and domination of nature so brilliantly analyzed by Susan Griffin in her book, *Pornography and Silence*. Culture is a body of developing and decaying interpretations and strategies created by people for understanding and interacting with human and nonhuman aspects of nature and with other aspects of culture. Not only can the personal be political, for example, but both politics and personal life are bound up with other matters not easily classifiable either as political or as personal. Not only are our bodies ourselves (rather than being something that we, as minds, possess), but the bodies, intellects, emotions, souls, characters, and configurations of relationships that we are can be adequately understood only in relation to one another.

ONTOLOGY OF THE PERSON

The model of the person that I propose is a relational and historical model but, unlike the relational and historical models of patriarchy, one that takes seriously everyone's creativity and moral integrity. On this view it is the exercise of human creativity in the realization of aspirations and the maintenance of moral integrity, rather than success-ful performance of an externally definable role, that are the key elements in a person's well-being.

On this view relationships to other people are fundamental to being a person, and one cannot become a person without relationships to other people. A person is an historical being whose history is funda-mentally a history of relationships to other people.[16] This feature of people or persons is not adequately captured by saying that people are cultural beings, although the latter statement is also true. By virtue of being the cultural beings we are, we possess the languages we do; but the history of the relationships which, in part, constitute us, is some-thing over and above our cultural heritage.

It is important to emphasize that the relationships I am discuss-ing are *lived* relationships, not legal or biological relationships, although relationships in the latter sense may influence lived relation-ships. The concept of a relationship also contrasts with the notion of a role as something that a person can take on and later reject and be no more affected by than the clothing one has temporarily worn.

This notion of relationship has some affinities with the notions of practice I discussed in the first section of this essay. Something is lost, however, when the relationships that constitute and are constituted by those practices are not given a primary place in the discussion. Perhaps the tendency to emphasize practices rather than relationships is due to the relative ease with which one can ignore what is taken to be the secondary private world in discussing practices: in discussing practices it is relatively easy to confine attention to practices in the so-called real public world, whereas lived relationships are personal and involve much that is regarded as private. If so, the tendency rests on the acceptance of an opposition of public and private. If relationships are necessary to the emergence of a person, then the existence of social practices requires the prior emergence of the people who participate in those practices, and hence the existence of relationships among people.

The ontology based upon a self-others relation is adequate to represent many facts that have been anomalous from the point of view of dualistic ontology, and thus have regularly escaped notice. For example, the customary views of the family, both the sentimental view of it as a haven in a heartless world ministered to by an angel mother-wife, and the disenchanted view of it as a hell-hole in which the neuroses of one generation are visited upon the next, fail to take account of the extent to which all family members, including the youngest, are typically involved in caring for the others. Sociologist Elise Boulding puts the point in the following way:

> We expect parents to nurture children, but forget that children also nurture parents. Even the fact that children often nurse sick and temporarily bedridden parents [or siblings] is by a pathological twist of the social memory simply forgotten. Each act of healing becomes a part of the personality of both the healer and the healed, a part of each person's future [Boulding 1978].

I submit that what Boulding calls "a pathological twist of social memory" is a predictable consequence of an ontology that views matters in terms of dualistic oppositions so that one and only one member of any dyad can be creative in any except competitive relations.

A related finding that is also recalcitrant to representation in dualistic ontologies is the finding that for some clients of psychotherapy, who were themselves children of disturbed parents whom they as children experienced no success in healing, progress in therapy occurred only as the therapist was able to accept healing by the client (Searles 1980).[17]

Other findings that show the inadequacy of the dichotomy between egoism and altruism that arises from the self-other opposition are the facts that led to the World Health Organization's construction of the concept of maternal-child health. One might suppose that if any aspect of a person's well-being could be construed individualistically, it would be health (as contrasted with such things as status or economic security), but the health of the mother and of the child are so intimately connected that neither can be influenced without influencing the other.

THE ETHICS

It is a measure of how impoverished the view of the person has become in contemporary philosophical discussions that an increasing number of writers now use the term person to mean nothing more than a being with certain rights, particularly a right to life.[18] This restricted view of the moral person arises as the attempt is made to model all moral requirements on the rights that proved so central in arguing for the legitimacy of the "rule of the sons" that replaced patriarchy. The view that the notion of a right is the fundamental notion in ethics is what I call "the rights view of ethics." The overreliance upon and/or loose use of the concept of rights in contemporary ethics has been pointed out by a number of authors, some of whom, like MacIntyre (1981), and Ladd (1979, 1982) specifically link their criticisms to a criticism of modern individualism. It is Ladd's account that I find most helpful in outlining an alternative view of ethics compatible with the ontological viewpoint presented here. That John Ladd has developed this view of ethics, or one very much like it, gives a concrete demonstration that the philosophical viewpoint I am proposing is not unavailable to men.[19]

According to the rights view of ethics, the concept of a moral right is the fundamental moral notion, or at least the one of preeminent significance. People are viewed as social and moral atoms, armed with rights and reason, and actually or potentially in competition and conflict with one another. (It is a testimony to this culture's obsession with competition that so often aspiration is rendered in competitive terms; for example, "I am competing with myself." A key difference between aspiration and competition is that the goals of competition are achieved by making the competitor fail.) If any attention is given to relationships on the rights view, it is assumed they exist on a contractual or quasi-contractual basis and that the moral requirements arising from them are limited to rights and obligations.

In contrast to obligations that generally specify what acts or conduct are morally required, permitted, or forbidden, responsibilities (in the prospective sense of "responsibility for") specify the ends to be achieved rather than the conduct required. Thus, responsibilities require an exercise of discretion on the part of their bearers. People without the knowledge to exercise discretion in some matter can have only moral obligation and not moral responsibilities in that matter. What I call "the responsibilities view" of ethics takes the moral responsibilities arising out of a relationship as the fundamental moral notion, and regards people as beings who can (among other things) act for moral reasons, and who come to this status through relationships with other people. Such relationships are not assumed to be contractual. The relationship of children to their parents is a good example of a relationship that is not contractual. In general, relationships between people place moral responsibilities on both parties, and these responsibilities change over time with changes in the parties and their relationship. (Newborns cannot have any responsibilities, and for that reason may be regarded as immanent people.) Each party in a relationship is responsible for ensuring some aspect of the other's welfare or, at least, for achieving some ends that contribute to the other's welfare or achievement. This holds even in asymmetrical relationships (whether personal or occupational), such as the relationship between parent and child or between client and lawyer.

Rights and obligations do have a place within the responsibilities view. Human rights are claims upon society and upon other people that are necessary if a person is to be able to meet the responsibilities of her or his relationships. Although only moral agents can have moral responsibilities and thus can have moral rights, according to this view, moral agents may, and probably do, have some moral obligations toward, or responsibility for, the welfare of other beings who are not moral agents, that is, beings who do not themselves have the moral status of people. For example, people may have a moral obligation to treat corpses with respect, or not to be cruel to animals.

I maintain that a rights view of ethics yields an inadequate view of the moral status of people or "persons" and disregards the importance of the special responsibilities that go with affectional and occupational relationships. In some cases, notably in situations involving adults who are strangers, the situation may be described adequately in terms of rights and obligations alone. (The question of whether anyone is ever a total stranger is answered differently in different ethical and religious frameworks.) When the relationships between the parties are significant, or even necessary in order for one of the parties to become a moral agent, the moral responsibilities arising out of relationships are of central importance.[20]

It is important that the description of a relationship and the responsibilities that attend the relationship begin with that of the parties to it (although such a description is criticizable by others so that, for example, there may be grounds for saying that a child is being abused even if initially neither the child nor parent sees the relationship that way). This means that the responsibilities approach to ethics has a greater potential for cross-cultural applicability than does the rights approach, which has no means for representing variation in moral requirements with variation in lived relationships. Since the fulfillment of the responsibilities for the welfare of others that attends one's relationships to them is essential to the maintenance of moral integrity, each person's moral integrity is integrally related to the maintenance of the moral integrity of others. Thus, on this view their self-interest is not something that can be neatly separated from the interests of others.

In contrast to the usual dualist accounts, *all* parties to the relationship and participants in the practice emerge and develop and, therefore, the relationships and practices also develop. Furthermore, what counts as *proper* development is itself partially specified in terms of acquisition of the very virtues necessary to engage in the key practices of mutual realization.

The liberation of women's relationships and practices requires that those practices and relationships be so reconstituted that the skills, sensitivities, and virtues, which make it possible for people to contribute to one another's development, be the primary traits developed in everyone. This liberation is a social task, and for this reason communities committed to this transformation have often undertaken to separate from those unwilling to take part in it. Faithfulness in relationships and the advancement of liberated practices does require that one sometimes contest another's actions, or cause the other pain or disappointment. As Jean Baker Miller has argued (1976), the liberation of women's practice will mean that developing others will no longer be a matter of self-sacrifice on the part of those engaged in the practice, a self-sacrifice that ultimately contributes to the perpetuation of practices and relationships of domination and competition. It follows that among the virtues that are necessary to engage in and sustain the liberated practices are strengths to resist domination and co-optation of one's development of others.

SUMMARY OF THE ONTOLOGY

In view of the foregoing arguments it may be clear that in spite of the intuitive plausibility and even obviousness of some features of the proposed ontology, a thorough-going replacement of dualistic ontologies with an ontology such as this has major implications for both theory and practice. The ontology is based on an understanding of the relation of self and other as a relation between analogous beings. The nature and extent of the analogy is something to be determined in each case. Therefore, the distinction between the self and an other does not turn on construing the other as opposite; another distinct being may, and usually does, possess some of the same characteristics as the self. Because the distinction between the self and an other does not turn on an opposition, the characteristics of the self do not define a unique other by opposition. There may be many others who differ in character from one another as well as being numerically distinct from one another and from the self. In place of the self-other opposition, therefore, we have the relation of the self and others, and in place of the previously mentioned dualistic oppositions that figure so prominently in "western thought," we have multifactorial interactive models. Since there is no assumed opposition between the self and other, there is no general motivation to either deny the existence of others, reduce all others to the self—"one soul in two bodies"—or to interpret the other as mere material for the self's designs.

On this view the person is understood as a relational and historical being. One becomes a person in and through relationships with other people; being a person requires that one have a history of relationships with other people, and the realization of the self can be achieved only in and through relationships and practices. The fundamental moral notion is that of the responsibility for (some aspect of) another's welfare arising from one's relationship to that person. Responsibilities are mutual, although the parties to a relationship may have different responsibilities. Rights (and the correlative obligations) receive their warrant as the claims upon institutions and other people that must be honored if people are to be able to meet the responsibilities of their relationships.

NOTES

I thank Margaret Rhodes, Spencer Carroll, Nona Lyons, Carol Gould, and Mary Vetterling-Braggin for helpful criticisms of earlier versions of this essay.

1. For an early and important feminist critique of dualistic thinking, see Ruether (1972). I believe that I heard all or part of the argument of this paper presented at Yale around 1970. A number of the other essays in this volume criticize one or another of these dualistic oppositions. Hilde Hein's critique of the spirit-matter opposition, which is the only one that I have seen at the time of this writing, is very illuminating. Carolyn Merchant's major historical study of the period 1500–1700 both transcends the customary spirit-matter dichotomy and gives an account of some of its historical antecedents (Merchant 1980). Sherry Ortner has discussed the relation between the culture-nature opposition and the male-female opposition in masculist thought (Ortner 1974). A number of other early essays by feminist anthropologists and other feminist scholars outside of philosophy, which deal with dualisms in different cultures, are contained in Rosaldo and Lamphere (1974). Sandra Harding has written on the knower-known dichotomy as it affects investigations in the social sciences (Harding 1981), and numerous feminist and nonfeminist philosophers in the last ten years have argued against the mind-body dualism of Descartes and modern philosophy. Not all these treatments are consistent with the view presented in this paper. This is particularly true of those accounts that rely heavily on theories that incorporate dualistic thinking while arguing against some particular polarity or dichotomy. Another recent work on dualism is Glennon (1979). I am indebted to Linda Gardiner for bringing it to my attention.

I regard feminist philosophy as primarily concerned with the construction and development of concepts and models adequate for the articulation of women's experience and women's practices. Many of the most important influences on my work have been the practices and new ways of living that many women have helped to create, and it is difficult to find ways adequately to acknowledge those creations and their creators. In addition to the influence of writers and thinkers mentioned in previous papers, I would like to acknowledge the influence of women's music on the practices in which I have participated and on my theoretical reflections on those practices. I am particularly impressed with the range of women's experience that Holly Near, and Sweet Honey in The Rock have expressed, and with the representation of the self in transformation in Chris Williamson's work. Women's music is all the more impressive in its ability to speak to many people.

In arguing that reality should not be understood dualistically, I am not arguing that oppositional thinking is never helpful in the continuing struggle to liberate our thinking. It may sometimes be important to temporarily reorganize one's experience in terms of an opposition of the self and the oppressive other in order to liberate oneself from fatalistic acceptance of oppression, as Paulo Freire suggests (1973). I am indebted to Kate Lindemann for demonstrating some of the general applicability of Freire's scheme (Lindemann and Oliver 1982).

2. My definition is indebted to MacIntyre's, although Ruddick's use of the term is similar in many ways, and her use is influenced by that of Habermas (Ruddick 1980). Carol Gould's expression "joint action" (Gould 1981) is more likely to highlight the departure from individualism than MacIntyre's "cooperative activity," but for that reason may seem more obscure. MacIntyre defines a practice as follows: "By 'a practice' I am going to mean any coherent and complex form of socially established cooperative human activity through which goods internal to that activity are realized in the course of trying to achieve those standards of excellence which are appropriate to, and partially definitive of, that form of activity, with the result that human powers to achieve excellence, and human conceptions of ends and goods involved, are systematically extended" (MacIntyre 1981, p. 175).

3. Elsewhere I have used the expression "calling forth" for infant care, to emphasize the creativity of the mother in creating the relationships that will make the infant capable of relationship. There is a danger that this way of speaking may obscure the point that "calling forth" involves exquisite sensitivity to the initiatives of the infant. Nona Lyons and Carol Gilligan use the term "response" following H. Richard Neibuhr. The latter avoids the disadvantages of "calling forth," but may be misunderstood to suggest response to the exclusion of initiation. My accounts of mothering and family life are strongly influenced by my own experience of rearing a daughter in community with other women (while working in the male academic world). My accounts of nursing are a result of both academic research and the first-person experiences of nurses and allied health workers who have been my friends and my students, especially Patricia Comer, who created family life with us and with whom I came to understand the influences of the practices in our occupations upon our life together. A brief, readable account of family life that provides an historical and cross-cultural perspective is contained in Boulding 1978. A detailed but less-readable account is contained in Boulding 1977.

4. This same hierarchal organization is also found in many branches of Eastern thought; for example, in the *I Ching*, one of the oldest sources of Taoist thought, the *yang* principal is explicitly viewed as superior and the *yin* as inferior. This hierarchy is less evident in some Taoist practices, such as *Tai Chi*, that make use of the *yin-yang* symbolism.

5. For a discussion of the prevalence and function of the view that rape is a normal sexual behavior, see Peterson (1977).

6. An interesting discussion of the thought of Nietzsche and Bachofen on this point is contained in a paper by Rebekah S. Perry, "Nietzsche and Bachofen:

The Sexual Roots of Morality and Culture," presented at the SWIP session of the 1982 Eastern APA meeting. I disagree with the author's attempt to categorize theirs as a proto-feminist view, however.

7. I am indebted to Mitchell Aboulofia for several discussions on Hegel's thought. Perhaps Aboulofia and other Hegelians can arrive at a nondualistic ontology beginning where Hegel began, even as those who begin with individualism may work their way out with arguments that no man is an island, but I see no reason to "enter that fly bottle," to use Wittgenstein's metaphor.

8. What I have described as individualism has developed over centuries. I have not attempted to do justice to the history of that development here. Were I to do so, however, I would trace it from the late Middle Ages, rather than from the 17th century. It shows the strength of the ideas of individualism that anyone would feel obliged to argue that "no man is an island," as John Donne did at the beginning of the 17th century.

9. I choose the term "peer" mindful of the application of the term both to dukes, marquesses, earls, etc., who asserted their right vis-à-vis the monarch before propertied citizens took on and transformed the role of rebellious "sons," and of the literature on peer relations in developmental psychology.

10. I cannot do justice here to the complex relation and distinction between concepts of selfhood and personhood.

11. *The Declaration of Independence* speaks of the rights of "all men," but civil rights were not extended to male slaves until the passage of the Fourteenth Amendment.

12. Elsewhere I have shown how the patriarchal view that women and women's bodies are a resource to be controlled by men and/or the state is very prevalent in our "individualistic" society as well as in socialist "state patriarchies" (where the availability of contraceptive and abortive services are manipulated to serve state interests), and argued that the individualistic position that is represented as the alternative view to patriarchal control of women's bodies is also inadequate to represent women's concerns about pregnancy and childbirth. The interested reader is referred to Whitbeck 1983a.

13. Arguments for this point are contained in Miller 1976, Gilligan 1982, and Whitbeck 1983b.

14. It may be that some women have internalized a dualistic view of gender, and that may even be common among women exposed to a great deal of masculist theory, but the absence of a nurturer with whom the infant shares characteristics that are socially significant would tend to generate in him a dualistic view of the self-other relation in the cases in which the mother did not see him as opposite, and engages in a great deal of mirroring and teaching by example, as many mothers do with children of both sexes.

15. The extent of such social reinforcement varies and may be minimal in some cases; for example, in the case of upper-class girls reared by women of a lower class.

16. There are some parallels to this notion of a person in the thought of some major thinkers in western philosophy. For example, I might have taken the notion of an historical object from the middle period of Whitehead's thought, and elaborated the notion of a person using that starting point. It would be an enormous and unrewarding task to discuss the views of each

philosopher individually, however, and to draw out the meager parallels and to suggest appropriate epicycles to their formulations. I know no really *close* parallels in western thought to the ontology that I find in feminist practice and thought. The nondual ontology of Tibetan Buddhism looks somewhat promising, but I am too dependent on a few translations and interpretations to assert this with confidence.

Of particular interest among contemporary philosophical formulations is the account of the person or "individual" that Carol Gould develops in connection with her view of the ontological foundations of democracy and property (Gould 1979, 1980). Although her characterization of persons as "individuals-in-relation" and her notion of joint action (see note 2 above) are quite compatible with the ontology outlined here, there are some difficulties in reading her views as operating out of a similar framework. Gould criticizes the social ontologies of individualism and "socialist holism" (which I take to be similar to what I have called "state patriarchy") and constructs an alternative designed to avoid the inadequacies of each that she has identified. Many of the terms that Gould uses are borrowed from the positions that she criticizes, and therefore often suggest the same self-other opposition, and individualism in particular. Since these terms may have been chosen to communicate to the audiences she was addressing, I have tried translating her terminology—words such as "individual," "choice," "right," and "self-realization"—in ways that make explicit the interconnectedness of selves. When this is done, however, some of her central theses lose their plausibility. For example, if self-realization is understood to be the realization of aspirations to participate in certain sorts of practices and relationships, then the right to personal possessions or "individual property" (which she distinguishes from social property—including the means of production) does not seem to be required. What is required, instead, is the existence of the relevant practices and relationships, or the people interested in creating those practices and relationships. It is difficult to see how there could be a *right* to the requisite practices, relationships and/or people, since these might not even exist. Although it is easy to see why such things as health care might be important to a person's self-realization, and in this society medical care is a commodity to which people are viewed as having property rights, it is difficult to see why such services would be regarded as personal possessions in a society in which women's practices were central. It would seem, instead, that healing would be an integral part of the life of a community, as Ehrenreich and English suggest (p. 292).

17. I am grateful to Carol Gilligan for this reference.

18. For example, Michael Tooley in "A Defense of Abortion and Infanticide," *Philosophy and Public Affairs* 2, p. 40, stipulates "In my usage the sentence 'X is a person' will be synonymous with the sentence 'X has a (serious) moral right to life'"; and Edward A. Langerak, in his article "Abortion: Listening to the Middle," *Hastings Center Report* 9, p. 25, stipulates that by the term "person" he means a human being that has "as strong a right to life as a normal adult."

19. It is significant, I think, that John Ladd is experienced in the practice of rearing children, in contrast to the bachelors who are seen as the great figures of modern philosophy (and to contemporary philosophers who left to their wives—*not* "spouses"—the rearing of children who were born early in their

academic careers) and who found the philosophical framework of individualism so congenial. Ladd has been at a further advantage in participating in the
practice of childrearing with his wife, Rosalind Ladd who, being an analytic
philosopher herself, could make that practice clear to an analytic philosopher. In
keeping with the dichotomization of the public and private, it has been thought
impolite or irrelevant to mention a philosopher's experience of relationships,
though not the philosopher's intellectual or class background, but the dichotomy between the public and the private is one I reject. (Elsewhere I have
discussed some other ways in which the practice of doing philosophy might be
transformed in conformity with a feminist vision of reality [Whitbeck 1983b].
Major statements on the subject of doing feminist theory are contained in a paper
by María C. Lugones and Elizabeth V. Spelman [Lugones and Spelman 1983].)

20. Nona Lyons and Carol Gilligan, in their major empirical studies
investigating both women's conception of the self and the ways in which
women tend to formulate moral issues, found that consideration of interrela-
tionships among people and responsibility for the welfare of all involved
figures prominently in many women's thinking (Lyons 1983 and Gilligan 1982).

REFERENCES

Addelson, Kathryn. "Respect and Impartiality." Unpublished manuscript.

Aristotle. 1942 ed. *Generation of Animals*. English translation by A. L. Peck.
Cambridge: Harvard University Press.

———. 1962 ed. *Physics*. Translated by Richard Hope. Lincoln: University
of Nebraska Press.

Boulding, Elise. 1977. *Women in the Twentieth Century World*. Beverly Hills:
Sage Publications.

———. 1978. *The Family As a Way Into the Future*. Wallingford, Penn.:
Pendle Hill Publications.

Brown, Norman O. 1966. *Love's Body*. New York: Random House.

Caplan, A. C., H. T. Engelhardt, Jr., and J. J. McCartney, eds. 1981. *Concepts
of Health and Disease: Interdisciplinary Perspectives*. Reading, Mass.: Addison-
Wesley Co.

Chodorow, Nancy. 1978. *The Reproduction of Mothering, Psychoanalysis and
the Sociology of Gender*. Berkeley: University of California Press.

Christ, Carol, and Judith Plaskow. 1979. *Womanspirit Rising: A Feminist
Reader on Religion*. New York: Harper & Row.

Collins, Margery, and Christine Pierce. 1973–74. "Holes and Slime: Sexism
in Sartre's Psychoanalysis." *Philosophical Forum* 5, nos. 1–2. Reprinted 1976 in
Gould and Wartofsky, eds., *Women and Philosophy*.

Condren, Mary T. 1982. "Patriarchy and Death." Paper presented at the
American Academy of Religion Meetings, New York, December.

Ehrenreich, Barbara, and Deirdre English. 1978. *For Her Own Good: 150
Years of the Experts' Advice to Women*. New York: Anchor Press/Doubleday.

Freire, Paulo. 1973. *Pedagogy of the Oppressed*. Translated by Myra Bergman
Ramos. New York: Seabury Press.

————. 1974. "Education as the Practice of Freedom." In *Education for Critical Consciousness*, ed. Paulo Freire. New York: Seabury Press.

Gilligan, Carol. 1982. *In a Different Voice: Psychological Theory and Women's Development*. Cambridge: Harvard University Press.

Glennon, Lynda M. 1979. *Women and Dualism*. White Plains, N.Y.: Longman Press.

Gould, Carol C. 1979. "Ontological Foundations of Democracy." Paper presented to the Metaphysical Society of America. Manhattanville College, March 15.

————. 1980. "Contemporary Legal Conceptions of Property and Their Implications for Democracy." *Journal of Philosophy* 7, no. 11 (November).

Gould, Carol C., and Marx Wartofsky, eds. 1976. *Women and Philosophy: Toward A Theory of Liberation*. New York: G. P. Putnam's Sons.

Griffin, Susan. 1981. *Pornography and Silence: Culture's Revenge Against Nature*. New York: Harper & Row.

Harding, Sandra. 1981. "The Norms of Social Inquiry and Masculine Experience." *PSA 1980*, vol. 2. Edited by P. D. Asquith and R. N. Giere. East Lansing, Mich.: Philosophy of Science Association.

Hartsock, Nancy C. M. 1981. "Social Life and Social Science: The Significance of the Naturalist/Intentionalist Dispute." *PSA 1980*, vol. 2. Edited by P. D. Asquith and R. N. Giere, East Lansing, Mich.: Philosophy of Science Association.

Hegel, G. W. F., ed. 1977. *Phenomenology of Spirit*. Translated by A. V. Miller. Oxford: Clarendon Press.

Hesse, Mary B. 1966. *Models and Analogies in Science*. Notre Dame, Ind.: University of Notre Dame Press.

Holmes, Helen B., Betty Hoskins, and Michael Gross, eds. 1981. *The Custom-Made Child?: Women-Centered Perspectives*. Vol. 2 of the Proceedings of the Conference on Ethical Issues in Human Reproduction Technology: Analysis by Women. Clifton, N.J.: Humana Press.

Ladd, John. 1979. "Legalism and Medical Ethics." In *Contemporary Issues in Biomedical Ethics*, ed. J. W. Davis, Barry Hoffmaster, and Sarah Shorten. Clifton, N.J.: Humana Press.

————. 1982. "The Distinction Between Rights and Responsibilities: A Defense." *Linacre Quarterly*. May.

Lindemann, S. K., and Elizabeth Oliver. 1982. "Consciousness, Liberation, and Health Delivery Systems." *Journal of Medicine and Philosophy* 7, no. 4.

Lodge, George C. 1977. *The New American Ideology*. New York: Alfred A. Knopf.

Lyons, Nona. 1983. "Two Perspectives: On Self, Relationships and Morality." *Harvard Educational Review* 53, no. 2. May.

Lugones, María, and Elizabeth V. Spelman. 1983. "Have We Got A Theory for You!" Feminist Theory, Cultural Imperialism, and the Demand for "The Woman's Voice." *Hypatia* 1, no. 1. Published as the fall 1983 issue of *Women's Studies International*.

MacIntyre, Alasdair. 1981. *After Virtue*. Notre Dame, Ind.: University of Notre Dame Press.

Mahowald, Mary Briody. 1978. *Philosophy of Women: Classical to Current Concepts*. Indianapolis: Hackett Publishing Co.

McBride, Angela B. 1972. *The Growth and Development of Mothers*. New York: Harper & Row.

Merchant, Carolyn. 1980. *The Death of Nature*. San Francisco: Harper & Row.

Miller, Jean Baker. 1976. *Toward A New Psychology of Women*. Boston: Beacon Press.

————. 1982. *Women and Power*. "Work in Progress," no. 82–01. Wellesley Mass.: Wellesley College.

O'Faolain, Julia, and Lauro Martines, eds. 1973. *Not in God's Image: Women in History from the Greeks to the Victorians*. New York: Harper & Row.

Ortner, Sherry B. 1974. "Is Female to Male as Nature Is to Culture?" in Rosaldo and Lamphere, eds., *Woman, Culture, and Society*.

Peterson, Susan. 1977. "Rape and Coercion: The State as a Male Protection Racket." In *Feminism and Philosophy*, edited by Mary Vetterlin-Braggin et al. Totôwa, N.J.: Littlefield, Adams & Co.

Rawlinson, Mary. 1982. "Psychiatric Discourse and the Feminine Voice." *Journal of Medicine and Philosophy* 7, no. 2.

Rich, Adrienne. 1976. *Of Woman Born: Motherhood as Experience and Institution*. New York: Bantam Books.

Ringelheim, Joan. 1983. "Communities in Distress: Women and the Holacaust." *Netzach* 1, no. 1.

Rosaldo, Michelle Zimbalist, and Louise Lamphere, eds. 1974. *Woman, Culture, and Society*. Stanford, Calif.: Stanford University Press.

Ruddick, Sara. 1980. "Maternal Thinking." *Feminist Studies* 6, no. 2.

Ruether, Rosemary Radford. 1972. 'Motherearth and the Megamachine: A Theology of Liberation in a Feminine, Somatic and Ecological Perspective." *Christianity and Crisis*. April 12. Reprinted 1979 in Christ and Plaskow. *Womanspirit Rising*.

Searles, Harold F. 1979. "Patient as Therapist." In *Counter-Transference and Related Subjects*, ed. Harold F. Searles. New York: International University Press.

Surrey, Janet L. 1983. "The Relation Self in Women: Clinical Implications." *"Work in Progress,"*, no. 82–02. Wellesley, Mass.: Wellesley College.

Warren, Mary Ann. 1980. *The Nature of Woman. An Encyclopedia and Guide to the Literature*. Michigan: Edgewood Press.

Whitbeck, Caroline. 1969. "Simultaneity and Distance." *The Journal of Philosophy* 66, no. 11.

————. 1973–74. "Theories of Sex Difference." *The Philosophical Forum* 5, nos. 1 & 2. Reprinted in Gould and Wartofsky, eds. *Women and Philosophy*.

————. 1975. "The 'Maternal Instinct.'" *Philosophical Forum* 6, nos. 1 & 2.

————. 1981a. "Introduction" and "Response" on the Neonate. In Holmes, Hoskins, and Gross, eds., *The Custom-Made Child?*

————. 1981b. "A Theory of Health." In Caplan, Engelhardt, and McCartney, eds., *Concepts of Health and Disease*.

————. 1982. "Women and Medicine: An Introduction." *Journal of Medicine and Philosophy* 7, no. 4.

————. 1983a. "The Moral Implication of Regarding Women as People: New Perspectives on Pregnancy and Personhood." In *Abortion and the Status of the Fetus*, edited by W. B. Bondeson, H. T. Engelhardt, Jr., S. F. Spicker, and D. Winship. Dordrecht: Reidel Publ. Co.

————. 1983b. "Afterword to the 'Maternal Instinct'." In *Mothering: Essays in Feminist Theory*, edited by Joyce Trebilcot. Totowa, N.J.: Rowman & Allanheld.

Chapter 5

To See and be Seen:
The Politics of Reality

Marilyn Frye

—————————————————————————————————————

I

*I*n the Spring of 1978, at a meeting of the Midwestern Division of the Society for Women in Philosophy, Sarah Hoagland read a paper entitled "Lesbian Epistemology," in which she sketched the following picture:

> In the conceptual schemes of phallocracies there is no category of woman-identified-woman, woman-loving-woman or woman-centered-woman; that is, there is no such thing as a lesbian. This puts a lesbian in the interesting and peculiar position of being something that doesn't exist, and this position is a singular vantage point with respect to the reality which does not include her. It affords her a certain freedom from constraints of the conceptual system; it gives her access to knowledge which is inaccessible to those whose existence *is* countenanced by the system. Lesbians can therefore undertake kinds of criticism and description, and kinds of intellectual invention, hitherto unimagined.

Hoagland was urging lesbian-feminists to begin this work, and she did not try to say in advance what could be seen from that exceptional epistemic position.

Some critics of that paper, bridling at the suggestion that lesbians might be blessed with any exotic powers or special opportunities, were quick to demand a definition of the word "lesbian." They knew that if a definition of "lesbian" featured certain patterns of physical contacts as definitive, then the claim that phallocratic conceptual schemes do not include lesbians would be obviously false, since phallocrats obviously can and do wrap their rapacious minds around verbal and visual

Source: From *The Politics of Reality: Essays in Feminist Theory,* by Marilyn Frye (Trumansburg, N.Y.: The Crossing Press, 1983), 152–175. Copyright © 1983 by Marilyn Frye. Reprinted by permission of the author and of The Crossing Press.

images of females so positioned physically, with respect to each other. And they knew also, on the other hand, that any definition that is more spiritual, such as *woman-identified-woman*, will be flexible enough to permit almost any woman to count herself a lesbian and claim for herself these exciting epistemological privileges.

Other critics, who found Hoagland's picture engaging but were loathe to glorify the conditions of exile, pressed for a definition of "lesbian" that would be both accurate and illuminating—a definition that would shed light on what it means to say lesbians are excluded from phallocratic conceptual schemes, and that might even provide some clue as to what lesbians might see from this strange nonlocation beyond the pale.

These pressures combined with the philosopher's constitutional propensity to view all orderly procedure as beginning with definitions, and the assembly was irresistibly drawn into trying to define the term "lesbian." But to no avail. That term is extraordinarily resistant to standard procedures of semantic analysis. It finally dawned on me that the elusiveness of the meaning of the term was itself a clue that Hoagland's picture was right. If indeed lesbians' existence is not countenanced by the dominant conceptual scheme, it would follow that we could not construct a definition of the term "lesbian" of the sort we might recommend to well-intentioned editors of dictionaries. If a conceptual scheme excludes something, the standard vocabulary of those whose scheme it is will not be adequate to the defining of a term that denotes it. If Hoagland's picture is right, then whatever we eventually do by way of defining the word "lesbian," that definition will evolve within a larger enterprise and cannot be the *beginning* of understanding and assessing that picture.

Another way of beginning is suggested by the observation that women of all stripes and colors, including lesbians but also including nonlesbians, suffer erasure. This is true, but it also seems to me that Hoagland is right: the exclusion of lesbians from phallocratic reality is different and is related to unusual knowing. The difficulty lies in trying to say just what this *means*. In order to get a handle on this we need to explore the differences and the connections between the erasure of women generally and the erasure of lesbians.

This inquiry, about what is *not* encompassed by a conceptual scheme, presents problems that arise because the scheme in question is, at least in the large, the inquirer's own scheme. The resources for the inquiry are, in the main, drawn from the very scheme whose limits we are already looking beyond in order to conceive the project. This undertaking therefore engages me in a sort of flirtation with meaninglessness—dancing about a region of cognitive gaps and negative semantic spaces,[1] kept aloft only by the rhythm and momentum of my own motion, trying to plumb abysses which are generally agreed not to exist and to map the tensions which create them. The danger is of falling into incoherence. But conceptual schemes have saving complexities such that their structures and substructures imitate and reflect each other and one thus can locate holes and gaps indirectly that cannot, in the nature of the thing, be directly named.

I start with a semantic reminder.

II

Reality is that which is.

The English word "real" stems from a word that meant *regal*, of or pertaining to the king.

"Real" in Spanish means *royal*.

Real property is that which is proper to the king.

Real estate is the estate of the king.

Reality is that which pertains to the one in power, is that over which he has power, is his domain, his estate, is proper to him.

The ideal king reigns over everything as far as the eye can see. His eye. What he cannot see is not royal, not real.

He sees what is proper to him.

To be real is to be visible to the king.

The king is in his counting house.

III

I say, "I am a lesbian. The king does not count lesbians. Lesbians are not real. There are no lesbians." To say this, I use the word "lesbian," and hence one might think that there is a word for this thing, and thus that the thing must have a place in the conceptual scheme. But this is not so. Let me take you on a guided tour of a few standard dictionaries, to display some reasons for saying that lesbians are not named in the lexicon of the King's English.

If you look up the word "lesbian" in *The Oxford English Dictionary*, you find an entry that says it is an adjective that means *of or pertaining to the island of Lesbos*, and an entry describing at length and favorably an implement called a lesbian rule, which is a flexible measuring device used by carpenters. Period.

Webster's Third International offers a more pertinent definition. It tells us that a lesbian is a homosexual female. And going on, one finds that "homosexual" means *of or pertaining to the same sex*. The elucidating example provided is the phrase "homosexual twins" which means *same-sex twins*. The alert scholar can conclude that a lesbian is a same-sex female.

A recent edition of *Webster's Collegiate Dictionary* tells us that a lesbian is a woman who has sex, or sexual relations, with other women. Such a definition would be accepted by many speakers of the language and at least seems to be coherent, even if too narrow. But the appearance is deceptive, for this account collapses into nonsense, too. The key word in this definition is "sex": having sex or having sexual relations. But what is having sex? It is worthwhile to follow this up because the pertinent dictionary entries obscure an important point about the logic of sex. Getting clear about that point helps one see that there is semantic closure against recognition of the existence of lesbians, and it also prepares the way for understanding the connection between the place of *woman* and the place of *lesbian* with respect to the phallocratic scheme of things.[2]

Dictionaries generally agree that "sexual" means something on the order of *pertaining to the genital union of a female and a male animal*, and that "having sex" is having intercourse—intercourse being defined as the penetration of a vagina by a penis, with ejaculation. My own observation of usage leads me to think these accounts are inadequate and misleading. Some uses of these terms do fit this dictionary account. For instance, parents and counselors standardly remind young women that if they are going to be sexually active they must deal responsibly with the possibility of becoming pregnant. In this context, the word "sexually" is pretty clearly being used in a way that accords with the given definition. But many activities and events fall under the rubric "sexual," apparently without semantic deviance, though they do not involve penile penetration of the vagina of a female human being. Penile penetration of almost anything, especially if it is accompanied by ejaculation, counts as having sex or being sexual. Moreover, events that cannot plausibly be seen as pertaining to penile erection, penetration and ejaculation will, in general, not be counted as sexual, and events that do not involve penile penetration or ejaculation will not be counted as having sex. For instance, if a girlchild is fondled and aroused by a man, and comes to orgasm, but the man refrains from penetration and ejaculation, the man can say, and speakers of English will generally agree, that he did not have sex with her. No matter what is going on, or (it must be mentioned) *not* going on, with respect to female arousal or orgasm, or in connection with the vagina, a pair can be said without semantic deviance to have had sex, or not to have had sex; the use of that term turns entirely on what was going on with respect to the penis.

When one first considers the dictionary definitions of "sex" and "sexual," it seems that all sexuality is heterosexuality, by definition, and that the term "homosexual" would be internally contradictory. There are uses of the term according to which this is exactly so. But in the usual and standard use, there is nothing semantically odd in describing two men as having sex with each other. According to that usage, any situation in which one or more penises are present is one in which something could happen which could be called having sex. But on this apparently broader definition there is nothing women could do in the absence of men that could, without semantic oddity, be called "having sex." Speaking of women who have sex with other women is like speaking of ducks who engage in arm wrestling.

When the dictionary defines lesbians as women who have sex or sexual relations with other women, it defines lesbians as logically impossible.

Looking for other words in the lexicon that might denote these beings which are non-named "lesbians," one thinks of terms in the vernacular, like "dyke," "bulldagger" and so on. Perhaps it is just as well that standard dictionaries do not pretend to provide relevant definitions of such terms. Generally, these two terms are used to denote women who are perceived as imitating, dressing up like, or trying to be men. Whatever the extent of the class of women who are perceived to do such things, it obviously is not coextensive with the class of lesbians. Nearly every feminist, and many other women as well, has been perceived as wishing to be a man, and a great many lesbians are not so perceived. The term "dyke" has been appropriated by some lesbians as a term of pride and solidarity, but in that use it is unintelligible to most speakers of English.

One of the current definitions of "lesbianism" among lesbians is *woman-loving*—the polar opposite of misogyny. Several dictionaries I checked have entries for "misogyny" (hatred of women), but not for "philogyny" (love of women). I found one which defines "philogyny" as *fondness for women*, and another dictionary defines "philogyny" as *Don Juanism*. Obviously neither of these means *love of women* as it is intended by lesbians combing the vocabulary for ways to refer to themselves. According to the dictionaries, there is no term in English for the polar opposite of misogyny nor for persons whose characteristic orientation toward women is the polar opposite of misogyny.

Flinging the net wider, one can look up the more Victorian words, like sapphism and sapphist. In *Webster's Collegiate*, "sapphism" is defined just as *lesbianism*. But *The Oxford English Dictionary* introduces another twist. Under the heading of "sapphism" is an entry for "sapphist" according to which sapphists are those addicted to unnatural sexual relations between women. The fact that these relations are characterized as unnatural is revealing. For what is unnatural is contrary to the laws of nature, or contrary to the nature of the substance of entity in question. But what is contrary to the laws of nature cannot happen: this is what it means to call these laws the laws of nature. And I cannot do what is contrary to my nature, for if I could do it, it would be in my nature to do it. To call something "unnatural" is to say it cannot be. This definition defines sapphists, that is lesbians, as *naturally* impossible as well as *logically* impossible.

The notion that lesbianism is not possible in nature, that it is nobody's nature to be a lesbian, has a life of its own even among some people who do know factually that there are certain women who do and are inclined to do certain things with other women and who sincerely avow certain feelings and attitudes toward women. Lesbianism can be seen as not natural in that if someone lives as a lesbian, it is not assumed that that is just who, or how, she *is*. Rather, it is presumed to be some sort of affliction, or is a result of failed attempts to solve some sort of problem or resolve some sort of conflict (and if she could find another way, she would take it, and then would not be a lesbian). Being a lesbian is understood as something that could be nobody's natural configuration but must be a configuration one is twisted into by some sort of force that is in some basic sense "external" to one. "Being a lesbian" is understood here as certain sorts of people understand "being a delinquent" or "being an alcoholic." It is not of one's nature the way illness is not of one's nature. To see this sense of "unnatural," one can contrast it with the presumed "naturalness" of the heterosexuality of women. As most people see it, being heterosexual is just being. It is not *interpreted*. It is not understood as a consequence of anything. It is not viewed as possibly a solution to some problem, or as a way of acting and feeling that one worked out or was pushed to by circumstances. On this sort of view, all women *are* heterosexual, and some women somehow come to *act* otherwise. On this view, no one *is*, in the same sense, a lesbian.

There are people who do believe in the real existence of perverts and deviants. What they share with those who do not is the view that the behaviors and attitudes in question are not natural to *humans*. One's choice then, when confronted with someone who says she is a lesbian, is to believe her and class her as not fully or really human, or to class her as fully and really human and not believe that she is a lesbian.

Lesbian.

One of the people of the Isle of Lesbos.

It is bizarre that when I try to name myself and explain myself, my native tongue provides me with a word that is so foreign, so false, so hopelessly inappropriate. Why am I referred to by a term which means *one of the people of Lesbos?*

The use of the word "lesbian" to name us is a quadrifold evasion, a laminated euphemism. To name us, one goes by way of a reference to the island of Lesbos, which in turn is an indirect reference to the poet Sappho (who used to live there, they say), which in turn is itself an indirect reference to what fragments of her poetry have survived a few millenia of patriarchy, and this in turn (if we have not lost you by now) is a prophylactic avoidance of direct mention of the sort of creature who would write such poems or to whom such poems would be written . . . assuming you happen to know what is in those poems written in a dialect of Greek over two thousand five hundred years ago on some small island somewhere in the wine dark Aegean Sea.

This is a truly remarkable feat of silence.

The philosopher John Langshaw Austin, commenting on the connection between language and conceptions of reality, said the following: "Our common stock of words embodies all the distinctions men have found worth drawing, and the connections they have found worth marking, in the lifetimes of many generations."[3]

our

common stock of words

men have found

distinction is not worth drawing
connection is not worth marking

Revealing as this is, it still dissembles. It is not that the connections and distinctions are not worth drawing and marking, it is that men do not want to draw and mark them, or do not dare to.

IV

When one says that some thing or some class is not countenanced by a certain conceptual scheme, or that it is not "among the values over which the variables of the system range," or that it is not among the ontological commitments of the system, there are at least three things this can mean. One is just that there is no simple direct term in the system for the thing or class, and no very satisfactory way to explain it. For example, it is in this sense that western conceptual schemes do not countenance the forces or arrangements called "karma." Indeed, I don't know whether it is suitable to say "forces or arrangements" here, and that is part of the point. A second thing that can be meant when it is said that something is not in the scope of the concepts of the scheme is that the term that ostensibly denotes the thing is internally self-contradictory, as in the case of round squares. Nothing can be in both the class denoted by "round" and the class denoted by "square," given what those words mean. A third thing one can mean when one says a scheme does not encompass a certain thing is that according to principles that are fundamental to the most general picture of how things are in the world, the thing could not exist in nature. An example of this is the denial that there could be a beast that was a cross between a dog and a cat. The belief that such a thing could exist would be inconsistent with beliefs about the nature of the world and of animals that underlie vast chunks of the rest of our world view.

Lesbian is the only class I have ever set out to define, the only concept I have ever set out to explain, that seemed to be shut out in more than one of these ways. As the considerations reviewed here seem to show, it is shut out in all three. You can "not believe in lesbians" as you don't believe in the possibility of "doggie-cats" or as you don't believe in round squares; or you can be just unable to accommodate lesbianism in the way I cannot accommodate the notion of karma—it doesn't articulate suitably with the rest of my concepts; it can't be worked into my active conceptual repertoire.

The redundancy of the devices of closure that are in place here is one of the things that leads me to say that lesbians are *excluded* from the scheme. The overdetermination, the metaphysical overkill, signals a manipulation, a scurrying to erase, to divert the eye, the attention, the mind. Where there is manipulation there is motivation, and it does not seem plausible to me that the reason lies with the physical details of certain women's private lives. The meaning of this erasure and of the totality and conclusiveness of it has to do, I think, with the maintenance of phallocratic reality as a whole, and with the situation of women generally apropos of that reality.

V

At the outset I said lesbians are not real, that there are no lesbians. I want to say also that women in general are not countenanced by the phallocratic scheme, are not real; there are no women. But the predicament of women apropos the dominant reality is complex and paradoxical, as is revealed in women's mundane experience of the seesaw of demand and neglect, of being romanced and assaulted, of being courted and being ignored. The observations that lead me to say there are no women in phallocratic reality themselves also begin to reveal the elements of the paradox. These observations are familiar to feminists; they are among the things we come back to again and again as new layers of their meanings become accessible to our understanding.

There are two kinds of erasure of women that have by now become "often noted." One is the conception of human history as a history of the acts and organizations of men, and the other is a long and sordid record in western civilization of the murder and mutilation of women. Both of these erasures are extended into the future, the one in fiction and speculation, the other in the technological projects of sperm selection for increasing the proportion of male babies, of extrauterine gestation, of cloning, of male to female transsexual reconstruction. Both sorts of erasure seem entwined in the pitched religious and political battle between males who want centralized male control of female reproductive functions, and males who want individualized male control of female reproductive functions. (I speak of the fights about abortion, forced sterilization, the conditions of birthing, etc.)

A reasonable person might think that these efforts to erase women reveal an all-too-vivid recognition that there *are* women—that the projects of ideological and material elimination of women presuppose belief in the existence of the objects to be eliminated. In a way, I agree. But also, there is a peculiar mode of relating belief and action that I think is characteristic of the construction of phallocratic reality, according to which a project of annihilation can be seen to presuppose the nonexistence of the objects being eliminated. This mode is an insane reversal of the reasonable procedure of adjusting one's views so that they accord with reality as actively discovered: it is a mode according to which one begins with a firmly held view, composed from fabulous images of oneself, and adopts as one's project the alteration of the world to bring it into accord with that view.

A powerful example of this strange practice was brought to my attention by Harriet Desmoines who had been reading about the United States' expansion across the North American continent. It seems that the white men, upon encountering the vast and rich midcontinental prairie, called the prairie a *desert*. They conceived a desert, they took it to be a desert, and a century later it is a desert (a fact that is presently somewhat obscured by the annual use of megatons of chemical fertilizers). Did they *really* believe that what they were seeing was a desert? It is a matter of record that that is what they *said* they saw.

There is another example of this sort of practice to be found in the scientific and medical realm, which was brought to my attention by the work of Eileen Van Tassell. It is a standard assumption in the disciplines of human biology and human medicine that the species consists of two sexes, male and female. Concrete physical evidence that there are individuals of indeterminate sex and that "sex-characteristics" occur in spectrums and not as all-or-nothing phenomena is not acknowledged as existent evidence but is removed, erased, through chemical and surgical "cures" and "corrections."[4] In this case, as in the case of the rich and living prairie, erasure of fact and destruction of concrete objects does not demonstrate recognition of the fact or object; it is, on the contrary, direct manifestation of the belief that those are not the facts and the belief that no such individual objects exist.

If it is true that this mode of connection of belief and action is characteristic of phallocratic culture, then one can construct or reconstruct beliefs that are fundamental to that culture's conceptual/scientific system by inspecting the culture's projects and reasoning that what is believed is what the projects would make to be true. As noted before, there are and have long been ongoing projects whose end will be a world with no women in it. Reasoning back, one can conclude that those whose projects these are believe there are no women.

For many of us, the idea that there are no women, that we do not exist, began to dawn when we first grasped the point about the nongeneric so-called generic "man." The word "woman" was supposed to mean *female of the species*, but the name of the species is "Man." The term "female man" has a tension of logical impossibility about it that is absent from parallel terms like "female cat" and "female terrier." It makes one suspect that the concept of the species that is operative here is one according to which there are no females of the species. I think one can begin to get a handle on what this means by seeing how it meshes with another interesting phenomenon, namely the remarkable fact that so many men from so many stations in life have so often declared that women are unintelligible to them.

Reading or hearing the speeches of men on the unintelligibility of women, I imagine the men are like people who for some reason can see everything but automobiles and are constantly and painfully perplexed by blasts and roars, thumps and bumps, which they cannot avoid, control or explain. But it is not quite like that, for such men do seem to recognize our physical existence, or at least the existence of some of our parts. What they do not see is our souls.

The phallocratic scheme does not admit women as authors of perception, as seers. Man understands his own perception as simultaneously generating and being generated by a point of view. Man is understood to author names; men have a certain status as points of intellectual and perceptual origin. Insofar as the phallocratic scheme permits the understanding that women perceive at all, it features women's perceptions as passive, repetitive of men's perception, nonauthoritative. Aristotle said it outright: Women are rational, but do not have authority.[5]

Imagine two people looking at a statue, one from the front, the other from the back, and imagine that the one in front thinks the one in back must be seeing exactly what he is seeing. He cannot fathom how the other can come up with a description so different from his own. It is as though women are assumed to be robots hooked up to the senses of men—not using senses of our own, not authoring perception, not having and generating a point of view. And then they cannot fathom how we must be wired inside, that we could produce the output we produce from the input they assume to be identical with their own. The hypothesis that we are seeing from a different point of view, and hence simply seeing something he cannot see, is not available to a man, is not in his repertoire, so long as his total conception of the situation includes a conception of women as not authoritative perceivers like himself, that is, so long as he does not count women as men. And no wonder such a man finds women incomprehensible.

VI

For the reasons given, and in the ways indicated, I think there is much truth in the claim that the phallocratic scheme does not include women. But while women are erased in history and in speculation, physically liquidated in gynocidal purges and banished from the community of those with perceptual and semantic authority, we are on the other hand regularly and systematically invited, seduced, cajoled, coerced and even paid to be in intimate and constant association with men and their projects. In this, the situation of women generally is radically different from the situation of lesbians. Lesbians are not invited to join—the family, the party, the project, the procession, the war effort. There is a place for a woman in every game. Wife, secretary, servant, prostitute, daughter, assistant, babysitter, mistress, seamstress, proofreader, nurse, confidante, masseusse, indexer, typist, mother. Any of these is a place for a woman, and women are much encouraged to fill them. None of these is a place for a lesbian.

The exclusion of women from the phallocratic scheme is impressive, frightening, and often fatal, but it is not simple and absolute. Women's existence is both absolutely necessary to and irresolvably problematic for the dominant reality and those committed to it, for our existence is *presupposed* by phallocratic reality, but it is not and cannot be *encompassed* by or countenanced by that reality. Women's existence is a background against which phallocratic reality is a foreground.

A foreground scene is created by the motion of foreground figures against a static background. Foreground figures are perceptible, are defined, have identity, only in virtue of their movement against a background. The space in which the motion of foreground figures takes place is created and defined by their movement with respect to each other and against the background. But nothing of the background is *in* or is *part of* or is *encompassed by* the foreground scene and space. The background is unseen by the eye which is focused on foreground figures, and if anything somehow draws the eye to the background, the foreground dissolves. What would draw the eye to the background would be any sudden or well-defined motion in the background. Hence there must be either no motion at all in the background, or an unchanging buzz of small, regular and repetitive motions. The background must be utterly un*event*ful if the foreground is to continue to hang together, that is, if it is to endure as *a space* within which there are discrete *objects* in relation to each other.

I imagine phallocratic reality to be the space and figures and motion that constitute the foreground, and the constant repetitive uneventful activities of women to constitute and maintain the background against which this foreground plays. It is essential to the maintenance of the foreground reality that nothing within it refer in any way to anything in the background, and yet it depends absolutely upon the existence of the background. It is useful to carry this metaphor on in a more concrete mode—thinking of phallocratic reality as a dramatic production on a stage.

The motions of the actors against the stage settings and backdrop constitute and maintain the existence and identities of the characters in a play. The stage setting, props, lights and so forth are created, provided, maintained and occasionally rearranged (according to the script) by stagehands. The stagehands, their motions and the products of those motions, are neither in nor part of the play, are neither in nor part of the reality of the characters. The reality in the framework of which Hamlet's actions have their meaning would be rent or shattered if anything Hamlet did or thought referred in any way to the stage-hands or their activities, or if that background blur of activity were in any other way to be resolved into attention-catching events.

The situation of the actors is desperately paradoxical. The actors are absolutely committed to the maintenance of the characters and the characters' reality: participation as characters in the ongoing creation of Reality is their *raison d'être*. The reality of the character must be lived with fierce concentration. The actor must be immersed in the play and undistracted by any thought for the scenery, props or stagehands, lest the continuity of the characters and the integrity of their reality be dissolved or broken. But if the character must be lived so intently, who will supervise the stagehands to make sure they don't get rowdy, leave early, fall asleep or walk off the job? (Alas, there is no god nor heavenly host to serve as Director and Stage Managers.) Those with the most intense commitment to the maintenance of the reality of the play are precisely those most interested in the proper deportment of the stagehands, and this interest competes directly with that commitment. There is nothing the actor would like better than that there be no such thing as stagehands, posing as they do a constant threat to the very existence, the very life, of the character and hence to the meaning of the life of the actor; and yet the actor is irrevocably tied to the stagehands by his commitment to the play. Hamlet, of course, has no such problems; there are no stagehands in the play.

To escape his dilemma, the actor may throw caution to the wind and lose himself in the character, whereupon stagehands are unthinkable, hence unproblematic. Or he may construct and embrace the belief that the stagehands share exactly his own perceptions and interests and that they are as committed to the play as he—that they are like robots. On such a hypothesis he can assume them to be absolutely dependable and go on about his business single-mindedly and without existential anxiety. A third strategy, which is in a macabre way more sane, is that of trying to solve the problem technologically by constructing actual robots to serve as stagehands.[6] Given the primacy of his commitment to the play, all solutions must involve one form or another of annihilation of the stagehands. Yet all three require the existence of stagehands; the third, he would hope, requiring it only for a while longer.

The solution to the actor's problem that will appear most benign with respect to the stagehands, because it erases the erasure, is that of training, persuading and seducing the stagehands into *loving* the actors and taking actors' interests and commitments unto themselves as their own. One significant advantage to this solution is that the actors can carry on without the guilt or confusion that might come with annihilating, replacing or falsely forgetting the stagehands. As it turns out, of course, even this is a less than perfect solution. Stagehands, in the thrall of their commitment, can become confused and think of themselves as actors—and then they may disturb the play by trying to enter it as characters, by trying to participate in the creation and maintenance of Reality. But there are various well-known ways to handle these intrusions and this seems to be, generally speaking, the most popular solution to the actor's dilemma.

VII

All eyes, all attention, all attachment must be focused on the play, which is Phallocratic Reality. Any notice of the stagehands must be oblique and filtered through interest in the play. Anything which threatens the fixation of attention on the play threatens a cataclysmic dissolution of Reality into Chaos. Even the thought of the possibility of a distraction is a distraction. It is necessary to devise devices and construct systems that will lock out the thought-crime of conceiving the possibility of a direct and attentive focus on anything but Reality.

The ever-present potential for cosmological disaster lies with the background. There is nothing in the nature of the background that disposes it to be appropriately tame: it is not made to serve the foreground, it is just there. It therefore is part of the vocation of phallocratic loyalists to police *attention*. They must make it radically impossible to attend to anything in the background; they must make it impossible to think it possible to fasten one's eye on anything in the background.

We can deduce from this understanding of their motivation *what it is* that phallocratic loyalists are motivated to forbid conceiving. What must not be conceived is a *seer* for whom the background is eventful, dramatic, compelling—whose attention fastens upon stagehands and their projects. The loyalists cannot just identify such seers and kill them, for that would focus the loyalists' own attention on the criminal, hence the crime, hence the object of the crime, and that would interrupt the loyalists' own attention to Reality.

The king is in his counting house. The king is greedy and will count for himself everything he dares to. But his greed itself imposes limits on what he dares to count.

VIII

What the king cannot count is a seer whose perception passes the plane of the foreground Reality and focuses upon the background. A seer whose eye is attracted to the ones working as stagehands—the women. A seer in whose eye the woman has authority, has interests of her own, is not a robot. A seer who has no motive for wanting there to be no women; a seer who is not loyal to Reality. We can take the account of the seer who must be unthinkable if Reality is to be kept afloat as the beginning of an account of what a lesbian is. One might try saying that a lesbian is one who, by virtue of her focus, her attention, her attachment, is disloyal to phallocratic reality. She is not commited to its maintenance and the maintenance of those who maintain it, and worse, her mode of disloyalty threatens its utter dissolution in the mere flick of the eye. This sounds extreme, of course, perhaps even hysterical. But listening carefully to the rhetoric of the fanatic fringe of the phallocratic loyalists, one hears that they do think that feminists, whom they fairly reasonably judge to be lesbians, have the power to bring down civilization, to dissolve the social order as we know it, to cause the demise of the species, by our mere existence.

Even the fanatics do not really believe that a lone maverick lesbian can in a flick of her evil eye atomize civilization, of course. Given the collectivity of conceptual schemes, the way they rest on agreement, a maverick perceiver does not have the power to bring one tumbling down—a point also verified by my own experience as a not-so-powerful maverick. What the loyalists fear, and in this I think they are more-or-less right, is a contagion of the maverick perception to the point where the agreement in perception that keeps Reality afloat begins to disintegrate.

The event of becoming a lesbian is a reorientation of attention in a kind of ontological conversion. It is characterized by a feeling of a world dissolving, and by a feeling of disengagement and re-engagement of one's power as a perceiver. That such conversion happens signals its possibility to others.

Heterosexuality for women is not simply a matter of sexual prefer-ence, any more than lesbianism is. It is a matter of orientation of attention, as is lesbianism, in a metaphysical context controlled by neither heterosexual nor lesbian women. Attention is a kind of passion. When one's attention is on something, one is present in a particular way with respect to that thing. This presence is, among other things, an element of erotic presence. The orientation of one's attention is also what fixes and directs the application of one's physical and emotional work.

If the lesbian sees the woman, the woman may see the lesbian seeing her. With this, there is a flowering of possibilities. The woman, feeling herself seen, may learn that she *can be* seen; she may also be able to know that a woman can see, that is, can author perception. With this, there enters for the woman the logical possibility of assuming her authority as a perceiver and of shifting her own attention. With that there is the dawn of choice, and it opens out over the whole world of women. The lesbian's seeing undercuts the mechanism by which the production and constant reproduction of heterosexuality for women was to be rendered *automatic*. The nonexistence of lesbians is a piece in the mechanism that is supposed to cut off the possibility of choice or alternative at the root, namely at the point of conception.

The maintenance of phallocratic reality requires that the attention of women be focused on men and men's projects—the play; and that attention not be focused on women—the stagehands. Woman-loving, as a spontaneous and habitual orientation of attention is then, both directly and indirectly, inimical to the maintenance of that reality. And therein lies the reason for the thoroughness of the ontological closure against lesbians, the power of those closed out, and perhaps the key to the liberation of women from oppression in a male-dominated culture.

IX

My primary goal here has not been to state and prove some rigid thesis, but simply to *say* something clearly enough, intelligibly enough, so that it can be understood and thought about. Lesbians are outside the conceptual scheme, and this is something done, not just the way things are. One can begin to see that lesbians are excluded by the scheme, and that this is *motivated,* when one begins to see what purpose the exclusion might serve in connection with keeping women generally in their metaphysical place. It is also true that lesbians are in a position to see things that cannot be seen from within the system. What lesbians see is what makes them lesbians and their seeing is why they have to be excluded. Lesbians are women-seers. When one is suspected of seeing women, one is spat summarily out of reality, through the cognitive gap and into the negative semantic space. If you ask what became of such a woman, you may be told she became a lesbian, and if you try to find out what a lesbian is, you will be told there is no such thing.

But there is.

NOTES

1. Phrase due to Julia Penelope Stanley.
2. The analysis that follows is my own rendering of an account developed by Carolyn Shafer. My version of it is informed also by my reading of "Sex and Reference," by Janice Moulton, *Philosophy and Sex*, edited by Robert Baker and Frederick Elliston (Prometheus Books, Buffalo, New York, 1975).
3. From "A Plea for Excuses," *Philosophical Papers* (Oxford: Oxford University Press, 1961).
4. See my *The Politics of Reality: Essays in Feminist Theory* (Trumansburg, N.Y.: The Crossing Press, 1983), 39, n. 3.
5. *Politics* I 13, 1260 a13. My attention was first brought to this by a paper, "Aristotle's Views On Women In The *Politics*," presented at the meetings of the Western Division of the Society For Women In Philosophy, Fall 1974, by Jan Bidwell, Susan Ekstrom, Sue Hildebrand and Rhoda H. Kotzin.
6. This solution is discussed in *The Transsexual Empire: The Making of The She-Male*, by Janice G. Raymond (Beacon Press, Boston, 1979).

Chapter 6 ───────────────────────────────

A Feminist Aspect Theory of the Self

Ann Ferguson

───

*T*he contemporary women's movement has generated major new theories of the social construction of gender and male power. The feminist attack on the masculinist assumptions of cognitive psychology, psychoanalysis and most of the other academic disciplines has raised questions about some basic assumptions of those fields. For example, feminist economists have questioned the public/private split of much of mainstream economics that ignores the social necessity of women's unpaid housework and childcare.[1] Feminist psychologists have challenged cognitive and psychoanalytic categories of human moral and gender development arguing that they are biased toward the development of male children rather than female children.[2] Feminist anthropologists have argued that sex/gender systems, based on the male exchange of women in marriage, have socially produced gender differences in sexuality and parenting skills, which have perpetuated different historical and cultural forms of male dominance.[3] Feminist philosophers and theorists have suggested that we must reject the idea of a gender-free epistemological standpoint from which to understand the world.[4] Finally, radical feminists have argued that the liberal state permits a pornography industry that sexually objectifies women, thus legitimizing male violence against women.[5]

Though each of these feminist approaches to understanding the social perpetuation of male dominance is insightful, they are based on overly simplistic theories of the self and human agency. As a result they tend to give us misleading ideas of what is required for social change. For one thing, they don't allow us to understand how women who are socialized into subordinate gender roles nonetheless can develop the sense of self-respect and the personal power necessary to be strong feminists able to effectively change institutional sexism. In order to

───

Source: Reprinted with the permission of the author and of the editors from *Science, Morality and Feminist Theory*, ed. Marsha Hanen and Kai Nielsen, *Canadian Journal of Philosophy* Supplementary Volume 13:339–356, 1988. Copyright © 1988 by *Canadian Journal of Philosophy*.

grasp what is necessary to develop a strong and powerful sense of self, we must have the correct theory of what the self is. I shall defend an Aspect theory of the self in this paper.

DEVELOPING A SENSE OF SELF

Most feminists would take it to be a truism that women's sense of self-worth, and consequently our personal power, has been weakened by a male-dominant society that has made us internalize many demeaning images of women. Thus, part of every feminist program must involve a process of feminist education that allows women to develop—some would say, reclaim—a self-integrity and self-worth that will provide each of us with the psychological resources we need to develop full self-realization. Since individuals who lack a sense of self-worth are timid and afraid to take risks, women face the problem of contributing to our own subordination because of not even trying to achieve goals we really want, thus falling victim to the adage "nothing ventured, nothing gained." But how do we conceive of the process of constructing self-respect? In what follows, I am going to present three different theories of the self that feminist theories have presupposed. I shall give the answers they give to the question of how women can develop a strong sense of self, critique the first two, and defend my own view.

THE RATIONAL MAXIMIZER THEORY OF THE SELF

There is a view of self prevalent in American society today that derives from the views of such classical liberal philosophers as John Locke and Thomas Jefferson. This view, characteristic of many contemporary Americans of both liberal and conservative bent, holds that the self is a unified rational thinking subject, possessed of free will and the ability to choose life goals and means to achieve them, as long as fate or external social coercion do not interfere. Examples of such social coercion include government legal restrictions against certain actions or strong social groups (e.g., large corporations or community groups) whose actions or policies restrict one from certain courses of action.

On this view of self, which I call the Rational Maximizer view of self, humans are unified selves, rational maximizers, who operate to maximize their own self-interest as defined by their goals, within the external constraints laid down by force of circumstance, government or society. Social oppression of a group, for example women or Black people, is then explained by external constraints placed in the way of individuals achieving their goals. These constraints can range from the personal prejudices of employers and potential friends and lovers to the institutional sexism involved in lesser pay for work defined socially as "women's work," or the fact that housework, defined as women's work, is unpaid labor, which makes the exchanges between men and women in the household economy unequal.

On the Rational Maximizer view of self, women do not differ from men in terms of personal identity and the human ability to choose reasonable goals and means to them. Thus, if men and women make different choices as to how to develop what economists call their "human capital," that is, their skills and abilities, including their degree of formal education and job training, this is due not to innate gender preferences and skills (e.g., that men are more competitive and aggressive and women more nurturant and submissive). Rather, it is a result of the realistic options that society and the individual circumstances of women provide. Thus, more men than women choose to pursue graduate studies, or careers in management and other high-paying careers in business, politics and medicine because women choosing as men do would have to face much sexism and would have to work twice as hard and be twice as lucky to succeed. In a male-dominant society, it is not rationally maximizing for women to make the same choices as men, especially since most women want to be wives and mothers—whether this is socialized or innate—and these goals are more difficult to combine with the typical high-paying masculine career.

The explanation of women's lesser sense of self-worth on this view is that women lack the skills that are highly valued in our society as well as access to the wages that are necessary to achieve status and economic independence in our society. Furthermore men, because of their comparative social and economic advantage, treat women as inferiors.

On the view that both men and women are rational maximizers, there are two social conditions necessary to develop a better sense of self for women. First is a feminist social policy that makes it less worth men's while to continue their sexist treatment of women, and second are feminist education programs that compensate women for the lack of skills society has denied them by encouraging the development of those skills necessary to compete in a man's world.

Affirmative action programs are a good example of feminist social policy that provides opportunities for qualified women to learn the skills hitherto reserved for men, in higher education and in on-the-job training. Such opportunities help those women involved to change their self-concept. Men will be persuaded to overcome their sexist attitudes when they see that women can do men's jobs as well as women, and will stop treating women as inferiors.

Another kind of training need is psychological re-training: women need consciousness-raising types of education, like assertiveness training and counseling programs that advocate the goal of economic independence for women. Such programs can provide the survival skills to replace those self-denigrating traditional skills that are characteristic of most women under patriarchy, those that involve habits of deference to men and the myriad skills of indirect manipulation that we have been taught to create the greater likelihood of "catching a man," and in gaining indirect power through men's favors in a patriarchal world.

Since most women want to be wives and mothers, feminists must support state legislation providing affordable, quality child care centers. At the same time, feminist education must combat the traditional prejudice against combining a career with motherhood. The most important feminist goal should be to create social structures that help women learn to become more like men—in motivations, personalities and job skills—so that we can get ahead in the system and thus achieve economic parity with men.

DIFFERENCE THEORY

The second theory of the self that I want to discuss is that of those I call the Difference theorists. Unlike Rational Maximizer theory, which argues that men and women are basically the same underneath though we develop different skills and goals as means to achieving social success, this theory argues that there really are extreme personality and skills differences between the genders. These differences, whether originally innate or socialized in early infancy, are so much a part of the identities of men and women that they cannot be changed. People's identities are not analogous to little atoms of consciousness that can, chameleon-like, take on or shed their personal properties as it is expedient. Rather, since human personal identity is essentially relational, a personal identificaton with one's gender is an essential characteristic of personal identity. Men and women essentially define ourselves in relation to different social standards learned in childhood. Since a man or woman's sense of self-worth is essentially connected to success or failure in meeting gender-related standards, women's sense of self-worth cannot be ultimately achieved by imitating men or by adopting masculine goals and skills. Rather, women must find collective ways to socially re-valorize feminine-identified values and skills in order that individual women can reclaim a sense of self-worth denied by patriarchy.

There are two schools of thought among Difference theorists on the question of the inevitability of gender differences. One school, the biological determinists, e.g., those such as Mary Daly,[6] Mary O'Brien[7] and others,[8] maintain that it is inevitable that masculine traits and inner sense of self be different from feminine ones. Testosterone makes men more aggressive than women, while women's reproductive biology not only creates womb envy in men but makes women more nurturant and altruistic in relation to others.[9] Thus, universally, men have a motivation to dominate women and the nasty personality skills capable of doing so, while women have a motivation to relate more to children than to men (thus setting up a universal conflict in male and female motivations), as well as to each other (as like understands and empathizes better with like). Thus, given these biologically based gender conflicts, systems of compulsory heterosexuality are set up for the benefit of men to keep women from bonding with each other and children to the exclusion of men.

The social schools of Difference include feminist psychoanalytic theory as well as some radical feminist theory.[10] These theorists argue that the personality differences between men and women, though they are central to personal identity and difficult to change, are not biological. Rather, they are socially produced through the sexual division of labor, particularly in parenting. This sexual division creates in women a more altruistic and relational sense of self than men, who are produced with a more oppositional and autonomous, hence more competitive and self-interested, sense of self.

The biological determinist school of feminism tends toward a separatist solution for women. Men, after all, are incorrigible! Indeed, in her latest book, Mary Daly goes so far as to suggest that they are tantamount to a separate species from women, and consequently women owe them no personal or political obligations.[11] Women should learn to value our authentic selves by relating to each other as friends and lovers, thus dropping out of, and thereby challenging the dominant patriarchal culture by providing an example to other women of a freer life—one more in tune with women-centered values.

Not all Difference theorists believe that such an extreme separatism is the political solution for feminists. Jan Raymond, in her latest book, *A Passion for Friends*,[12] maintains that women have an authentic Self (her capital "S") different from men's. Thus if women are to be true to themselves they must prioritize being for other women. This means that we should prioritize friendships with women rather than accept the socially constructed patterns of what she calls "heteroreality," all of which socialize women to define our selves and our meaning in life in relationships with men.

Though Raymond wants a certain kind of cultural separatism for women, she does not advocate a "drop out" separatism. Rather than dropping out of the world, women must strive to change the political and economic priorities of a patriarchal society by working in careers that have hitherto involved only males and male-defined values.

It is never made clear in Raymond's book whether she thinks women's authentic Self is more like other women's than like men's for biological or for social reasons. Other Difference theorists who clearly reject the biological gender difference argument are Nancy Chodorow,[13] Dorothy Dinnerstein,[14] Carol Gilligan[15] and Sara Ruddick.[16] These thinkers argue that the psychology of women differs from that of men because women rather than men mother. By "mothering" they do not mean childbearing, that biological function that women cannot share with men, but mothering in the social sense of the nurturing and direct physical care for infants in early childrearing. The fact that women and not men mother in this sense creates a different sense of self in little girls than in little boys. Girls have an immediate role model for what it is to be female: one who is engaged in the concrete chores involved in housework and regular nurturant interaction with children. Consequently the girl defines a sense of self that is relational or incorporative (i.e., I am like mom in these ways). Girls also must identify with, rather than absolutely oppose, that aspect of mother that is resented and feared: the fact that she can never meet all of the infant's myriad needs. This tends to make females turn anger originally directed at mother inward on themselves in ways that weaken self-esteem.

Gender identity for the boy comes out differently. Society teaches him that to be male is not to be female, and due to the relative or complete absence of his father he lacks a male role model as immediate for him as is the mother for the little girl. Thus he learns to define himself oppositionally instead of relationally (I am not-mother, I am not-female). He can thus project infantile anger not only on mother but on the class of women in general. Thus, the crosscultural constant, the asymmetrical parenting of women, explains the crosscultural male deprecating of women.

Carol Gilligan argues that women tend to have a different style of moral reasoning then men—what she calls a different "moral voice." When presented with hypothetical moral dilemmas, females tend to find a contextual solution while males formulate abstract principles and prioritize justifying one solution rather than the other.

The idea that women have a different moral voice than men's is pursued by Sara Ruddick, who argues that the socialization for, and actual experience of, mothering creates a maternal thinking in women that prioritizes the life preservation, growth, and social acceptability of the child under her care. When women generalize from the values embedded in this concrete mothering experience, they develop a more care-oriented ethic, concerned with peacemaking and concrete life preserving, than men. These latter, with their gender identity and masculine training in the abstract skills necessary to do well in competitive male groups and careers, are more likely to fall prey to the militaristic thinking of the sort that justifies war, the arms race and other life- and species-endangering activities.

Social difference theory has two conflicting tendencies within it in regard to the question of how individual women can reclaim a personal power denied by the standards of femininity built into heterosexual desires. Feminist psychoanalytic theory suggests that women should have recourse to feminist therapy to undo the damages of being denied the proper nurturance for self-autonomy in early childhood. The collective strategies of radical feminism, however, tend to reject this individual solution in favor of a collective process in which women bond with other women to re-value feminine work and values, thus allowing women's self, based as it is on the worth of the feminine itself, to gain power. Thus the importance of comparable worth campaigns and women-only peace protests that reclaim the value of maternal thinking as opposed to militaristic thinking.

The general strategy of this line of Difference thought is opposed to the strategies of those liberal feminists who assume a rational maximizer theory of self. Rather than striving to make women more like men so we have a better chance of succeeding in a male-dominant world, the feminist empowerment process involves affirming the socially insufficiently recognized value of the feminine. Indeed, ideally, men should become more like women by committing themselves to learn so-called feminine skills. Only by so identifying with the feminine can they cease their deprecation of women. Further, only by an individual commitment of this sort, for example, the commitment to learn mothering skills by co-parenting, can a man create the kind of love relationship with a woman that will allow her the maximum opportunity of obtaining a sense of self-worth.

But it is at this point that Difference theory can provide us with no clear answers on how and why men are going to be motivated to make such a dramatic change in the conception of masculinity. And even if they were, how can they be expected to succeed in learning feminine skills if these demand a permeable, or incorporative, personality as opposed to an oppositional one? And, given these problems, why and how can women who are concerned to increase their sense of self-worth work with individual men to encourage change?

PROBLEMS WITH THE FIRST TWO THEORIES
OF THE SELF

Although both the Rational Mazimizer and Difference theories of the Self have important insights, they are inadequate in other ways. Though the first explains why women remain oppressed because of the external constraints that society places on them, it cannot explain why those few women in economically and socially privileged positions in society still defer to men. Why, if a woman is independently wealthy, would she be content to be a wife and mother rather than embarking on a professional or political career that would give her an even greater social effect on the world? Why do some such women even allow themselves to be battered wives? Such behavior does not seem to be rationally maximizing! Why then do these women who are economically independent continue to pursue less rewarding lives that require deferring to men? And why do many women who can afford higher education choose less well paying careers in literature, nursing and elementary school teaching rather than business, physics, medical school or engineering? In short, the Rational Maximizer theory under-estimates the way in which people are not rational maximizers when it comes to their ultimate goals in life, which for most are gender-defined and socially engineered.

Though the Difference school can answer this question—women after all are constructed with essentially different senses of self, skills, and desires from men—this group is overly deterministic about the static nature of this social molding. Consequently they cannot answer the historical question of how and why a women's movement should have arisen just now in American history. If women are so different from men, why should women now be demanding the opportunity to enter male spheres? Why should the idea of developing independence and autonomy, long considered the special purview of masculine identity, suddenly be a goal for feminists as well?

My view is at odds with both the Rational Maximizer and the Difference theorist theories. Both of them are *static* and *essentialist*. That is, they conceive of the self as a given unity with certain fixed qualities, though they disagree about what those fixed qualities are. Thus, they both have *atomistic* views of the self. Whether the self is a rational calculator or a phenomenal center that defines itself in relation to others, the self is seen as having an essence fixed by human nature or by early childhood.

Many Difference theorists maintain that there is a split between the authentic and inauthentic parts of the self. This model does suggest that radical change is possible by spurning the inauthentic self. But their claim that there is such an authentic aspect of self, and speculations as to the nature of its preferences and interests, are wildly metaphysical and unprovable. Indeed, they have seemed elitist and culture-bound to some. For example, since most women continue to prefer men to women as love-mates, how can it be proved that it is more authentic for those women to prefer women, as some Difference theories maintain? How do we decide whether the authentic female self is a lesbian, heterosexual, pansexual or asexual?

THE ASPECT THEORY OF SELF

My alternative theory, which I call the Aspect theory of self, rejects the idea that the self is an unchanging, unified consciousness that has a two-tiered set of properties: those that are necessary and essential, and those that are accidental. Rather, conscious selfhood is an ongoing process in which both unique individual priorities and social constraints vie in limiting and defining one's self-identity.[17]

Humans may be rational maximizers if placed in the sort of social practices that encourage such a type of thinking strategy. But that is only one aspect of a self that is more like a bundle of parts or aspects than it is like a uni-dimensional means/ends calculator. Gender differences in personality, in life choices, and in moral reasoning are characteristic of only one aspect of a complicated human psyche that is often at odds with itself, and therefore, cannot be thought, comfortingly, to have only one essence.

If we think of the self as having many parts or aspects, some of which are in conflict, we can make better sense out of Gilligan's claim that there is a dichotomy of masculine and feminine moral voices. Most male and female psyches, created in standard gender-dichotomous childrearing practices, have at least one characteristic difference that is reflected by a difference in moral voices. But many adult women who engage in similar social practices with adult men, e.g., as business or professional colleagues, may also share with them the so-called masculine voice of moral reasoning. And men influenced enough by feminist women to attempt co-parenting may develop a feminine voice of moral reasoning due to this practice. These men and women will have both so-called masculine and feminine aspects of self as developed by their ongoing social practices, and while they will be likely to find these opposing perspectives incongruous, and indeed inharmonious, there is no reason to say that they are thus "denying their essence" in the social practice in which they are doing the gender-anomalous job.

If the self is seen as having many aspects, then it cannot be determined universally which are prior, more fundamental, or more or less authentic. Rather, aspects of our selves are developed by participating in social practices that insist on certain skills and values. Furthermore the *contents* of masculinity and femininity vary with the social practices they are connected to. A woman defending her child against attack (for example in the movie *Cujo* or *Aliens*) is supposed to be showing her feminine protective maternal instinct. But a similar aggressive, perhaps violent act against a man who has made deprecating sexist remarks is not considered feminine.

Where different social practices encourage skills and values that are in conflict, those participating in them will develop conflicting aspects of self. And where certain social practices are taken to be paradigmatic of one's personal identity (as in self-effacing mothering activities for women in our society and self-aggrandizing aggressive or competitive activities for men), then those who develop gender-anomalous aspects of self can be disempowered by attributing the inharmonious combination of the two aspects to a personal neurosis. Though the feminist strategy of conceiving of certain aspects of self as inauthentic (for example, manipulative skills or heterosexual charm) is a more empowering approach than this, it does not follow that the view of self as having an authentic core and inauthentic outer layers is correct. Rather, one's sense of self and one's core values may change at different times and in different contexts. How then do we understand what it is to increase a sense of self-worth and personal power when the self is conceived of, as the Aspect theory suggests, as an *existential process* in which incongruities and lack of power are due to participation in conflicting social practices? Let us take a concrete example to discuss.

Professional women in the helping professions are a good example of those whose concrete social practices are in conflict. Those in jobs in higher education, nursing and social work must develop our ability to emphathize with concrete others—students, patients, or clients—to do our job well. But since most of us work in large bureaucratic settings where impersonal rules of the game apply to job hiring, promotions and allocations, we must develop a competitive, impersonal, meritocratic set of values and principles in self-defense. Thus one aspect of our jobs encourages the caring ethic connected to a contextual concern for concrete others that Gilligan claims is typical of the feminine role, and another aspect requires adopting the masculine ethic characterized by a universalistic rights/justice approach. Thus we have two moral voices, both in unhappy and unharmonious juxtaposition in our consciousness. What is alienating is not that our authentic self is thus denied, but the psychological incongruity of having to operate with conflicting values.

This contradiction in ways of thinking and valuing is a feature not only of women's work in the helping professions but of the work of those in male-dominated fields such as business, politics, and the law who face the second-shift problem as working mothers.

Ironically, the juggling of incorporative aspects of self in nurturant work at home with oppositional and individualistic ways of being in such careers is also a problem for some men who, in sharing housework and childcare with feminist partners, find their modus operandi different from their more conservative male colleagues at the office. Black and other minority women, no matter whether employed or not, could be expected to develop a rights/justice orientation in self-defense against the social opposition of racist whites, toward whom they cannot afford to take a simple caring orientation.

The way to understand personal empowerment of an oppressed group faced with social practices that involve conflicting values is to combine the insights of the Rational Maximizer and Difference theories of Self with a historical perspective. The traditional sexual division of labor in public and private spheres is breaking down for many women and some men. Where it is no longer clear what exactly is men's and women's work, gender identities defined in terms of the different standards of self-worth attached to men's and women's work are put in crisis. It is precisely this developing conflict in gender roles, in conjunction with the American democratic ideology of the right of equality for all based on merit, that has spawned both the women's movement and the possibility for greater empowerment for women. Though the initial phase of capitalist development in America perpetuated male dominance by relegating women to the private, less socially valued, dependent, and relatively powerless sphere of the home, advanced capitalism and consumerist standards of living have been pulling women into part- and full-time labor. Though this has created the second-shift problem for working mothers and the incongruity of women, brought up to do individualized, caring work, placed in impersonal and uncaring bureaucracies and anonymous institutions, it has also allowed many women to gain economic independence from men.

An existential process of resolving this incongruity of personal identity can take many forms. The New Right women may decide that homemaking in economic and social dependency on a man is a better way to resolve the incongruity in her life than to strive for a career and economic independence from men. As Phyllis Schafly notes, most women would really rather cuddle a baby than a typewriter!

If the Aspect theory of the self is correct, the feminist cannot challenge the New Right woman's choice by claiming it is inauthentic, for there is no way to prove what the authentic female self would choose. Nonetheless, due to the social crisis in gender roles, all women in the United States today are likely to have developed rational maximizer as well as incorporative (i.e., traditionally feminine) aspects of self. This is so because when traditional life styles are no longer rigidly followed, individuals are forced to a more self-conscious means/ends calculation of what in the long run will serve their interests.

Feminists can appeal to the rational maximizer aspect of women to argue that women who take the New Right solution to the gender crisis face a high risk of failing to achieve their goals of security and well being. This is so because of the rise in divorce rates, low welfare payments, low-paid wage labor work for most women and the small amount of child support most women receive from former husbands. Thus a woman who places all her eggs in the homemaker basket is increasingly likely to end up a single mother who is one of the statistics in the feminization of poverty.

With respect to women's traditional feminine identification as nurturers, feminists can argue that the only way to really have these values be effective today is not to retreat to private motherhood but to influence public policy by gaining individual and collective power in careers and politics that will allow for a public challenge to a militarism spawned by an excessive masculine thinking. Only by gaining public power as women can we have the collective power, through unionizing women and feminist political networks, to demand that those feminine values of caring and contextual moral decision-making be incorporated into the rules of the game of our economic and government institutions. In the long run, only a more decentralized, worker (and client, patient, and student) -controlled type of decision making can incorporate the caring and contextual considerations needed into the more abstract meritocratic but often inhumane rules by which our public institutions operate.

Such a feminist program will require radical structural changes in the present relation between public and private. We will need to educate the American public to the idea that the raising of children is not a private luxury but a public responsibility. Employers should thus be required to reorganize wage work so as to allow flextime jobs, with no career penalty for mothers and fathers of young children, as well as maternity and paternity leave and quality affordable child care.

Our ultimate goal must be the de-genderizing of every aspect of social life. Only this can empower women to develop our potentials as unique individuals not constrained by a social definition that sees our essential nature to be to serve men. However, we cannot achieve this goal without a collective, public process that first empowers women by creating a higher public value for feminine skills and interests. Though assertiveness training and economic independence are key for women, they must be supplemented by comparable worth, social security for homemakers, and other such campaigns that set a higher value on women's traditional work.

While feminist collective networking and public feminist political campaigns can start the empowerment process that allows a woman to re-define a core sense of self that can perceive itself as valuable and able to control her life independently of men, there are many other private issues that remain to be negotiated if she is to develop full personal empowerment.

For example, should a woman cut herself off from, or just try to ignore, her parents if they are very sexist? Should she pursue mother-hood, given the social costs and dangers of motherhood, indeed the likelihood of being a single mother in a sexist world? Should she give up a heterosexual life style and choose a woman lover in order to create a more equal context for love? Should she choose an alternative living arrangement with a man that does not involve marriage, to avoid the sexist social and psychological expectations that may be involved? Or should she eschew sexual love relationships altogether and prioritize platonic friendships with women (and perhaps men)?[18]

There is no general answer as to which of these paths a woman should take to personal empowerment. Only trial and error and the experience of juggling the various aspects of her self by trying out different private commitments can lead to what is most personally empowering to different women. The Aspect theory of the self, based as it is on the view that the self is an existential process whose integration may be different for different women, must assume an ethical pluralism on such matters of personal choice.

The position of ethical pluralism is a consequence of the rejection of the essentialist idea that all women have the same inner and authentic self that can only be empowered by the same choices. But, nonetheless, we can still draw a few important generalizations about what this empowerment process must minimally entail for women in the contem-porary United States: first, collective networking with other women around feminist campaigns; and second, prioritizing friendships with other women that value personal autonomy and the elimination of self-definitions that define self-worth exclusively in terms of relation-ships with men, whether they be fathers, employers, sons, workmates, friends, husbands or lovers. Given the fragmented aspects of self and the general deprecation of the feminine that pervades all our social life, these steps are necessary, to empower both the rational maximizing aspect of self, which gains when women find ways to gain material equality with men, and the incorporative aspect of self, which finds empowerment when it finds a secure yet self-affirming way to ally one's self-interests in nurturing and supportive connections to others.

NOTES

1. For a survey of this literature, see Natalie Sokoloff, *Between Money and Love: The Dialectics of Women's Home and Market Work* (New York: Praeger, 1980). Also cf. Heidi Hartmann, "The Unhappy Marriage of Marxism and Feminism," in Lydia Sargent, ed., *Women and Revolution* (Boston, MA: South End Press, 1981) and the responses to Hartmann in the same volume; Christine Delphy, *Close to Home: A Materialist Analysis of Women's Oppression* (Amherst, MA: University of Massachusetts Press, 1984) and the articles by Jean Gardiner, "Women's Domestic Labor," Batya Weinbaum and Amy Bridges, "The Other Side of the Paycheck: Monopoly Capital and the Structure of Consumption," Heidi Hartmann, "Capitalism, Patriarchy and Job Segregation by Sex" and Margery Davies "Women's Place Is at the Typewriter: The Feminization of the Clerical Labor Force," all in Zillah R. Eisenstein, ed., *Capitalist Patriarchy and the Case for Socialist-Feminism* (New York: Monthly Review Press, 1979).

2. Cf. Nancy Chodorow, *The Reproduction of Mothering* (Berkeley, CA: University of California Press, 1978); Carol Gilligan, *In a Different Voice* (Cambridge, MA: Harvard University Press, 1982); Jean Baker Miller, *Toward a New Psychology of Women* (Boston: Beacon Press, 1976), Jean Baker Miller, ed. *Psychoanalysis and Women* (Baltimore, MD: Penguin, 1973).

3. Perhaps the most original and influential article of the new feminist anthropology is that by Gayle Rubin, "The Traffic in Women," in Rayna Reiter, ed., *Toward a New Anthropology of Women* (New York: Monthly Review Press, 1975). Other important contributions are the rest of the articles in Reiter as well as those in Michelle Zimbalist Rosaldo and Louise Lamphere, eds., *Woman, Culture and Society* (Stanford, CA: Stanford University Press, 1974). See also Peggy Reeves Sanday, *Female Power and Male Dominance: On the Origins of Sexual Inequality* (New York: Cambridge University Press, 1981).

4. Cf. Nancy Hartsock, *Money, Sex and Power* (New York: Longman's, 1983); Mary O'Brien, *The Politics of Reproduction* (Boston: Routledge and Kegan Paul, 1981); Sandra Harding and Merrill Hintikka, eds., *Discovering Reality: Feminist Perspectives on Epistemology, Metaphysics, Methodology and Philosophy of Science* (Boston: Reidel, 1983); Sandra Harding, *The Science Question in Feminism* (Ithaca, NY: Cornell University Press, 1987).

5. Cf. Andrea Dworkin, *Womanhating* (New York: Dutton, 1974); Andrea Dworkin, *Pornography: Men Possessing Women* (New York: Perigee, 1981); Kathleen Barry, *Female Sexual Slavery* (Englewood Cliffs, NJ: Prentice-Hall, 1979); Susan Griffin, *Pornography and Silence* (New York: Harper, 1981); Laura Lederer, ed., *Take Back the Night: Women on Pornography* (New York: Wm. Morrow, 1980); Andrea Dworkin, "Against the Male Flood: Censorship, Pornography and Equality," *Harvard Women's Law Journal* 8 (Spring 1985): 1–29; and Catharine A. MacKinnon, "Pornography, Civil Rights and Speech," *Harvard Civil Rights-Civil Liberties Law Review* 20 (Winter 1985): 1–70.

6. Mary Daly, *Gyn/Ecology: The Meta-ethics of Radical Feminism* (Boston, MA: Beacon Press, 1978).

7. See O'Brien, *The Politics of Reproduction*.

8. Simone de Beauvoir, *The Second Sex* (New York: Bantam, 1952); Laurel

Holliday, *The Violent Sex: Male Psychobiology and the Evolution of Consciousness* (Guerneville, CA: Bluestocking Press, 1978); Kathleen Barry.

9. Alice Rossi, "A Biosocial Perspective on Parenting," *Daedulus* 106, 2 (Spring 1977): 1–32; Melvin Konner, "She & He," *Science* (Sept. 1982): 54–61; Laurel Holliday; Adrienne Rich, *Of Woman Born* (New York: Norton, 1976).

10. Nancy Chodorow; Juliet Mitchell, *Psychoanalysis and Feminism* (New York: Pantheon, 1974); Janice Raymond, *The Transexual Empire: The Making of the She-Male* (Boston: Beacon Press, 1979); Carol Gilligan.

11. Mary Daly, *Pure Lust: Elemental Feminist Philosophy* (Boston: Beacon Press, 1984).

12. Janice Raymond, *A Passion for Friends: Toward a Philosophy of Female Affection* (Boston: Beacon Press, 1986).

13. Chodorow, *The Reproduction of Mothering.*

14. Dorothy Dinnerstein, *The Mermaid and the Minotaur: Sexual Arrangements and Human Malaise* (New York: Harper and Row, 1976).

15. Gilligan, *In a Different Voice.*

16. Sara Ruddick, "Maternal Thinking," *Feminist Studies* 6, 2 (Summer 1980): 342–67; reprinted in Joyce Trebilcot, ed., *Mothering: Essays in Feminist Theory* (Totowa, NJ: Rowman and Allenheld, 1984).

17. Cf. Ann Ferguson, *Blood at the Root: Motherhood, Sexuality and Male Dominance* (Boston: Pandora/Unwin Hyman, 1988) as well as Ferguson, "Motherhood and Sexuality: Some Feminist Questions," *Hypatia: A Journal of Feminist Philosophy* 1, 2 (Fall 1986): 322.

18. For a discussion of some of these feminist ethical questions, see Ferguson, *Blood at the Root*, and the articles in Ann Ferguson, ed., "Motherhood and Sexuality" issue, *Hypatia: A Journal of Feminist Philosophy* 1, 2 (Fall 1986).

Part III ——————————————
Theory of Knowledge

_____

Many philosophers consider theory of knowledge—(epistemology) to be the core of philosophy. Questions about what we can know, the reliability of claims to know, the role that reason and sense experience play in knowledge, and the relation among belief, knowledge, and truth, are among those that have continued to occupy philosophers. Although there have always been controversies among philosophers about the proper role of reason both as an ideal and in the everyday acquisition of knowledge, the dominant tradition in western philosophy has placed a very high value on reason and rationality, and has characterized them in ways that are inextricably tied to being male.

Feminist philosophers have come to understand that one cannot set about righting the wrongs of traditional male epistemologists by simply proclaiming that both men and women possess reason, knowledge and emotion. For, as Genevieve Lloyd points out about the cultural ideal of reason, the very definitions of the key terms grow from ideals of maleness and femaleness within structures of male dominance.[1] A lesser value is given to the female traits, and then reason is defined in opposition to those traits. Because of the pervasiveness of this pattern, one must be suspect about any gender-neutral concept of reason currently proposed.

The paper of Lloyd's included here is the most historically oriented of any in this collection. She focuses on the seventeenth century "man of reason," particularly Descartes, while taking a more cursory look at the relations among maleness, femaleness, and rationality in other periods. It is important to examine Descartes and the seventeenth century not only because this period is a turning point in the history of philosophy, but also because the Cartesian tradition is severely criticized by feminist philosophers as well as others.

One contrast with the "man of reason" is, of course, the identification of woman with emotion. Alison Jaggar points out some of the ways in which reason and emotion have been contrasted and emotion has been denigrated. In opposition to views that emotion hinders the acquisition of knowledge, Jaggar maintains that emotion is indispensable for knowledge and that women are especially well situated to use their recognition of emotions in the pursuit of knowledge.

In feminist epistemology one finds good examples of the ways in which feminist scholars learn from integrating different fields of inquiry. Feminist epistemologists tend not to separate epistemology from other areas such as philosophy of science; they often see the connection between ethics and theory of knowledge, and want to draw on work done in other disciplines, for example, sociology of knowledge or psychology. For example, both feminist psychologists and epistemologists explore women as knowers and investigate knowledge of women's experiences. Readers unfamiliar with feminist psychological literature might want to look at *Women's Ways of Knowing*[2] as an example of some of the psychological studies done on the distinctive ways women think and feel about themselves as knowers and about their styles of acquiring knowledge.

Lorraine Code approaches the topics of women as knowers and knowledge of women's experiences from a feminist epistemological point of view. She argues that in order to find appropriate ways of knowing women's experiences we must counteract the stereotypes about women's nature that limit women's ability to know. Code seeks a theory of knowledge that is informed by women's experiences; it will focus on understanding rather than on "justification, verification, and control" and will find value in first person experiential stories.

Notes

1. Genevieve Lloyd, *The Man of Reason: "Male" and "Female" in Western Philosophy* (Minneapolis, Minn. University of Minnesota Press, 1984).

2. Mary Field Belenky et al., *Women's Ways of Knowing: The Development of Self, Voice, and Mind* (New York: Basic Books, 1986).

Chapter 7

The Man of Reason

Genevieve Lloyd

*B*y the Man of Reason I mean the ideal of rationality associated with the rationalist philosophies of the seventeenth century. And, secondly, something more nebulous—the residue of that ideal in our contemporary consciousness, our inheritance from seventeenth century rationalism. This is, I think, a substantial component in what reason has come to be. But it is not, of course, the only component. In focusing on it to the exclusion of any other developments in the notion of reason since the seventeenth century, this paper inevitably presents an incomplete picture of reason, but one that does highlight, I think, some aspects of reason that are of considerable relevance to philosophical aspects of feminism.

The main feature of the Man of Reason that I am concerned to bring into focus is his maleness. This in itself, I think, is a matter of philosophical interest. More is involved here than the supposedly "neutral" sense of "man" to include women. We are all familiar with the fact that linguistic usage commonly fails to recognize that humanity comprises two sexes. But there is something deeper to the maleness of the Man of Reason; something more deeply engrained in consciousness. He is after all a creation of reflective consciousness. When the Man of Reason is extolled, philosophers are not talking about idealizations of human beings. They are talking about ideals of manhood.

What I want to do in this paper is to bring this undoubted maleness of the Man of Reason into clearer focus. There are, I think, reasons that belong in the history of philosophy for the association between reason and masculinity. Some parts of the history of philosophy can throw light here on a very confused and tension-ridden area of human experience. Past philosophical reflection has after all helped form our present thought structures. And the creature I am calling the Man of

Source: First published in *Metaphilosophy* 10, 1 (January 1979): 18–37. Copyright © 1979 by *Metaphilosophy.* Reprinted by permission of the author and of the publisher.

Reason embodies some of the fundamental ideals of our culture. Let us try then to bring him into sharper focus.

THE ASSOCIATION OF "MALE" WITH "RATIONAL"

The associations between "male" and "rational" and between "female" and "non-rational" have, of course, a very long history. The idea that the rational is somehow specially associated with masculinity goes back to the Greek founding fathers of rationality as we know it. Aristotle thought that woman was "as it were an impotent male, for it is through a certain incapacity that the female is female."[1] This intrinsic female incapacity was a lack in the "principle of soul"[2] and hence associated with an incapacity in respect of rationality. The claim is not of course that women do not have rationality, but they have it in an inferior, fainter way. They have rationality; they are distinguished from the animals by being rational. Yet they are not equal to men. They are somehow *lesser* men, lesser in respect of the all-important thing: rationality.

Later Augustine in *The Confessions* displays a similar reluctance to fully extend the privilege of male rationality to women:

> And finally we see man, made in your image and likeness ruling over all the irrational animals for the very reason that he was made in your image and resembles you, that is because he has the power of reason and understanding. And just as in man's soul there are two forces; one which is dominant because it deliberates and one which obeys because it is subject to such guidance, in the same way in the physical sense, woman has been made for man. In her mind and her rational intelligence she has a nature the equal of man's, but in sex she is physically subject to him in the same way as our natural impulses need to be subjected to the reasoning power of the mind, in order that the actions to which they lead may be inspired by the principles of good conduct.[3]

And, two chapters later:

> Then you took man's mind, which is subject to none but you and needs to imitate no human authority, and renewed it in your own image and likeness. You made rational action subject to the rule of the intellect, as woman is subject to man.[4]

Being rational, woman ought to share a common nature with man and hence, unlike the animals, to be equal to him. But of course she is not equal to man. Augustine accommodates this tension by making a division within the rational faculty between a dominant and a passive mode of rationality, whose relationship mirrors that of woman to man.

These tensions surrounding woman's status as a rational being come to the surface during the Renaissance period, with prolonged debate centering on the vexed question "Does mankind include woman?" The rediscovery of ancient thought changed the character of education for the nobility and there was no lack of learned ladies. The acquisition of book learning by women was no doubt seen as a threat to male dominance and much of the debate of the period about woman's status as a rational being perhaps springs from this threat.

Charlotte de Brachart, in an attack on those who want to forbid knowledge to women, written in 1604, complains

> these gentlemen would like to see us plain imbeciles so that we could serve as shadows to set off better their fine wits.[5]

However that may be, the existence of women posed questions for the Renaissance world view. There was controversy over how they fitted into the scheme of things. The dignity, the perfection of man was a favorite theme of the age. For some, that meant the perfection of man alone. But there were many, men as well as women, at this period who insisted that "man" here covered the whole of the human race. Woman, her defenders of the period argue, cannot be called an imperfect animal, produced by chance through some error of nature. The divine image is perfect in her and in man equally. One man cannot be more wholly man than another, or the male more perfect in substance than the female, for both belong to the same species: man. As Marie de Gournay, a French woman writing on the equality of men and women early in the seventeenth century sums it up: "Nothing is more like a cat in a window than another cat."[6]

Such recognition of a common nature for men and women and the repudiation of Aristotle's views on the inferior natures of women did not however bring with them any automatic recognition of their equality. And widespread recognition of their common nature and equal capacities was small comfort to the ladies of the period. Nor did it prevent the endorsement of a different morality for women. There was an emphasis on different virtues, especially chastity, which was, for women, the central virtue around which all others revolved. Works on education for women at this time often focus on chastity as the principal justification for bothering with the education of women at all. A complex of social and economic factors, chiefly the fact that women were still the property of someone who therefore had special rights over them, ensured that they remained subject to a different array of moral restraints, obligations, and correlative virtues. It was by no means critically assumed at this time that the dignity of man meant the dignity of males only. But the prolonged debate on the nature and rationality of women was of little consequence for sexual equality. Much of the debate in this Renaissance "war of the sexes" was conducted in theological terms, centering on the exegesis of Genesis. And what prevailed, in terms of the Genesis debate, was that *Man* was made in God's image. And that woman was made as his literal and metaphorical "offsider." Whether she also was made fully in the likeness of God paled into social insignificance compared with the fact that her *role* was to be man's companion and helpmate and hence subject to his rule.

But if reflection on the nature and extent of rationality did not help further the cause of sexual equality at this stage—as perhaps it should have done were rational considerations the only ones involved—it cannot be said that, in itself, it provided a hindrance either. In the seventeenth century, with the emergence of a special, more sharply defined, kind of reason, and the associated emergence of the Man of Reason as a character ideal, we find developing a rather different situation in the relationship between philosophical thought and social reality

REASON IN THE SEVENTEENTH CENTURY

One of the most striking things that happens to reason in the seventeenth century is the attempt to encapsulate it in a systematic method for attaining certainty. The paradigm of this approach to reason is Descartes's *Regulae*, the *Rules for the Direction of the Mind*, written in 1628. Here there emerges a new conception of what is involved in knowledge. The acquisition of knowledge is a matter of the systematic pursuit of an orderly method. The essence of the method is to break down all the complex operations involved in reasoning into their most basic constituents and to render the mind adept in performing these simple operations—intuition and deduction. Intuition is the undoubting conception of an unclouded and attentive mind which comes from the light of reason alone. This is the basis for Descartes's later influential doctrine of clear and distinct ideas. Deduction is the process by which we extend knowledge beyond intuitions by connecting them in series. These are the only mental operations Descartes will admit into his method; but the proper understanding and use of them will, he thinks, yield all that lies within the province of knowledge. Anything else is in fact an impediment to knowledge:

nothing can be added to the pure light of reason which does not in some way obscure it.[7]

The method is universally applicable, regardless of any difference in subject matter:

> we must not fancy that one kind of knowledge is more obscure than another, since all knowledge is of the same nature throughout, and consists solely in combining what is self evident.[8]

This universality of Cartesian method is emphasized in the *Discourse on Method*, published in 1637:

> provided only that we abstain from receiving anything as true which is not so, and always retain the order which is necessary in order to deduce the one conclusion from the other, there can be nothing so remote that we cannot reach to it, nor so recondite that we cannot discover it.[9]

For Descartes, then, all knowledge consists in self-evident intuition and necessary deduction. We are to break down the complex and obscure into what is simple and self-evident, then combine the resultant units in an orderly manner. In order to know we must isolate the "simple natures," the objects of intuition, and "scrutinise them separately with steadfast mental gaze." We then combine them in chains of deductions. The whole of human knowledge consists in a distinct perception of the way in which these simple natures combine in order to build up other objects.[10]

There is a deeper, metaphysical, dimension to the Cartesian treatment of reason. In the course of elaborating a method for attaining certain knowledge Descartes thinks he is uncovering the unity of all the sciences, the unity of knowledge. For him this is identical with the order of thought itself, with the very structure of the knowing mind. And this order of thought is taken as transparently reflecting the order of things. In the *Regulae* there is no gap between intuitions and the simple natures that are their objective correlates. In the later *Meditations* (1641) the possibility of radical doubt opens a gap between ideas and the material world, between the structure of the mind and the structure of the reality it attempts to know. But this gap is then closed by the existence of a veracious God. Introspection of the nature of thought in an individual mind ultimately yields access to universal reason, God given and God guaranteed, and hence to the structure of reality itself, conceived by Cartesian rationalism to be identical with that of the mind.

This isomorphism, between reason and reality, founded on a veracious God, gives reason a quasi-divine character. Reason is God imbued, the divine spark in man. This is the seventeenth century version of the treatment of man's rational faculty as reflecting the godhead, as that in virtue of which man is made in God's image.

Another feature of Descartes's treatment of reason that is crucial here is its connection with his antithesis between mind and matter. The basic units of Cartesian method are discrete, sharp edged and self-contained mental items. This becomes even more pronounced in his later works. The vehicles of knowledge are clear, precisely bordered mental states, sharply separated from one another:

> The distinct is that which is so precise and different from all other objects that it contains within itself nothing but what is clear.[11]

And this discrete, delineated character of the units of knowledge is grounded in Descartes's distinction between mind and matter. The absolute certainty that accompanies clear and distinct ideas derives from their purely mental character. Intuition, as Descartes puts it, is free of the "fluctuating testimony of the senses" and the "blundering constructions of imagination." Cartesian method is essentially a matter of forming the "habit of distinguishing intellectual from corporeal matters."[12] It is a matter of shedding the sensuous from thought.

The search for the "clear and distinct," the separating out of the emotional, the sensuous, the imaginative, now makes possible polarizations of previously existing contrasts—intellect versus the emotions; reason versus imagination; mind versus matter. We have seen that the claim that women are somehow lacking in respect of rationality, that they are more impulsive, more emotional, than men is by no means a seventeenth century innovation. But these contrasts were previously contrasts *within* the rational. What ought to be dominated by reason had not previously been so sharply delineated from the intellectual. The conjunction of Cartesian down-grading of the sensuous with the use of the mind-matter distinction to establish the discrete character of Cartesian ideas introduces possibilities of polarization that were not there before.

Another relevant factor here is that shedding the non-intellectual from our mental states is something that demands training. In earlier centuries too, of course, it was thought appropriate to give the education of women a different character from that of men. And it was possible to present this as justified by their being different in respect of rationality. But with the seventeenth century there is a new dimension. Women can now be excluded from training *in* reason, that is, from the acquisition of method. And since this training is explicitly a matter of learning to leave one's emotions, imagination, etc., out of account, there now emerges a new dimension to the idea that women are more emotional or more impulsive, etc., than men. If they are excluded from training in rationality, women are perforce *left* emotional, impulsive, fancy ridden. They are not trained out of the "blundering constructions of the imagination" to enter the rarified air of reason. So thought styles, that are in the seventeenth century sense pre-rational, can survive in women. This *makes* it true, in a way it need not have been before, that women are less rational than men.

Also, it now becomes possible, as it was not before, to have a reasoned basis for assigning the emotions, the imagination, the sensuous in general, to women as their special area of responsibility. The training of a Man of Reason does after all involve getting him to shed many of his normal characteristics. It can now be seen as woman's role to preserve for him the areas of warmth and sensuousness that training in reason demands that he himself transcend. A great deal happens of course between the time of Descartes and that of Rousseau. But we can see this theme, elaborated almost to the point of parody, in Rousseau's views on the education of women in *Emile*, which so outraged Mary Wollstonecraft in the *Vindication of the Rights of Women*:

> To be pleasing in his sight, to win his respect and love, to train him in childhood, to tend him in manhood, to counsel and console, to make his life pleasant and happy, these are the duties of woman for all time, and this is what she should be taught while she is young.[13]

The contrast involved in the idea that man was made in God's image and woman was made to be a companion for man thus takes on a new dimension in the seventeenth century. We now have a separation of functions backed by a theory of mind. Given an already existing situation of sexual inequality, reason—the godlike, the spark of the divine in man—is assigned to the male. The emotions, the imagination, the sensuous are assigned to women. They are to provide comfort, relief, entertainment and solace for the austerity that being a Man of Reason demands. Something like this had of course been the case before. Different training was given to men and women to fit them for different life styles. But now the transcending of the sensuous can be seen as an end in itself. It is not in order to fit him for the heroic that the Man of Reason is to be trained out of his soft emotions and his sensuousness, but because that is precisely what it is to be rational. The division between reason and the non-rational can now be seen as reflecting and as being reenacted in the division between the sexes—in a way it was not before.

The stage is now set for the emergence of the Man of Reason as a male character ideal.

THE MAN OF REASON AS AN ETHICAL IDEAL

Cartesian method has its ethical correlate. Descartes's grandiose expectations of what can be gained by the elimination of sensuous intrusions on the intellect are paralleled by grandiose expectations of what can be acquired in the practical realm by gaining mastery of one's thoughts. In a letter to Princess Elizabeth, Descartes says:

> True philosophy teaches that even amid the saddest disasters and most bitter pains a man can always be content, provided that he knows how to use his reason.[14]

His own mastery of reason over the passions, he claims, has cured him of his hereditary dry cough and pale color[15] and ensured that even his dreams are pleasant.[16]

But the full ethical dimensions of the seventeenth century cultivation of reason are found not in Descartes's works, but in Spinoza's *Ethics*. Here mastery of one's thoughts and the attaining of rational control over passion are no trivial pursuit of mental gymnastics for the maintenance of good health and pleasant dreams. Freeing oneself from the bondage of inadequate ideas to become a Man of Reason has as its goal nothing less than the attaining of eternity of the mind:

> the ignorant man is not only distracted in various ways by external causes without ever gaining the true acquiescence of his spirit, but moreover lives, as it were unwitting of himself, and of God, and of things, and as soon as he ceases to suffer ceases also to be.

> Whereas the wise man, in so far as he is regarded as such, is scarcely at all disturbed in spirit, but, being conscious of himself, and of God, and of things, by a certain eternal necessity, never ceases to be, but always possesses true acquiescence of his spirt.[17]

The details of Spinoza's account of the rewards to be gained from the cultivation of reason lie beyond the scope of this paper. What I wish to focus on here are some features of his treatment of the relationship between reason and emotion.

It would not be true to say that Spinoza recommends that the Man of Reason ignore his passions. The task is not to ignore his emotions but, on the contrary, to understand them, thereby transforming them from passivities into active, rational emotions:

> An emotion, which is a passion, ceases to be a passion, as soon as we form a clear and distinct idea thereof.[18]

An emotion therefore becomes more under our control, and the mind is less passive in respect of it, in proportion as it is more known to us.[19]

Emotions in their original state, that is as passions, are confused modes of perception of reality. When this confusion is replaced by clear and distinct perception the emotions cease to be passions. This process is bound up with the understanding of the causality of our passions and hence, for Spinoza, with the recognition of necessities. And this recognition of necessity is at the same time the means of attaining freedom. The transition from passion to active, intellectual emotion through the understanding of necessities is the transition to individual autonomy. Despite his metaphysical rejection of a plurality of individual substances, Spinoza's ethic is highly individualistic. But the achievement of individuality is at the cost of a detachment from the particular, the specific, the transient, in order to turn one's attention increasingly to the general, the universal, the unchanging, to what is common to all:

an emotion which springs from reason is necessarily referred to the common properties of things, . . . which we always regard as present (for there can be nothing to exclude their present existence) and which we always conceive in the same manner. Wherefore an emotion of this kind always remains the same.[20]

So it is his increasing detachment from the transient and his increasing attachment to the unchanging that renders Spinoza's Man of Reason acquiescent and thereby free. The Man of Reason's attachments become increasingly directed away from the contingencies and vicissitudes of interactions with individuals and towards what is common to all. And he moves increasingly in a realm where the appearance of contingency gives way to the recognition of necessity:

the strong man has ever first in his thoughts that all things follow from the necessity of the divine nature; so that whatsoever he deems to be hurtful and evil, and whatsoever, accordingly seems to him impious, horrible, unjust or base, assumes that appearance owing to his own disordered, fragmentary and confused view of the universe. Wherefore he strives before all things to conceive things as they really are, and to remove the hindrances to true knowledge, such as are hatred, anger, envy, derision, pride and similar emotions . . . Thus he endeavours, as far as in him lies, to do good and go on his way rejoicing.[21]

This sounds like a commendable exercise in tolerance of perception. And indeed it is that. The Man of Reason endeavors to transcend the distortions of his own self-centred perception to perceive things as they

really are. But if Spinoza's "strong man" recognizes the particular
objects of his hate as seeming hateful only because of his own
inadequate ideas, the same goes for the objects of his love. As Reason
acquires dominance, changeable transient objects of affection are
gradually cast aside:

> spiritual unhealthiness and misfortunes can generally be traced to exces-
> sive love for something which is subject to many variations, and which we
> never become masters of. For none is solicitous or anxious about anything,
> unless he loves it; neither do wrongs, suspicions, enmities, etc. arise,
> except in regard to things whereof no one can be really master.

> We may thus readily conceive the power which clear and distinct knowl-
> edge, and especially this third kind of knowledge . . . founded on the
> actual knowledge of God, possesses on the emotions: if it does not
> absolutely destroy them, in so far as they are passions; at any rate it causes
> them to occupy a very small part of the mind. . . . Further, it begets a love
> towards a thing immutable and eternal, whereof we may really enter into
> possession; neither can it be defiled by those faults which are inherent in
> ordinary love; but it may grow from strength to strength and may engross
> the greater part of the mind and deeply penetrate it.[22] Something else the
> Man of Reason sheds along the way is pity. Pity in a man who lives under
> the guidance of reason is in itself bad and useless.[23]

> He who rightly realizes that all things follow from the necessity of the
> divine nature, and come to pass in accordance with the eternal laws and
> rules of nature, will not find anything worthy of hatred, derision or
> contempt, nor will he bestow pity on anything. . . .[24]

In another section Spinoza described pity as "womanish."[25]

The ideal, again, is a masculine one. The ultimate horror for
Spinoza's Man of Reason is to be "womanish," which is equated with
being under the sway of passions, untransformed by reason. The full
picture is of a man detached from changeable objects of passion to the
point where temporal transience, including the fact of death, is of no
consequence:

> In so far as the mind conceives a thing under the dictates of reason, it is
> affected equally, whether the idea be of a thing future, past or present.[26]

> A free man thinks of death least of all things; and his wisdom is a
> meditation not of death but of life.[27]

Here we have the ultimate glorification of reason in its ethical
dimension. But although the cultivation of reason is the means by
which we attain to freedom, the motivating force for this effort is

self-interest, the desire to persist in one's being. This emphasis on self-interest as the underlying ethical force is in some ways an anticipation of the more utilitarian spirit of the eighteenth century attitudes to the passions. The very essence of a man, according to Spinoza, resides in his endeavor to persist in his being. And, as a thinking being, his overriding self-interest is in preserving the coherence and continuity of his own thought against the flow of unconnected, fragmentary ideas that result from his limited, individual standpoint within the order of things. The more active his thought processes, the less he is at the mercy of the impingement of what is not himself, including, as we have seen, the demands of pity and the ravages of "meretricious" love. And the more autonomous, the more himself, he becomes. So integral is this connection between reason and the endeavor to persist in one's being that for Spinoza the rational mind simply cannot will not to be.[28]

All this gives to the *Ethics* a life-affirming character and an emphasis on individuality that cannot be underestimated. But as we have seen, this is in fact achieved at the cost of a detachment from changeable, individual objects of concern. It is true that the life style described by Spinoza contains positive compensations for the apparent impoverishment of individual life his ethical system involves. But what remains with us as the character ideal expressed in his Man of Reason is mainly the negative detachment from all that gives warmth and compassion to human existence—his ultimate detachment from the impingement of all that is not himself.

There is indeed much that is appealing and impressive in the picture Spinoza presents of the Man of Reason—the transcending of self-centered and hence dependent, jealous love; the pursuit of a detached perception of the truths of himself and his situation, transcending the distortions of his limited, unreflective perspective on things; the location of moral worth in a certain style of perception rather than in the will. Spinoza's attempt to combine a recognition of self interest as the basis of ethics—the rejection of false altruism and false sentiment—with the effort to transcend the distortions of a limited, individual perspective on the world remains of enduring significance. But the Man of Reason, we have seen, sheds not merely selfish, obsessive love, but also individuals as proper objects of love. This, along with his repudiation of "womanish" pity, may well seem too much to pay for liberation from the bondage of passion.

There is of course no suggestion that any man of reason will actually live like that. Pure specimens of the breed were no doubt nonexistent. "All things excellent are as difficult as they are rare," Spinoza says at the end of the *Ethics*. But it is the conception of the Man of Reason as an ideal that we are considering here. And we may well, I think, find the rarity of his particular kind of moral excellence no great cause for regret.

REASON AND INTUITION

Another area of relevance to the maleness of the Man of Reason concerns the relationship between reason and intuition. Spinoza identifies the pursuit of freedom with the cultivation of reason, in a broad sense. But, strictly, the higher levels of freedom that lead on to eternity of the mind are attained not through reason by which he means, roughly, ratiocination—the reason of Descartes's *Regulae*—but through what he calls "Scientia Intuitiva." This is a kind of knowledge superior to reason. It gives adequate knowledge of the essences of things and proceeds from an adequate idea of the absolute essence of the attributes of God. The exact nature of Spinoza's "intuition" need not concern us. What is important about it here is that Spinoza, in treating it as the highest form of knowledge, recognizes the limitations of the systematized reason of Cartesian method. This is of course a very different sense of the limitations of reason from that of later nineteenth century thought, which saw reason as limited in contrast to the access to reality provided by the will or the imagination. "Scientia intuitiva," whatever its exact nature, is clearly a mode of thought more closely related to Cartesian reason than to imagination. But Spinoza's treatment of intuition amounts nonetheless to a recognition of the limitations of the style of thinking systematized by Descartes. Intuitions for Descartes were the basic clear and distinct perceptions which were systematized by reason. For Spinoza intuition became a different form of thought, superior to reason.

Spinoza's recognition of the limitations of reason may seem surprising in a seventeenth century rationalist. But this is not as novel as it at first appears. In his letters to Princess Elizabeth, Descartes himself shows some awareness of the limitations of the style of thought he has developed. Although the purely intellectual can be separated out from the sensuous to yield clear and distinct ideas, the ideas thus obtained cannot, he admits, yield the whole truth. Clear and distinct perception demands the separation of mind from matter. But we have not grasped the whole truth unless we grasp also the union of mind and body. And to understand that, clearness and distinctness are of no use. Indeed, he goes on, it is only by refraining from metaphysical speculation that we can understand the union of mind and body.[29]

I am not sure how seriously Descartes should be taken here, though he is at pains to assure Elizabeth that he is not making fun of her. But there are in any case tensions within Descartes's treatment of the "intuitions" that are the very basis of his method, which give rise to some questions about the limitations of this style of reasoning.

Descartes saw himself as breaking with tradition, as shedding the stifling molds into which thought processes had been channelled by the excesses of the neo-scholastics. Method was to be above all a way of thinking originally, from one's own resources. This indeed was what his basic intuitions were supposed to be—the fresh, spontaneous, unclouded apprehensions of a mind operating in accordance with its understanding of its own nature. Yet in the fully developed Cartesian method, intuition becomes circumscribed by a process of ratiocination. Intuition becomes something the mind has to train itself to do; something it cannot be relied upon to do of its own untrained initiative. It becomes a legitimate question to ask, "Have I really managed to bring off in the approved manner a clear and distinct perception?" And with this arises the possibility of doubt about the reliability of reason itself. Authority, supposedly exorcised with the break from tradition, rears its head within method, intruding its demands into the inner recesses of consciousness itself. "This is how you must think if you wish to attain truth." Descartes begins from an emphasis on personal autonomous knowledge, the development of one's own judgments in a direct response to reality, untrammelled by appeals to authority. Yet Cartesian method itself shackles intuition within a method for knowing—a method in which the mind must be trained. This is partly of course just a matter of subjecting the erratic, unreliable vagaries of individual consciousness to the demands of rigor and discipline. But it is easy then to mistake the artificially created units Descartes has carved out of the flux of consciousness for the true nature of mind; as if mental life were really a succession of discrete, stabilized mental states.

This is partly why Descartes's "intuitions" break out of the bonds in which reason has put them. Descartes ties himself in knots attempting to validate the basic intuitions, to prove them reliable; moving, inevitably, in circles as he tries to establish the reliability of the mind's basic apprehensions by reasoning about them. The basic intuitions remain an unjustified base and Cartesian method is limited to ordering and systematizing them. A detailed critique of Descartes's attempt to justify the reliability of reason, on which a great deal has been written, is not my concern. What I want to emphasize is just that the rationalist's conception of reason does encapsulate thought artificially into discrete mental states, subject to rigorously disciplined order; and, especially from Descartes's treatment of reason, it then becomes easy to mistake this artificial creation for the real nature of consciousness.

Leibniz's treatment of knowledge shows a more explicit awareness of the pre-Rational underpinning of the sharply delineated constituents of seventeenth-century-style reasoning. His ideal of method coexists strikingly with a repeated insistence on the buzzing confusion of consciousness, incorporated into his system as the unconscious perceptions of the monads. Clear and distinct perception is a small isolated area of consciousness against a background of confusion:

> our confused sensations are the result of a variety of perceptions. This variety is infinite. It is almost like the confused murmuring which is heard by those who approach the shore of the sea. It comes from the continual beatings of innumerable waves.[30]

We have seen that the seventeenth century rationalists were aware of the limited, and limiting, character of systematized reason. Nonetheless what has come down to us as our unmistakable inheritance from seventeenth century rationalism is the ideal of method, construed as expressing the true nature of the mind. Although much has happened since in the development of reason, this rationalist model still underlies our "rational" thought styles. Conversely, "intuition" has come to mean the negation of all this—a thought style that is not sharpened and systematized in the manner of which Cartesian method is the paradigm. Intuition, inevitably, has come to be associated with specifically *female* thought styles.

If female minds are more intuitive, that is less rational, than male minds, it is mainly because rationality has been circumscribed to have no use for what, given the status quo, differentiates minds as female. If women's minds are less rational than men's, it is because the limits of reason have been set in a way that excludes qualities that are then assigned to women. It may well be true that thought styles that are not rational, in the seventeenth century sense, have survived more in women than in men as a result of their general exclusion from, at any rate, the more rarified levels of training in rationality. Here, in insisting on the existence and merits of "female intuition" women may in effect be trying to turn their own victimization into a false strength. "Female intuition" can, quite rightly, be a pejorative term.

An awareness of the claims of "intuition" can, nonetheless, be part of a constructive assessment of the claims and the ideals of reason. The Man of Reason is, after all, becoming in our times less able to bask in the glories of his self image, less confident in his self-style dignity. There is, of course, a lot to be said in praise of the Man of Reason. But it *has* all been said. In the increasing self-questioning of the ideals of reason, the feminist challenge to male sovereignty—to women's exclusion from the power structure, which is in some ways identifiable with rationality—can be sterile and self defeating unless it is conjoined with a critical assessment of reason itself.

THE CONTEMPORARY MAN OF REASON

The Man of Reason has, of course, had his crises before and been changed by them. In the eighteenth century he was stripped of his godlike character. The *philosophes* brought reason down to earth. No longer the spark of the divine in man, no longer dependent on nor guaranteed by God, reason was brought to bear critically on religion itself. But this did not really amount to a downgrading of reason. The result was rather, in some ways, to make a god of man himself. Optimism about reason survived the loss of its divine aura and much of the elitism associated with it in the seventeenth century. The *philosophes* were great popularizers of reason and this gave a new twist to women's relationship to reason in the eighteenth century. Woman was taken as the ultimate paradigm of "the common man."

The eighteenth century sees also a revaluation of the emotions. In the seventeenth century the passions were characteristically seen as a source of disorder and falsehood. Thought was the essence of the mind; the passions were seen as intruding distractions and disturbances resulting from the mind's union with the body. Although not necessarily disapproved of, they were seen as, at worst, threats to purity and clarity of thought; and, at best, as confused modes of thought itself. They were to be either transcended and kept in subjugation by reason or else transformed by reason into higher modes of thought. The eighteenth century saw a defense of the passions as the well springs of action, with reason providing the means for achieving the dictates of passion. Something like this, we have seen, was already present in Spinoza's treatment of thought and emotion. But there it coexisted with an insistence on an inner weakness, a lack of reality in the passions, which made them amenable not just to domination by reason but to complete transformation by it. From the eighteenth century on, the passions, and the nonrational in general, are more assured of their own reality. Even if controlled by reason passion remains something different from thought, a motivating force in its own right. And by the nineteenth century, with the Romantic movement, it could be seen as challenging the supremacy of reason.

With the Romantic revaluation of the passions and exaltation of imagination and feeling, we might expect a new evaluation of women along with the qualities associated with women. And so indeed there was, but one that proved disastrous for sexual equality—the pedestalizing of women, the revival of Romantic love. The Man of Reason stayed intact through the challenge of Romanticism, while going in search of his opposite to complete or complement his existence. The dichotomy between reason and feeling was preserved and in fact endorsed by the challenge of Romanticism.

What is distinctive about current disaffection with reason? It is not that the forces of unreason are stronger now. The Man of Reason was created in, and largely in response to, savage times. It is not that there is less faith in the basic reasonableness of human beings. What is new is the decline in optimism about the eventual victory of reason. Condorcet, an eighteenth century philosopher who died during the Terror, wrote the night before he left his hiding place in the expectation of his arrest, an affirmation of his faith in the eventual triumph of reason:

> How consoling for the philosopher who laments the errors, the crimes, the injustices which still pollute the earth and of which he is often the victim, is this view of the human race emancipated from its shackles, released from the empire of fate and from that of the enemies of its progress, advancing with a firm and sure step along the path of truth, virtue and happiness![31]

What is distinctive about current disaffection with reason is the sense that it will not all be solved by the progress of reason. It cannot any longer be said that the threats to humanity are threats posed by forces of unreason. Many of them have their source within reason itself. Man's reason is no longer an unequivocal object of his self esteem.

The nineteenth century reactions against reason—the polarizations we associate with the exaltation of the nonrational—have, however, left a legacy in consciousness that makes it very difficult to engage in any critical assessment of the forms and structures of contemporary rationality. Critics of reason too easily fall into a sterile repudiation of the rational, a vacuous affirmation of the importance or superiority of feeling or imagination. A sense of the sterility of Romantic rejections of reason is no doubt a major reason for the lack of reasoned critiques of current forms of rationality. And any attempt to provide the notion of "intuition" with content can easily be seen in terms of such a repudiation of the rational.

This, for example, is a common reaction to Bergson's treatment of intuition and his associated critique of the limitations of rationality.[32] Bergson's "intuition" is not, as is often suggested, merely an aesthetic notion. For him it is the essential nature of metaphysics. His affirmation of intuition is not a repudiation of rationality but an attempt to get beneath the segmentation of thought involved in "clear and distinct" thinking. The project is not to reject clear and distinct Cartesian-style thought in favor of some nonrational mode of access to reality. Bergson sees clear and distinct conceptualized thought, which achieved its most self-conscious articulation in the seventeenth century, as a development in thought essential for utilitarian purposes—a development without which human beings could not have managed to cope with their environment; but, for all that, a limited thought style, especially for the purpose of speculative metaphysical understanding. Bergsonian intuition, then, is not meant to be anything mystical, but rather an attempt to get below the spatialized, discrete representations into which seventeenth century rationalism has carved up reality; an attempt to grasp duration free of the spatializations that that form of reasoning has imposed on consciousness; an attempt to grasp the continuities rather than the separations.

More recently Robert Pirsig's book *Zen and the Art of Motorcycle Maintenance* represents an attempt to get at the unity underlying "Classical" and "Romantic" thought styles. This is a very different kind of critique of reason from that attempted by the Romantics, who were concerned rather with affirming one side of the dichotomy. Pirsig's book points to the possibility of an expansion of reason, rather than an abandoning of it.

Another danger which besets any attempt to engage in a critique of the Man of Reason from a specifically feminist standpoint is that such critique becomes a catalogue of the atrocities he has perpetrated on women. It is easy to see the Man of Reason as just the post seventeenth century variant on the historical role of male oppressor. But men and women are jointly responsible for his continued status as an ideal of rationality, for he represents women's ideals too. What is needed is critique of his standing as an ideal, whether as an object of male self-esteem or of female envy. The impoverishment of woman through the imposition of sexual stereotypes is obvious. Exclusion from reason has meant exclusion from power. The corresponding impoverishment of men is rather less obvious, for what they miss out on has been downgraded. What is needed for the Man of Reason is realization of his limitations as a *human* ideal, in the hope that men and women alike might come to enjoy a more human life, free of the sexual stereotypes that have evolved in his shadow.

NOTES

1. Aristole, *Generation of Animals*, Book I, Ch. 20, 727a15.

2. ibid., Book II, Ch. 3, 737a25.

3. Augustine, *The Confessions*, trans. R. S. Pine-Coffin (Baltimore: Penguin Classics, 1961), 344.

4. ibid., 345.

5. Ruth Kelso, *Doctrine for the Lady of the Renaissance* (Urbana: University of Illinois Press, 1956), 64. (This work is the source for much of the material in this section.)

6. ibid., 17.

7. *Rules for the Direction of the Mind*, Rule IV in *Descartes: Philosophical*

Works, trans. E. S. Haldane and G. R. T. Ross (Cambridge: Cambridge Univeristy Press, 1968) 1:10.

8. ibid., Rule XIII, 47.

9. *Discourse on Method*, Part II, 92.

10. *Rules for the Direction of the Mind*, Rule XII, 47.

11. Replies to the Second Set of Objections in *Descartes: Philosophical Works*, Vol. II, 32.

12. *Rules for the Direction of the Mind*, Rule III, 7.

13. Jean Jacques Rousseau, *Emile*, Book V, trans. B. Foxley (New York: E. P. Dutton, 1974) 328.

14. Descartes to Elizabeth, 6 October 1645; in *Descartes: Philosophical Letters*, ed. and trans. Anthony Kenny (Oxford: Oxford University Press, 1970), 180.

15. Descartes to Elizabeth, May or June 1645; ibid., 163.

16. Descartes to Elizabeth, 1 September 1645; ibid., 168.

17. Spinoza, *The Ethics*, trans. R. H. M. Elwes (Mineola, N.Y.: Dover, 1955) 2: Part V, Prop. XLII, 270.

18. ibid., Part V, Prop. III, 248.

19. loc. cit.

20. ibid., Part V, Prop. VII, 251.

21. ibid., Part IV, Prop. LXXIII, 236.

22. ibid., Part V, Prop. XX, 258.

23. ibid., Part IV, Prop. L. 221.

24. loc cit.

25. ibid., Part IV, Prop. XXXVII, Note 1, 213.

26. ibid., Part IV, Prop. LXII, 229.

27. ibid., Part IV, Prop. LXVII, 232.

28. ibid.

29. Descartes to Elizabeth, 28 June 1643, in *Descartes: Philosophical Letters*, 141.

30. *Discourse on Metaphysics*, in *Leibniz: Basic Writings*, trans. G. R. Montgomery (LaSalle, I 11.: Open Court 1962), Ch. XXXIII, 57.

31. Quotation in R. J. White, *The Antiphilosophers* (New York: Macmillan, 1970), 153.

32. See especially Henri Bergson, *Creative Evolution* (New York: Macmillan, 1913); *An Introduction to Metaphysics* , trans. T. E. Hulme (New York: G. P. Putnam's Sons, 1912); and "Philosophical Intuition," in *The Creative Mind* (Secaucus, N.J.: Citadel, 1946).

Chapter 8

Love and Knowledge:
Emotion in Feminist Epistemology

Alison M. Jaggar

INTRODUCTION: EMOTION IN WESTERN EPISTEMOLOGY

Within the western philosophical tradition, emotions usually have been considered as potentially or actually subversive of knowledge.[1] From Plato until the present, with a few notable exceptions, reason rather than emotion has been regarded as the indispensable faculty for acquiring knowledge.[2]

Typically, although again not invariably, the rational has been contrasted with the emotional, and this contrasted pair then often has been linked with other dichotomies. Not only has reason been contrasted with emotion, but it has also been associated with the mental, the cultural, the universal, the public and the male, whereas emotion has been associated with the irrational, the physical, the natural, the particular, the private, and of course, the female.

Although western epistemology has tended to give pride of place to reason rather than emotion, it has not always excluded emotion completely from the realm of reason. In the *Phaedrus*, Plato portrayed emotions, such as anger or curiosity, as irrational urges (horses) that must always be controlled by reason (the charioteer). On this model, the emotions did not need to be totally suppressed, but rather needed to be directed by reason: for example, in a genuinely threatening situation, it was thought not irrational but foolhardy not to be afraid.[3] The split between reason and emotion was not absolute, therefore, for the Greeks. Instead, the emotions were thought to provide indispensable

Source: This paper was written originally as a contribution to the Women's Studies Chair Seminar at Douglass College, Rutgers University. It has been published previously in *Inquiry: An Interdisciplinary Journal of Philosophy* (June 1989), and in *Gender/Body/ Knowledge: Feminist Reconstructions of Being and Knowing*, ed. Alison M. Jaggar and Susan R. Bordo (New Brunswick, N.J.: Rutgers University Press, 1989). Copyright © 1989 by Alison M. Jaggar. Reprinted by permission of the author.

motive power that needed to be channeled appropriately. Without horses, after all, the skill of the charioteer would be worthless.

The contrast between reason and emotion was sharpened in the seventeenth century by redefining reason as a purely instrumental faculty. For both the Greeks and the medieval philosophers, reason had been linked with value insofar as reason provided access to the objective structure or order of reality, seen as simultaneously natural and morally justified. With the rise of modern science, however, the realms of nature and value were separated: nature was stripped of value and reconceptualized as an inanimate mechanism of no intrinsic worth. Values were relocated in human beings, rooted in human preferences and emotional responses. The separation of supposedly natural fact from human value meant that reason, if it were to provide trustworthy insight into reality, had to be uncontaminated by or abstracted from value. Increasingly, therefore, though never universally,[4] reason was reconceptualized as the ability to make valid inferences from premises established elsewhere, the ability to calculate means but not to determine ends. The validity of logical inferences was thought independent of human attitudes and preferences; this was now the sense in which reason was taken to be objective and universal.[5]

The modern redefinition of rationality required a corresponding reconceptualization of emotion. This was achieved by portraying emotions as nonrational and often irrational urges that regularly swept the body, rather as a storm sweeps over the land. The common way of referring to the emotions as the "passions" emphasized that emotions happened to or were imposed upon an individual, something she suffered rather than something she did.

The epistemology associated with this new ontology rehabilitated sensory perception that, like emotion, typically had been suspected or even discounted by the western tradition as a reliable source of knowledge. British empiricism, succeeded in the nineteenth century by positivism, took its epistemological task to be the formulation of rules of inference that would guarantee the derivation of certain knowledge from the "raw data" supposedly given directly to the senses. Empirical testability became accepted as the hallmark of natural science; this, in turn, was viewed as the paradigm of genuine knowledge. Epistemology often was equated with the philosophy of science, and the dominant methodology of positivism prescribed that truly scientific knowledge must be capable of intersubjective verification. Because values and emotions had been defined as variable and idiosyncratic, positivism stipulated that trustworthy knowledge could be established only by methods that neutralized the values and emotions of individual scientists.

Recent approaches to epistemology have challenged some fundamental assumptions of the positivist epistemological model. Contemporary theorists of knowledge have undermined once-rigid distinctions between analytic and synthetic statements, between theories and observations and even between facts and values. Thus far, however, few challenged the purported gap between emotion and knowledge. In this paper, I wish to begin bridging this gap through the suggestion that emotions may be helpful and even necessary rather than inimical to the construction of knowledge. My account is exploratory in nature and leaves many questions unanswered. It is not supported by irrefutable arguments or conclusive proofs; instead, it should be viewed as a preliminary sketch for an epistemological model that will require much further development before its workability can be established.

EMOTION

What are emotions?
The philosophical question, "What are emotions?" requires both explicating the ways in which people ordinarily speak about emotion and evaluating the adequacy of those ways for expressing and illuminating experience and activity. Several problems confront someone trying to answer this deceptively simple question. One set of difficulties results from the variety, complexity, and even inconsistency of the ways in which emotions are viewed, both in daily life and in scientific contexts. It is in part this variety that makes emotions into a "question" and at the same time precludes answering that question by simple appeal to ordinary usage. A second difficulty is the wide range of phenomena covered by the term "emotion": these extend from apparently instantaneous "knee-jerk" responses of fright to lifelong dedication to an individual or a cause; from highly civilized aesthetic responses to undifferentiated feelings of hunger and thirst;[6] from background moods such as contentment or depression to intense and focused involvement in an immediate situation. It may well be impossible to construct a manageable account of emotion to cover such apparently diverse phenomena.

A further problem concerns the criteria for preferring one account of emotion to another. The more one learns about the ways in which other cultures conceptualize human faculties, the less plausible it becomes that emotions constitute what philsophers call a "natural kind." Not only do some cultures identify emotions unrecognized in the west, but there is reason to believe that the concept of emotion itself is a historical invention, like the concept of intelligence (Lewontin 1982) or even the concept of mind (Rorty 1979). For instance, anthropologist Catherine Lutz argues that the "dichotomous categories of 'cognition' and 'affect' are themselves Euroamerican cultural constructions, master symbols that pariticpate in the fundamental organization of our ways of looking at ourselves and others, both in and outside of social science" (Lutz 1987: 308, citing Lutz 1985, 1986). If this is true, then we have even more reason to wonder about the adequacy of ordinary western ways of talking about emotion. Yet we have no access either to our own emotions or to those of others independent of or unmediated by the discourse of our culture.

In the face of these difficulties, I shall sketch an account of emotion with the following limitations. First, it will operate within the context of western discussions of emotion: I shall not question, for instance, whether it would be possible or desirable to dispense entirely with anything resembling our concept of emotion. Second, although this account attempts to be consistent with as much as possible of western understandings of emotion, it is intended to cover only a limited domain, not every phenomenon that may be called an emotion. On the contrary, it excludes as genuine emotions both automatic physical responses and nonintentional sensations, such as hunger pangs. Third, I do not pretend to offer a complete theory of emotion; instead, I focus on a few specific aspects of emotion that I take to have been neglected or misrepresented, especially in positivist and neopositivist accounts. Finally, I would defend my approach not only on the ground that it illuminates aspects of our experience and activity that are obscured by positivist and neopositivist construals but also on the ground that it is less open than these to ideological abuse. In particular, I believe that recognizing certain neglected aspects of emotion makes possible a better and less ideologically biased account of how knowledge is, and so ought to be, constructed.

Emotions as intentional

Early positivist approaches to understanding emotion assumed that an adequate account required analytically separating emotion from other human faculties. Just as positivist accounts of sense perception attempted to distinguish the supposedly raw data of sensation from their cognitive interpretations, so positivist accounts of emotion tried to separate emotion conceptually from both reason and sense perception. As one way of sharpening these distinctions, positivist construals of emotion tended to identify emotions with the physical feelings or involuntary bodily movements that typically accompany them, such as pangs or qualms, flushes or tremors; emotions were also assimilated to the subduing of physiological function or movement, as in the case of sadness, depression, or boredom. The continuing influence of such supposedly scientific conceptions of emotion can be seen in the fact that "feeling" is often used colloquially as a synonym for emotion, even though the more central meaning of "feeling" is physiological sensation. On such accounts, emotions were not seen as being *about* anything; instead, they were contrasted with and seen as potential disruptions of other phenomena that *are* about some thing, phenomena such as rational judgments, thoughts, and observations. The positivist approach to understanding emotion has been called the Dumb View (Spelman 1982).

The Dumb View of emotion is quite untenable. For one thing, the same feeling or physiological response is likely to be interpreted as various emotions, depending on the context of experience. This point often is illustrated by reference to the famous Schachter and Singer experiment; excited feelings were induced in research subjects by the injection of adrenalin, and the subjects then attributed to themselves appropriate emotions depending on their context (Schachter and Singer 1969). Another problem with the Dumb View is that identifying emotions with feelings would make it impossible to postulate that a person might not be aware of her emotional state, because feelings by definition are a matter of conscious awareness. Finally, emotions differ from feelings, sensations, or physiological responses in that they are dispositional rather than episodic. For instance, we may assert truthfully that we are outraged by, proud of, or saddened by certain events, even if at that moment we are neither agitated nor tearful.

In recent years, contemporary philosophers have tended to reject the Dumb View of emotion and have substituted more intentional or cognitivist understandings. These newer conceptions emphasize that intentional judgments as well as physiological disturbances are integral elements in emotion.[7] They define or identify emotions not by the quality or character of the physiological sensation that may be associated with them but rather by their intentional aspect, the associated judgment. Thus, it is the content of my associated thought or judgment that determines whether my physical agitation and restlessness are defined as "anxiety about my daughter's lateness" rather than as "anticipation of tonight's performance."

Cognitivist accounts of emotion have ben criticized as overly rationalist and inapplicable to allegedly spontaneous, automatic, or global emotions, such as general feelings of nervousness, contentedness, angst, ecstasy, or terror. Certainly, these accounts entail that infants and animals experience emotions, if at all, in only a primitive, rudimentary form. Far from being unacceptable, however, this entailment is desirable because it suggests that humans develop and mature in emotions as well as in other dimensions, increasing the range, variety and subtlety of their emotional responses in accordance with their life experiences and their reflections on these.

Cognitivist accounts of emotion are not without their own problems. A serious difficulty with many is that they end up replicating within the structure of emotion the very problem they are trying to solve—namely, that of an artificial split between emotion and thought—because most cognitivist accounts explain emotion as having two "components": an affective or feeling component and a cognition that supposedly interprets or identifies the feelings. Such accounts, therefore, unwittingly perpetuate the positivist distinction between the shared, public, objective world of verifiable calculations, observations, and facts, and the individual, private, subjective world of idiosyncratic feelings and sensations. This sharp distinction breaks any conceptual links between our feelings and the "external" world: if feelings still are conceived as blind or raw or undifferentiated, then we can give no sense to the notion of feelings fitting or failing to fit our perceptual judgments, that is, being appropriate or inappropriate. When intentionality is viewed as intellectual cognition and moved to the center of our picture of emotion, the affective elements are pushed to the periphery and become shadowy conceptual danglers whose relevance to emotion is obscure or even negligible. An adequate cognitive account of emotion must overcome this problem.

Most cognitivist accounts of emotion thus remain problematic insofar as they fail to explain the relation between the cognitive and the affective aspects of emotion. Moreover, insofar as they prioritize the intellectual aspect over feelings, they reinforce the traditional western preference for mind over body.[8] Nevertheless, they do identify a vital feature of emotion overlooked by the Dumb View—namely, its intentionality.

Emotions as social constructs

We tend to experience our emotions as involuntary individual responses to situations, responses that are often (though, significantly, not always) private in the sense that they are not perceived as directly and immediately by other people as they are by the subject of the experience. The apparently individual and involuntary character of our emotional experience often is taken as evidence that emotions are presocial, instinctive responses, determined by our biological constitution. This inference, however, is quite mistaken. Although it is probably true that the physiological disturbances characterizing emotions (facial grimaces, changes in the metabolic rate, sweating, trembling, tears and so on) are continuous with the instinctive responses of our prehuman ancestors, and also that the ontogeny of emotions to some extent recapitulates their phylogeny, mature human emotions are neither instinctive nor biologically determined. Instead, they are socially constructed on several levels.

The most obvious way in which emotions are socially constructed is that children are taught deliberately what their culture defines as appropriate responses to certain situations: to fear strangers, to enjoy spicy food, or to like swimming in cold water. On a less conscious level, children also learn what their culture defines as the appropriate ways to express the emotions that it recognizes. Although there may be cross-cultural similarities in the expression of some apparently universal emotions, there are also wide divergences in what are recognized as expressions of grief, respect, contempt, or anger. On an even deeper level, cultures construct divergent understandings of what emotions are. For instance, English metaphors and metonymies are said to reveal a "folk" theory of anger as a hot fluid contained in a private space within an individual and liable to dangerous public explosion (Lakoff and Kovecses 1987). By contrast, the Ilongot, a people of the Philippines, apparently do not understand the self in terms of a public/private distinction and consequently do not experience anger as an explosive internal force: for them, rather, it is an interpersonal phenomenon for which an individual may, for instance, be paid (Rosaldo 1984).

Further aspects of the social construction of emotion are revealed through reflection on emotion's intentional structure. If emotions necessarily involve judgments, then obviously they require concepts, which may be seen as socially constructed ways of organizing and making sense of the world. For this reason, emotions simultaneously are made possible and limited by the conceptual and linguistic re-sources of a society. This philosophical claim is borne out by empirical observation of the cultural variability of emotion. Although there is considerable overlap in the emotions identified by many cultures (Wierzbicka 1986), at least some emotions are historically or culturally specific, including perhaps *ennui*, *angst*, the Japanese *amai* (in which one clings to another, affiliative love) and the response of "being a wild pig," which occurs among the Gururumba, a horticultural people living in the New Guinea Highlands (Averell 1980:158). Even apparently uni-versal emotions, such as anger or love, may vary crossculturally. We have just seen that the Ilongot experience of anger apparently is quite different from the contemporary western experience. Romantic love was invented in the Middle Ages in Europe and since that time has been modified considerably; for instance, it is no longer confined to the nobility, and it no longer needs to be extramarital or unconsummated. In some cultures, romantic love does not exist at all.[9]

Thus there are complex linguistic and other social preconditions for the experience, that is, for the existence of human emotions. The emotions that we experience reflect prevailing forms of social life. For instance, one could not feel or even be betrayed in the absence of social norms about fidelity: it is inconceivable that betrayal or indeed any distinctively human emotion could be experienced by a solitary individual in some hypothetical presocial state of nature. There is a sense in which any individual's guilt or anger, joy or triumph, presupposes the existence of a social group capable of feeling guilt, anger, joy, or triumph. This is not to say that group emotions historically precede or are logically prior to the emotions of individuals; it is to say that individual experience is simultaneously social experience.[10] In later sections, I shall explore the epistemological and political implications of this social rather than individual understanding of emotion.

Emotions as active engagements

We often interpret our emotions as experiences that overwhelm us rather than as responses we consciously choose: that emotions are to some extent involuntary is part of the ordinary meaning of the term "emotion." Even in daily life, however, we recognize that emotions are not entirely involuntary and we try to gain control over them in various ways, ranging from mechanistic behavior modification techniques designed to sensitize or desensitize our feeling responses to various situations to cognitive techniques designed to help us think differently about situations. For instance, we might try to change our response to an upsetting situation by thinking about it in a way that will either divert our attention from its more painful aspects or present it as necessary for some larger good.

Some psychological theories interpret emotions as chosen on an even deeper level, interpreting them as actions for which the agent disclaims responsibility. For instance, the psychologist Averell likens the experience of emotion to playing a culturally recognized role: we ordinarily perform so smoothly and automatically that we do not realize we are giving a performance. He provides many examples demonstrating that even extreme and apparently totally involving displays of emotion in fact are functional for the individual and/or the society.[11] For example, when students were asked to record their experiences of anger or annoyance over a two-week period, they came to realize that their anger was not as uncontrollable and irrational as they had assumed previously, and they noted the usefulness and effectiveness of anger in achieving various social goods. Averell, notes, however, that emotions often are useful in attaining their goals only if they are interpreted as passions rather than as actions. He cites the case of one subject led to reflect on her anger, who later wrote that it was less useful as a defense mechanism when she became conscious of its function.

The action/passion dichotomy is too simple for understanding emotion, as it is for other aspects of our lives. Perhaps it is more helpful to think of emotions as habitual responses that we may have more or less difficulty in breaking. We claim or disclaim responsibility for these responses depending on our purposes in a particular context. We could never experience our emotions entirely as deliberate actions, for then they would appear nongenuine and inauthentic, but neither should emotions be seen as nonintentional, primal, or physical forces with which our rational selves are forever at war. As they have been socially constructed, so may they be reconstructed, although describing how this might happen would require a long and complicated story.

Emotions, then, are wrongly seen as necessarily passive or involuntary responses to the world. Rather, they are ways in which we engage actively and even construct the world. They have both "mental" and "physical" aspects, each of which conditions the other; in some respects, they are chosen, but in others they are involuntary; they presuppose language and a social order. Thus, they can be attributed only to what are sometimes called "whole persons," engaged in the ongoing activity of social life.

Emotion, evaluation and observation

Emotions and values are closely related. The relation is so close, indeed, that some philosophical accounts of what it is to hold or express certain values reduce these phenomena to nothing more than holding or expressing certain emotional attitudes. When the relevant conception of emotion is the Dumb View, then simple emotivism certainly is too crude an account of what it is to hold a value; on this account, the intentionality of value judgments vanishes and value judgments become nothing more than sophisticated grunts and groans. Nevertheless, the grain of important truth in emotivism is its recognition that values presuppose emotions to the extent that emotions provide the experiential basis for values. If we had no emotional responses to the world, it is inconceivable that we should ever come to value one state of affairs more highly than another.

Just as values presuppose emotions, so emotions presuppose values. The object of an emotion—that is, the object of fear, grief, pride, and so on—is a complex state of affairs that is appraised or evaluated by the individual. For instance, my pride in a friend's achievement necessarily incorporates the value judgment that my friend has done something worthy of admiration.

Emotions and evaluations, then, are logically or conceptually connected. Indeed, many evaluative terms derive directly from words for emotions: "desirable," "admirable," "contemptible," "despicable," "respectable," and so on. Certainly it is true (pace J. S. Mill) that the evaluation of a situation as desirable or dangerous does not entail it is universally desired or feared but it does entail that desire (or fear) is viewed generally as an appropriate response to the situation. If someone is unafraid in a situation generally perceived as dangerous, her lack of fear requires further explanation; conversely, if someone is afraid without evident danger, than her fear is denounced as irrational or pathological. Thus, every emotion presupposes an evaluation of some aspect of the environment while, conversely, every evaluation or appraisal of the situation implies that those who share that evaluation will share, *ceteris paribus*, a predictable emotional response to the situation.

The rejection of the Dumb View and the recognition of intentional elements in emotion already incorporate a realization that observation influences and indeed partially constitutes emotion. We have seen already that distinctively human emotions are not simple instinctive responses to situations or events; instead, they depend essentially on the ways that we perceive those situations and events, as well on the ways that we have learned or decided to respond to them. Without characteristically human perceptions of and engagements in the world, there would be no characteristically human emotions.

Just as observation directs, shapes, and partially defines emotion, so too emotion directs, shapes, and even partially defines observation. Observation is not simply a passive process of absorbing impressions or recording stimuli; instead, it is an activity of selection and interpretation. What is selected and how it is interpreted are influenced by emotional attitudes. On the level of individual observation, this influence always has been apparent to common sense, which notes that we remark very different features of the world when we are happy, depressed, fearful, or confident. Social scientists are now exploring this influence of emotion on perception. One example is the so-called Honi phenomenon, named after the subject Honi who, under identical experimental conditions, perceived strangers' heads as changing in size but saw her husband's head as remaining the same.[12]

The most obvious significance of this sort of example is to illustrate how the individual experience of emotion focuses our attention selectively, directing, shaping and even partially defining our observations, just as our observations direct, shape and partially define our emotions. In addition, the example argues for the social construction of what are taken in any situation to be undisputed facts. It shows how these facts rest on intersubjective agreements that consist partly in shared assumptions about "normal" or appropriate emotional responses to situations (McLaughlin 1985). Thus these examples suggest that certain emotional attitudes are involved on a deep level in all observation, in the intersubjectively verified and so supposedly dispassionate observations of science as well as in the common perceptions of daily life. In the next section, I shall elaborate this claim.

EPISTEMOLOGY

The myth of dispassionate investigation

As we have seen already, western epistemology has tended to view emotion with suspicion and even hostility.[13] This derogatory western attitude towards emotion, like the earlier western contempt for sensory observation, fails to recognize that emotion, like sensory perception, is necessary to human survival. Emotions prompt us to act appropriately, to approach some people and situations and to avoid others, to caress or cuddle, fight or flee. Without emotion, human life would be unthinkable. Moreover, emotions have an intrinsic as well as an instrumental value. Although not all emotions are enjoyable or even justifiable, as we shall see, life without any emotion would be life without any meaning.

Within the context of western culture, however, people often have been encouraged to control or even suppress their emotions. Consequently, it is not unusual for people to be unaware of their emotional state or to deny it to themselves and others. This lack of awareness, especially combined with a neopositivist understanding of emotion that construes it just as a feeling of which one is aware, lends plausibility to the myth of dispassionate investigation. But lack of awareness of emotions certainly does not mean that emotions are not present subconsciously or unconsciously, or that subterranean emotions do not exert a continuing influence on people's articulated values and observations, thoughts and actions.[14]

Within the positivist tradition, the influence of emotion usually is seen only as distorting or impeding observation or knowledge. Certainly it is true that contempt, disgust, shame, revulsion, or fear may inhibit investigation of certain situations or phenomena. Furiously angry or extremely sad people often seem quite unaware of their surroundings or even their own conditions; they may fail to hear or may systematically misinterpret what other people say. People in love are notoriously oblivious to many aspects of the situation around them.

In spite of these examples, however, positivist epistemology recognizes that the role of emotion in the construction of knowledge is not invariably deleterious and that emotions may make a valuable contribution to knowledge. But the positivist tradition will allow emotion to play only the role of suggesting hypotheses for emotion. Emotions are allowed this because the so-called logic of discovery sets no limits on the idiosyncratic methods that investigators may use for generating hypotheses.

When hypotheses are to be tested, however, positivist epistemology imposes the much stricter logic of justification. The core of this logic is replicability, a criterion believed capable of eliminating or cancelling out what are conceptualized as emotional as well as evaluative biases on the part of individual investigators. The conclusions of western science thus are presumed "objective," precisely in the sense that they are uncontaminated by the supposedly "subjective" values and emotions that might bias individual investigators (Nagel 1968: 33–4).

But if, as has been argued, the positivist distinction between discovery and justification is not viable, then such a distinction is incapable of filtering out values in science. For example, although such a split, when built into the western scientific method, generally is successful in neutralizing the idiosyncratic or unconventional values of individual investigators, it has been argued that it does not, indeed cannot, eliminate generally accepted social values. These values are implicit in the identification of the problems that are considered worthy of investigation, in the selection of the hypotheses that are considered worthy of testing, and in the solutions to the problems that are considered worthy of acceptance. The science of past centuries provides ample evidence of the influence of prevailing social values, whether seventeenth century atomistic physics (Merchant 1980) or nineteenth century competitive interpretations of natural selection (Young 1985).

Of course, only hindsight allows us to identify clearly the values that shaped the science of the past and thus to reveal the formative influence on science of pervasive emotional attitudes, attitudes that typically went unremarked at the time because they were shared so generally. For instance, it is now glaringly evident that contempt for (and perhaps fear of) people of color is implicit in nineteenth century anthropology's interpretations and even constructions of anthropological facts. Because we are closer to them, however, it is harder for us to see how certain emotions, such as sexual possessiveness or the need to dominate others, currently are accepted as guiding principles in twentieth century sociobiology or even defined as part of reason within political theory and economics (Quinby 1986).

Values and emotions enter into the science of the past and the present not only on the level of scientific practice but also on the metascientific level, as answers to various questions: What is science? How should it be practiced? And what is the status of scientific investigation versus nonscientific modes of enquiry? For instance, it is claimed with increasing frequency that the modern western conception of science, which identifies knowledge with power and views it as a weapon for dominating nature, reflects the imperialism, racism and misogyny of the societies that created it. Several feminist theorists have argued that modern epistemology itself may be viewed as an expression of certain emotions alleged to be especially characteristic of males in certain periods, such as separation anxiety and paranoia (Flax 1983; Bordo 1987) or an obsession with control and fear of contamination (Scheman 1985; Schott 1988).

Positivism views values and emotions as alien invaders that must be repelled by a stricter application of the scientific method. If the forgoing claims are correct, however, the scientific method and even its positivist construals themselves incorporate values and emotions. Moreover, such an incorporation seems a necessary feature of all knowledge and conceptions of knowledge. Therefore, rather than repressing emotion in epistemology it is necessary to rethink the relation between knowledge and emotion and construct a conceptual model that demonstrates the mutually constitutive rather than opposi-tional relation between reason and emotion. Far from precluding the possibility of reliable knowledge, emotion as well as value must be shown as necessary to such knowledge. Despite its classical antecedents and like the ideal of disinterested enquiry, the ideal of dispassionate enquiry is an impossible dream, but a dream nonetheless, or perhaps a myth that has exerted enormous influence on western epistemology. Like all myths, it is a form of ideology that fulfills certain social and political functions.

The ideological function of the myth

So far, I have spoken very generally of people and their emotions, as though everyone experienced similar emotions and dealt with them in similar ways. It is an axiom of feminist theory, however, that all generalizations about "people" are suspect. The divisions in our society are so deep, particularly the divisions of race, class, and gender, that many feminist theorists would claim that talk about people in general is ideologically dangerous because such talk obscures the fact that no one is simply a person but instead is constituted fundamentally by race, class and gender. Race, class, and gender shape every aspect of our lives, and our emotional constitution is not excluded. Recognizing this helps us to see more clearly the political functions of the myth of the dispassionate investigator.

Feminist theorists have pointed out that the western tradition has not seen everyone as equally emotional. Instead, reason has been associated with members of dominant political, social, and cultural groups and emotion with members of subordinate groups. Prominent among those subordinate groups in our society are people of color, except for supposedly "inscrutable orientals," and women.[15]

Although the emotionality of women is a familiar cultural stereotype, its grounding is quite shaky. Women appear to be more emotional than men because they, along with some groups of people of color, are permitted and even required to express emotion more openly. In contemporary western culture, emotionally inexpressive women are suspect as not being real women,[16] whereas men who express their emotions freely are suspected of being homosexual or in some other way deviant from the masculine ideal. Modern western men, in contrast with Shakespeare's heroes, for instance, are required to present a facade of coolness, lack of excitement, even boredom, to express emotion only rarely and then for relatively trivial events, such as sporting occasions, where the emotions expressed are acknowledged to be dramatized and so are not taken entirely seriously. Thus, women in our society form the main group allowed or even expected to feel emotion. A woman may cry in the face of disaster, and a man of color may gesticulate, but a white man merely sets his jaw.[17]

White men's control of their emotional expression may go to the extremes of repressing their emotions, failing to develop emotionally, or even losing the capacity to experience many emotions. Not uncommonly, these men are unable to identify what they are feeling, and even they may be surprised, on occasion, by their own apparent lack of emotional response to a situation, such as a death, where emotional reaction is perceived appropriate. In some married couples, the wife implicitly is assigned the job of feeling emotion for both of them. White, college-educated men increasingly enter therapy in order to learn how to "get in touch with" their emotions, a project other men may ridicule as weakness. In therapeutic situations, men may learn that they are just as emotional as women but less adept at identifying their own or others' emotions. In consequence, their emotional development may be relatively rudimentary; this may lead to moral rigidity or insensitivity. Paradoxically, men's lacking awareness of their own emotional responses frequently results in their being more influenced by emotion rather than less.

Although there is no reason to suppose that the thoughts and actions of women are any more influenced by emotion than the thoughts and actions of men, the stereotypes of cool men and emotional women continue to flourish because they are confirmed by an uncritical daily experience. In these circumstances, where there is a differential assignment of reason and emotion, it is easy to see the ideological function of the myth of the dispassionate investigator. It functions, obviously, to bolster the epistemic authority of the currently dominant groups, composed largely of white men, and to discredit the observations and claims of the currently subordinate groups including, of course, the observations and claims of many people of color and women. The more forcefully and vehemently the latter groups express their observations and claims, the more emotional they appear and so the more easily they are discredited. The alleged epistemic authority of the dominant groups then justifies their political authority.

The previous section of this paper argued that dispassionate inquiry was a myth. This section has shown that the myth promotes a conception of epistemological justification vindicating the silencing of those, especially women, who are defined culturally as the bearers of emotion and so are perceived as more "subjective," biased, and irrational. In our present social context, therefore, the ideal of the dispassionate investigator is a classist, racist, and especially masculinist myth.[18]

Emotional hegemony and emotional subversion

As we have seen already, mature human emotions are neither instinctive nor biologically determined, although they may have developed out of presocial, instinctive responses. Like everything else that is human, emotions in part are socially constructed; like all social constructs, they are historical products, bearing the marks of the society that constructed them. Within the very language of emotion, in our basic definitions and explanations of what it is to feel pride or embarrassment, resentment or contempt, cultural norms and expectations are embedded. Simply describing ourselves as angry, for instance, presupposes that we view ourselves as having been wronged, victimized by the violation of some social norm. Thus, we absorb the standards and values of our society in the very process of learning the language of emotion, and those standards and values are built into the foundation of our emotional constitution.

Within a hierarchical society, the norms and values that predominate tend to serve the interest of the dominant groups. Within a capitalist, white supremacist, and male-dominant society, the predominant values will tend to be those that serve the interests of rich white men. Consequently, we are all likely to develop an emotional constitution that is quite inappropriate for feminism. Whatever our color, we are likely to feel what Irving Thalberg has called "visceral racism"; whatever our sexual orientation, we are likely to be homophobic; whatever our class, we are likely to be at least somewhat ambitious and competitive; whatever our sex, we are likely to feel contempt for women. The emotional responses may be rooted in us so deeply that they are relatively impervious to intellectual argument and may recur even when we pay lip service to changed intellectual convictions.[19]

By forming our emotional constitution in particular ways, our society helps to ensure its own perpetuation. The dominant values are implicit in responses taken to be precultural or acultural, our so-called gut responses. Not only do these conservative responses hamper and disrupt our attempts to live in or prefigure alternative social forms but also, and insofar as we take them to be natural responses, they limit our vision theoretically. For instance, they limit our capacity for outrage; they either prevent us from despising or encourage us to despise; they lend plausibility to the belief that greed and domination are inevitable human motivations; in sum, they blind us to the possibility of alternative ways of living.

This picture may seem at first to support the positivist claim that the intrusion of emotion only disrupts the process of seeking knowledge and distorts the results of that process. The picture, however, is not complete; it ignores the fact that people do not always experience the conventionally acceptable emotions. They may feel satisfaction rather than embarrassment when their leaders make fools of themselves. They may feel resentment rather than gratitude for welfare payments and hand-me-downs. They may be attracted to forbidden modes of sexual expression. They may feel revulsion for socially sanctioned ways of treating children or animals. In other words, the hegemony that our society exercises over people's emotional constitution is not total.

People who experience conventionally unacceptable, or what I call "outlaw," emotions often are subordinated individuals who pay a disproportionately high price for maintaining the status quo. The social situation of such people makes them unable to experience the conventionally prescribed emotions: for instance, people of color are more likely to experience anger than amusement when a racist joke is recounted, and women subjected to male sexual banter are less likely to be flattered than uncomfortable or even afraid.

When unconventional emotional responses are experienced by isolated individuals, those concerned may be confused, unable to name their experience; they may even doubt their own sanity. Women may come to believe that they are "emotionally disturbed" and that the embarrassment or fear aroused in them by male sexual innuendo is prudery or paranoia. When certain emotions are shared or validated by others, however, the basis exists for forming a subculture defined by perceptions, norms, and values that systematically oppose the prevailing perceptions, norms, and values. By constituting the basis for such a subculture, outlaw emotions may be politically (because epistemologically) subversive.

Outlaw emotions are distinguished by their incompatibility with the dominant perceptions and values, and some, though certainly not all, of these outlaw emotions are potentially or actually feminist emotions. Emotions become feminist when they incorporate feminist perceptions and values, just as emotions are sexist or racist when they incorporate sexist or racist perceptions and values. For example, anger becomes feminist anger when it involves the perception that the persistent importuning endured by one woman is a single instance of a widespread pattern of sexual harassment, and pride becomes feminist pride when it is evoked by realizing that a certain person's achievement was possible only because that individual overcame specifically gendered obstacles to success.[20]

Outlaw emotions stand in a dialectical relation to critical social theory: at least some are necessary to developing a critical perspective on the world, but they also presuppose at least the beginnings of such a perspective. Feminists need to be aware of how we can draw on some of our outlaw emotions in constructing feminist theory and also of how the increasing sophistication of feminist theory can contribute to the reeducation, refinement, and eventual reconstruction of our emotional constitution.

Outlaw emotions and feminist theory

The most obvious way in which feminist and other outlaw emotions can help in developing alternatives to prevailing conceptions of reality is by motivating new investigations. This is possible because, as we saw earlier, emotions may be long-term as well as momentary; it makes sense to say that someone continues to be shocked or saddened by a situation, even if she is at the moment laughing heartily. As we have seen already, theoretical investigation is always purposeful, and observation is always selective. Feminist emotions provide a political motivation for investigation and so help to determine the selection of problems as well as the method by which they are investigated. Susan Griffin makes the same point when she characterizes feminist theory as following "a direction determined by pain, and trauma, and compassion and outrage" (Griffin 1979:31).

As well as motivating critical research, outlaw emotions may also enable us to perceive the world differently than we would from its portrayal in conventional descriptions. They may provide the first indications that something is wrong with the way alleged facts have been constructed, with accepted understandings of how things are. Conventionally unexpected or inappropriate emotions may precede our conscious recognition that accepted descriptions and justifications often conceal as much as reveal the prevailing state of affairs. Only when we reflect on our initially puzzling irritability, revulsion, anger, or fear, may we bring to consciousness our "gut-level" awareness that we are in a situation of coercion, cruelty, injustice, or danger. Thus, conventionally inexplicable emotions, particularly, though not exclusively, those experienced by women, may lead us to make subversive observations that challenge dominant conceptions of the status quo. They may help us to realize that what are taken generally to be facts have been constructed in a way that obscures the reality of subordinated people, especially women's reality.

But why should we trust the emotional responses of women and other subordinated groups? How can we determine which outlaw emotions we should endorse or encourage and which reject? In what sense can we say that some emotional responses are more appropriate than others? What reason is there for supposing that certain alternative perceptions of the world, perceptions informed by outlaw emotions, are to be preferred to perceptions informed by conventional emotions? Here I can indicate only the general direction of an answer, whose full elaboration must await another occasion.[21]

I suggest that emotions are appropriate if they are characteristic of a society in which all humans (and perhaps some nonhuman life too) thrive, or if they are conducive to establishing such a society. For instance, it is appropriate to feel joy when we are developing or exercising our creative powers, and it is appropriate to feel anger and perhaps disgust in those situations where humans are denied their full creativity or freedom. Similarly, it is appropriate to feel fear if those capacities are threatened in us.

This suggestion obviously is extremely vague and may even verge on the tautological. How can we apply it in situations where there is disagreement over what is or is not disgusting or exhilarating or unjust? Here I appeal to a claim for which I have argued elsewhere: the perspective on reality that is available from the standpoint of the oppressed, which in part at least is the standpoint of women, is a perspective that offers a less partial and distorted and therefore more reliable view (Jaggar 1983: chap. 11). Oppressed people have a kind of epistemological privilege insofar as they have easier access to this standpoint and therefore a better chance of ascertaining the possible beginnings of a society in which all could thrive. For this reason, I would claim that the emotional responses of oppressed people in general, and often of women in particular, are more likely to be appropriate than the emotional responses of the dominant class. That is, they are more likely to incorporate reliable appraisals of situations.

Even in contemporary science, where the ideology of dispassionate inquiry is almost overwhelming, it is possible to discover a few examples that seem to support the claim that certain emotions are more appropriate than others in both a moral and epistemological sense. For instance, Hilary Rose claims that women's practice of caring, even though warped by its containment in the alienated context of a coercive sexual division of labor, nevertheless has generated more accurate and less oppressive understandings of women's bodily functions, such as menstruation (Rose 1983). Certain emotions may be both morally appropriate and epistemologically advantageous in approaching the nonhuman and even the inanimate world. Jane Goodall's scientific contribution to our understanding of chimpanzee behavior seems to have been made possible only by her amazing empathy with or even love for these animals (Goodall 1987). In her study of Barbara

McClintock, Evelyn Fox Keller describes McClintock's relation to the objects of her research—grains of maize and their genetic properties—as a relation of affection, empathy and "the highest form of love: love that allows for intimacy without the annihilation of difference." She notes that McClintock's "vocabulary is consistently a vocabulary of affection, of kinship, of empathy" (Keller 1984:164). Examples like these prompt Hilary Rose to assert that a feminist science of nature needs to draw on heart as well as hand and brain.

Some implications of recognizing the epistemic potential of emotion

Accepting that appropriate emotions are indispensable to reliable knowledge does not mean, of course, that uncritical feeling may be substituted for supposedly dispassionate investigation. Nor does it mean that the emotional responses of women and other members of the underclass are to be trusted without question. Although our emotions are epistemologically indispensable, they are not epistemologically indisputable. Like all our faculties, they may be misleading, and their data, like all data, are always subject to reinterpretation and revision. Because emotions are not presocial, physiological responses to unequivocal situations, they are open to challenge on various grounds. They may be dishonest or self-deceptive, they may incorporate inaccurate or partial perceptions, or they may be constituted by oppressive values. Accepting the indispensability of appropriate emotions to knowledge means no more (and no less) than that discordant emotions should be attended to seriously and respectfully rather than condemned, ignored, discounted, or suppressed.

Just as appropriate emotions may contribute to the development of knowledge so the growth of knowledge may contribute to the development of appropriate emotions. For instance, the powerful insights of feminist theory often stimulate new emotional responses to past and present situations. Inevitably, our emotions are affected by the knowledge that the women on our faculty are paid systematically less than the men, that one girl in four is subjected to sexual abuse from heterosexual men in her own family, and that few women reach orgasm in heterosexual intercourse. We are likely to feel different emotions towards older women or people of color as we reevaluate our standards of sexual attractiveness or acknowledge that Black is beautiful. The new emotions evoked by feminist insights are likely in turn to stimulate further feminist observations and insights, and these may generate new directions in both theory and political practice. There is a continuous feedback loop between our emotional constitution and our theorizing such that each continually modifies the other and is in principle inseparable from it.

The ease and speed with which we can reeducate our emotions unfortunately is not great. Emotions are only partially within our control as individuals. Although affected by new information, they are habitual responses not quickly unlearned. Even when we come to believe consciously that our fear or shame or revulsion is unwarranted, we may still continue to experience emotions inconsistent with our conscious politics. We may still continue to be anxious for male approval, competitive with our comrades and sisters and possessive with our lovers. These unwelcome, because apparently inappropriate, emotions should not be suppressed or denied; instead, they should be acknowledged and subjected to critical scrutiny. The persistence of such recalcitrant emotions probably demonstrates how fundamentally we have been constituted by the dominant world view, but it may also indicate superficiality or other inadequacy in our emerging theory and politics.[22] We can only start from where we are—beings who have been created in a cruelly racist, capitalist, and male-dominated society that has shaped our bodies and our minds, our perceptions, our values and our emotions, our language and our systems of knowledge.

The alternative epistemological model that I suggest displays the continuous interaction between how we understand the world and who we are as people. It shows how our emotional responses to the world change as we conceptualize it differently and how our changing emotional responses then stimulate us to new insights. The model demonstrates the need for theory to be self-reflexive, to focus not only on the outer world but also on ourselves and our relation to that world, to examine critically our social location, our actions, our values, our perceptions and our emotions. The model also shows how feminist and other critical social theories are indispensable psychotherapeutic tools because they provide some insights necessary to a full understanding of our emotional constitution. Thus, the model explains how the reconstruction of knowledge is inseparable from the reconstruction of ourselves.

A corollary of the reflexivity of feminist and other critical theory is that it requires a much broader construal than positivism accepts of the process of theoretical investigation. In particular, it requires acknowledging that a necessary part of theoretical process is critical self-examination. Time spent in analyzing emotions and uncovering their sources should be viewed, therefore, neither as irrelevant to theoretical investigation nor even as a prerequisite for it; it is not a kind of clearing of the emotional decks, "dealing with" our emotions so that they will not influence our thinking. Instead, we must recognize that our efforts to reinterpret and refine our emotions are necessary to our theoretical investigation, just as our efforts to reeducate our emotions are necessary to our political activity. Critical reflection on emotion is not a self-indulgent substitute for political analysis and political action. It is itself a kind of political theory and political practice, indispensable for an adequate social theory and social transformation.

Finally, the recognition that emotions play a vital part in developing knowledge enlarges our understanding of women's claimed epistimic advantage. We can now see that women's subversive insights owe much to women's outlaw emotions, themselves appropriate responses to the situations of women's subordination. In addition to their propensity to experience outlaw emotions, at least on some level, women are relatively adept at identifying such emotions, in themselves and others, in part because of their social responsibility for caretaking, including emotional nurturance. It is true that women (like all subordinated peoples, especially those who must live in close proximity with their masters) often engage in emotional deception and even self-deception as the price of their survival. Even so, women may be less likely than other subordinated groups to engage in denial or suppression of outlaw emotions. Women's work of emotional nurturance has required them to develop a special acuity in recognizing hidden emotions and in understanding the genesis of those emotions. This emotional acumen can now be recognized as a skill in political analysts and validated as giving women a special advantage both in understanding the mechanisms of domination and in envisioning freer ways to live.

CONCLUSION

The claim that emotion is vital to systematic knowledge is only the most obvious contrast between the conception of theoretical investigation that I have sketched here and the conception provided by positivism. For instance, the alternative approach emphasizes that what we identify as emotion is a conceptual abstraction from a complex process of human activity that also involves acting, sensing, and evaluating. This proposed account of theoretical construction demonstrates the simultaneous necessity for and interdependence of faculties that our culture has abstracted and separated from each other: emotion and reason, evaluation and perception, observation and action. The model of knowing suggested here is nonhierarchical and antifoundationalist; instead, it is appropriately symbolized by the radical feminist metaphor of the upward spiral. Emotions are neither more basic than observation, reason, or action in building theory, nor secondary to them. Each of these human faculties reflects an aspect of human knowing inseparable from the other aspects. Thus, to borrow a famous phrase from a Marxian context, the development of each of these faculties is a necessary condition for the development of all.

In conclusion, it is interesting to note that acknowledging the importance of emotion for knowledge is not an entirely novel suggestion within the western epistemological tradition. The archrationalist, Plato himself, came to accept in the end that knowledge required a (very purified form of) love. It may be no accident that in the *Symposium* Socrates learns this lesson from Diotima, the wise woman!

NOTES

I wish to thank the following individuals who commented helpfully on earlier drafts of this paper or made me aware of further resources: Lynne Arnault, Susan Bordo, Martha Bolton, Cheshire Calhoun, Randy Cornelius, Shelagh Crooks, Ronald De Sousa, Tim Diamond, Dick Foley, Ann Garry, Judy Gerson, Mary Gibson, Sherry Gorelick, Marcia Lind, Helen Longino, Catherine Lutz, Andy McLaughlin, Uma Narayan, Linda Nicholson, Bob Richardson, Sally Ruddick, Laurie Shrage, Alan Soble, Vicky Spelman, Karsten Struhl, Joan Tronto, Daisy Quarm, Naomi Quinn and Alison Wylie. I am also grateful to my colleagues in the fall of 1985 Women's Studies Chair Seminar at Douglass College, Rutgers University, and to audiences at Duke University, Georgia University Centre, Hobart and William Smith Colleges, Northeastern University, the University of North Carolina at Chapel Hill and Princeton University, for their responses to earlier versions of this paper. In addition, I received many helpful comments from members of the Canadian Society for Women in Philosophy and from students in Lisa Heldke's classes in feminist epistemology at Carleton College and Northwestern University. Thanks, too, to Delia Cushway, who provided a comfortable environment in which I wrote the first draft.

1. Philosophers who do not conform to this generalization and constitute part of what Susan Bordo calls a "recessive" tradition in western philosophy include Hume and Nietzsche, Dewey and James (Bordo 1987:114–118).

2. The western tradition as a whole has been profoundly rationalist, and much of its history may be viewed as a continuous redrawing of the boundaries of the rational. For a survey of this history from a feminist perspective, see Lloyd 1984.

3. Thus, fear and other emotions were seen as rational in some circumstances. To illustrate this point, E. V. Spelman quotes Aristotle as saying (in the *Nicomachean Ethics*, Bk. IV, ch. 5): "[Anyone] who does not get angry when there is reason to be angry, or who does not get angry in the right way at the right time and with the right people, is a dolt" (Spelman 1982:1).

4. Descartes, Leibnitz, and Kant are among the prominent philosophers who did not endorse a wholly stripped-down, instrumentalist conception of reason.

5. The relocation of values in human attitudes and preferences in itself was not grounds for denying their universality, because they could have been

conceived as grounded in a common or universal human nature. In fact, however, the variability, rather than the commonality, of human preferences and responses was emphasized; values gradually came to be viewed as individual, particular, and even idiosyncratic rather than as universal and objective. The only exception to the variability of human desires was the supposedly universal urge to egoism and the motive to maximize one's own utility, whatever that consisted of. The value of autonomy and liberty, consequently, was seen as perhaps the only value capable of being justified objectively because it was a precondition for satisfying other desires.

6. For instance, Julius Moravcsik has characterized as emotions what I would call "plain" hunger and thirst, appetites that are not desires for any particular food or drink (Moravcsik 1982:207–224). I myself think that such states, which Moravcsik also calls instincts or appetites, are understood better as sensations than emotions. In other words, I would view so-called instinctive, nonintentional feelings as the biological raw material from which full-fledged human emotions develop.

7. Even adherents of the Dumb View recognize, of course, that emotions are not entirely random or unrelated to an individual's judgments and beliefs; in other words, they note that people are angry or excited *about* something, afraid or proud *of* something. On the Dumb View, however, the judgments or beliefs associated with an emotion are seen as its causes and thus as related to it only externally.

8. Cheshire Calhoun pointed this out to me in private correspondence.

9. Recognition of the many levels on which emotions are socially constructed raises the question whether it makes sense even to speak of the possibility of universal emotions. Although a full answer to this question is methodologically problematic, one might speculate that many of what we westerners identify as emotions have functional analogues in other cultures. In other words, it may be that people in every culture behave in ways that fulfill at least some social functions of our angry or fearful behavior.

10. The relationship between the emotional experience of an individual and the emotional experience of the group to which the individual belongs may perhaps be clarified by analogy to the relation between a word and the language of which it is a part. That a word has meaning presupposes that it is part of a linguistic system without which it has no meaning; yet the language itself has no meaning over and above the meaning of the words of which it is composed, together with their grammatical ordering. Words and language presuppose and mutually constitute each other. Similarly, both individual and group emotion presuppose and mutually constitute each other.

11. Averell cites dissociative reactions by military personnel at Wright Paterson Air Force Base and shows how these were effective in mustering help to deal with difficult situations while simultaneously relieving the individual of responsibility or blame (Averell 1980:157).

12. These and similar experiments are described in Kilpatrick 1961: ch. 10, cited by McLaughlin 1985:296.

13. The positivist attitude toward emotion, which requires that ideal investigators be both disinterested and dispassionate, may be a modern variant of older traditions in western philosophy that recommended that people seek to

minimize their emotional responses to the world and develop instead their powers of rationality and pure contemplation.

14. It is now widely accepted that the suppression and repression of emotion has damaging if not explosive consequences. There is general acknowledgement that no one can avoid at some time experiencing emotions she or he finds unpleasant, and there is also increasing recognition that the denial of such emotions is likely to result in hysterical disorders of thought and behavior, in projecting one's own emotions on to others, in displacing them to inappropriate situations, or in psychosomatic ailments. Psychotherapy, which purports to help individuals recognize and "deal with" their emotions, has become an enormous industry, especially in the U.S. In much conventional psychotherapy, however, emotions still are conceived as feelings or passions, "subjective" disturbances that afflict individuals or interfere with their capacity for rational thought and action. Different therapies, therefore, have developed a wide variety of techniques for encouraging people to "discharge" or "vent" their emotions, just as they would drain an abscess. Once emotions have been discharged or vented, they are supposed to be experienced less intensely, or even to vanish entirely, and consequently to exert less influence on individuals' thoughts and actions. This approach to psychotherapy clearly demonstrates its kinship with the "folk" theory of anger mentioned earlier, and it equally clearly retains the traditional western assumption that emotion is inimical to rational thought and action. Thus, such approaches fail to challenge and indeed provide covert support for the view that "objective" knowers are not only disinterested but also dispassionate.

15. E. V. Spelman (1982) illustrates this point with a quotation from the well known contemporary philosopher, R. S. Peters, who wrote "we speak of emotional outbursts, reactions, upheavals and women" (*Proceedings of the Aristotelian Society*, New Series, vol. 62).

16. It seems likely that the conspicuous absence of emotion shown by Mrs Thatcher is a deliberate strategy she finds necessary to counter the public perception of women as too emotional for political leadership. The strategy results in her being perceived as a formidable leader, but as an Iron Lady rather than a real woman. Ironically, Neil Kinnock, leader of the British Labor Party and Thatcher's main opponent in the 1987 General Election, was able to muster considerable public support through television commercials portraying him in the stereotypically feminine role of caring about the unfortunate victims of Thatcher economics. Ultimately, however, this support was not sufficient to destroy public confidence in Mrs Thatcher's "masculine" competence and gain Kinnock the election.

17. On the rare occasions when a white man cries, he is embarrassed and feels constrained to apologize. The one exception to the rule that men should be emotionless is that they are allowed and often even expected to experience anger. Spelman (1982) points out that men's cultural permission to be angry bolsters their claim to authority.

18. Someone might argue that the viciousness of this myth was not a logical necessity. In the egalitarian society, where the concepts of reason and emotion were not gender-bound in the way they still are today, it might be argued that the ideal of the dispassionate investigator could be epistemologically

beneficial. Is it possible that, in such socially and conceptually egalitarian circumstances, the myth of the dispassionate investigator could serve as a heuristic device, an ideal never to be realized in practice but nevertheless helping to minimize "subjectivity" and bias? My own view is that counterfactual myths rarely bring the benefits advertised and that this one is no exception. This myth fosters an equally mythical conception of pure truth and objectivity, quite independent of human interests or desires, and in this way it functions to disguise the inseparability of theory and practice, science and politics. Thus, it is part of an antidemocratic world view that mystifies the political dimension of knowledge and unwarrantedly circumscribes the arena of political debate.

19. Of course, the similarities in our emotional constitutions should not blind us to systematic differences. For instance, girls rather than boys are taught fear and disgust for spiders and snakes, affection for fluffy animals, and shame for their naked bodies. It is primarily, though not exclusively, men rather than women whose sexual responses are shaped by exposure to visual and sometimes violent pornography. Girls and women are taught to cultivate sympathy for others; boys and men are taught to separate themselves emotionally from others. As I have noted already, more emotional expression is permitted for lower-class and some nonwhite men than for ruling-class men, perhaps because the expression of emotion is thought to expose vulnerability. Men of the upper classes learn to cultivate an attitude of condescension, boredom, or detached amusement. As we shall see shortly, differences in the emotional constitution of various groups may be epistemologically significant in so far as they both presuppose and facilitate different ways of perceiving the world.

20. A necessary condition for experiencing feminist emotions is that one already be a feminist in some sense, even if one does not consciously wear that label. But many women and some men, even those who would deny that they are feminist, still experience emotions compatible with feminist values. For instance, they may be angered by the perception that someone is being mistreated just because she is a woman, or they may take special pride in the achievement of a woman. If those who experience such emotions are unwilling to recognize them as feminist, their emotions are probably better described as potentially feminist or prefeminist emotions.

21. I owe this suggestion to Marcia Lind.

22. Within a feminist context, Berenice Fisher suggests that we focus particular attention on our emotions of guilt and shame as part of a critical reevaluation of our political ideals and our political practice (Fisher 1984).

REFERENCES

Averell, James R. 1980. "The Emotions." In *Personality: Basic Aspects and Current Research*, ed. Ervin Staub. Englewood Cliffs, N.J.: Prentice Hall.

Bordo, Susan R. 1987. *The Flight to Objectivity: Essays on Cartesianism and Culture*. Albany, N.Y.: SUNY Press.

Fisher, Berenice. 1984. "Guilt and Shame in the Women's Movement: The

Radical Ideal of Action and its Meaning for Feminist Intellectuals." *Feminist Studies* 10:185–212.

Flax, Jane. 1983. "Political Philosophy and the Patriarchal Unconscious: A Psychoanalytic Perspective on Epistemology and Metaphysics." In *Discovering Reality: Feminist Perspectives on Epistemology, Metaphysics, Methodology and Philosophy of Science*, ed. Sandra Harding and Merrill Hintikka. Dordrecht, Holland: D. Reidel Publishing.

Goodall, Jane. 1986. *The Chimpanzees of Bombe: Patterns of Behavior*. Cambridge, Mass.: Harvard University Press.

Griffin, Susan. 1979. *Rape: The Power of Consciousness*. San Francisco: Harper & Row.

Hinman, Lawrence. 1986. "Emotion, Morality and Understanding." Paper presented at Annual Meeting of the Central Division of the American Philosophical Association, St. Louis, Missouri, May 1986.

Jaggar, Alison M. 1983. *Feminist Politics and Human Nature*. Totowa, N.J.: Rowman and Allanheld; Brighton, UK: Harvester Press.

Keller, Evelyn Fox. 1984. *Gender and Science*. New Haven, Conn.: Yale University Press.

Kilpatrick, Franklin P., ed. 1961. *Explorations in Transactional Psychology*. New York: New York University Press.

Lakoff, George and Zoltan Kovecses. 1987. "The Cognitive Model of Anger Inherent in American English." In *Cultural Models in Language and Thought*, ed. N. Quinn and D. Holland. New York: Cambridge University Press.

Lewontin, R. C. 1982. "Letter to the Editor." *New York Review of Books*, 4 (February): 40–1. This letter was drawn to my attention by Alan Soble.

Lloyd, Genevieve. 1984. *The Man of Reason: 'Male' and 'Female' in Western Philosophy*. Minneapolis: University of Minnesota Press.

Lutz, Catherine. 1985. "Depression and the Translation of Emotional Worlds." In *Culture and Depression: Studies in the Anthropology and Cross-cultural Psychiatry of Affect and Disorder*, ed. A. Kleinman and B . Good. Berkeley, Calif: University of California Press, 63–100.

Lutz, Catherine. 1986. "Emotion, Thought, and Estrangement: Emotion as a Cultural Category." *Cultural Anthropology* 1:287–309.

Lutz, Catherine. 1987. "Goals, Events and Understanding in Ifaluck and Emotion Theory." In *Cultural Models in Language and Thought*, ed. N. Quinn and D. Holland. New York: Cambridge University Press.

McLaughlin, Andrew. 1985. "Images and Ethics of Nature." *Environmental Ethics* 7:293–319.

Merchant, Carolyn M. 1980. *The Death of Nature: Women, Ecology and the Scientific Revolution*. New York: Harper & Row.

Moravcsik, J. M. E. 1982. "Understanding and the Emotions." *Dialectica* 36, 2–3:207–224.

Nagel, Ernest. 1968. "The Subjective Nature of Social Subject Matter." In *Readings in the Philosophy of the Social Sciences*, ed. May Brodbeck. New York: Macmillan.

Quinby, Lee. 1986. Discussion following talk at Hobart and William Smith Colleges, April 1986.

Rorty, Richard. 1979. *Philosophy and the Mirror of Nature*. Princeton: Princeton University Press.

Rosaldo, Michelle Z. 1984. "Toward an Anthropology of Self and Feeling." In *Culture Theory*, ed. Richard A. Shweder and Robert A. LeVine. New York: Cambridge University Press.

Rose, Hilary. 1983. "Hand, Brain, and Heart: A Feminist Epistemology for the Natural Sciences." *Signs: Journal of Women in Culture and Society* 9, 1:73–90.

Schachter, Stanley and Jerome B. Singer. 1969. "Cognitive, Social and Psychological Determinants of Emotional State." *Psychological Review* 69: 379–399.

Scheman, Naomi. "Women in the Philosophy Curriculum." Paper presented at the Annual Meeting of the Central Division of the American Philosophical Association, Chicago, April, 1985.

Schott, Robin M. 1988. *Cognition and Eros: A Critique of the Kantian Paradigm*. Boston, Mass: Beacon Press.

Spelman, Elizabeth V. 1982. "Anger and Insubordination." Manuscript; early version read to mid-western chapter of the Society for Women in Philosophy, Spring 1982. (Later version appears as Chapter Sixteen of this volume.)

Wierzbicka, Anna. 1986. "Human Emotions: Universal or Culture-Specific?" *American Anthropologist* 88:584–594.

Young, Robert M. 1985. *Darwin's Metaphor: Nature's Place in Victorian Culture*. Cambridge: Cambridge University Press.

Chapter 9

Experience, Knowledge, and Responsibility

Lorraine Code

INTRODUCTION

*T*wo central, interconnected tasks that face feminist philosophers working in theory of knowledge are that of finding appropriate ways of knowing women's experiences and the structures that shape them; and that of developing theoretical accounts of knowledge that retain continuity with those experiences. To perform the first task adequately, it is necessary, among other things, to break out of stereotyped perceptions of woman's "nature" that work, persistently, to constrain the possibilities of knowing well. In this connection, I shall argue that ways of knowing can be judged "appropriate" partly on the basis of responsibility manifested by cognitive agents in making knowledge claims, and in acting upon assumptions that they know. Adequate performance of the second task requires a shift in perspective about the purpose of "the epistemological project." It involves moving away from theoretical positions that advocate a purity in knowledge that would leave experience behind in a search for an epistemic ideal of unrealizable clarity.

To perform these tasks successfully it will be useful, too, to eschew any idea that ethics and epistemology are separate and distinct areas of enquiry. This could provide scope both for the view that knowing well is good for its own sake—a moral *and* an epistemological point—and for a recognition of the extent to which the explanatory capacities of moral theories and of policies based upon them depend upon their having a basis in responsible knowledge of human experience. Hence, in the elaboration of feminist epistemological concerns that I shall present here, epistemic responsibility will figure as a central intellectual virtue,

Source: From *Feminist Perspectives in Philosophy,* ed. Morwenna Griffiths and Margaret Whitford (Bloomington, IN: Indiana University Press, 1988), 187–204. Copyright © 1988 by Morwenna Griffiths and Margaret Whitford. Reprinted by permission of the author, the editors, and the publisher.

with the potential to play a regulatory role in cognitive activity analogous to the role moral virtues can play in moral activity.

Certain preliminary points need to be made before proceeding to a more detailed discussion of these tasks. First, in naming the task of coming to know women's experiences as one of the two central tasks I shall discuss, I mean to indicate from the outset that the notion of women's experience (in the singular) is an artificial construct. While it may often be expedient, in the course of the discussion, to use the term in the singular, it should always be read with a sensitivity to the fact that there is no such singular entity. To assume that there could be would be to mask crucial differences between and among women, and hence to break that continuity with experiences that it is important to maintain.

Secondly, it needs to be made clear that the point of this exploration is neither to provide a female-experience-based nor a responsibility-based epistemology, designed to *supplant* traditional epistemological modes, though running parallel to them in structure and content. Nor is it simply to *add* an account of female experiences and of the workings of epistemic responsibility to "traditional" epistemological theories, leaving their presuppositions and structures otherwise intact. While it is by no means clear what theory of knowledge might look like when attention is directed towards maintaining continuity with experience(s) and clarifying the implications of epistemic responsibility, it seems to be highly probable that it must differ markedly, both in its aims and in its conclusions, from traditional epistemological enterprises. Some of these differences will become apparent in the discussion that follows; but my purpose is much more to offer an exploration, from a feminist perspective, of certain epistemological problems, and to give some indication of the directions one might take in trying to solve them, than it is to present a fully articulated feminist theory of knowledge.

These points reflect my conviction that, while feminist epistemological practice may indeed reject and/or seek to render problematic much of traditional "malestream" epistemology, it can most fruitfully do so by remaining in dialogue with that tradition. In genuine dialogue, as contrasted both with polite conversation and with adversarial confrontation, both of the participants are changed.[1] So the process I envisage does not involve simply turning away from the malestream tradition in order to celebrate "the feminine," however that might be understood. Rather, it involves engaging with that tradition, trying to see what can be learned from reading it "against the grain" so that different of its facets are highlighted, and its gaps and exclusions understood and elaborated.[2]

But engagement with the *philosophical* tradition alone will not enable feminists to perform these tasks successfully. Disciplinary boundaries constitute some of the most intractable exclusionary structures impeding possibilities of insight and illumination. It is becoming a well-established aspect of feminist practice to move back and forth across such boundaries with the aims both of demonstrating their artificiality, and of tapping sources of understanding that fall outside the scope of traditional disciplinary orthodoxy. Hence feminist epistemological practice engaged in from a philosophical perspective is continuous with the epistemological concerns of feminists working in such traditionally disparate areas as sociology, anthropology, history and political theory. Feminists have much to learn from each other.

With respect to the practical effects that such learning might have, it should be mentioned that in commenting upon the *artificiality* of a conception of women's experience (in the singular), and upon the artificiality of disciplinary boundaries, my point is not to equate goodness with "naturalness." Rather, it is to draw attention to a connection between artificiality and contingency. What has been labeled or created by human beings out of contingent circumstances can likewise be labeled and understood differently by them, or altered when its flaws are revealed. Suspending such artificial constructs may reveal other possibilities, perhaps more creative ones, just as reading traditional texts, theories and presuppositions against the grain may reveal other perspectives on seemingly entrenched ideas.

STEREOTYPES AND RESPONSIBILITY

Stereotyped perceptions of women's nature, and actions based upon them, count amongst the most intransigent of constructs that shape women's experiences and make it difficult for women to move "beyond domination."[3] Manifestations of such perceptions are perhaps best known as they come across in anthropological, psychological and sociological studies and the (often unquestioned) assumptions about gender differences in terms of which such studies are conducted. But it is clear from a closer perusal of some of these studies that their implications are as much ontological, in their structuring effects upon women's possibilities of being, and epistemological, in their constraints upon responsible knowing, as they are practical. Indeed, such studies often work as self-fulfilling prophecies, leading people to *be* much as stereotype-governed research takes them to be.[4] It is because of these consequences that a principal requirement of epistemically responsible knowing centers about the need to become aware of the extent to which stereotypes govern perception and shape alleged knowledge (both one's own, and those of other members of one's epistemic community). It is part of responsible epistemic practice to

work towards freeing cognitive activity from such constraining influences: this is an indispensable first step in the project of developing
an epistemological approach that can maintain continuity with experience.

The point is not, however, that if stereotypes are stripped away,
then experience will present itself pure and untainted. Experience is
always mediated by the location of experiencing subjects within a
certain time, place, culture and environment, and it is always shaped as
much by unconscious considerations and motivations. It is, arguably,
also shaped by the gender of the experiencer. But stereotypes constitute
a particular sort of knower-adopted overlay upon these structures, of
whose effects one can become aware, and which one can work to
rethink and restructure. It is especially for this reason that it makes
sense to illustrate something of what is involved in epistemic responsibility by looking at some of the epistemological and political effects of
stereotypes.

I have spelled out the features and implications of epistemic
responsibility more extensively elsewhere.[5] My belief in its importance
stems from my view that the Kantian conception of the creative
synthesis of the imagination is one of the most important innovations
in the history of philosophy, and that to think of knowledge as arising
out of that synthesis is to take human cognition to be an active process
of *taking* and *structuring* experience. Such activity is constrained by the
(often fluid) nature of human cognitive equipment, and by the (also
fluid) nature of reality. But within these constraints there is considerable freedom in making sense of the world. To take an example
particularly relevant to this context, one is free to know, conduct one's
life, and interact with other people on the basis of the alleged knowledge that women are deficient in reason by comparison with an alleged
masculine norm. Certainly it is possible to make sense of many aspects
of the world on these terms, and to construct a view of human relations
and possibilities that depends upon this alleged knowledge. Yet feminists are showing how serious a bias is at the basis of such knowledge
claims, and how they provide the cognitive basis for devastatingly
oppressive practices. And many other analogous examples can be cited
from a wide variety of contexts. They show why imperatives are
required to limit the kinds of sense that can responsibly be made of
experience; and I take the notion of *epistemic responsibility* to stand for a
cluster of considerations that work to constitute such imperatives.

Evidence for such responsibility is to be found in intellectual virtue,
and in the recognition of a normative force that attaches to "realism."
By the former, I mean a certain kind of orientation to the world and to
one's knowledge-seeking self as part of the world. An intellectually
virtuous person would value knowing and understanding how things

"really" are, to the extent that this is possible, renouncing both the temptation to live with partial explanations when fuller ones are attainable, and the temptation to live in fantasy or illusion. Such a person would consider it better to *know*, despite the comfortable complacency that a life indiscriminately governed by fantasy, and illusion might offer. And this connects directly to the idea that "realism" has normative force. In terms of this idea, the value of understanding how things are, to the best possible extent, is greater than, and supersedes, any value that might be taken to attach to consistent adherence to established theory or received opinion about how things might be. To achieve the "right" perceptions implied by such an approach requires honesty and humility, the courage not to pretend to know what one does not know, the wisdom not to ignore its relevance, and the humility not to yield to temptations to suppress facts damaging to a cherished theoretical stance.

Now it seems to be beyond dispute that claims to know based in stereotypical perceptions and conceptions fail in just this respect. In their extreme crudity as epistemological tools, stereotypes violate the requirements of epistemic responsibility, opting, in its place, for what one might term both epistemic indolence and epistemic imperialism. The former is manifested in a stereotype-user's conviction that s/he knows what s/he is talking about and is absolved from any need to attempt to know better. This encourages a kind of intellectual *akrasia*, an entrenched reluctance to enquire further lest one face the necessity of having to "reconsider a range of treasured beliefs."[6] The latter is manifested in a belief that a stereotyped person or situation is summed up, that the putative knower has labeled it for what it is, and has thus claimed it as part of his/her stock of cognitive concerns.

From the minimal concern with knowing well that is apparent in such epistemic postures, it is clear that these are epistemically irresponsible ways of claiming to know. Here there is none of the humility, openness, and concern with the normative force of realism that marks responsible cognitive endeavor. In fact, stereotypes close off possibilities of understanding; and this feature of their functioning is attributable, in part at least, to their resemblance, at once, to products of hasty generalizations, and to illegitimate appeals to authority. Both in its manner of selecting accidental characteristics of people and stretching them to sum up all people of that sort (be they women, Blacks, or men), and in its posing as a finished product, not open to amendment, the use of a stereotype has all the reprehensible features of pronouncements based upon hasty generalizations. Yet it is unlikely to have been derived by the overly simple (empiricist) process of simple enumeration by which hasty generalizations, in the main, are formed. Stereotypes are just as much the products of accumulated cultural lore, acquired as part of an acculturation process, and, as such, both deep-seated and tenacious. To allow them to pass for knowledge is to grant that cultural tradition undue authority and to abandon the critical perspective characteristic of responsible knowing.

Yet having said this, it is perhaps paradoxical to observe that something very like stereotypes is in fact needed if knowledge, or language, are to be possible at all. Categories and classifications, derived both from cultural traditions and from generalizations based on particular experiences, are part of the essential stuff of which both language and knowledge are made. So it is part of this epistemological task to devise responsible ways to distinguish open, potentially "fallibilist" categories and classificatory devices from rigid, dogmatism-evincing stereotypes. It is as much part of responsible knowing to become mindful of the possibilities of acting according to stereotypes oneself, and of succumbing to stereotyped self-perceptions, as it is to avoid stereotyping others.

With special reference to stereotypes of women, feminists in several disciplines have documented the way in which actions and attitudes shaped by such stereotypes structure the ways in which women are perceived and known, and come thereby to know themselves. Much of this documentation is philosophically pertinent just because it shows, precisely with reference to people's experience of themselves as participants in the world, that how one comes to know oneself through received doctrine has profound effects upon one's possibilities of being. In a complex process of reciprocal structuring and restructuring, what a person comes to believe that she (or he) *is* affects what that person can know, and to a large extent, structures what s/he is. In short, a stereotype is an unjust tyrant whose effects are both ontological and ethical. Two examples of such documentation are worth citing here to show something of what I mean.[7]

Margaret Rossiter's historical study of *Women Scientists in America: Struggles and Strategies to 1940* (1982) takes as one of its central themes a demonstration of the tyranny of stereotypes as they work to construct women's lives and to confine them both within certain possibilities for using their qualifications, and within certain modes of self-awareness that reinforce the stereotypes. Rossiter shows, for example, that if women can bring themselves to "know," even within their professional lives, that it is more appropriate to seek employment compatible with what it is (stereotypically) to be a woman (the "helpmate" role of a research assistant is an obvious example), then they make themselves less threatening to social structures, and hence more employable. In this mode, one simply buys into the "complementarity" thesis and engages gratefully in mediocre work allegedly more suited to one's own different (=inferior) female capacities. One's possibilities of knowing both one's own experiences and "the world" responsibly are thereby diminished.

A somewhat different manifestation of the feminine stereotype is evident in the case of Christine English who was found not guilty of murder but of manslaughter in the 1981 killing of her lover. She successfully pleaded diminished responsibility as a result of severe premenstrual tension. Initial feminist enthusiasm for the decision in this case arose out of belief that doctors and lawyers had in fact granted reality to women's experiences of menstrual and premenstrual sufferings, long dismissed (on a common reading of the stereotype) as "all in her mind." But in a subtler way the decision contributes to a re-entrenchment of the very stereotype it appears to challenge. For the stereotype of female hysteria, emotional immaturity and irrationality might readily, now, be reinstated, on the basis of the expertise of highly accredited authorities.[8] Despite their rigidity, on the basis of which one is rightly critical of their usage, stereotypes also have a curious elasticity that enables them to stretch and shift so as to accommodate (and condemn) quite contradictory ways of behaving.

To return, then, to the complex interrelation between the avoidance of stereotypes and epistemic responsibility, ordinarily I would take some version of the ancient Greek injunction "Know thyself" to be one of the imperatives that responsible knowers would try to follow. I think one can work towards observing this injunction even while acknowledging that "selves" are not fixed and are never fully conscious entities, and that claims to self-knowledge are not absolutely privileged by contrast with other people's claims to know one. Selves are constructed and reconstructed out of narratives, perspectives, experiences and events; and out of first-, second- and third-person accounts. But even within these acknowledgments there is a place for some version of self-knowledge, however provisionally it may need to be construed.

But when it comes to knowing oneself responsibly in defiance of stereotypes, the examples just cited indicate that this is an even more convoluted requirement than it seems to be, even with the ephemerality of "selves" taken into account. Particularly in cases such as that of the scientific helpmate, *not* knowing oneself may be conducive to survival. On the other hand, to undermine a stereotype strengthened by evidence from the English case, the most responsible approach would seem indeed to be to know oneself as well as possible, to work to acquire a just perception of one's own capacities and incapacities, starting from the well-justified assumption that the authority of the experts is as fallible as any other human posture. Plainly there are no straightforward or universal solutions to the puzzles posed by efforts to know women's experiences, or to challenge structures that systematically distort them.

EXPERIENCE AND KNOWLEDGE

In Carol Gilligan's work on the responses of female moral agents to Lawrence Kohlberg's tests for measuring levels of moral maturity, it is the clash between the moral experiences of those female subjects and the requirements of the Kohlberg theory that leads her to conclude that women speak in a *different* (moral) voice (Gilligan 1982). In fact, within the terms of the present discussion, one might take it to be Gilligan's (implicit) working hypothesis that the epistemological assumptions of Kohlberg's work preclude the possibility of accounting for women's experiences within the theoretical conclusions he draws.

Very much in keeping with traditional Kantian morality, Kohlberg assumes that moral maturity is characterized by a capacity for the autonomous endorsement of universalizable moral principles. The worthiness of such principles will be apparent from their applicability, with impartiality and following the dictates of duty alone, across all situations where moral judgment is required. Epistemologically speaking, it is tacitly assumed, although the question itself is not raised, that situations requiring moral judgment will be *known* in just the same way by all moral agents.[9] But it is a serious oversimplification to take for granted that perceptions are always unproblematically "right." Indeed, the moral quality of an action is dependent upon the cognition in which it is based, and this cognition is itself a proper object of evaluation.

Now Kohlberg's female and male subjects differ from one another as much in their *apprehensions* of the situations upon which they are called to pronounce as they do in their moral judgments. This cognitive asymmetry evidenced in their disparate responses seems to inspire much of Gilligan's dissatisfaction with the way those responses have been read so as to reinforce traditional stereotypes of the rational and morally mature male, and the irrational and morally immature female. Rather than considering an equally plausible interpretation to the effect that the complexity of female responses to Kohlberg's tests (statistically speaking) might be read as evidence of a finely tuned moral sense and a high level of moral sophistication, readers of these responses have tended automatically to favor the conclusion that female respondents are too much immersed in particularity to achieve the principled impartiality characteristic of mature moral being. It can at least be suggested that there has been a failure to maintain a responsible degree of openness on the part of these readers, too easy a willingness to structure their readings so as to confirm entrenched stereotypes and theoretical presuppositions.

In claiming that Gilligan's work lends itself to this kind of epistemological interpretation, I do not mean either to suggest that there *are* intrinsically incommensurable "masculine" and "feminine" ways of knowing, or that such statistical differences as emerge from female and male responses are essentially and/or naturally female and male. Gilligan herself argues that although the moral voices she discerns have traditionally been differentiated along gender lines, this is a matter of historical contingency rather than biological necessity.[10] It is partially consequent, she suggests, upon the ways in which gender has been constituted in mother-dominated western childrearing practices.[11] Both voices, she maintains, are at least in principle accessible to women and to men.

Nonetheless, a distinctive mode of moral discourse is discernible in Gilligan's work, especially in women's responses to her abortion study. This mode is markedly different from the kinds of deliberation commonly conducted within the rubric either of a Kantian or of a utilitarian approach to moral questions. While it is difficult to specify exactly how it differs, and quite inappropriate to see it either as arising out of, or as constituting a rival moral *theory*, certain of its features can be sketched out.

Both in the perceptions of relevance they reflect, and in their manner of apprehending and structuring situations, the responses Gilligan records are characterizable by what might be described as an analogue of practical reasoning (*phronesis*).[12] This is manifested in a kind of reflective posture, a thoughtfulness, which contrasts markedly with the Kantian-derived concentration upon achieving a principled moral stance that carries over into Kohlberg's work. But this is not the standard utilitarian contrast. The concern at its core is not so much with the consequences as with the *implications* both of motives and of actions, as much for other people, with whom one recognizes a complex network of affinities and connections, as for oneself.

The possibility of discerning these implications seems to involve attempting to position oneself reflectively within a situation, in relation to various of its aspects, so as to achieve a stance which will allow one to take account of as many of these implications as possible, while not destroying one's capacity to act. To do this well one needs to cultivate an attitude perhaps best described, borrowing Annette Kuhn's useful and evocative phrase, as one of "passionate detachment" (Kuhn 1982, ch. 1). It is rather like the attitude a good therapist brings to a client: a kind of "objective" sympathy, a mode of participation without intervention, of compassion without passion, which, at its best, succeeds at once in being involved and maintaining an appropriate distance. It is a matter of positioning and repositioning oneself within a situation until the best course of action comes to suggest itself; but always at points within the situation, for there is no removed, God's-eye vantage point. Whether such a mode of moral response is "naturally" or contingently female remains an open question.

It is an advantage of Gilligan's methodological approach that she makes it possible for this moral voice to be heard, not as affording evidence of stereotypically muddled female thinking, but as worthy of a hearing equivalently thoughtful to that accorded to products of male deliberation. There is an evident *concern*, in her work, to maintain contact with, and derive insights from, accounts that not only arise out of experience and are firmly grounded in it, but that stay in touch with that experience in drawing their conclusions. This contrasts with methods of epistemological and moral theory construction that aim to transcend experience, to move beyond it, allegedly towards greater clarity and accuracy but at the expense, I believe, of the insight and understanding that a maintained continuity with experience can afford.

Gilligan listens to people's stories (to *women's* stories) as they recount their experiences; and her aim seems to be the laudable one of listening responsively, and so, I would maintain, responsibly, to these stories.[13] For responsiveness seems to be a necessary component of any approach that purports to retain continuity with experience: it signals an appropriate receptiveness and humility towards that recounted experience, from which one moves only cautiously in the direction of interpretation. Such caution is enjoined in recognition of the fact that subjective factors are bound to structure any interpretation, and it is important to be cognizant of them, to the extent that one can. By no means the least significant of such factors is in the fact that a subject's account of her/his own experiences is as much structured by un-conscious and semiconscious forces as it is by conscious ones; and this is true, too, of any interpretation. Listening to, responding to and interpreting stories are acquired capacities. One has to put some effort into learning how to exercise them well. The need for *responsibility* in their exercise is particularly clear when one considers that there can be no uniquely true story, nor is there any uniquely right interpretation. But some are clearly better, or worse, than others, at least for now, and one can learn to recognize which ones.

In elaborating the potential value of Gilligan's methodological approach through these considerations, I do not mean to suggest that she herself shows a sensitivity to all of them. But the story-listening techniques she uses could be adapted and amplified so as to be more tentative, more qualified and nuanced in their interpretative moves. And even within the limitations of her own use of the approach, one sees some indication of how both epistemological and moral thinking might begin to move away from a preoccupation with transcending experience, not bothering about *who* the knowing subject, or that acting subject, really is.[14] Extrapolating from what Gilligan has done, it is possible to make sense of how it is that actual, historically situated, gendered epistemological and moral subjects know and respond to actual, complex experiences.

Clearly if any conclusions, however tentative and provisional, are to be derived from the process of telling and listening to stories, then the subject matter, the theme, of these stories must be specified, at least roughly. It is unlikely that randomly collected stories could be of much use in providing solutions—even tentative ones—to specific theoretical problems. So the investigator who would use such an approach must take a good deal of care to select stories both open enough *and* theoretically specified enough to elicit a range of responses that will neither predetermine possible conclusions, nor offer no possibility of discerning a common thread. If Gilligan is indeed committed to the view that this "different" moral voice is accessible equally to women and to men, then I think one must have serious reservations about her use of a study of women's responses to abortion as a means of making it audible. She makes too little of an epistemological constraint that is built into the structure of the investigation.[15]

Leaving open the question as to whether there are essentially "feminine" and "masculine" ways of knowing, it is nonetheless reasonable to maintain that there is a range of experiences that could not be known in ways similar enough, from knower to knower, to produce "common" knowledge in differently gendered subjects. Experiences that depend upon natural biological differences, in areas of sexuality, parenthood, and some aspects of physical and emotional being, must be different for women and for men to the extent that it would be impossible for them to know them in anything like "the same" way.[16] Hence it cannot make sense to imply that conclusions about moral maturity *per se* could be drawn from biologically specific experiences available only to women, particularly if one grants the point that the quality of moral action is dependent upon, and a direct reflection of, the cognitive activity in which it is based. The abortion study could only work to generate a universally relevant new perspective on moral maturity if one could assume, with respect to the questions that arise within it, that women and men count as a group who have to make this kind of decision *as equals*. But to make such an assumption is to ignore the crucial practical respects in which women and men are not equally implicated in and affected by decisions about abortion. It is to gloss over the unequal impact upon women's and men's lives, at least within current social structures, of childbearing and rearing. Hence it creates an intolerable discontinuity between experience and theory.[17]

On the other hand, stories must be specified sufficiently to provide experiential accounts of a *certain kind* of situation, if any substantive conclusions at all are to be drawn from them. And there is good reason to think that it is imperative to hear stories drawn from undervalued aspects of women's experiences, in view of the age-old imbalance in the standard selection of examples from stereotypically masculine experience. So the question arises as to what Gilligan's primary purpose is. If it is to make the "different" voice audible as one in which both women and men can speak, then the abortion study does not serve her well. In advocating that a necessarily female kind of experience, and hence knowledge and moral judgment, be allowed to generate an alternative standard of moral maturity she creates a structure for judging moral practice in which male knowledge, and hence male moral judgment, must equally necessarily be Other.

If, however, it is Gilligan's purpose to develop a specifically female morality, then perhaps the abortion stories are well chosen after all. But such a project would, I think, be of doubtful worth in the long run. Any celebration of specifically "feminine" modes that would aim to revalue them, yet leave them intact, would be in danger of obscuring the constraints commonly attendant upon their manifestation. If "connectedness," for example, were selected as a primary value, it would be important to keep in mind that, at least in the past, women's concentration upon "connection" within the domestic sphere has limited their capacity to contest exploitation, and has contributed to their powerlessness and oppression. So if the project is to open the way for the development of an ethics of care and responsibility that could be juxtaposed *against* an ethics of rights and justice, the most likely consequences would be to reinstate and reinforce precisely those stereotypes Gilligan sets out to undermine. It would be but a short step towards the contention that the former—the caring morality—is female morality, attuned to women's softer, more emotional, and lesser concerns; the latter—the rights and justice morality—is male morality; appropriate to men's more serious moral endeavors.

Gilligan would, I think, be better advised to choose themes for her stories that might enable male and female responses to be more nearly commensurable. Then her readers could more readily entertain the possibility that her work contributes to a long-needed challenge to the tyranny of feminine *and* masculine stereotypes.

CONCLUSION

My discussion has centered on the question of how people and situations are known; and I have made a particular plea in favor of taking seriously a certain kind of story—first-person accounts of experiences. Such stories provide access to a kind of knowledge not ordinarily regarded as appropriate for epistemological consideration. Indeed, this is one of the gaps that shows up when one reads standard, "male-stream" epistemology against the grain, and wonders what has become of the *people* whose knowledge it allegedly analyzes and explains. I have suggested that reflection upon epistemological and moral matters that is responsibly attuned to such narratives might be able to retain a kind of contact with human lives that is often lost in formalistic and abstract theoretical structures. Moreover, the subtlety and variety of narrative of this kind is such as to highlight the crudity of stereotypes, and their ineffectuality as putative cognitive devices. Responsible knowing simply has no place for them.[18]

The rejection of stereotypes as cognitive tools does not force one to fall back upon a belief in pure, unmediated experiences. Indeed, it would be a complete mistake to believe that stories, narratives, some-how provide unmediated access to experiences. Stories, even first-person stories, are not necessarily *truer* either than stereotypes or than standard philosophical analyses. Nor is there any kind of reliable criterion for determining their truth. Rather, the main point is that stories convey something about cognitive and moral experiences, in their manifold manifestations, that slips through the formalist nets of moral principles and duties, or standards of evidence and justification. The modest proposal urged here is that perhaps, by taking stories into account, theorists will be better able to repair some of the rifts in continuity that are so glaringly evident between moral theory and moral experiences, and theory of knowledge and cognitive experiences.

It is unlikely that this project could ever result in a seamless, invisible mending of these rifts. Theoretical structures and patterns that emerge from responsible reflection upon experience will more likely be piecemeal, comprised of interpretations of stories, and interpretations of interpretations. The point is not to generate a neat, comprehensive theoretical structure, but to learn how to let experience shape and reshape theory. In a word, the aim is to *understand* rather than to find methods of justification, verification, and control. So the price to be paid in terms of loss of certainty, clarity and precision is, admittedly, high. The position is a vertiginous one, and understanding is fleeting. But the certainty, clarity and precision claimed for dominant theoretical structures is as illusory as the truth claimed for stereotypes. And the vertigo will not be the source of dismay that it may at first sight seem to be, if cognitive activity does, in fact, begin to move towards thoughtful, responsible practice. Such practice can generate theoretical accounts of knowledge that stand a good chance of retaining contact with women's experiences without, carelessly and dismissively, simply slotting them into stereotyped categories.[19]

NOTES

1. In her article, "A Paradigm of Philosophy: The Adversary Method," Janice Moulton (1983, reprinted in this volume) shows how adversarial argumentation, which is characteristic of most present-day philosophical discourse, is minimally productive of understanding, insight or change.

2. Some of the most significant of these gaps and exclusions are made clear in Lloyd (1984), where it is argued that reason itself is defined by exclusion of character-traits traditionally associated with femaleness.

3. Here I cite the title of Carol Gould's book, *Beyond Domination* (1983). Stereotyped perception of women's nature is, of course, continuous with stereotyping of any sort and shares its reprehensibly dogmatic, unthinking character. Nor could one argue that only women are stereotyped and hence, by implication, that it is only men who stereotype. Women are prone to stereotyping each other, anti-feminists to stereotyping feminists, and vice versa. It is the stereotyping of women that concerns me here, whether by men or by other women. But epistemologically speaking, the use of stereotypes is always a crude and irresponsible way of not bothering to know, yet posing as though one does.

4. Classic feminist discussions of such practices are found in Hubbard (1983), Weisstein (1972), and Rubin (1975).

5. See Code (1983a, 1983b and 1984). The theory is more fully elaborated in my *Epistemic Responsibility* (1987a). In the account given here, I borrow from the discussion of this idea that appears in Code (1983b).

6. This is Amélie Rorty's phrase in Rorty (1983).

7. For the sake of clarity, these examples are taken from patriarchal structures, where stereotypes are imposed upon women from the vantage point of male experience and alleged expertise. In coming to a philosophical understanding of the problem of stereotypes as such, one would have to take account of the facts, already mentioned, that women, too, stereotype other women; and that people are prone, also to stereotype themselves. So the problem is more complex than these examples might suggest. But I think its solution would follow the same lines for its various manifestations, all of which, I think, are evidence of irresponsible cognitive practice.

8. I discuss these examples more fully in Code (1987b).

9. Hence Lawrence Blum (1979) argues that there are two aspects to any occasion of moral judgement: the apprehension of a situation, and the action(s) based upon that apprehension.

10. Cf. Gilligan (1982), 2. But it should be noted, as Debra Nails (1983) points out, that the book is "characterized by generalizations about the sexes, offered as descriptions of differences," hence that it has "the power to exaggerate existing differences" (662).

11. In this connection, Gilligan draws upon the work of Nancy Chodorow (1978).

12. Gilligan is not a philosopher, and would be unlikely to characterize them in this way. But it seems to be a potentially fruitful way of understanding something of what is at issue.

13. That she is not always successful in achieving this aim does not detract from its commendability as a guiding methodological principle. Gilligan seems

often to interpret too swiftly, and it has been suggested that she quotes too selectively, and unjustifiably out of context (cf. Nails, 1983, esp. 640–52). But the aim itself could be pursued somewhat differently, and its worthiness become more clearly apparent.

14. The use of narrative partially to effect this move is analogous to Alasdair MacIntyre's advocacy of the importance of narrative in understanding moral judgments and actions within the context of a life (see MacIntyre 1981).

15. These reservations are also expressed in Code (1983b).

16. This is not to suggest that all women and all men would know these situations and aspects of their being in the same (stereotypical) way—only that the lines of difference would be differently drawn in terms of their common starting points within one sex, and between the sexes.

17. I am indebted in my formulation of this point to Jean Grimshaw's discussion of philosophical writings on the ethics of abortion in her *Feminist Philosophers* (1986), 31–3.

18. I discuss the epistemological value of story-telling in greater detail in Code (1986).

19. Work on this paper was made possible by a Strategic Grant from the Social Sciences and Humanities Research Council of Canada, and by a Visiting Fellowship at the Humanities Research Centre at the Australian National University in Canada.

REFERENCES

Blum, Lawrence (1979), *Friendship, Altruism and Morality* (London: Routledge & Kegan Paul).

Chodorow, Nancy (1978), *The Reproduction of Mothering: Psychoanalysis and the Sociology of Gender* (Berkeley: University of California Press).

Code, Lorraine (1983a), "Father and Son: A Case Study in Epistemic Responsibility," *The Monist*, vol. 66, 268–82.

Code, Lorraine (1983b), "Responsibility and the Epistemic Community: Woman's Place," *Social Research*, vol. 50, no. 3, 537–55.

Code, Lorraine (1984), "Toward a 'Responsibilist' Epistemology," *Philosophy and Phenomenological Research*, vol. 45, no. 1, 29–50.

Code, Lorraine (1987a), *Epistemic Responsibility* (Hanover, New Hampshire: University Press of New England).

Code Lorraine (1986), "Stories People Tell," *New Mexico Law Review* 16 (fall 1986), 599–606.

Code, Lorraine (1987b) "The Tyranny of Stereotypes," in Kathleen Storrie (ed.), *Women, Isolation and Bonding: The Ecology of Gender* (Toronto: Methuen).

Gilligan, Carol (1982), *In a Different Voice: Psychological Theory and Women's Development* (Cambridge, Mass.: Harvard University Press).

Gould, Carol C. (ed.) (1983). *Beyond Domination: New Perspectives on Women and Philosophy* (Totowa, NJ: Littlefield Adams).

Grimshaw, Jean (1986), *Feminist Philosophers: Women's Perspectives on Philosophical Traditions* (Brighton: Wheatsheaf).

Harding, Sandra and Hintikka, Merrill B. (eds.) (1983), *Discovering Reality: Feminist Perspectives on Epistemology, Metaphysics, Methodology, and Philosophy of Science* (Dordrecht: Reidel).

Hubbard, Ruth (1983), "Have Only Men Evolved?" in S. Harding and M. Hintikka (eds.) 45–69.

Kuhn, Annette (1982), *Women's Pictures: Feminism and Cinema* (London: Routledge & Kegan Paul).

Lloyd, Genevieve (1984), *The Man of Reason: "Male" and "Female" in Western Philosophy* (London: Methuen).

MacIntyre, Alasdair (1981), *After Virtue: A Study in Moral Theory* (London: Duckworth).

Moulton, Janice (1983), "A Paradigm of Philosophy: The Adversary Method," in S. Harding and M. Hintikka (eds.), 149–64. Reprinted as Chapter One of this volume.

Nails, Debra (1983), "Social Scientific Sexisms: Gilligan's Mismeasure of Man," *Social Research*, vol. 50, no. 3, 643–64.

Rorty, Amélie (1983), "Akratic Believers," *The American Philosophical Quarterly*, vol. 20, no. 2, 174–83.

Rossiter, Margaret (1982), *Women Scientists in America: Struggles and Strategies to 1940* (Baltimore: Johns Hopkins University Press).

Rubin, Gayle (1975), "The Traffic in Women: Notes on the Political Economy of Sex," in Rayna Rapp Reiter (ed.), *Toward an Anthropology of Women* (New York: Monthly Review Press), 157–210.

Weisstein, Naomi (1972), "Psychology Constructs the Female," in Vivian Gornick and Barbara K. Moran (eds.), *Women in Sexist Society* (New York: Signet Books), 207–24.

Part IV ──────────────

Philosophy of Science

───────────────────────────

Philosophers of science are interested in questions that are presupposed by the practices of science—for example, conceptions of scientific inquiry, theory, and paradigms; what counts as proper scientific method; the connection between theory and observation; models; causality; and rationality, objectivity, and values in science. Feminist philosophers and historians of science have added their perspectives to the many ongoing debates in philosophy of science, particularly concerning the role that values play in science.

Feminist philosophers and historians of science have also raised new issues for consideration. For example, we point out that the practices of science have a broad variety of gender implications, ranging from the structure of laboratory work to the most fundamental scientific concepts. We examine androcentric bias in its myriad forms in theories, models, and experiments. We ask whether science can serve what Sandra Harding calls "emancipatory ends" for gender, race, and class. Flowing from the critique of the gendered character of science, we raise many epistemological questions about objectivity, about rationality, about the possibility of a value-free science, and about the ways in which beliefs and knowledge are related to social experience.

The three papers included here all focus in some way on the relation between objectivity in science and feminist values. Evelyn Fox Keller maintains that the feminist criticisms of science that carry the greatest liberating potential for science are those that conflict most deeply with our conventional notions of science. She focuses on issues surrounding objectivity in science. She rejects the idea that science is purely a social product bearing no objectivity; she wants instead to redefine the effort to understand the world in rational terms. For Keller, one thing required by this redefinition is that we see the ways that objectivity has been linked with masculinity, and the goals of science linked with power and domination. Keller maintains that although two conceptions of science can be found historically—domination over nature and conversation with nature—the domination view was most often selected. Feminists can draw on this historical plurality to help transform science today.

Sandra Harding explains two feminist strategies that try to answer important epistemological questions in philosophy of science. One such question is "How can feminist (politicized) inquiry increase the objectivity of our explanations and understandings in science?" She first considers feminist empiricism, which builds upon traditional empiricism, but undermines many of its basic assumptions. Next she focuses on feminist standpoint epistemologies, which claim that the point of view of women is an advantaged one for knowledge. Among the criticisms she offers of these views are those of feminist postmodernism. Harding believes that although all of these strategies, including postmodernism, have weaknesses, feminists cannot afford to forsake any one entirely.

"What sort of sense does it make to talk of a feminist science?" is Helen Longino's topic. Longino focuses on the practice and process of science rather than on its content as she discusses the possibility of a value-free science. She believes that it is possible in principle to do science as a feminist, but that in practice we cannot do it until we change current conditions. Her reasoning rests on the ways in which values both can and do influence our choice of models and theories in science.

Chapter 10

Feminism and Science

Evelyn Fox Keller

In recent years, a new critique of science has begun to emerge from a number of feminist writings. The lens of feminist politics brings into focus certain masculinist distortions of the scientific enterprise, creating, for those of us who are scientists, a potential dilemma. Is there a conflict between our commitment to feminism and our commitment to science? As both a feminist and a scientist, I am more familiar than I might wish with the nervousness and defensiveness that such a potential conflict evokes. As scientists, we have very real difficulties in thinking about the kinds of issues that, as feminists, we have been raising. These difficulties may, however, ultimately be productive. My purpose in the present essay is to explore the implications of recent feminist criticism of science for the relationship between science and feminism. Do these criticisms imply conflict? If they do, how necessary is that conflict? I will argue that those elements of feminist criticism that seem to conflict most with at least conventional conceptions of science may, in fact, carry a liberating potential for science. It could therefore benefit scientists to attend closely to feminist criticism. I will suggest that we might even use feminist thought to illuminate and clarify part of the substructure of science (which may have been historically conditioned into distortion) in order to preserve the things that science has taught us, in order to be more objective. But first it is necessary to review the various criticisms that feminists have articulated.

The range of their critique is broad. Though they all claim that science embodies a strong androcentric bias, the meanings attached to this charge vary widely. It is convenient to represent the differences in meaning by a spectrum that parallels the political range characteristic of feminism as a whole. I label this spectrum from right to left, beginning somewhere left of center with what might be called the liberal position.

Source: First published in *Signs: Journal of Women in Culture and Society* 7, 3 (1982): 589–602. Copyright © The University of Chicago. All rights reserved. Reprinted by permission of the author and of The University of Chicago Press.

From the liberal critique, charges of androcentricity emerge that are relatively easy to correct. The more radical critique calls for correspondingly more radical changes; it requires a reexamination of the underlying assumptions of scientific theory and method for the presence of male bias. The difference between these positions is, however, often obscured by a knee-jerk reaction that leads many scientists to regard all such criticism as a unit—as a challenge to the neutrality of science. One of the points I wish to emphasize here is that the range of meanings attributed to the claim of androcentric bias reflects very different levels of challenge, some of which even the most conservative scientists ought to be able to accept.

First, in what I have called the liberal critique, is the charge that is essentially one of unfair employment practices. It proceeds from the observation that almost all scientists are men. This criticism is liberal in the sense that it in no way conflicts either with traditional conceptions of science or with current liberal, egalitarian politics. It is, in fact, a purely political criticism, and one that can be supported by all of us who are in favor of equal opportunity. According to this point of view, science itself would in no way be affected by the presence or absence of women.

A slightly more radical criticism continues from this and argues that the predominance of men in the sciences has led to a bias in the choice and definition of problems with which scientists have concerned themselves. This argument is most frequently and most easily made in regard to the health sciences. It is claimed, for example, that contraception has not be given the scientific attention its human importance warrants and that, furthermore, the attention it has been given has been focused primarily on contraceptive techniques to be used by women. In a related complaint, feminists argue that menstrual cramps, a serious problem for many women, have never been taken seriously by the medical profession. Presumably, had the concerns of medical research been articulated by women, these particular imbalances would not have arisen.[1] Similar biases in sciences remote from the subject of women's bodies are more difficult to locate—they may, however, exist. Even so, this kind of criticism does not touch our conception of what science is, nor our confidence in the neutrality of science. It may be true that in some areas we have ignored certain problems, but our definition of science does not include the choice of problem—that, we can readily agree, has always been influenced by social forces. We remain, therefore, in the liberal domain.

Continuing to the left, we next find claims of bias in the actual design and interpretation of experiments. For example, it is pointed out that virtually all of the animal-learning research on rats has been performed with male rats.[2] Though a simple explanation is offered—

namely, that female rats have a four-day cycle that complicates experiments—the criticism is hardly vitiated by the explanation. The implicit assumption is, of course, that the male rat represents the species. There exist many other, often similar, examples in psychology. Examples from the biological sciences are somewhat more difficult to find, though one suspects that they exist. An area in which this suspicion is particularly strong is that of sex research. Here the influence of heavily invested preconceptions seems all but inevitable. In fact, although the existence of such preconceptions has been well documented historically,[3] a convincing case for the existence of a corresponding bias in either the design or interpretation of experiments has yet to be made. That this is so can, I think, be taken as testimony to the effectiveness of the standards of objectivity operating.

But evidence for bias in the interpretation of observations and experiments is very easy to find in the more socially oriented sciences. The area of primatology is a familiar target. Over the past fifteen years women working in the field have undertaken an extensive reexamination of theoretical concepts, often using essentially the same methodological tools. These efforts have resulted in some radically different formulations. The range of difference frequently reflects the powerful influence of ordinary language in biasing our theoretical formulations. A great deal of very interesting work analyzing such distortions has been done.[4] Though I cannot begin to do justice to that work here, let me offer, as a single example, the following description of a single-male troop of animals that Jane Lancaster provides as a substitute for the familiar concept of "harem": "For a female, males are a resource in her environment which she may use to further the survival of herself and her offspring. If environmental conditions are such that the male role can be minimal, a one-male group is likely. Only one male is necessary for a group of females if his only role is to impregnate them."[5]

These critiques, which maintain that a substantive effect on scientific theory results from the predominance of men in the field, are almost exclusively aimed at the "softer," even the "softest," sciences. Thus they can still be accommodated within the traditional framework by the simple argument that the critiques, if justified, merely reflect the fact that these subjects are not sufficiently scientific. Presumably, fair-minded (or scientifically minded) scientists can and should join forces with the feminists in attempting to identify the presence of bias—equally offensive, if for different reasons, to both scientists and feminists—in order to make these "soft" sciences more rigorous.

It is much more difficult to deal with the truly radical critique that attempts to locate androcentric bias even in the "hard" sciences, indeed in scientific ideology itself. This range of criticism takes us out of the liberal domain and requires us to question the very assumptions of objectivity and rationality that underlie the scientific enterprise. To challenge the truth and necessity of the conclusions of natural science on the grounds that they too reflect the judgment of men is to take the Galilean credo and turn it on its head. It is not true that "the conclusions of natural science are true and necessary, and the judgement of man has nothing to do with them";[6] it is the judgment of woman that they have nothing to do with.

The impetus behind this radical move is twofold. First, it is supported by the experience of feminist scholars in other fields of inquiry. Over and over, feminists have found it necessary, in seeking to reinstate women as agents and as subjects, to question the very canons of their fields. They have turned their attention, accordingly, to the operation of patriarchal bias on ever deeper levels of social structure, even of language and thought.

But the possibility of extending the feminist critique into the foundations of scientific thought is created by recent developments in the history and philosophy of science itself.[7] As long as the course of scientific thought was judged to be exclusively determined by its own logical and empirical necessities, there could be no place for any signature, male or otherwise, in that system of knowledge. Furthermore, any suggestion of gender differences in our thinking about the world could argue only too readily for the further exclusion of women from science. But as the philosophical and historical inadequacies of the classical conception of science have become more evident, and as historians and sociologists have begun to identify the ways in which the development of scientific knowledge has been shaped by its particular social and political context, our understanding of science as a social process has grown. This understanding is a necessary prerequisite, both politically and intellectually, for a feminist theoretic in science.

Joining feminist thought to other social studies of science brings the promise of radically new insights, but it also adds to the existing intellectual danger a political threat. The intellectual danger resides in viewing science as pure social product; science then dissolves into ideology and objectivity loses all intrinsic meaning. In the resulting cultural relativism, any emancipatory function of modern science is negated, and the arbitration of truth recedes into the political domain.[8] Against this background, the temptation arises for feminists to abandon their claim for representation in scientific culture and, in its place, to invite a return to a purely "female" subjectivity, leaving rationality and objectivity in the male domain, dismissed as products of a purely male consciousness.[9]

Many authors have addressed the problems raised by total relativism;[10] here I wish merely to mention some of the special problems added by its feminist variant. They are several. In important respects, feminist relativism is just the kind of radical move that transforms the political spectrum into a circle. By rejecting objectivity as a masculine ideal, it simultaneously lends its voice to an enemy chorus and dooms women to residing outside of the realpolitik modern culture; it exacerbates the very problem it wishes to solve. It also nullifies the radical potential of feminist criticism for our understanding of science. As I see it, the task of a feminist theoretic in science is twofold: to distinguish that which is parochial from that which is universal in the scientific impulse, reclaiming for women what has historically been denied to them; and to legitimate those elements of scientific culture that have been denied precisely because they are defined as female.

It is important to recognize that the framework inviting what might be called the nihilist retreat is in fact provided by the very ideology of objectivity we wish to escape. This is the ideology that asserts an opposition between (male) objectivity and (female) subjectivity and denies the possibility of mediation between the two. A first step, therefore, in extending the feminist critique to the foundations of scientific thought is to reconceptualize objectivity as a dialectical process so as to allow for the possibility of distinguishing the objective effort from the objectivist illusion. As Piaget reminds us:

> Objectivity consists in so fully realizing the countless intrusions of the self in everyday thought and the countless illusions which result—illusions of sense, language, point of view, value, etc.—that the preliminary step to every judgement is the effort to exclude the intrusive self. Realism, on the contrary, consists in ignoring the existence of self and thence regarding one's own perspective as immediately objective and absolute. Realism is thus anthropocentric illusion, finality—in short, all those illusions which teem in the history of science. So long as thought has not become conscious of self, it is a prey to perpetual confusions between objective and subjective, between the real and the ostensible.[11]

In short, rather than abandon the quintessentially human effort to understand the world in rational terms, we need to refine that effort. To do this, we need to add to the familiar methods of rational and empirical inquiry the additional process of critical self-reflection. Following Piaget's injunction, we need to "become conscious of self." In this way, we can become conscious of the features of the scientific project that belie its claim to universality.

The ideological ingredients of particular concern to feminists are found where objectivity is linked with autonomy and masculinity, and in turn, the goals of science with power and domination. The linking of objectivity with social and political autonomy has been examined by many authors and shown to serve a variety of important political functions.[12] The implications of joining objectivity with masculinity are less well understood. This conjunction also serves critical political functions. But an understanding of the sociopolitical meaning of the entire constellation requires an examination of the psychological processes through which these connections become internalized and perpetuated. Here psychoanalysis offers us an invaluable perspective, and it is to the exploitation of that perspective that much of my own work has been directed. In an earlier paper, I tried to show how psychoanalytic theories of development illuminate the structure and meaning of an interacting system of associations linking objectivity (a cognitive trait) with autonomy (an affective trait) and masculinity (a gender trait).[13] Here, after a brief summary of my earlier argument, I want to explore the relation of this system to power and domination.

Along with Nancy Chodorow and Dorothy Dinnerstein, I have found that branch of psychoanalytic theory known as object relations theory to be especially useful.[14] In seeking to account for personality development in terms of both innate drives and actual relations with other objects (i.e., subjects), it permits us to understand the ways in which our earliest experiences—experiences in large part determined by the socially structured relationships that form the context of our developmental processes—help to shape our conception of the world and our characteristic orientations to it. In particular, our first steps in the world are guided primarily by the parents of one sex—our mothers; this determines a maturational framework for our emotional, cognitive, and gender development, a framework later filled in by cultural expectations.

In brief, I argued the following: Our early maternal environment, coupled with the cultural definition of masculine (that which can never appear feminine) and of autonomy (that which can never be compromised by dependency) leads to the association of female with the pleasures and dangers of merging, and of male with the comfort and loneliness of separateness. The boy's internal anxiety about both self and gender is echoed by the more widespread cultural anxiety, thereby encouraging postures of autonomy and masculinity, which can, indeed may, be designed to defend against that anxiety and the longing that generates it. Finally, for all of us, our sense of reality is carved out of the same developmental matrix. As Piaget and others have emphasized the capacity for cognitive distinctions between self and other (objectivity) evolves concurrently and interdependently with the development of psychic autonomy; our cognitive ideals thereby become subject to the same psychological influences as our emotional and gender ideals. Along with autonomy the very act of separating subject from object— objectivity itself—comes to be associated with masculinity. The combined psychological and cultural pressures lead all three ideals—affective, gender, and cognitive—to a mutually reinforcing process of exaggeration and rigidification.[15] The net result is the entrenchment of an objectivist ideology and a correlative devaluation of (female) subjectivity.

This analysis leaves out many things. Above all it omits discussion of the psychological meanings of power and domination, and it is to those meanings I now wish to turn. Central to object relations theory is the recognition that the condition of psychic autonomy is double edged: it offers a profound source of pleasure, and simultaneously of potential dread. The values of autonomy are consonant with the values of competence, of mastery. Indeed competence is itself a prior condition for autonomy and serves immeasurably to confirm one's sense of self. But need the development of competence and the sense of mastery lead to a state of alienated selfhood, of denied connectedness, of defensive separateness? To forms of autonomy that can be understood as protections against dread? Object relations theory makes us sensitive to autonomy's range of meanings; it simultaneously suggests the need to consider the corresponding meanings of competence. Under what circumstances does competence imply mastery of one's own fate and under what circumstances does it imply mastery over another's? In short, are control and domination essential ingredients of competence, and intrinsic to selfhood, or are they correlates of an alienated selfhood?

One way to answer these questions is to use the logic of the analysis summarized above to examine the shift from competence to power and control in the psychic economy of the young child. From that analysis, the impulse toward domination can be understood as a natural concomitant of defensive separateness—as Jessica Benjamin has written, "A way of repudiating sameness, dependency and closeness with another person, while attempting to avoid the consequent feelings of aloneness."[16] Perhaps no one has written more sensitively than psychoanalyst D. W. Winnicott of the rough waters the child must travel in negotiating the transition from symbiotic union to the recognition of self and other as autonomous entities. He alerts us to a danger that others have missed—a danger arising from the unconscious fantasy that the subject has actually destroyed the object in the process of becoming separate.

Indeed, he writes, "It is the destruction of the object that places the object outside the area of control. . . . After 'subject relates to object' comes 'subject destroys object' (as it becomes external); then may come 'object survives destruction by the subject.' But there may or may not be survival." When there is, "because of the survival of the object, the subject may now have started to live a life in the world of objects, and so the subject stands to gain immeasurably; but the price has to be paid in acceptance of the ongoing destruction in unconscious fantasy relative to object-relating."[17] Winnicott, of course, is not speaking of actual survival but of subjective confidence in the survival of the other. Survival in that sense requires that the child maintain relatedness; failure induces inevitable guilt and dread. The child is poised on a terrifying precipice. On one side lies the fear of having destroyed the object, on the other side, loss of self. The child may make an attempt to secure this precarious position by seeking to master the other. The cycles of destruction and survival are reenacted while the other is kept safely at bay, and as Benjamin writes, "the original self assertion is . . . converted from innocent mastery to mastery over and against the other."[18] In psychodynamic terms, this particular resolution of preoedipal conflicts is a product of oedipal consolidation. The (male) child achieves his final security by identification with the father—an identification involving simultaneously a denial of the mother and a transformation of guilt and fear into aggression.

Aggression, of course, has many meanings, many sources, and many forms of expression. Here I mean to refer only to the form underlying the impulse toward domination. I invoke psychoanalytic theory to help illuminate the forms of expression that impulse finds in science as a whole, and its relation to objectification in particular. The same questions I asked about the child I can also ask about science. Under what circumstances is scientific knowledge sought for the pleasures of knowing, for the increased competence it grants us, for the increased mastery (real or imagined) over our own fate, and under what circumstances is it fair to say that science seeks actually to dominate nature? Is there a meaningful distinction to be made here?

In his work *The Domination of Nature* William Leiss observes, "The necessary correlate of domination is the consciousness of subordination in those who must obey the will of another; thus properly speaking only other men can be the objects of domination."[19] (Or women, we might add.) Leiss infers from this observation that it is not the domination of physical nature we should worry about but the use of our knowledge of physical nature as an instrument for the domination of human nature. He therefore sees the need for correctives, not in science but in its uses. This is his point of departure from other authors of the Frankfurt school, who assume the very logic of science to be the logic of domination. I agree with Leiss's basic observation but draw a somewhat different inference. I suggest that the impulse toward domination does find expression in the goals (and even in the theories and practice) of modern science, and argue that where it finds such expression the impulse needs to be acknowledged as projection. In short, I argue that not only in the denial of interaction between subject and other but also in the access of domination to the goals of scientific knowledge, one finds the intrusion of a self we begin to recognize as partaking in the cultural construct of masculinity.

The value of consciousness is that it enables us to make choices— both as individuals and as scientists. Control and domination are in fact intrinsic neither to selfhood (i.e., autonomy) nor to scientific knowledge. I want to suggest, rather, that the particular emphasis western science has placed on these functions of knowledge is twin to the objectivist ideal. Knowledge in general, and scientific knowledge in particular, serves two gods: power and transcendence. It aspires alternately to mastery over and union with nature.[20] Sexuality serves the same two gods, aspiring to domination and ecstatic communion—in short, aggression and eros. And it is hardly a new insight to say that power, control, and domination are fueled largely by aggression, while union satisfies a more purely erotic impulse.

To see the emphasis on power and control so prevalent in the rhetoric of western science as projection of a specifically male consciousness requires no great leap of the imagination. Indeed, that perception has become a commonplace. Above all, it is invited by the rhetoric that conjoins the domination of nature with the insistent image of nature as female, nowhere more familiar than in the writings of Francis Bacon. For Bacon, knowledge and power are one, and the promise of science is expressed as "leading to you Nature with all her children to bind her to your service and make her your slave,"[21] by means that do not "merely exert a gentle guidance over nature's course; they have the power to conquer and subdue her, to shake her to her foundations."[22] In the context of the Baconian vision, Bruno Bettelheim's conclusion appears inescapable: "Only with phallic psychology did aggressive manipulation of nature become possible."[23]

The view of science as an oedipal project is also familiar from the writings of Herbert Marcuse and Norman O. Brown.[24] But Brown's preoccupation, as well as Marcuse's is with what Brown calls a "morbid" science. Accordingly, for both authors the quest for a nonmorbid science, an "erotic" science, remains a romantic one. This is so because their picture of science is incomplete: it omits from consideration the crucial, albeit less visible, erotic components already present in the scientific tradition. Our own quest, if it is to be realistic rather than romantic, must be based on a richer understanding of the scientific tradition, in all its dimensions, and on an understanding of the ways in which this complex, dialectical tradition becomes transformed into a monolithic rhetoric. Neither the oedipal child nor modern science has in fact managed to rid itself of its preoedipal and fundamentally bisexual yearnings. It is with this recognition that the quest for a different science, a science undistorted by masculinist bias, must begin.

The presence of contrasting themes, of a dialectic between aggressive and erotic impulses, can be seen both within the work of individual scientists and, even more dramatically, in the juxtaposed writings of different scientists. Francis Bacon provides us with one model;[25] there are many others. For an especially striking contrast, consider a contemporary scientist who insists on the importance of "letting the material speak to you," of allowing it to "tell you what to do next"—one who chastises other scientists for attempting to "impose an answer" on what they see. For this scientist, discovery is facilitated by becoming "part of the system," rather than remaining outside; one must have a "feeling for the organism."[26] It is true that the author of these remarks is not only from a different epoch and a different field (Bacon himself was not actually a scientist by most standards), she is also a woman. It is also true that there are many reasons, some of which I have already suggested, for thinking that gender (itself constructed in an ideological context) actually does make a difference in scientific inquiry. Nevertheless, my point here is that neither science nor individuals are totally bound by ideology. In fact, it is not difficult to find similar sentiments expressed by male scientists. Consider, for example, the following remarks: "I have often had cause to feel that my hands are cleverer than my head. That is a crude way of characterizing the dialectics of experimentation. When it is going well, it is like a quiet conversation with Nature."[27] The difference between conceptions of science as "dominating" and as "conversing with" nature may not be a difference primarily between epochs, nor between the sexes. Rather it can be seen as representing a dual theme played out in the work of all scientists, in all ages. But the two poles of this dialectic do not appear with equal weight in the history of science. What we therefore need to attend to is the evolutionary process that selects one theme as dominant.

Elsewhere I have argued for the importance of a different selection process.[28] In part, scientists are themselves selected by the emotional appeal of particular (stereotypic) images of science. Here I am arguing for the importance of selection within scientific thought—first of preferred methodologies and aims, and finally of preferred theories. The two processes are not unrelated. While stereotypes are not binding (i.e., they do not describe all or perhaps any individuals), and this fact creates the possibility for an ongoing contest within science, the first selection process undoubtedly influences the outcome of the second. That is, individuals drawn by a particular ideology will tend to select themes consistent with that ideology.

One example in which this process is played out on a theoretical level is in the fate of interactionist theories in the history of biology. Consider the contest that has raged throughout this century between organismic and particulate views of cellular organization—between what might be described as hierarchical and nonhierarchical theories.

Whether the debate is over the primacy of the nucleus or the cell as a whole, the genome or the cytoplasm, the proponents of hierarchy have won out. One geneticist has described the conflict in explicitly political terms:

> Two concepts of genetic mechanisms have persisted side by side throughout the growth of modern genetics, but the emphasis has been very strongly in favor of one of these. . . . The first of these we will designate as the "Master Molecule" concept. . . . This is in essence the Theory of the Gene, interpreted to suggest a totalitarian government. . . . The second concept we will designate as the "Steady State" concept. By this term . . . we envision a dynamic self-perpetuating organization of a variety of molecular species which owes its specific properties not to the characteristic of any one kind of molecule, but to the functional interrelationships of these molecular species.[29]

Soon after these remarks, the debate between "master molecules" and dynamic interactionism was foreclosed by the synthesis provided by DNA and the "central dogma." With the success of the new molecular biology such "steady state" (or egalitarian) theories lost interest for almost all geneticists. But today, the same conflict shows signs of reemerging—in genetics, in theories of the immune system, and in theories of development.

I suggest that method and theory may constitute a natural continuum, despite Popperian claims to the contrary, and that the same processes of selection may bear equally and simultaneously on both the means and aims of science and the actual theoretical descriptions that emerge. I suggest this in part because of the recurrent and striking consonance that can be seen in the way scientists work, the relation they take to their object of study, and the theoretical orientation they favor. To pursue the example cited earlier, the same scientist who allowed herself to become "part of the system," whose investigations were guided by a "feeling for the organism," developed a paradigm that diverged as radically from the dominant paradigm of her field as did her methodological style.

In lieu of the linear hierarchy described by the central dogma of molecular biology, in which the DNA encodes and transmits all instructions for the unfolding of a living cell, her research yielded a view of the DNA in delicate interaction with the cellular environment— an organismic view. For more important than the genome as such (i.e., the DNA) is the "overall organism." As she sees it, the genome functions "only in respect to the environment in which it is found."[30] In this work the program encoded by the DNA is itself subject to change. No longer is a master control to be found in a single component of the cell; rather, control resides in the complex interactions of the entire system. When first presented, the work underlying this vision was not understood, and it was poorly received.[31] Today much of that work is undergoing a renaissance, although it is important to say that her full vision remains too radical for most biologists to accept.[32]

This example suggests that we need not rely on our imagination for a vision of what a different science—a science less restrained by the impulse to dominate—might be like. Rather, we need only look to the thematic pluralism in the history of our own science as it has evolved. Many other examples can be found, but we lack an adequate understanding of the full range of influences that lead to the acceptance or rejection not only of particular theories but of different theoretical orientations. What I am suggesting is that if certain theoretical interpretations have been selected against, it is precisely in this process of selection that ideology in general, and a masculinist ideology in particular, can be found to effect its influence. The task this implies for a radical feminist critique of science is, then, first a historical one, but finally a transformative one. In the historical effort, feminists can bring a whole new range of sensitivities, leading to an equally new consciousness of the potentialities lying latent in the scientific project.

NOTES

1. Notice that the claim is not that the mere presence of women in medical research is sufficient to right such imbalances, for it is understood how readily women, or any "outsiders" for that matter, come to internalize the concerns and values of a world to which they aspire to belong.

2. I would like to thank Lila Braine for calling this point to my attention.

3. D. L. Hall and Diana Long, "The Social Implications of the Scientific Study of Sex," *Scholar and the Feminist* 4 (1977): 11–21.

4. See, e.g., Donna Haraway, "Animal Sociology and a Natural Economy of the Body Politic, Part I: A Political Physiology of Dominance"; and "Animal Sociology and a Natural Economy of the Body Politic, Part II: The Past Is the Contested Zone: Human Nature and Theories of Production and Reproduction in Primate Behavior Studies," *Signs: Journal of Women in Culture and Society* 4, no. 1 (Autumn 1978): 21–60.

5. Jane Lancaster, *Primate Behavior and the Emergence of Human Culture* (New York: Holt, Rinehart & Winston, 1975), 34.

6. Galileo Galilei, *Dialogue on the Great World Systems*, trans. T. Salusbury, ed. G. de Santillana (Chicago: University of Chicago Press, 1953), 63.

7. The work of Russell Hanson and Thomas S. Kuhn was of pivotal importance in opening up our understanding of scientific thought to a consideration of social, psychological, and political influences.

8. See, e.g., Paul Feyerabend, *Against Method* (London: New Left Books, 1975); and *Science in a Free Society* (London: New Left Books, 1978).

9. This notion is expressed most strongly by some of the new French

feminists (see Elaine Marks and Isabelle de Courtivron, eds., *New French Feminisms: An Anthology* [Amherst: University of Massachusetts Press, 1980]), and is currently surfacing in the writings of some American feminists. See, e.g., Susan Griffin, *Woman and Nature: The Roaring Inside Her* (New York: Harper & Row, 1978).

10. See, e.g., Steven Rose and Hilary Rose, "Radical Science and Its Enemies," *Socialist Register 1979*, ed. Ralph Miliband and John Saville (Atlantic Highlands, N.J.: Humanities Press, 1979), 317–35. A number of the points made here have also been made by Elizabeth Fee in "Is Feminism a Threat to Objectivity?" (paper presented at the American Association for the Advancement of Science meeting, Toronto, January 4, 1981).

11. Jean Piaget, *The Child's Conception of the World* (Totowa, N.J.: Littlefield, Adams & Co., 1972).

12. Jerome R. Ravetz, *Scientific Knowledge and Its Social Problems* (London: Oxford University Press, 1971); and Hilary Rose and Steven Rose, *Science and Society* (London: Allen Lane, 1969).

13. Evelyn Fox Keller, "Gender and Science," *Psychoanalysis and Contemporary Thought* 1 (1978): 409–33.

14. Nancy Chodorow, *The Reproduction of Mothering: Psychoanalysis and the Sociology of Gender* (Berkeley: University of California Press, 1978); and Dorothy Dinnerstein, *The Mermaid and the Minotaur: Sexual Arrangements and Human Malaise* (New York: Harper & Row, 1976).

15. For a fuller development of this argument, see n. 12 above. By focusing on the contributions of individual psychology, I in no way mean to imply a simple division of individual and social factors, or to set them up as alternative influences. Individual psychological traits evolve in a social system and, in turn, social systems reward and select for particular sets of individual traits. Thus if particular options in science reflect certain kinds of psychological impulses or personality traits, it must be understood that it is in a distinct social framework that those options, rather than others, are selected.

16. Jessica Benjamin has discussed this same issue in an excellent analysis of the place of domination in sexuality. See "The Bonds of Love: Rational Violence and Erotic Domination," *Feminist Studies* 6, no. 1 (Spring 1980): 144–74, esp. 150.

17. D. W. Winnicott, *Playing and Reality* (New York: Basic Books, 1971), 89–90.

18. Benjamin, 165.

19. William Leiss, *The Domination of Nature* (Boston: Beacon Press, 1974), 122.

20. For a discussion of the different roles these two impulses play in Platonic and in Baconian images of knowledge, see Evelyn Fox Keller, "Nature as 'Her'" (paper delivered at the Second Sex Conference, New York Institute for the Humanities, September 1979).

21. B. Farrington, "*Temporis Partus Masculus:* An Untranslated Writing of Francis Bacon," *Centaurus* 1 (1951): 193–205, esp. 197.

22. Francis Bacon, "Description of the Intellectual Globe," in *The Philosophical Works of Francis Bacon*, ed. J. H. Robertson (London: Routledge & Sons, 1905). 506.

23. Quoted in Norman O. Brown, *Life against Death* (New York: Random House, 1959), 280.

24. Brown; and Herbert Marcuse, *One Dimensional Man* (Boston: Beacon Press, 1964).

25. For a discussion of the presence of the same dialectic in the writings of Francis Bacon, see Evelyn Fox Keller, "Baconian Science: A Hermaphrodite Birth," *Philosophical Forum* 11, no. 3 (Spring 1980): 299–308.

26. Barbara McClintock, private interviews, December 1, 1978, and January 13, 1979.

27. G. Wald, "The Molecular Basis of Visual Excitation," *Les Prix Nobel en 1967* (Stockholm: Kungliga Boktryckerlet, 1968), 260.

28. Keller, "Gender and Science."

29. D. L. Nanney, "The Role of the Cyctoplasm in Heredity," in *The Chemical Basis of Heredity*, ed. William D. McElroy and Bentley Glass (Baltimore: Johns Hopkins University Press, 1957), 136.

30. McClintock, December 1, 1978.

31. McClintock, "Chromosome Organization and Genic Expression," *Cold Spring Harbor Symposium of Quantitative Biology* 16 (1951): 13–44.

32. See McClintock, "Modified Gene Expressions Induced by Transposable Elements," in *Mobilization and Reassembly of Genetic Information*, ed. W. A. Scott, R. Werner, and J. Schultz (New York: Academic Press, 1980).

Chapter 11 ———————————————————————

Feminist Justificatory Strategies

Sandra Harding

EPISTEMOLOGIES AND JUSTIFICATORY STRATEGIES

*I*n the last 15 years, feminist-inspired research in the natural and social sciences has challenged many beliefs that had been thought to be well-supported by empirical evidence and, therefore, to be free of sexism and androcentrism. No longer is it noncontroversial to assume that "man the hunter" created human culture, that females are an evolutionary drag on the species, that human families and human sexuality are precultural and outside history, that women's destinies are determined by biology but men's are determined by history, and so forth. This paper is not about these substantive shifts in scientific belief, but about the strategies used to justify the new claims.

Epistemologies—theories of knowledge—are one kind of justificatory strategy. Epistemologies make normative claims; they tell us that one should do *x* to obtain the best kinds of belief. Traditionally they have appealed to such notions as divine revelation, common sense, observations, certainty, verifiability, and falsifiability. But justificatory strategies need make no normative claims or, indeed, any claims at all. If one is powerful enough, one can gain legitimacy for one's views by having one's critics put to death in the dark of the night, or by denying literacy to potential critics—both common ways to "justify" one's beliefs in the past as well as today. In either case, one's own claims are left "justified" by default. More attractive strategies could include social practices that would maximize participatory democracy in the production of belief, and—since power corrupts in science as well as in other forms of politics—even ones that would weight more heavily a belief's fit with the goals of a culture's "lease-advantaged" persons.

Here I want to reflect on the emergence from the natural and social sciences of two conflicting feminist epistemologies: how each is embedded in a different justificatory strategy, and how each undermines the nonfeminist, traditional epistemology from which it borrows. I begin by posing a problem to which these epistemologies

189

provide responses so that we can see how these theories of knowledge arise in the context of challenges to controversial claims.

AN EPISTEMOLOGICAL PROBLEM FOR FEMINISM

Feminism is a political movement for social change. Viewed from the perspective of the assumptions of science's self-understanding, "feminist knowledge," "feminist science," and "feminist philosophy of science" should be contradictions in terms. Scientific knowledge-seeking is supposed to be value-neutral, objective, dispassionate, and disinterested. It is supposed to be protected from political interests by the norms of science. These norms are said to include commitments to, and well-tested sociological and logical methods for, maintaining rigid separations between the goals of "special-interest" political movements (as feminism is often perceived) and the conduct of scientific research. Of course, a few people familiar with the history or practices of science really believe these sociological and logical norms have ever been effective. Nevertheless, for better or worse, appeal to these norms serves as a resource to justify whatever social relations and logical habits the scientific community in fact practices.

However, some social scientists and biologists have made claims that clearly have been produced through research guided by feminist concerns. Many of these claims appear more plausible (better sup-ported, more reliable, less false, more likely to be confirmed by evidence, etc.) than the beliefs they would replace. These claims appear to increase the objectivity of our understandings of nature and social life. I alluded to some of these claims earlier—the ones about the evolutionary importance of gathering activities and of female activities more generally, about the social construction of families and of sexuali-ties, and so forth. (While one need not find any particular claim more plausible than the beliefs it would replace, one must find *some* such feminist-inspired claim or other more plausible, less false, more likely to be confirmed by evidence, etc. in order to enter the discourse of this essay. It is the justification of this kind of claim that is at issue. If you cannot find *any* scientific claim generated by feminist-inspired research to be reasonable, then do not waste your time reading further!)

These claims raise fundamental epistemological questions. How can politicized inquiry be increasing the objectivity of our explanations and understandings? On what grounds should these claims be justi-fied? What are the accounts of the processes of objective inquiry that will explain the apparently bizarre phenomenon of politically guided research producing more adequate explanations, less biased results of inquiry? An examination of the reports of this research reveals two

main justificational strategies. Each of these responses to the epistemological questions has its virtues and its problems. Each also reveals
more clearly than have other critiques the problems in the "parental
discourse" on which each draws.

FEMINIST EMPIRICISM

The argument here is that it is social biases—sexism and
androcentrism—that are responsible for the false claims that have been
made in biology and the social sciences. Sexism and androcentrism are
prejudices that arise from false beliefs (ones that originate in supersti-
tion, custom, ignorance, or miseducation) and from hostile attitudes.
They enter research particularly at the stage of the identification of
scientific problems, but also in the design of research and the collection
and interpretation of evidence. Researchers can eliminate sexism and
androcentrism by stricter adherence to the existing methodological
norms of inquiry. It is "bad science" that is responsible for the sexist
and androcentric results of research. Movements for social liberation
"make it possible for people to see the world in an enlarged perspective
because they remove the covers and blinders that obscure knowledge
and observation." (Millman and Kanter 1975, p. vii.) Thus the women's
movement creates the opportunity for such an enlarged perspective.
Furthermore, the women's movement creates more women scientists
and more feminist scientists (both male and female feminists) who are
more likely than are sexists to notice androcentric biases. These
considerations explain how it is that this kind of politically guided
research can produce less biased results.

This epistemology has great strengths. Its appeal is obvious: many
of the claims emerging from feminist research in biology and the social
sciences are capable of accumulating better empirical support than the
claims they replace. This research better meets the overt standards of
"good science" than do the purportedly gender-blind studies. Should
not the weight of this empirical support be valued more highly than the
ideal of "value-neutrality" that was advanced, we are told, only in order
to increase empirical support for hypotheses? It is not that all feminist
claims are automatically preferable because they are feminist; rather,
when the results of such research show good empirical support, the fact
that they were produced through politically guided research should not
count against them. Moreover, feminist empiricism leaves intact
empiricist understandings of the principles of scientific inquiry that are
de rigeur for most practicing natural and social scientists. It appears to
challenge only the incomplete way empiricism has been practiced, not
the norms of empiricism themselves: science bereft of feminist guid-

ance does not rigorously enough adhere to its own norms. Further-more, one can appeal to historical precedents to increase the plausi-bility of this kind of claim. After all, wasn't it the bourgeois revolution of the fifteenth to seventeenth centuries that made it possible for early modern thinkers to see the world in an enlarged perspective, because this great social revolution from feudalism to modernism removed the covers and blinders that obscured earlier knowledge-seeking and obser-vation? Wasn't the proletarian revolution of the late nineteenth and early twentieth centuries responsible for yet one more leap in the objectivity of knowledge claims as it permitted an understanding of the effects of class relations on social relations and on our beliefs? Doesn't the post-1960s deconstruction of European and U.S. colonialism have positive effects on the growth of scientific knowledge? From this perspective, the contemporary women's movement is bringing about the most recent of these revolutions, each of which moves us yet closer to achieving the goals of the creators of science.

However, further consideration reveals that the feminist com-ponent deeply undercuts the assumptions of empiricism in several ways. In the first place, empiricism insists that the social identity of the observer is irrelevant to the "goodness" of the results of research. It is not supposed to make a difference to the explanatory power, objec-tivity, etc., of the results of research if the inquirer and his or her community of scientists are white or Black, American or Japanese, bourgeois or proletarian, masculine or feminine, sexist or feminist in social origin. Scientific method is supposed to be a reliable way to prevent the social interests of the scientist and his or her community of peers from biasing the results of research. But feminist empiricism argues that women (or feminists) as a group are more likely than men (or nonfeminists) as a group to produce unbiased, objective results of inquiry, and especially in the context of a women's movement. Feminist empiricism inadvertently reveals that empiricism has no conceptual space for recognizing that humans are fundamentally constituted by their positions in the relational networks of social life. For empiricism, humans appear as socially isolated individuals who are here and there contingently collected into social bundles we call cultures. Feminist empiricism challenges this metaphysics, epistemology, and politics by asserting that individuals are fundamentally women or men, feminists or (intentional or unintentional) sexists, as well as members of class, racial, and cultural groups. We live at distinctive historical moments, some of which have and some of which do not have a women's movement in the environment; our locations in these various kinds of historical and social relations give us different potentials for acquiring knowledge. The experience against which scientific hypotheses are tested is always historically specific social experience. Thus a "feminist biologist" is not a contradiction in terms, but a reasonable ideal of an objective observer. In an important sense, the legitimate scientific claims should be those with certain kinds of socially identifiable "authors."

In the second place, the biology and social science literatures show that a key origin of androcentric bias appears to lie in the selection of phenomena to be investigated in the first place, and in the definition of what is problematic about these phenomena. (See, e.g., Bleir 1984, Keller 1982, Lowe and Hubbard 1983, Millman and Kanter 1975.) But empiricism insists that its methodological norms are meant to apply only to the "context of justification," not to the "context of discovery" where problems are identified and defined. We are supposed to consider the origins of hypotheses irrelevant to the process of scientific inquiry; whether hypotheses come to one from sun worshipping, from moral or political interests and desires, or from the recognition of cognitive problems in the beliefs of one's scientific ancestors and peers should not matter. Scientific method will eliminate any social biases as a hypothesis goes through rigorous tests. But feminist empiricism argues that scientific method is not sufficient to do this; that an androcentric picture of nature and social life emerges from the testing only of hypotheses generated by what nonfeminists (that is, sexists or at least androcentrists) find problematic in the world around them. Missing from the set of alternative hypotheses nonfeminists consider are the ones that would most deeply challenge androcentric beliefs, ones that emerge to consciousness and appear plausible only from a feminist understanding of the gendered character of social experience. Thus the origins of scientific hypotheses do affect the collective results of scientific research.

Finally, appearances to the contrary, feminist empiricism is ambivalent about the potency of science's norms and methods to eliminate androcentric biases. While attempting to fit feminist research within these norms and methods, it also points to the fact that without the assistance of feminism, science's norms and methods regularly failed to detect these biases.

Thus feminist empiricism intensifies recent tendencies in the philosophy and social studies of science to problematize fundamental empiricist assumptions. It challenges the desirability of defining legitimate scientific claims as only those for which socially anonymous authorship is asserted. It questions the assumption that the origin of scientific problems has no effect on the results of research. It doubts the power to maximize objectivity of a scientific method that is supposedly committed to value-freedom. I have been arguing that feminist empiricism creates a misfit, an incoherence, between the substantive scientific claims of feminist-guided research and its own strategies to justify these claims. It is recognition of this incoherence that has lead to the development of the next feminist epistemology I shall discuss, the feminist standpoint approaches.

The Feminist Standpoint

This justificatory approach originates in Hegel's insight into the relationship between the master and the slave, and in the development of Hegel's analysis into the proletarian standpoint by Marx, Engels, and Lukacs. (Marx 1964, 1970; Engels 1972; Lukacs 1971. The feminist standpoint epistemologies are developed in Hartsock 1983; Rose 1982; Smith 1987; and Harding 1983.) The argument here is that human activity not only structures but also sets limits on understanding. If social activity is structured in fundamentally opposing ways for two different groups, "one can expect that the vision of each will represent an inversion of the other, and in systems of domination the vision available to the rulers will be both partial and perverse" (Hartsock 1983, p. 285). Those theorists observe that knowledge is supposed to be based on experience. Thus, the reason the feminist claims can turn out to be scientifically preferable is that they originate in, and are tested against, a more complete and less distorting kind of social experience. The experience arising from the activities assigned to women, seen through feminist theory, provide a grounding for potentially more complete and less distorted knowledge claims than do men's experiences. This kind of politicized inquiry increases the objectivity of the results of research.

Consider Dorothy Smith's form of the argument. (She writes about sociology, but her argument can be generalized to all sciences, including natural science, though this claim requires a more extended argument than I can present here.) In our society, women have been assigned kinds of work that men do not want to do. Several aspects of this division of activity by gender have consequences for how knowledge can be generated. "Women's work" relieves men of the need to take care of their bodies and of the local places where men exist—their environments. It frees men to immerse themselves in the world of abstract concepts. The labor of women thereby "articulates" and shapes men's concepts of the world into those appropriate for managing other people's work—for administrative work. Moreover, the more successfully women perform our work, the more invisible does it become to men. Men who are relieved of the need to maintain their own bodies and the local places where these bodies exist can now see as real only what corresponds to their abstracted mental world. Men see "women's work" not as real human activity—self-chosen and consciously willed—but only as natural activity, an instinctual labor of love. Women are thus excluded from men's conceptions of culture. Furthermore, women's actual experiences of our own activities are incomprehensible and inexpressible within the distorted abstractions of men's conceptual schemes. Western thought alienates women from our own experiences.

However, for women sociologists, a "line of fault" opens up between their experiences and the dominant conceptual schemes. Smith points out that this disjuncture is the break along which much major work in the women's movement has focused. The politics of the women's movement has drawn attention to the lack of fit between women's experience and the dominant conceptual schemes. It is to the "bifurcated consciousness" of women researchers, who benefit from the politics of the women's movement (and presumably, to those who see the world from their perspectives), that we can attribute the greater adequacy of the results of feminist inquiry. Looking at nature and social relations from the perspective of administrative "men's work" can provide only partial and distorted understandings. (Of course, only white, western, professional/managerial class men are in general permitted this work, though it holds a cental place in more widespread ideals of masculinity.) Research *for* women must recover the understanding of women, men, and social relations available from the perspective of women's activities.

To give an example Smith discusses, the concept "housework," which appears in historial, sociological, and economic studies and is part of what liberal philosophers include in the "private" (vs. the "public"), at least recognizes that what women do at home is neither instinctual activity nor necessarily always a labor of love. However, it inaccurately conceptualizes the activity assigned to women in our society on the model of men's activities, which are divided into paid work and leisure. Is housework work? Yes! However, it has no fixed hours or responsibilities, no qualifications, wages, days off for sickness, retirement, or retirement benefits. Is it leisure? No, though even under the worst of conditions it has rewarding and rejuvenating aspects. As social scientists and liberal political philosophers use the term, "housework" includes raising one's children, entertaining friends, caring for loved ones, and other activities not appropriately understood through the wage-labor vs. leisure construct. Smith argues that this activity should be understood through concepts that arise from women's experience of it, not through concepts selected to account for men's experience of *their* work. Moreover, our understanding of men's activities also is distorted by reliance on conceptual schemes arising only from administrative-class men's experiences. How would our understanding of love, warfare, or how universities operate be expanded and transformed if it were structured by questions and concepts arising from those activities assigned predominantly to women that make possible the ways men participate in love, warfare, and higher education?

Women's distinctive social activities provide the possibility for more complete and less perverse human understanding—but only the possibility. Feminism provides the theory and motivation for inquiry, and the direction of political struggle through which increasingly more adequate descriptions are produced of the underlying causal tendencies of male domination. Only through feminist inquiry and struggle can the perspective of women be transformed into a feminist standpoint—a morally and scientifically preferable site from which to observe, explain, and design social life.

Standpoint theories have the virtue of providing a general theory of the greater objectivity that can result from research that begins in questions arising from the perspective of women's activities; a general theory that regards this perspective as an important part of the data on which the evidence for all knowledge claims should be based. This theory of knowledge resolves more satisfactorily certain problems within feminist empiricism. It sets within a larger social theory its explanation of the importance of the origin of scientific problems (of the "context of discovery") for the eventual picture of science. It eschews blind allegiance to scientific method, observing that no method, at least in the sciences' sense of this term, is powerful enough to eliminate kinds of social bias that are as widely held as in the scientific community itself. Moreover, it draws attention to why feminist politics can be a valuable guide in scientific inquiry, and to the way in which sexist politics is inherently anti-scientific (its focus on the "line of fault").

Before turning to the problems with the feminist standpoint epistemology, I draw attention to two points. First, the feminist standpoint, like feminist empiricism, clearly asserts that objectivity never has been and could not be increased by the exclusion or elimination of social values from inquiry—at least not in the cultures in which science has existed and in which it will exist in the foreseeable future. Instead, it is commitment to anti-authoritarianism, anti-elitism, and anti-domination tendencies that has increased the objectivity of science and will continue to do so. The emergence of modern science itself can be accounted for in these terms, as can later leaps in our understandings of nature and social life (Van den Daele 1977; Zilsel 1942).

Moreover, one might be tempted to relativist defenses of feminist claims on standpoint grounds. However, this temptation should be resisted. One cannot simply add to the claim that the earth is flat the hypothesis that the earth is round. Analogously, feminist inquirers are never saying that sexist and anti-sexist claims are equally plausible—for example, that it's equally plausible to regard women's situation as primarily biological and as primarily social. Historically, relativism appears as an intellectual possibility, and as a "problem," only for dominating groups at the point where the legitimacy and hegemony of their views is being challenged. Relativism as an intellectual position or a "problem" is fundamentally a moral and political issue, not a cognitive or logical issue, as traditional philosophy of science and epistemology discourses would have it.

There are several kinds of issues raised by this standpoint epistemology. Like feminist empiricism, the feminist standpoint reveals key problems in its parental discourse. Where Marxism insisted that sexism was entirely a consequence of class relations, a problem within only the superstructural social institutions and bourgeois ideology, the standpoint theorists see gender relations as at least as causal as economic relations in creating forms of social life and belief. More accurately, in sexist cultures, all gender relations have economic consequences and all economic relations have gender consequences. Like feminist empiricism, the standpoint approach takes women and men to be fundamentally "gender classes." In contrast to Marxism, women and men are not merely (or perhaps even primarily) members of economic classes, though class (like race and culture) does mediate our opportunities to gain empirically preferable understandings of nature and social life.

Another issue arises when we ask how effective the standpoint theories are as justificatory strategies. After all, a justificatory strategy is intended to convince. Those wedded to empiricism (those who are resistant to countenancing the possibility that the social identity of the observer can be an important variable in the potential objectivity of the results of research) are likely to find feminist empiricism at least mildly plausible, but the feminist standpoint beyond the pale. One might counter this resistance in two ways. One could point out that it is not just feminists who claim that the best scientists are those with certain social characteristics. After all, empiricist practices create distinctive kinds of social persons as scientists. Science takes young folks who are often eager to pursue science as a moral calling, and it transforms them into something quite different—professionals, who have been systematically trained to be preoccupied only with instrumental rationality. They are trained to justify their activity in mechanical terms though they have been attracted into a scientific career by a vision of knowledge seeking in the service of social progress (Kuhn 1970). This personality structure—cool, dispassionate, socially unengaged—marks a distinctive kind of social person. It does not indicate the absence of a person, but the presence of a certain kind of person. Thus empiricism is wrong to claim that only feminism argues for certain kinds of social persons as scientists; empiricists do, too. So the standpoint theorists are reasonable to ask if the empiricists' ideal scientists are the best kinds of social persons to "author" scientific claims.

Moreover, one might also point out that the novelty of an epistemology provides no guide to its eventual fate. After all, Descartes,

Locke, Hume, and Kant were not uncontroversial thinkers in their own days, but today their views provide much of the "folk wisdom"—certainly not the *critical* theory—of modern, western cultures. Nevertheless, this strategic problem with the standpoint epistemologies is a main reason that feminist empiricism has appeared to be a more powerful resource within biology and the social sciences for grounding feminist knowledge claims—in spite of the internal contradictions I pointed out in that approach.

Yet another set of questions about the feminist standpoint arises from the feminist critiques of Enlightenment assumptions. Feminist postmodernists ask whether there should be feminist sciences and epistemologies at all. Is it realistic to imagine that the western science traditions can be harnessed in ways that will advance women's situations? Jane Flax locates the mainstream origins of postmodernism in such otherwise diverse thinkers as Nietzsche, Derrida, Foucault, Lacan, Rorty, Cavell, Feyerabend, Gadamer, Wittgenstein, and Unger, and in such otherwise disparate discourses as those of semiotics, deconstruction, psychoanalysis, structuralism, archeology/geneology, and nihilism. She points out that these thinkers and movements "share a profound skepticism regarding universal (or universalizing) claims about the existence, nature and powers of reason, progress, science, language and the 'subject/self'" (Flax 1987). The nonfeminist expositions of postmodernism frequently are preoccupied with the issue of just what postmodernism is. Does it mark the end of the intellectual assumptions of the post-romantic literary and art worlds, or perhaps even of the consciousness explored by Locke and Kant? Does postmodernism arise to replace modernism, or is it only a necessary moment in the cycles of modernism? Are its fundamental political tendencies progressive or regressive? Feminist postmodernism does not resolve these issues, though a lengthier exposition than the present one could show how it poses some of them more sharply.

In feminist hands, this theoretical tendency to criticize Enlightenment assumptions has a number of different foci originating in the different intellectual and political projects of its authors. One focus that is important for our purposes here is the criticism of the idea that the feminist mind, like the Enlightenment one about which Richard Rorty and other nonfeminist postmodernists are skeptical, is a glassy mirror that can reflect a world that is ready-made and "out there" for the reflecting. Instead, feminist claims should be held not as "approximations to truth" that can be woven into a seamless web of representation of the world "out there," but as permanently partial instigators of rupture, of rents and unravelings in the dominant schemes of representation. From this perspective, if there can be "a" feminist standpoint, it can only be what emerges from the political struggles of "oppositional consciousness"—oppositional precisely to the longing for "one true story" that has been the psychic motor for western science. Once the Archimedean, transhistorical agent of knowledge is deconstructed into constantly shifting, wavering, recombining, historical groups, then the world that can be understood and navigated with the assistance of Archimedes's map of perfect perspective also disappears. As Jane Flax puts the issue,

> perhaps "reality" can have "a" structure only from the falsely universalizing perspective of the master. That is, only to the extent that one person or group can dominate the whole, can "reality" appear to be governed by one set of rules or be constituted by one privileged set of social relationships (Flax 1987).

However, even if the feminist postmodernists are right, there will be no safety for those who might be tempted to retreat back to the justificatory strategies of feminist empiricism or to prefeminist grounds for knowledge claims. After all, these kinds of postmodernist criticisms are even more powerful against those epistemologies, since the latter are even more firmly grounded in Englightenment assumptions than are the feminist standpoint approaches. This is an extraordinary moment in history when no traditional assumptions appear to be immune to reasonable criticism. The feminist postmodern critiques show us how our theories of knowledge must even more radically break with many of the assumptions that underly not only traditional views of western science, but also feminist attempts to improve scientific inquiry.

But do they require the abandonment not only of mainstream western scientific projects, but also of feminist attempts to generate less false and distorting images of nature and social relations? My answer is "no"; paradoxically, feminist postmodernism itself has a positive epistemological program. It, too, wants to produce less false and distorting images of nature and social relations for purposes of social progress. It can be understood to be arguing that feminist standpoint approaches simply haven't gone far enough in this respect. It does indeed pose a radical alternative to the standpoint theories and also, of course, to feminist empiricism. To defend these claims and explore further these important issues requires consideration of a more complex set of issues than is possible here. (See Harding 1989 and the collection that contains it.)

CONCLUSION

Meanwhile, how should we justify the less false and less distorting results of research that feminist-inspired inquiry is producing? The two theories of knowledge discussed have different strengths and weaknesses. Once we conceptualize an epistemology as a kind of justificatory strategy, we are led to think of justifiers, of audiences for those justifications, and of contexts and purposes of justification. Feminist empiricism, the feminist standpoint theory—indeed, feminist postmodernism, too—assume different speakers, audiences, contexts and purposes for their analyses. I think feminists cannot afford to give up any of the quite different projects to which these analyses respond. In a world so deeply permeated by scientific rationality, we need feminist empiricism to degender as far as it can the science we have. In a world in which that scientific rationality advances partial and distorted understandings of nature and social relations, we need feminist standpoint approaches to reveal the relationship between the social activities in which traditional scientists engage and the kinds of partial and distorting beliefs those activities produce. In a world where science has far too intimate links to power, we need to take seriously postmodernist skepticism about the relationship between knowledge and power in the worlds in which we live and in the ones we hope for and plan.

NOTE

This paper was originally prepared for the session on "Women and the Epistemology of Science" at the December 1985 Eastern Division meetings of the American Philosophical Association. The issues raised by this paper are discussed more fully in *The Science Question in Feminism* (Cornell University Press and Open University Press, 1986; forthcoming in Italian and German translations). Other versions of this discussion have subsequently been published in other places (see, e.g., Harding 1987a). Research for this essay was supported by the National Science Foundation, a Mina Shaughnessy Fellowship from the Fund for the Improvement of Post-Secondary Education, a Mellon Fellowship at the Center for Research on Women at Wellesley, and a University of Delaware Faculty Research Grant.

REFERENCES

Bleier, R. 1984. *Science and Gender: A Critique of Biology and Its Theories on Women.* New York: Pergamon Press.

Engels, F. 1972. "Socialism: Utopian and Scientific." In *The Marx and Engels Reader*, ed. R. Tucker. New York: Norton.

Flax, J. 1987. "Postmodernism and Gender Relations in Feminist Theory." *Signs: Journal of Women in Culture and Society* Vol. 12, no. 4.

Harding, S. 1989. "Feminism, Science, and the Anti-Enlightenment Critique." In *Feminism/Postmodernism*, L. Nicholson, ed. New York: Methuen/ Routledge & Kegan Paul.

———. 1986. *The Science Question in Feminism*. Ithaca: Cornell University Press; Milton Keynes: Open University Press.

———. 1987a. *Feminism and Methodology: Social Science Issues*. Bloomington: Indiana University Press.

———. 1987b. "Feminism and Theories of Scientific Knowledge." *American Philosophical Association Feminism and Philosophy Newsletter*, no. 1.

———. 1983. "Why Has the Sex/Gender System Become Visible Only Now?" In Harding and Hintikka.

——— and M. Hintikka, eds. 1983. *Discovering Reality: Feminist Perspectives on Epistemology, Metaphysics, Methodology and Philosophy of Science*. Dordrecht: Reidel Publishing Co.

——— and J. O'Barr, eds. 1987. *Sex and Scientific Inquiry*. Chicago: University of Chicago Press.

Hartsock, N. 1983 "The Feminist Standpoint: Developing the Ground for a Specifically Feminist Historical Materialism." In Harding and Hintikka. See also her "Chapter 10" in *Money, Sex and Power*. Boston: Northeastern University Press.

Keller, E. F. 1984. *Reflections on Gender and Science*. New Haven: Yale University Press.

Kuhn, T. S. 1970. *The Structure of Scientific Revolution.* Chicago: University of Chicago Press.

Lowe, M. and R. Hubbard, eds. 1983. *Woman's Nature: Rationalizations of Inequality*. New York: Pergamon Press.

Lukacs, G. 1971. *History and Class Consciousness*. Cambridge: The MIT Press.

Marx, K. 1984. *Economic and Philosophic Manuscripts of 1844*. Edited by Dirk Struik. New York: International Publishers.

———. 1970. *The German Ideology*. Edited by C. J. Arthur, New York: International Publishers.

Millman, M. and R. M. Kanter, eds. 1975. *Another Voice: Feminist Perspectives on Social Life and Social Science*. New York: Anchor Books.

Rose, H. 1983. "Hand, Brain and Heart: A Feminist Epistemology for the Natural Sciences." *Signs: Journal of Women in Culture and Society* 9:1.

Smith, D. 1987. *The Everyday World as Problematic*. Boston: Northeastern University Press.

Chapter 12 ——————————————

Can There Be A Feminist Science?

Helen E. Longino

I

The question of this title conceals multiple ambiguities. Not only do the sciences consist of many distinct fields, but the term "science" can be used to refer to a method of inquiry, a historically changing collection of practices, a body of knowledge, a set of claims, a profession, a set of social groups, etc. And as the sciences are many, so are the scholarly disciplines that seek to understand them: philosophy, history, sociology, anthropology, psychology. Any answer from the perspective of some one of these disciplines will, then, of necessity, be partial. In this essay, I shall be asking about the possibility of theoretical natural science that is feminist and I shall ask from the perspective of a philosopher. Before beginning to develop my answer, however, I want to review some of the questions that could be meant, in order to arrive at the formulation I wish to address.

The question could be interpreted as factual, one to be answered by pointing to what feminists in the sciences are doing and saying: "Yes, and this is what it is." Such a response can be perceived as question-begging, however. Even such a friend of feminism as Stephen Gould dismisses the idea of a distinctively feminist or even female contribution to the sciences. In a generally positive review of Ruth Bleier's book, *Science and Gender*, Gould (1984) brushes aside her connection between women's attitudes and values and the interactionist science she calls for. Scientists (male, of course) are already proceeding with wholist and interactionist research programs. Why, he implied, should women or feminists have any particular, distinctive, contributions to make? There is not masculinist and feminist science, just good and bad science. The question of a feminist science cannot be settled by pointing, but involves a deeper, subtler investigation.

Source: First published in *Hypatia* 2, 3 (fall 1987): 51–64. Copyright © 1987 by Helen E. Longino. Reprinted with permission.

The deeper question can itself have several meanings. One set of meanings is sociological, the other conceptual. The sociological meaning proceeds as follows. We know what sorts of social conditions make misogynist science possible. The work of Margaret Rossiter (1982) on the history of women scientists in the United States and the work of Kathryn Addelson (1983) on the social structure of professional science detail the relations between a particular social structure for science and the kinds of science produced. What sorts of social conditions would make feminist science possible? This is an important question, one I am not equipped directly to investigate, although what I can investigate is, I believe, relevant to it. This is the second, conceptual, interpretation of the question: what sort of sense does it make to talk about a feminist science? Why is the question itself not an oxymoron, linking, as it does, values and ideological commitment with the idea of impersonal, objective, value-free, inquiry? This is the problem I wish to address in this essay.

The hope for a feminist theoretical natural science has concealed an ambiguity between content and practice. In the content sense the idea of a feminist science involves a number of assumptions and calls a number of visions to mind. Some theorists have written as though a feminist science is one the theories of which encode a particular world view, characterized by complexity, interaction and wholism. Such a science is said to be feminist because it is the expression and valorization of a female sensibility or cognitive temperament. Alternatively, it is claimed that women have certain traits (dispositions to attend to particulars, interactive rather than individualist and controlling social attitudes and behaviors) that enable them to understand the true character of natural processes (which are complex and interactive).[1] While proponents of this interactionist view see it as an improvement over most contemporary science, it has also been branded as soft— misdescribed as nonmathematical. Women in the sciences who feel they are being asked to do not better science, but inferior science, have responded angrily to this characterization of feminist science, thinking that it is simply new clothing for the old idea that women can't do science. I think that the interactionist view can be defended against this response, although that requires rescuing it from some of its proponents as well. However, I also think that the characterization of feminist science as the expression of a distinctive female cognitive temperament has other drawbacks. It first conflates feminine with feminist. While it is important to reject the traditional derogation of the virtues assigned to women, it is also important to remember that women are *constructed* to occupy positions of social subordinates. We should not uncritically embrace the feminine.

This characterization of feminist science is also a version of recently propounded notions of a "women's standpoint" or a "feminist stand-point" and suffers from the same suspect universalization that these ideas suffer from. If there is one such standpoint, there are many: as María Lugones and Elizabeth Spelman spell out in their tellingly entitled article, "Have We Got a Theory for You: Feminist Theory, Cultural Imperialism, and the Demand for 'The Woman's Voice,'" women are too diverse in our experiences to generate a single cognitive framework (Lugones and Spelman 1983). In addition, the sciences are themselves too diverse for me to think that they might be equally transformed by such a framework. To reject this concept of a feminist science, however, is not to disengage science from feminism. I want to suggest that we focus on science as practice rather than content, as process rather than product; hence, not on feminist science, but on doing science as a feminist.

The doing of science involves many practices: how one structures a laboratory (hierarchically or collectively), how one relates to other scientists (competitively or cooperatively), how and whether one en-gages in political struggles over affirmative action. It extends also to intellectual practices, to the activities of scientific inquiry, such as observation and reasoning. Can there be a feminist scientific inquiry? This possibility is seen to be problematic against the background of certain standard presuppositions about science. The claim that there could be a feminist science in the sense of an intellectual practice is either nonsense because oxymoronic as suggested above or the claim is interpreted to mean that established science (science as done and dominated by men) is wrong about the world. Feminist science in this latter interpretation is presented as correcting the errors of masculine, standard science and as revealing the truth that is hidden by masculine "bad" science, as taking the sex out of science.

Both of these interpretations involve the rejection of one approach as incorrect and the embracing of the other as the way to a truer understanding of the natural world. Both trade one absolutism for another. Each is a side of the same coin, and that coin, I think, is the idea of a value-free science. This is the idea that scientific methodology guarantees the independence of scientific inquiry from values or value-related considerations. A science or a scientific research program informed by values is *ipso facto* "bad science." "Good science" is inquiry protected by methodology from values and ideology. This same idea underlies Gould's response to Bleier, so it bears closer scrutiny. In the pages that follow, I shall examine the idea of value-free science and then apply the result of that examination to the idea of feminist scientific inquiry.

II

I distinguish two kinds of values relevant to the sciences. Constitutive values, internal to the sciences, are the source of the rules determining what constitutes acceptable scientific practice or scientific method. The personal, social and cultural values, those group or individual preferences about what ought to be, I call contextual values, to indicate that they belong to the social and cultural context in which science is done (Longino 1983c). The traditional interpretation of the value-freedom of modern natural science amounts to a claim that its constitutive and contextual features are clearly distinct from and independent of one another, that contextual values play no role in the inner workings of scientific inquiry, in reasoning and observation. I shall argue that this construal of the distinction cannot be maintained.

There are several ways to develop such an argument. One scholar is fond of inviting her audience to visit any science library and peruse the titles on the shelves. Observe how subservient to social and cultural interests are the inquiries represented by the book titles alone! Her listeners would soon abandon their ideas about the value-neutrality of the sciences, she suggests. This exercise may indeed show the influence of external, contextual considerations on what research gets done/ supported (i.e., on problem selection). It does not show that such considerations affect reasoning or hypothesis acceptance. The latter would require detailed investigation of particular cases or a general conceptual argument. The conceptual arguments involve developing some version of what is known in philosophy of science as the underdetermination thesis, i.e., the thesis that a theory is always underdetermined by the evidence adduced in its support, with the consequence that different or incompatible theories are supported by or at least compatible with the same body of evidence. I shall sketch a version of the argument that appeals to features of scientific inference.

One of the rocks on which the logical positivist program foundered was the distinction between theoretical and observational language. Theoretical statements contain, as fundamental descriptive terms, terms that do not occur in the description of data. Thus, hypotheses in particle physics contain terms like "electron," "pion," "muon," "electron spin," etc. The evidence for a hypothesis such as "A pion decays sequentially into a muon, then a positron" is obviously not direct observations of pions, muons and positrons, but consists largely in photographs taken in large and complex experimental apparati: accelerators, cloud chambers, bubble chambers. The photographs show all sorts of squiggly lines and spirals. Evidence for the hypotheses of particle physics is presented as statements that describe these photographs. Eventually, of course, particle physicists point to a spot on a photograph and say things like "Here a neutrino hits a neutron." Such an assertion, how-ever, is an interpretive achievement that involves collapsing theoretical and observational moments. A skeptic would have to be supplied a complicated argument linking the elements of the photograph to traces left by particles themselves. What counts as theory and what as data in a pragmatic sense change over time, as some ideas and experimental procedures come to be securely embedded in a particular framework and others take their place on the horizons. As the history of physics shows, however, secure embeddedness is no guarantee against over-throw.

Logical positivists and their successors hoped to model scientific inference formally. Evidence of hypotheses, data, were to be repre-sented as logical consequences of hypotheses. When we try to map this logical structure onto the sciences, however, we find that hypotheses are, for the most part, not just generalizations of data statements. The links between data and theory, therefore, cannot be adequately repre-sented as formal or syntactic, but are established by means of assump-tions that make or imply substantive claims about the field over which one theorizes. Theories are confirmed via the confirmation of their constituent hypotheses, so the confirmation of hypotheses and theories is relative to the assumptions relied upon in asserting the evidential connection. Conformation of such assumptions, which are often un-articulated, is itself subject to similar relativization. And it is these assumptions that can be the vehicle for the involvement of considera-tions motivated primarily by contextual values (Longino 1979, 1983a).

The point of this extremely telescoped argument is that one can't give an a priori specification of confirmation that effectively eliminates the role of value-laden assumptions in legitimate scientific inquiry without eliminating auxiliary hypotheses (assumptions) altogether. This is not to say that all scientific reasoning involves value-related assumptions. Sometimes auxiliary assumptions will be supported by mundane inductive reasoning. But sometimes they will not be. In any given case, they may be metaphysical in character; they may be untestable with present investigative techniques; they may be rooted in contextual, value-related considerations. If, however, there is no a priori way to eliminate such assumptions from evidential reasoning generally, and, hence, no way to rule out value-laden assumptions, then there is no formal basis for arguing that an inference mediated by contextual values is thereby bad science.

A comparable point is made by some historians investigating the origins of modern science. James Jacob (1977) and Margaret Jacob (1976) have, in a series of articles and books, argued that the adoption of conceptions of matter by 17th century scientists like Robert Boyle was inextricably intertwined with political considerations. Conceptions of matter provided the foundation on which physical theories were developed and Boyle's science, regardless of his reasons for it, has been fruitful in ways that far exceed his imaginings. If the presence of contextual influences were grounds for disallowing a line of inquiry, then early modern science would not have gotten off the ground.

The conclusion of this line of argument is that constitutive values conceived as epistemological (i.e., truth-seeking) are not adequate to screen out the influence of contextual values in the very structuring of scientific knowledge. Now the ways in which contextual values do, if they do, influence this structuring and interact, if they do, with constitutive values has to be determined separately for different theories and fields of science. But this argument, if it's sound, tells us that this sort of inquiry is perfectly respectable and involves no shady assumptions or unargued intuitively based rejections of positivism. It also opens the possibility that one can make explicit value commitments and still do "good" science. The conceptual argument doesn't show that all science is value-laden (as opposed to metaphysics-laden) —that must be established on a case-by-case basis, using the tools not just of logic and philosophy but of history and sociology as well. It does show that not all science is value-free and, more importantly, that it is not necessarily in the nature of science to be value-free. If we reject that idea we're in a better position to talk about the possibilities of feminist science.

III

In earlier articles (Longino 1981, 1983b; Longino and Doell 1983), I've used similar considerations to argue that scientific objectivity has to be reconceived as a function of the communal structure of scientific inquiry rather than as a property of individual scientists. I've then used these notions about scientific methodology to show that science displaying masculine bias is not *ipso facto* improper or "bad" science; that the fabric of science can neither rule out the expression of bias nor legitimate it. So I've argued that both the expression of masculine bias in the sciences and feminist criticism of research exhibiting that bias are—shall we say—business as usual; that scientific inquiry should be expected to display the deep metaphysical and normative commitments of the culture in which it flourishes; and finally that criticism of the deep assumptions that guide scientific reasoning about data is a proper part of science.

The argument I've just offered about the idea of a value-free science is similar in spirit to those earlier arguments. I think it makes it possible to see these questions from a slightly different angle.

There is a tradition of viewing scientific inquiry as somehow inexorable. This involves supposing that the phenomena of the natural world are fixed in determinate relations with each other, that these relations can be known and formulated in a consistent and unified way. This is not the old "unified science" idea of the logical positivists, with its privileging of physics. In its "unexplicated" or "pre-analytic" state, it is simply the idea that there is one consistent, integrated or coherent, true theoretical treatment of all natural phenomena. (The indeterminacy principle of quantum physics is restricted to our understanding of the behavior of certain particles that themselves underlie the fixities of the natural world. Stochastic theories reveal fixities, but fixities among ensembles rather than fixed relations among individual objects or events.) The scientific inquirer's job is to discover those fixed relations. Just as the task of Plato's philosophers was to discover the fixed relations among forms and the task of Galileo's scientists was to discover the laws written in the language of the grand book of nature, geometry, so the scientist's task in this tradition remains the discovery of fixed relations however conceived. These ideas are part of the realist tradition in the philosophy of science.

It's no longer possible, in a century that has seen the splintering of the scientific disciplines, to give such a unified description of the objects of inquiry. But the belief that the job is to discover fixed relations of some sort, and that the application of observation, experiment and reason leads ineluctably to unifiable, if not unified, knowledge of an independent reality, is still with us. It is evidenced most clearly in two features of scientific rhetoric: the use of the passive voice as in "it is concluded that . . ." or "it has been discovered that . . ." and the attribution of agency to the data, as in "the data suggest. . . ." Such language has been criticized for the abdication of responsibility it indicates. Even more, the scientific inquirer, and we with her, become passive observers, victims of the truth. The idea of a value-free science is integral to this view of scientific inquiry. And if we reject that idea we can also reject our roles as passive onlookers, helpless to affect the course of knowledge.

Let me develop this point somewhat more concretely and autobiographically. Biologist Ruth Doell and I have been examining studies in three areas of research on the influence of sex hormones on human behavior and cognitive performance: research on the influence of pre-natal, *in utero*, exposure to higher or lower than normal levels of androgens and estrogens on so-called "gender-role" behavior in children, influence of androgens (pre- and post-natal) on homosexuality in women, and influence of lower than normal (for men) levels of androgen at puberty on spatial abilities (Doell and Longino 1988).

The studies we looked at are vulnerable to criticism of their data and their observation methodologies. They also show clear evidence of androcentric bias—in the assumption that there are just two sexes and two genders (us and them), in the designation of appropriate and inappropriate behaviors for male and female children, in the caricature of lesbianism, in the assumption of male mathematical superiority. We did not find, however, that these assumptions mediated the inferences from data to theory that we found objectionable. These sexist assumptions did affect the way the data were described. What mediated the inferences from the alleged data (i.e., what functioned as auxiliary hypotheses or what provided auxiliary hypotheses) was what we called the linear model—the assumption that there is a direct one-way causal relationship between pre- or post-natal hormone levels and later behavior or cognitive performance. To put it crudely, fetal gonadal hormones organize the brain at critical periods of development. The organism is thereby disposed to respond in a range of ways to a range of environmental stimuli. The assumption of unidirectional programming is supposedly supported by the finding of such a relationship in other mammals; in particular, by experiments demonstrating the dependence of sexual behaviors—mounting and lordosis—on peri-natal hormone exposure and the finding of effects of sex hormones on the development of rodent brains. To bring it to bear on humans is to ignore, among other things, some important differences between human brains and those of other species. It also implies a willingness to regard humans in a particular way—to see us as produced by factors over which we have no control. Not only are we, as scientists, victims of the truth, but we are the prisoners of our physiology.[2] In the name of extending an explanatory model, human capacities for self-knowledge, self-reflection, self-determination are eliminated from any role in human action (at least in the behaviors studied).

Doell and I have therefore argued for the replacement of that linear model of the role of the brain in behavior by one of much greater complexity that includes physiological, environmental, historical and psychological elements. Such a model allows not only for the interaction of physiological and environmental factors but also for the interaction of these with a continuously self-modifying, self-representational (and self-organizing) central processing system. In contemporary neurobiology, the closest model is that being developed in the group selectionist approach to higher brain function of Gerald Edelman and other researchers (Edelman and Mountcastle 1978). We argue that a model of at least that degree of complexity is necessary to account for the human behaviors studies in the sex hormones and behavior research and that if gonadal hormones function at all at these levels, they will probably be found at most to facilitate or inhibit neural processing in general. The strategy we take in our argument is to show that the degree of intentionality involved in the behaviors in question is greater than is presupposed by the hormonal influence researchers and to argue that this degree of intentionality implicates the higher brain processes.

To this point Ruth Doell and I agree. I want to go further and describe what we've done from the perspective of the above philosophical discussion of scientific methodology.

Abandoning my polemical mood for a more reflective one, I want to say that, in the end, commitment to one or another model is strongly influenced by values or other contextual features. The models themselves determine the relevance and interpretation of data. The linear or complex models are not in turn independently or conclusively supported by data. I doubt for instance that value-free inquiry will reveal the efficacy or inefficacy of intentional states or of physiological factors like hormone exposure in human action. I think instead that a research program in neuroscience that assumes the linear model and sex-gender dualism will show the influence of hormone exposure on gender-role behavior. And I think that a research program in neuroscience and psychology that proceeds on the assumption that humans do possess the capacities for self-consciousness, self-reflection, and self-determination, and then asks how the structure of the human brain and nervous system enables the expression of these capacities, will reveal the efficacy of intentional states (understood as very complex sorts of brain states).

While this latter assumption does not itself contain normative terms, I think that the decision to adopt it is motivated by value-laden considerations—by the desire to understand ourselves and others as self-determining (at least some of the time), that is, as capable of acting on the basis of concepts or representations of ourselves and the world in which we act. (Such representations are not necessarily correct, they are surely mediated by our cultures; all we wish to claim is that they are efficacious.) I think further that this desire on Ruth Doell's and my part is, in several ways, an aspect of our feminism. Our preference for a neurobiological model that allows for agency, for the efficacy of intentionality, is partly a validation of our (and everyone's) subjective experience of thought, deliberation and choice. One of the tenets of feminist research is the valorization of subjective experience, and so our preference in this regard conforms to feminist research patterns. There is, however, a more direct way in which our feminism is expressed in this preference. Feminism is many things to many people, but it is at its core in part about the expansion of human potentiality. When feminists talk of breaking out and do break out of socially prescribed sex-roles, when feminists criticize the institutions of domination, we are thereby insisting on the capacity of humans—male and female—to act on preceptions of self and society and to act to bring about changes in self and society on the basis of those perceptions. (Not overnight and not by a mere act of will. The point is that we act.) And so our criticism of theories of the hormonal influence or determination of so-called gender-role behavior is not just a rejection of the sexist bias in the description of the phenomena—the behavior of the children studied, the sexual lives of lesbians, etc.—but of the limitations on human capacity imposed by the analytic model underlying such research.[3]

While the argument strategy we adopt against the linear model rests on a certain understanding of intention, the values motivating our adoption of that understanding remain hidden in that polemical context. Our political commitments, however, presuppose a certain understanding of human action, so that when faced with a conflict between these commitments and a particular model of brain-behavior relationships we allow the political commitments to guide the choice.

The relevance of my argument about value-free science should be becoming clear. Feminists—in and out of science—often condemn masculine bias in the sciences from the vantage point of commitment to a value-free science. Androcentric bias, once identified, can then be seen as a violation of the rules, as "bad" science. Feminist science, by contrast, can eliminate that bias and produce better, good, more true, or gender-free science. From that perspective the process I've just des-cribed is anathema. But if scientific methods generated by constitutive values cannnot guarantee independence from contextual values, then that approach to sexist science won't work. We cannot restrict ourselves simply to the elimination of bias, but must expand our scope to include the detection of limiting and interpretive frameworks and the finding or construction of more appropriate frameworks. We need not, indeed should not, wait for such a framework to emerge from the data. In waiting, if my argument is correct, we run the danger of working unconsciously with assumptions still laden with values from the context we seek to change. Instead of remaining passive with respect to the data and what the data suggest, we can acknowledge our ability to affect the course of knowledge and fashion or favor research programs that are consistent with the values and commitments we express in the rest of our lives. From this perspective, the idea of a value-free science is not just empty, but pernicious.

Accepting the relevance to our practice as scientists of our political commitments does not imply simple and crude impositions of those ideas onto the corner of the natural world under study. If we recognize, however, that knowledge is shaped by the assumptions, values and interests of a culture and that, within limits, one can choose one's culture, then it's clear that as scientists/theorists we have a choice. We can continue to do establishment science, comfortably wrapped in the myths of scientific rhetoric, or we can alter our intellectual allegiances. While remaining committed to an abstract goal of understanding, we can choose to whom, socially and politically, we are accountable in our pursuit of that goal. In particular we can choose between being accountable to the traditional establishment or to our political comrades.

Such accountability does not demand a radical break with the science one has learned and practiced. The development of a "new" science involves a more dialectical evolution and more continuity with established science than the familiar language of scientific revolutions implies.

In focusing on accountability and choice, this conception of feminist science differs from those that proceed from the assumption of a congruence between certain models of natural processes and women's inherent modes of understanding.[4] I am arguing instead for the deliberate and active choice of an interpretive model and for the legitimacy of basing that choice on political considerations in this case. Obviously model choice is also constrained by (what we know of) reality, that is, by the data. But reality (what we know of it) is, I have already argued, inadequate to uniquely determine model choice. The feminist theorists mentioned above have focused on the relation between the content of a theory and female values or experiences, in particular on the perceived congruence between interactionist, wholist visions of nature and a form of understanding and set of values widely attributed to women. In contrast, I am suggesting that a feminist scientific practice admits political considerations as relevant constraints on reasoning, which, through their influence on reasoning and interpretation, shape content. In this specific case, those considerations in combination with the phenomena support an explanatory model that is highly interactionist, highly complex. This argument is so far, however, neutral on the issue of whether an interactionist and complex account of natural processes will always be the preferred one. If it is preferred, however, this will be because of explicitly political considerations and not because interactionism is the expression of "women's nature."

The integration of a political commitment with scientific work will be expressed differently in different fields. In some, such as the complex of research programs having a bearing on the understanding of human behavior, certain moves, such as the one described above, seem quite obvious. In others it may not be clear how to express an alternate set of values in inquiry, or what values would be appropriate. The first step, however, is to abandon the idea that scrutiny of the data yields a seamless web of knowledge. The second is to think through a particular field and try to understand just what its unstated and fundamental assumptions are and how they influence the course of inquiry. Knowing something of the history of a field is necessary to this process, as is continued conversation with other feminists.

The feminist interventions I imagine will be local (i.e., specific to a particular area of research); they may not be exclusive (i.e., different feminist perspectives may be represented in theorizing); and they will be in some way continuous with existing scientific work. The accretion of such interventions, of science done by feminists as feminists, and by members of other disenfranchised groups, has the potential, nevertheless, ultimately to transform the character of scientific discourse.

Doing science differently requires more than just the will to do so and it would be disingenuous to pretend that our philosophies of science are the only barrier. Scientific inquiry takes place in a social, political and economic context that imposes a variety of institutional obstacles to innovation, let alone to the intellectual working out of oppositional and political commitments. The nature of university career ladders means that one's work must be recognized as meeting certain standards of quality in order that one be able to continue it. If those standards are intimately bound up with values and assumptions one rejects, incomprehension rather than conversion is likely. Success requires that we present our work in a way that satisfies those standards and it is easier to do work that looks just like work known to satisfy them than to strike out in a new direction. Another push to conformity comes from the structure of support for science. Many of the scientific ideas argued to be consistent with a feminist politics have a distinctively nonproduction orientation.[5] In the example discussed above, thinking of the brain as hormonally programmed makes intervention and control more likely than does thinking of it as a self-organizing, complexly interactive system. The doing of science, however, requires financial support and those who provide that support are increasingly industry and the military. As might be expected they support research projects likely to meet their needs, projects that promise even greater possibilities for intervention in and manipulation of natural processes. Our sciences are being harnessed to the making of money and the waging of war. The possibility of alternate understandings of the natural worlds is irrelevant to a culture driven by those interests. To do feminist science we must change the social and political context in which science is done.

So: can there be a feminist science? If this means: is it in principle possible to do science as a feminist?, the answer must be: yes. If this means: can we in practice do science as feminists?, the answer must be: not until we change present conditions.

NOTES

I am grateful to the Wellesley Center for Research on Women for the Mellon Scholarship during which I worked on the ideas in this essay. I am also grateful to audiences at UC Berkeley, Northeastern University, Brandeis University and Rice University for their comments and to the anonymous reviewers for *Hypatia* for their suggestions. An earlier version appeared as Wellesley Center for Research on Women Working Paper #63.

1. This seems to be suggested in Bleier (1984), Rose (1983) and in Sandra Harding's (1980) early work.
2. For a striking expression of this point of view see Witelson (1985).
3. Ideological commitments other than feminist ones may lead to the same assumptions and the variety of feminisms means that feminist commitments can lead to different and incompatible assumptions.
4. Cf. note 1, above.
5. This is not to say that interactionist ideas may not be applied in productive contexts, but that, unlike linear causal models, they are several steps away from the manipulation of natural processes immediately suggested by the latter. See Keller (1985), especially Chapter 10.

REFERENCES

Addelson, Kathryn Pine. 1983. "The Man of Professional Wisdom." In *Discovering Reality*, ed. Sandra Harding and Merrill Hintikka. Dordrecht: Reidel.

Bleier, Ruth. 1984. *Science and Gender*. Elmsford, NY: Pergamon.

Doell, Ruth and Helen E. Longino. "Sex Hormones and Human Behavior: A Critique of the Linear Model." *Journal of Homosexuality* 15, 3/4: 55–78.

Edelman, Gerald and Vernon Mountcastle. 1978. *The Mindful Brain*. Cambridge, MA: MIT Press.

Gould, Stephen J. 1984. Review of Ruth Bleier, *Science and Gender*. *New York Times Book Review*, VVI, 7 (August 12): 1.

Harding, Sandra. 1980. "The Norms of Inquiry and Masculine Experience." In *PSA 1980*, Vol. 2, ed. Peter Asquith and Ronald Giere. East Lansing, MI: Philosophy of Science Association.

Jacob, James R. 1977. *Robert Boyle and English Revolution, A Study in Social and Intellectual Change*. New York: Franklin.

Jacob, Margaret C. 1976. *The Newtonians and the English Revolution, 1689–1720*. Ithaca, NY: Cornell University Press.

Keller, Evelyn Fox. 1985. *Reflections on Gender and Science*. New Haven, CT: Yale University Press.

Longino, Helen. 1979. "Evidence and Hypothesis." *Philosophy of Science* 46 (1): 35–56.

———. 1981. "Scientific Objectivity and Feminist Theorizing." *Liberal Education* 67 (3): 33–41.

————. 1983a. "The Idea of a Value-free Science." Paper presented to the Pacific Division of the American Philosophical Association, March 25, Berkeley, CA.

————. 1983b. "Scientific Objectivity and Logics of Science." *Inquiry* 26 (1): 85–106.

————. 1983c. "Beyond 'Bad Science.'" *Science, Technology and Human Values* 8 (1): 7–17.

Longino, Helen and Ruth Doell. 1983. "Body, Bias and Behavior." *Signs* 9 (2): 206–227

Lugones, Maria and Elizabeth Spelman. 1983. "Have We Got a Theory for You! Feminist Theory, Cultural Imperialism and the Demand for 'The Woman's Voice.'" *Hypatia 1*, published as a special issue of *Women's Studies International Forum* 6 (6): 573–581.

Rose, Hilary. 1983. "Hand, Brain, and Heart: A Feminist Epistemology for the Natural Sciences." *Signs* 9 (1): 73–90.

Rossiter, Margaret, 1982. *Women Scientists in America: Struggles and Strategies to 1940*. Baltimore, MD: Johns Hopkins University Press.

Witelson, Sandra. 1985. "An Exchange on Gender." *New York Review of Books* (October 24).

Part V

Philosophy of Language

Philosophy of language in the twentieth century has included a broad range of topics, among them the nature of language itself, the relation of language to the world, and what it is to have meaning. It has also encompassed more technical discussions of meaning and naming (reference), meaning and use, kinds of speech acts, and so on. These topics have traditionally been considered value-neutral; little attention has been paid to the values underlying the field itself.

Feminist philosophers as well as feminist linguists have explored how values are assumed in language use and how language can either clarify or obfuscate women's experiences. Linguists often do empirical work, for example, showing differences in men's and women's uses of language. Both philosophers and linguists have offered critiques of sexist language and an examination of the features that are oppressive to women in patriarchal linguistic practices. These critiques encompass not only examples of sexist discourse but also the background assumptions, beliefs, and practices that allow it to function.

Janice Moulton examines the use of "gender-neutral" terms such as "he," "man," and "mankind" when these are said to stand for both male and female persons. She calls into question whether there are, in fact, gender-neutral uses of such terms and shows how gender-neutral language fails us in most contexts.

Another concern of feminist philosophers is to find a means of understanding and overcoming the fact that women have been silenced in the patriarchal world. In her early work Mary Daly spoke of our having the power to name stolen from us. We were not allowed to name ourselves, our experience, or the world.[1] Women have taken back the power to name. We have been trying to discover ways to give linguistic expression to ourselves and our experiences. But what is to be the source of our language and the nature of our utterances: And if we have a women's language, what features will it have?

Andrea Nye asks whether there can be a feminist linguistics. She shows how traditional philosopohy of language will not accommodate feminist linguistic practices since it sees language as reflecting a male subject. She describes how certain French feminist thinkers have approached the question of language and women's experience, particularly their notion of woman as "speaking subject." Woman, who has been silenced as object, now can speak. Nye details the features of a feminist linguistics: language would not be a mode of domination (as in patriarchy), but a medium of exchange; it would be not an opposition but a "couple," a way of understanding each other.

NOTE

1. Mary Daly, *Beyond God the Father: Toward a Philosophy of Women's Liberation* (Boston: Beacon Press, 1973).

Chapter 13

The Myth of the Neutral "Man"

Janice Moulton

I

*H*ere are two riddles:

1. A man is walking down the street one day when he suddenly recognizes an old friend whom he has not seen in years walking in his direction with a little girl. They greet each other warmly and the friend says, "I married since I last saw you, to someone you never met, and this is my daughter, Ellen." The man says to Ellen, "You look just like your mother." How did he know that?
2. A boy and his father were driving when suddenly a large truck careened around a corner and hit their car head-on. The car was crushed, and when their bodies were removed from the wreck the father was already dead. The son, badly injured but still alive, was rushed to the hospital, where hasty preparations were made for immediate surgery. As the boy was brought in for the operation, the surgeon saw him and said, "I can't operate, that's my son." How is that possible?

If you have not heard these riddles before and they puzzle you, that's an important datum for this paper.

II

Recently it has been argued that the words "he," "man," etc. should not be used as gender-neutral terms because it is unfair to women; anyone who looks for the best *man* for the job or tells an applicant to

Source: Reprinted with revisions from *Feminism and Philosophy*, ed. Mary Vetterling-Braggin, Frederick Elliston, and Jane English (Totowa, NJ: Littlefield, Adams and Co., 1977) by permission of the author and publisher. Copyright © 1977, 1980 by Janice Moulton.

send *his* credentials is less likely or less able to consider a female candidate fairly.

Two claims should be distinguished here. The first accepts that there is a gender-neutral meaning for terms like "he," "man," etc. Adherents of this view consider the gender-neutral uses of these terms an *effect* of, and an unpleasant reminder of, the lower status of women, and urge that the gender-neutral use be eliminated as a sign of good will and for symptomatic relief.

The second claim denies that terms such as "he" and "man" have gender-neutral uses. It argues that using these terms as if they were neutral terms *causes* unfairness. This is because not really being gender-neutral, the use of such terms leads one to apply the context to males, and makes it difficult to apply it to females.

The first claim is sometimes followed up with a shift to the second claim: once the first claim has been articulated, the second claim is thought to become true. Refusing to adopt this sign of good will indicates a lack of good will—that is, sexism. Continued use of "he" and "man" as neutral terms indicates that the attitude of the speaker is not gender-neutral. It will be recognized on some level of awareness that the speaker intends men to be preferred to women, and intends terms such as "he" or "man," although hitherto neutral, to apply primarily to men. Only people who have these intentions will continue to use these terms as if they were neutral. Such an argument defends and reinforces the first claim by appeal to the second claim.

The first claim, that there *are* neutral uses but they are symptoms of unfairness and should be eliminated, has greater initial plausibility than the second. Using "he" and "man" as neutral terms may well be the result of the greater prominence of men in our culture. But once this use has been established, it appears that it can be both intended and understood neutrally. There is no initial reason to suppose that these terms are less likely to be applied to women than men, *if* used neutrally.

I am going to defend the second claim, but I would like to do so without appealing to any connection with the first claim. I believe that the second claim can be defended on its own, without appeal to sexist attitudes of the speakers. I shall try to show that however innocently and neutrally they are intended, the words "he," "man," etc. may not function as genuine gender-neutral terms; that their use is unavoidably somewhat gender-specific; and that male gender-specific descriptions make it difficult to recognize that descriptions in that context could apply to a female.

III

Let us first consider the criticism of the use of "he," "man," etc., as gender-neutral terms that, while allowing that the uses may be neutral, nevertheless requests relief from these symptoms of other injustices. This criticism reminds us that there are other neutral terms: One can look for the best *person* for the job, tell *applicants* to send their credentials to one, etc. It continues: If we change our language, we will increase awareness of past unfair treatment of women and save women from being constantly reminded of the male priority and domination that the neutral uses of "he" and "man" indicate. Although some of the suggested changes will be awkward at first, they will be signs of a spirit of sympathy and cooperation with the criticism and therefore with efforts of women to attain equal human status.

Once this request has been made, the continued use of "he" and "man" as gender-neutral terms does not *make* a person less likely to consider a woman for the job. Nevertheless it may be an indication that the person is not especially sympathetic to the problems of being automatically assigned a lower status, and therefore that the person may be less likely to consider a woman for the job. On this view, the gender-neutral use of "he," etc., is a consequence, or a symbol, not a cause, of existing unjust attitudes.

This request seems to be asking very little, just that a few words be changed, but is actually asking more than that. The change in language might also publicize a political position, or challenge friends and colleagues. In our language where a lower socioeconomic class is detectable by dialect variants such as the use of "gutter," "nylons," and "light bill," instead of "street" or "road," "stockings," and "electric bill," and a graduate education turns a "resume" into a "vita," a "convention" into "meetings," and "manuscripts" into "stuff" (as in "send me your stuff"), the change of a few words is likely to announce a life style, broadcast a political position, or misdirect attention to the wrong issue.

If, after their relation to male status has been pointed out, "he" and "man" continue to be used in place of other neutral terms, it does not necessarily follow that the user lacks good will toward females. Small variations in language may have great social significance. It may not be a lack of good will, but a desire to concentrate on more significant issues or a shyness about taking political stands in casual conversations, that leaves the request unfulfilled.

IV

Perhaps you've recognized by now that the above riddles are intended to illustrate that assuming that a description (a surgeon, the friend of a man) applies to a male makes it difficult to recognize that the description could also apply to a female.

The second riddle is frequently presented as an illustration of our sexist presuppositions. We automatically assume that the surgeon has to be a man. But the first riddle has a similar effect without the presence of a professional description to receive the blame. I do not believe that the surgeon riddle does show sexism. What it shows is that once the assumption is made that a description is of a man, it is very, very hard to change that assumption. In the first riddle the assumption is probably made merely because an old friend of a man is somewhat more likely to be a man than a woman. (The assumption about gender need not have any empirical basis. There appears to be a tendency to assume that "my cousin," if spoken by a woman, refers to a female, and if spoken by a man, refers to a male.) Yet however weak the basis for the assumption, the perplexity caused by the riddles shows that it is still very hard to change one's assumptions about gender.

Note that these riddles do not show that the use of "he" or "man" in their alleged neutral sense makes it difficult to realize that a description in that context could be of a female. The only thing the riddles show is that if one assumes that a description applies to a male, it is hard to realize that the description could apply to a female. But genuine gender-neutral terms should not foster such an assumption. Therefore I still have to show that the alleged gender-neutral uses of these terms are, in fact, somewhat gender-specific.

V

It is not legitimate to assume that any use of "he" makes people think of a male instead of a female. Language has an influence on thought, but there are many other influences, too. Consider another example: "being doctored" has worse connotations than "being nursed." Things that have been doctored are in a worse condition than if left alone, whereas things that have been nursed are frequently in a better condition as a result. However, such linguistic usage does not prevent people from seeking doctors rather than nurses for serious illnesses. It seems very likely that these verb forms are derived from the functions of doctors and nurses. Yet there is no reason to suppose that use of these expressions causes discrimination against doctors in favor of nurses.

So even though the use of "he" as a gender-neutral pronoun is related to the position of males as compared with that of females in this culture,[1] and even though women are in a position inferior to men, it still has to be shown that gender-neutral uses of "he," "man," etc., affect people's thinking by preventing them from applying the context in question to women.[2]

The claim that there is no really neutral use might not need defense if there were no other terms that had both a neutral and non-neutral use. But such is not the case. Many adjectives that refer to one of a pair of opposite qualities can be used neutrally to indicate the dimension whose extremes are the opposites. One can ask "How tall is she?" of a short person, and "How wide is that?" of a narrow object. "Tall" and "wide" are used not only as opposites of "short" and "narrow," but as neutral terms to describe the quality or dimension of which the opposites are extremes. One *can* ask "How short is she?" or "How narrow is that?" but doing so expresses the expectation that the answer will lie on one end of the range of possible answers. In contrast, any tendency to suppose that anyone of whom it is asked how tall they are is in fact a tall person, is certainly very slight. Such uses of "short," "narrow," as well as "young," "impure," "bad," and "small" are called *marked* while similar uses of the opposite terms, "tall" and "long," "wide," "old," "pure," "good," and "big" are termed *unmarked*.[3]

In this respect, unmarked and marked adjectives behave very much like the he-she, man-woman, his-her pairs. The use of "he" or "man" may be either gendered or neutral. However, if one uses "she" or "woman," one conveys the expectation that a person who fits the description will be female, not male.[4] If one is going to argue that "he" and "man" cannot function as gender-neutral terms, it cannot be merely because such terms also have gender-specific meanings.

VI

It might be argued that, given that there are other neutral terms ("they," "one," "human," "person"), perpetuation of a neutral use of one of a pair of opposites gives that quality a priority or superiority over the opposite quality. There is some evidence that the unmarked term of a pair of opposites has higher positive associations. The use of a marked term often has a pejorative tone.[5] It is not an accident that "good" and "pure" are unmarked, "bad" and "impure" marked. If by perpetuating the neutral uses of "he" and "man" one encouraged the continuation of the unfair priority of males, then there would be a sense in which such uses were not really neutral.

Granted that people usually do have higher positive associations for the term with the neutral use than with its opposite.[6] And people have higher positive associations for "he" than "she." But it is far from clear that the positive association is a *result* of the neutral use; it may well be the other way around. The neutral uses of "tall," "wide," "high," "long," "big," etc., tell us that, in general, the larger size is better, or standard, or ideal. I suspect the reason for this is that children, during the time of first language learning, are expected to increase in size and are often praised for doing so and worried over when they do not. Thus at the outset they learn the term for the extreme that is their goal, and then come to use it to stand for the whole dimension.[7] (This would explain why "old" is unmarked even though youth is so much admired and valued. The post-adolescent youth that is valued is many years older than the language-learning child.) When one uses an adjective that can stand for one end of a dimension neutrally to name the dimension, one presents that end of the dimension as expected or standard. For example, "How cold is it?" vs. "How hot is it?"; "How hard is it?" vs. "How soft is it?". If one end of a dimension is a standard independently of a particular context, the term for that end would acquire a neutral use. If this explanation of the origin of unmarked adjectives is correct, the similarity to unmarked adjectives is no reason to suppose that the more positive evaluation of "he" is the *result* of its neutral use. It indicates, instead, that men's being more highly re-garded than women promotes the neutral uses of male terms.

In any case, the higher positive associations of adjectives with neutral uses do not affect evaluations in particular cases. Although "wide" has a higher positive association for people than "narrow," wider objects are not necessarily valued more than narrower objects. For example, pocket calculators are touted for their narrow dimensions (although in advertisements one is more likely to hear the term "slim" than "narrow"). And so there is no reason to suppose that using "he" and "man" as unmarked neutral terms affects evaluations of females in particular cases. If one is going to argue that such uses are not really neutral, one has to show something more about these terms— something other than that they have the properties of other unmarked terms.

VII

There are important differences between unmarked adjectives and words like "he" and "man." The neutral use of adjectives is quite unambiguous, restricted to contexts in which a quantity or amount of that dimension is the topic (i.e., three inches *high*, 99 & 44/100% *pure*). The neutral uses of "he" and "man" have no restricted contexts to clarify them. Moreover, uses of these terms are frequently in need of clarification. We might be inclined to say that "man" in "The Neanderthal man was a hunter" was being used neutrally to mean "human." But this sentence could be used to describe just males. One might say, "The Neanderthal man was a hunter. The Neanderthal woman raised crops." In this context "man" is clearly intended to mean "male human." In an example from an introductory philosophy text, an apparently neutral use of "he" turns out to be intentionally gender-specific. This ambiguity is resolved only by the last word:

> Consider, firstly, two comparatively simple situations in which a cyberneticist might find himself. He has a servomechanism, or a computing machine, with no randomising element, and he also has a wife.[8]

Although "he" and "man" behave like unmarked adjectives in some respects, their double roles as both gender-specific and gender-neutral terms permit ambiguity in ways that the double roles of unmarked adjectives do not.

The ambiguity in the beginning of these examples allows an intended gender-specific "he" or "man" to be interpreted as a neutral term so that a context may be inadvertently applied to women. And ambiguity may also allow an intended neutral "he" to be interpreted as a gender-specific term so that the context is accidentally not applied to women. But if this is so, the culprit is ambiguity, which could be resolved without forsaking the neutral uses of male terms. Add that you are an equal-opportunity employer and there should be no gender-specific interpretation of "man" in "the best man for the job." One need not eliminate the neutral use of "he" and "man" in order to eliminate ambiguity. There will be other ways of resolving the ambiguity besides using other neutral terms that are not ambiguous.

VIII

Here's the problem: However the use of a term gets started, it would seem that if it was intended a certain way when used, and understood that way by others, then, on any available theory of meaning, that's what it means. If "man" or "he" are intended neutrally, as they often are, and if people know that, as they do, then it would seem that "man" and "he" do refer to the members of the human species, and that they are as neutral as "human" and "they."

In order to show that "man" and "he" and like terms are not really neutral, I propose to show that it is not enough that one *intend* a term to have a particular meaning for it to have that meaning; that intended neutral uses of "he," "man," etc., can fail to be neutral; and that such failures have implications for all other allegedly neutral uses.

Let's compare "he" and "man" with other terms whose gender neutrality is not in dispute, such as "one," "they," "human," and "person." One striking difference is the inability to use "he" and "man" to refer to a female human. It would be a rare person who could say without irony "She's the best *man* for the job" or say of a female, "He's the best." Yet the undisputed gender-neutral terms can indeed be used this way: "She's the best person;" "That one is the best" (of a female). If "he" and "man" are genuinely gender-neutral, then they ought to be applicable to any person regardless of gender.

One might argue that one does not say "he's the best" of a female for the same reason one does not merely say "I believe" when one knows. On Grice's account of the latter, it is not that believing *implies* not knowing, but that one does not usually convey less information than one can.[9] Therefore if one says one believes, people may assume one does not actually know. Similarly, one might argue, if it is clear in some context that the gender of a referent is known to the speaker, then the speaker is expected to specify that gender. It is not that uses of "he" and "man" *imply* that the referent is male, but simply that one does not convey less information than one can. If one uses "he" or "man," people may assume that either a male is being referred to or that the gender is not known.

This explanation, however, does not account for all the facts. It offers no explanation for why "She's the best man" is not permissible since gender *has* been specified. Moreover, it would predict that undisputed neutral terms could not be used if the gender were known. If the problem were only that speakers are expected to specify gender when known, the sentence "That's the best person" would be as inappropriate to say of either a male or a female as "That's the best man" is to say of a female.

On some theories of meaning, the meaning of a term is a function of its use. I have already pointed out that "he" and "man" do not have the same uses as undisputed gender-neutral terms. Recent theories of meaning have analyzed meaning as a function of the intentions of the speaker. Yet failures of gender-neutrality of "he" and "man" occur even though the speaker may intend a gender-neutral use. For example, Bertrand Russell in his classic paper "On Denoting" says:

Suppose now we wish to interpret the proposition, "I met a man." If this is true, I met some definite man; but that is not what I affirm. What I affirm is, according to the theory I advocate: " 'I met x and x is human' is not always false."[10]

If Russell were correct, then parents familiar with his theory would have no cause for anxiety if their young female child, on arriving home several hours late from kindergarten, said, "I met a man." Russell did not notice that "man" is not used neutrally in his context. This example shows that one cannot account entirely for the meaning of a term by the intentions of the speaker on a particular occasion. The meaning of a term involves, among other things, its expected interpretation, the way it functions with other terms, and its use in linguistic enterprises such as reasoning. This is important for the next point.

"He" and "man" cannot be used in some contexts where undisputedly gender-neutral terms can. But what about other contexts? Suppose it can be shown that a familiar and paradigmatic example of a gender-neutral use of "man" or "men" is not really neutral at all? Then I think it can be argued that there is no real gender-neutral meaning of these terms. Consider the first line of the familiar syllogism:

All men are mortal.

Most people would agree that the occurrence of "men" is intended to be neutral; this is a statement about the whole human species. But if it is a neutral use, then this syllogism, that paradigm of valid syllogisms, is invalid, for the second line usually reads,

Socrates is a man.

The occurrence of "man" in this sentence is *not* a neutral use. If it were a neutral use, then replacing "Socrates" with the name of a female human being or a child would not affect the syllogism. Yet the usual interpretation of

Sophia is a man

makes it false, or insulting. It is not taken to mean that Sophia is a member of the human species.

Let me add two explanations here. (1) The meaning of a term is not determined by the interpretation of one person alone. How others will understand it must be considered as well. Although some people might argue that in this context the syllogism "Sophia is a man" can be read as "Sophia is a human being," they will recognize that many other people will not take it this way (this is due in part to our inability to use "man" to refer to a female in other contexts). Although *some* people might be able to *read* "man" neutrally in this context, it does not follow that this is what it means. Further examples where "man" and "his" fail to be gender-neutral will be given to convince those who can make a gender-neutral reading in one case.

(2) It might be argued that I have changed the meaning of "man" in the syllogism by substituting "Sophia" for "Socrates." The original syllogism might have had a neutral occurrence of "man" that changed with the substitution. For example, if I substituted "The Outer Banks" for "savings and loan institutions" in "————are banks," I would

change the meaning of "banks." However, if "man" *has* a gender-neutral use, it should retain that use regardless of the gender of the referent. There is no reason to claim that it has a gender-neutral meaning unless it has a use that can be applicable to females as well as males. Gender-neutral terms such as "human" and "person" are not affected by the substitution of a female name in their context.

Thus the inference from "All men are mortal" and "Socrates is a man" to "Socrates is mortal" is invalid if the occurrence of "men" is intended to be gender-neutral in the first premise. Instead of a paradigm of valid inference we would have an equivocation, because the meaning of the terms has changed. It would be just like the argument:

All banks are closed on Sunday.
The Outer Banks are banks.
Therefore, the Outer Banks are closed on Sunday.

That the occurrence of "men" in the first premise is believed to be gender-neutral, and that the syllogism is believed to be neither enthymematic nor invalid, is evidence either that we are confused about neutral uses or that we are confused about validity even in the simplest cases. There is further evidence that it is the former. Consider another example:

Man is a mammal.

This use of "man" is neutral if any use is. But if this is conjoined with the dictionary definition of "mammalia":

the highest class of Vertebrata comprising man and all other animals that nourish their young with milk, that have the skin usu. more or less covered with hair, that have mammary glands . . .[11]

it should be legitimate to conclude:

Man has mammary glands.

But this conclusion is less acceptable than:

Humans have mammary glands.

because "man" doe not function in the same gender-neutral way as "human" in this context. A statement that members of the human species have mammary glands is not peculiar, but a statement that males have mammary glands is. Although both men and women have mammary glands, only the mature glands of women are ordinarily likely to be topics of conversation. If "man" could be used gender-neutrally, its occurrence in a context that applied to both male and female humans, particularly to female humans, would be given a gender-neutral interpretation. Instead, its occurrence in such a context is plainly gender-specific.

Alleged neutral uses of "he" are not as frequently found in syllogisms. But *if* it sounds strange to ask an applicant about the interests of his husband or wife, to instruct a child on the cleaning of his vagina or penis, or to compliment a guest on his gown or tuxedo, then something is less than neutral about "he" and "his" as well. Note that there is no ambiguity about these uses. The contexts make it clear that "man' and "his" are supposed to be understood to be gender-neutral, if possible. Other obvious failures of gender neutrality are:

> Man has two sexes.
> Some men are female.

There are many more contexts in which attempts to use terms such as "he" and "man" gender-neutrally produce false, funny, or insulting statements, even though the gender-neutrality was clearly intended.

The failure of "he," "man," etc., to be gender-neutral can be demonstrated in examples where a reference to a particular person, or a grammatical context in which these terms cannot be used neutrally occurs. But what about other cases? Surely I cannot *prove* that there is never a case in which "man" means human, you will say.

Similarly I could not prove that there was never a case in which "wash-bucket" meant "justice" or "Watch out!" (Imagine a feud in a laundry room.) But that's not the sense of meaning that's at issue here. As I've said earlier, the meaning of a term involves its expected interpretation, the way it functions with other terms, and its use in reasoning and other discourse. And what we've seen with "he" and "man," etc., is that some uses that may appear gender-neutral at first turn out to be gender-specific because of what is said in some other place.

To give an idea of the variety of ways that gender-neutrality can fail, or can be shown to have failed, let me offer another example first pointed out by Ruth Lucier:

> All men and all women are philosophers; or, let us say, if they are not conscious of having philosophical problems, they have, at any rate, philosophical prejudices. Most of these are theories which they unconsciously take for granted, or which they have absorbed from their intellectual environment or from tradition.
>
> Since few of these theories are consciously held, they are prejudices in the sense that they are held without critical examination, even though they may be of great importance for the practical actions of people, and for their whole life.
>
> It is an apology for the existence of professional philosophy that men are needed who examine critically these widespread and influential theories.[12]

In these three paragraphs by Karl Popper, he begins by speaking of men and women, using the pronoun "they" and then in the third paragraph switches to "men." Were it not for his talk of men *and women,* we might be tempted to interpret his use of "men" as intended gender-neutrally. But because there is a shift from men and women to men, whether deliberate or not, I believe that the reference to men is unquestionably gender-specific.

The difficulty is that there is no way of guaranteeing a gender-neutral use, because one cannot predict how that use will be connected with other discourse and behavior. One can imagine that an entire book might be written with attempted neutral uses of "he" and "man," while the title alone or some advertising copy shows that these uses are gender specific (for example, the *SPLEEN OF THE DIABETIC MALE,* or *MEN OF THE FUTURE*—"essential reading for their wives and girlfriends"—I. M. Mailer).

One might want to claim that the gender-specific contexts do not make the other neutral uses gender-specific. Instead there has been a change in meaning—as if one had switched from a discussion of different color greens to salad greens, from sand banks to commercial banks.

However, a shift in meaning, like a pun, is usually noticeable and often a bit funny. This is not the case for the alleged shift with "he," "man," etc. If there is a shift it takes place smoothly, and usually goes unnoticed, particularly by the people who are most likely to claim that there has been one. The noticeable and funny examples occur only when a gender-neutral use is attempted (as in "Man has two sexes") and not when a gender-specific reference is made. Because the gender-specific references are *not* noticeable shifts in meaning, I think it is justified to conclude that they were not genuinely neutral uses in the first place.

One might argue that all uses of "he," "man," and like terms are simply gender-specific. But I think a weaker conclusion is easier to support: that attempts at gender-neutrality with these terms fail, not because they are simply gender-specific but because something else is going on. This conclusion is supported by empirical studies that show the use of "he" rather than "they" or "he or she," makes it more likely, but not inevitable, that people will think of males. I try to explain what else is going on in the next section.

IX

How can the failure of gender-neutrality be accounted for when people think they are using "he," "man," etc., in a gender-neutral sense? Rather than attribute the failure to peculiar properties of each context in an ad hoc fashion, I believe it is the result of a broader linguistic phenomenon: Parasitic Reference. Tissues are called Kleenex;

petroleum jelly, Vaseline; bleach, Clorox; etc. to the economic benefit of the specific brands referred to and to the economic detriment of those brands that are ignored by this terminology. The alleged gender-neutral uses of "he," "man," etc. are just further examples of this common phenomenon. A gender-specific term, one that refers to a high-status subset of the whole class, is used *in place of* a neutral generic term. Many of us who deplore the efforts of drug companies to get us to use the brand name rather than the generic name of a product have failed to recognize that the use of "he," "man," etc., in place of "they," "one," "person," or "human" is a similar phenomenon with similar effects. Manufacturers realize that someone sent to buy "the cheapest Clorox" is less likely to return with the equal-strength half-price store brand than someone sent to buy the cheapest bleach. And this is true even when the term "Clorox" is intended and understood to be synonymous with "bleach." The failure of "Clorox" to be brand-neutral and the failure of "he" and "man" to be gender-neutral appear to be instances of the same phenomenon.[13]

Regardless of the intentions of the speakers and hearers, and regardless of their beliefs about the meanings of the terms, if the terms refer parasitically, subjectivity can fail, inferences may not go through, and equivocations will be produced. This is true not merely for brand names but for other terms, such as "he" and "man," whose neutral performances have been advertised by lexicographers but which break down easily even under normal speaking conditions. The existence of Parasitic Reference requires that theories of reference and meaning recognize that the functioning of terms in one context may be affected by their uses in other contexts that are not explicitly present.

NOTES

This paper owes a special thanks to G. M. Robinson and Cherin Elias for their comments and encouragement. Many other people at the Society for Women in Philosophy, the American Philosophical Association meetings, and the University of Maryland philosophy department gave me valuable comments. I would particularly like to thank Mary Vetterling-Braggin, Virginia Valian, Larry Stern, Christine Pierce, Susan Rae Peterson, Stan Munsat, Susan Moore, W. G. Lycan, Ron Laymon, Adele Laslie, Gale Justin, Carl Ginet, Alan Donagan, Richard Brandt, and H. D. Block.

1. Many people believe this claim, but Robin Lakoff in "Language and Woman's Place," *Language in Society* 2 (1973): 45–80, supports it with an impressive number of gender asymmetries in language whose best explanation appears to be the superior position of one gender in the culture. See also Mary Ritchie Key, *Male/Female Language* (Metuchen, N.J.: Scarecrow Press, 1975); and

Casey Miller and Kate Swift, *Words and Women* (Garden City, N.Y.: Anchor Press/Doubleday, 1976).

2. Even if the gender-neutral uses of "he," etc., prevent people from considering women in those contexts, there are some contexts where one does not want to be considered (for example, as a murder suspect). So one has also to show that the disadvantages of not being considered for jobs, awards, and consultation outweigh the advantages of not being considered for criminal activities, punishment, and obligations. Women who oppose the Equal Rights Amendment seem to disagree with other women, not on the actual unequal status of women, but rather on whether the advantages of this status outweigh the disadvantages.

3. Although this terminology was originally applied to phonological distinctions (e.g., the third-person singular of regular verbs is marked with an "s"), it has been extended to the use I cite. See John Lyons, *Introduction to Theoretical Linguistics* (Cambridge: Cambridge University Press, 1971), 79.

4. Porter G. Perrin and Karl W. Dykema, in *Writer's Guide and Index to English*, 3rd edition (Glenview, Ill.: Scott, Foresman, 1959), 538–539, 551–552, say: "As we must often refer to nouns that name either or both male and female, the language has developed . . . ways of making up for the lack of an accurate pronoun: The usual way is to use *he* or *his* alone even when some of the persons are female . . . Sometimes when the typical individuals or the majority of the group referred to would be women, *her* is used in the same way."

5. According to Lyons, *Theoretical Linguistics*, 467.

6. Evidence for this is to be found in C. E. Osgood, Suci, and Tannenbaum, *The Measurement of Meaning* (Urbana: University of Illinois Press, 1957), especially 36–62. Unmarked terms tend to be scored more positively by subjects on the semantic differential evaluative scale. But this is not always the case. It is worth remarking that "feminine" receives a higher positive evaluation than "masculine."

7. Eve V. Clark in "What's in a Word? On the Child's Acquisition of Semantics in his First Language," in *Cognitive Development and the Acquisition of Language*, T. E. Moore, ed. (New York: Academic Press, 1973), 65–110, points out that children learn to use the unmarked term of a pair before they learn the marked term.

8. L. Jonathan Cohen, "Can There Be Artificial Minds?" in *Reason and Responsibility*, 2nd ed., Joel Feinberg, ed. (Encino, Calif.: Dickenson Publishing Co., 1971), 288.

9. H. Paul Grice, "Logic and Conversation," in *Syntax and Semantics*, vol. 3, Peter Cole and Jerry L. Morgan, eds. (New York: Academic Press, 1975).

10. Bertrand Russell, "On Denoting," *Mind* 13 (1905): 479.

11. *Webster's Third New International Dictionary*.

12. Karl R. Popper, "How I See Philosophy," in *The Owl of Minerva*, Charles J. Bontempo and S. Jack Odell, eds. (New York: McGraw Hill, 1975), 48.

13. Elizabeth Lane Beardsley in "Referential Genderization," *Philosophical Forum* 5 (1973–74): 285–293, calls this phenomenon "linguistic imperialism."

Chapter 14

The Voice of the Serpent:
French Feminism and Philosophy of Language

Andrea Nye

C an there be a feminist linguistics? Is there a feminine language that confounds the semantics and syntax historically implicated in the denigration of women?[1] These questions, especially as they are raised in recent French feminist thought, have a mythic resonance. Can the father god, Yahweh, who installed his order and law in the Garden of Eden, be challenged by the alien voice of the serpent? Can the serpent, whispering to Eve in the sweet, sinuous words of desire, succeed in communicating a meaning outside Yahweh's orders? Is it possible to understand what no one can or dare say: Yahweh's threatened punishments cannot be carried out, the Father does not control life and death, carnal knowledge is to be desired for its own sake.

Raising similar questions, feminists such as Luce Irigaray and Hélène Cixous, listening for the forbidden whisper/hiss of the serpent, propose to break into the rigid symbolic order that supports male dominance and make a place for women. Also mythic, however, is the ordained punishment for such transgressions. The serpent is cast out, cursed to go upon its belly and eat dust all the days of its life. Can the serpent's speaking ever challenge the power of Yahweh? Or is the authority of logic necessary for speaking to have force? Are desire and power irrevocably opposed, so that Yahweh's viceroys, whether priests or professors, scientists or statesmen, must always be in control of bodies and pleasures? Must the voice of the serpent always become, as it does in *Genesis*, the rejected obscenity trod under foot?

Irigaray has proposed a fluid women's language "between ourselves" [*parler-entre-elles*]; Cixous, a women's writing [*écriture féminine*] that will reveal feminine desire, but it must be possible to make

Source: A shorter version of this paper appeared as "French Feminism and the Philosophy of Language," *Noûs* 20, 1 (1986): 45–51. Reprinted by permission of the author and of the editor of *Noûs*. Copyright © 1989 by Andrea Nye.

these heard against the sanctions of rationally ordered male discourse. Otherwise women, like the serpent, are reduced to silence. We must be sure that a feminine "textual" practice is truly feminist and not a return of women to the impotent marginality of poetry and hysteria.[2] But this concern cannot be addressed without raising deeper questions about the ways in which the philosophic tradition has understood the nature of language. Has any philosophy of language accommodated the voice of the serpent? Has any linguistics dealt with anything other than the grammatical and conceptual structures that are the fossilized remains of properly ordained speech? Has any language theorist captured the *power* that the serpent's speech has to move Eve to rebellion, or the *desire* that the serpent manages to put into words? In fact, philosophical discussion of language has avoided these questions. Their elision takes place in a variety of ways as the linguist separates emotional tone from sense, speech from language, pragmatics from structure, semiotic from symbolic. In the process of making these distinctions, desire and power are excluded from the analysis of language. Emotional tone is declared irrelevant to logical analysis.[3] Speech is rejected as a proper object of scientific research.[4] Pragmatics is claimed to have its own rules independent of semantic structure.[5] Physiological drives are allowed to interrupt but not inform semantic order.[6]

Certainly in our contemporary Anglo-American philosophical tradition, the relation between language, passion, and power has been neglected. Both poetic or emotional expression and political polemic are rejected as irrelevant glosses on logical form. Rational structure, in particular the structures of mathematical logic and physical science, are considered to be the proper objects of the philosopher of language's study. Linguistics, in the form of transformational grammars and generative semantics, produces the rules by which a plurality of well-formed grammatical surface structures can be generated from the philosopher's rationally structured propositions.[7] In these studies neither emotional tone, nor the practical force of expressions, nor their implication in oppressive social and political institutions is considered relevant. The linguist is interested in grammatical competence. The philosopher is interested in truth, which is equated with objective statements of fact and organized according to principles of logic. The person who speaks these facts, along with her motives, passions, designs has been removed.

The empirical verifications of science have taken her place. What is important is not who speaks or where and why she speaks, but "observations" and "experiments" that are independent of anyone's motives or desires. Even when the possibility of such incorrigible "sense data" is called into question, desire is not restored as a grounding for language. Although logicians have shown us that semantic truth is not only the formal satisfaction of truth-conditions (Tarski 1944), and philosophers that empirical data may support incommensurate conceptual schemes (Quine 1960) or that verification refers only to a system of meaning (Davidson 1984), the canonical status of objective logical-scientific language has not been questioned. Rational structures are admitted to be constitutive, creating their own objects and truths. At the same time, it is not doubted that, nevertheless, they provide the form for all meaningful language.

Nor do recent theories that emphasize pragmatic uses of language accommodate the power of desire. John Austin pointed out that we not only assert truths but also "do things with words," such as get married and christen ships (Austin 1962). But although the speech act theory that has developed out of this insight acknowledges the fact that we may intend to be married or to name a battle ship, those intentions are constituted by rules that leave no room for any serpentine rebellion. John Searle in his *Speech Acts* spells out in numbing detail the conditions and regulations that make "preformatives" such as "I promise" successful (Searle 1970, 54–71). Furthermore, in speech act theory logical form still is the core of meaning; at the heart of Searle's and Austin's illocutionary acts is not desire or intention but again the logician's proposition (Searle 1970, 97–123). Even for Wittgenstein, who in his later work rejected the logical view of language that he had so elegantly exhibited in his *Tractatus Logico-Philosophicus*, words have meaning only insofar as they are part of "forms of life" defined by criteria and rules for proper use (Wittgenstein 1953). If the serpent's insinuation is anathema within the reason of Yahweh's rule, it also must be a meaningless intrusion into the "language games" of command and obedience played out in Paradise. The wonder must be that Eve, even though the serpent speaks outside the form of life imposed by Yahweh, manages to understand.

Understand what? What is it that the serpent whispers? Here Derrida and Lacan, the intellectual fathers of French feminism, challenge Anglo-American philosophy of language. Is the logic that represents a supposedly neutral and objective truth really the expression of a parochial power? Is there in all language, even as it pretends to be most rational, a hidden writing of desire that expresses covertly sexual acts of desemination, penetration, fusion, desire? Is there at the very foundation of symbolic expression a passionate need transmuted to articulate demand? These questions must be foreign to a philosophy of language focused on the supposedly desireless and intentionless language of science. Lacan and Derrida agree with philosophers such as Quine and Davidson that a system of signifiers can never be firmly anchored in any empirical reality, but go further to examine the original motivations behind such a system, arguing that representation is an illusion motivated by desire. The point of language for Lacan is to construct a symbolic university where physical and emotional dependency on others and especially on the mother give way to the Law of the Father. Derrida sees a graphic transmutation of desire at work in the very constitution of linguistic meaning.

Lacan returns to origins. If Yahweh, the Father, presents himself as an autonomous legislator of meanings, his replicas, actual men, were once dependent sons locked into fusional dependence on their mothers. In order to become human they must escape from this animal intersubjectivity by way of a fragile mirror effect in which a split occurs between a feeling, needing "me" and a demanding linguistic "I." This mirror-stage prepares the way for full symbolic functioning as the subject goes on to "enter" a rational language structured around phallic presence and "The Law of the Father."[8]

Derrida also argues that there is a irrevocable break between animal expression and human language. But although there is no direct link between passions and words, he resurrects the serpent's graphic "trace" to deconstruct the hierarchies of Lacan's phallocentric rational discourse. In a kind of miming of the movements of an auto-erotic desire, meaning reverses (turns on, plays with itself). The surface order of grammar and rationality only cover up these necessarily pluralistic, ambivalent, and nonreferential sources of meaning that the practitioner of Derrida's technique of deconstruction exposes with his textual penetrations, feints, seductions, deseminations.[9]

Even though these reminders of the fragility of any rigid rational order offer no ultimate escape, they do raise the question of the relation between meaning, power, and desire. Lacan exposes logic as the *power* of the symbolic Father, if not of actual fathers. Derrida shows how a phallocentric symbolic order can only briefly armor itself against the anarchist vagaries of graphic spasms of desire. Power no longer resides only in a superficial choice of grammatical forms or of pre-constituted speech strategies but pervades the very symbolic function itself. Passion is no longer safely relegated to poets and mystics but interrupts the order of all discourse, including philosophy and science. Nevertheless, neither Lacan nor Derrida offers any hope for a feminist linguistics.

According to Lacan women can have no stable place in a symbolic order structured around phallic presense. Woman is less willing than man to give up regressive intersubjectivity to become a linguistic subject or "I" that objectifies and so symbolically controls objects of desire. Woman's role is speechless, the mute revelation of what cannot be expressed. Women are even, he suggested, unable to express the truth of their own feminine situation.[10] Although Derrida claimed to be the champion of the feminine in language against Lacan, his deconstruction, elegant if not tedious, is ultimately apolitical. Titillating, fun, naughty, it can do little to substantively relieve the anger and frustrated desires of women, excluded from political power, in danger from male violence, struggling to survive in a world of alien values. Whether there is no escape from the Law of the Father but only a realization of his clay feet, or whether we relieve the oppression of rigid categorizations in an iconoclastic play with phallocentric texts, feminist causes are not advanced. Either women remain semi-articulate, retreating into the mystic resonance of Lacan's female saints,[11] or they talk on and on, "making their voices resonate throughout the corridors" of academia.[12] In neither case is there much hope of a practical result. The possibility has been ruled out of a moving, direct expression of feminine desire, of any sympathetic communication between women that could give them the power of a common cause, of any power of words to tell a truth outside established concepts. What passes for communication is only possible when, according to Lacan, all submit to the Law of the Father, or when, according to Derrida, we spin out the threads of the text of another as if it were our own. The serpent has become only a dim memory of intersubjectivity haunting the Father's words, or, for Derrida, an anarchic writing that has lost its authentic voice. What it says remains unspeakable, unspeakable because there can be no symbolic expression outside Yahweh's rational order, only psychotic reversion or temporary diversion. In neither case is there any possibility of a revolutionary feminist linguistics.

In order to move towards such a linguistics, Hélène Cixous and Luce Irigaray must push poststructuralist analysis of language one step further. It is in this context that Cixous's *"écriture féminine"* and Irigaray's *"parler-entre-elles"* are of interest both as feminist strategy and as philosophy of language. In *La Jeune Née* Cixous calls for an escape from the oppositional hierarchies of reasoned, well-formed discourse. Like Lacan she points out the controlling contrast between male presence and female absence in foundational oppositions such as activity/passivity, sun/moon, culture/nature, day/night, rational/emotional.[13] But Cixous does not view these as universal semantic structures necessary in any symbolic expression, nor does she undermine the rational order of the texts in which they are found only to restore it again. Instead she notes that these oppositions are "couples." In other words semantic structure mimics the human institution of the male/female couple. Further, she notes that these contrasts are kept in place only with violence, as in the contrast between rich/poor, master/slave, civilized/primitive. Semantics is not a neutral analysis, it corresponds to power relations in the real world, relations that are maintained by force, a force applied by grammarians, linguists, and philosophers, as well as by police and armies. Semantic well-formedness does not reflect the power of the symbolic Father, so much as the power of men to establish and enforce hierarchical relations. Behind Yahweh are the priests. It is they who warn the Hebrew women not to be unfaithful to Yahweh by worshipping other gods, forbid them to eat of the fruit of the Goddess Asherah's sacred tree, and threaten punishment if they visit her shrines in the high leafy places. With this move away from the abstract authority of semantic categories to their grounding in the concrete power of men over women, the message of the serpent becomes more intelligible. The point is not wilful disobedience to divine authority, but an invitation to express and gratify a natural desire for wisdom and immortality forbidden in a theology and metaphysics maintained by men.

But how can this invitation be communicated? In her writing Cixous attempts to inaugurate a new kind of linguistic expression. The privileged medium for this expression is writing because speech situations are still dominated, according to Cixous, by the sexist constraints that prevent free expression. In a new "feminine" writing, she returns to the rhythm and tone of the human voice, searching for a language that can "speak the body."[14] Not only may feelings and emotions be directly expressed in such a language, but a speaker will be able to listen to others, and even to things, speaking themselves (Cixous 1980, 134ff). This project, as pursued in works such as *Illa* and *Angst*, might seem to place Cixous as a poet and not a philosopher. However, this is to ignore the radical thesis she holds. It is not that one should leave philosophers to their philosophizing and write poetry, but that a different kind of knowledge is possible and preferable. Expressive language, the language of desire, so long an embarassment to linguists and semanticists, can serve as a medium of discovery of truths.

In *Illa* Cixous does not make a futile attempt to maneuver in the textual thicket of established theories on women; instead she *listens* to some other train of thought that might help her to escape conventional logic. She looks in the very graphic lines of a word on a page for a new insight. She resists the temptation to fit phenomena into preestablished categories. Classification is, for Cixous, a way to kill off the object of knowledge. She tries to get back to a fresh seeing that allows things to speak themselves and to impose their own rhythms on consciousness.[15] This requires an abandonment of Lacan's masterful unitary "I." Instead the writer/knower is shaken by, traversed by, vulnerable to, other views, other voices, other writings. The thinker does not marshal a defensive battery of arguments to buttress an increasingly en-trenched position, but instead is an explorer, an undoer of simplistic logic. She does not edit or censor to reach a preset goal when a conceptual problem or tangle is encountered; she attempts to work through in the medium of language, not to a truth already known, but to a truth yet to be discovered. Such a writing and knowledge is only possible if words can carry the expression of those who speak them.

But is this sensuous explorative outpouring really the voice of the serpent, this passive speaking of the body traversed by other voices, other thoughts? Such an expression, for all the cathartic relief it may afford to the suffering oppressed, may not manage to tell a common truth, the truth that everyone knows but no one dares to say. The serpent does not speak a private language of the body nor does it give up its own voice, and what it says is immediately intelligible: You will not die if you break Yahweh's commandment; he knows that if you eat of the fruit of this tree you will no longer be willing to obey because "you shall be like a god, knowing good and evil" (Genesis 3,4–5). The serpent does not cry out or writhe with pain or abandon rationality; with this simple statement, it reveals to Eve the truth of Yahweh's bluff.

Irigaray comes closer to a view of language that can accommodate such passionate and powerful expression. In serpentine rebellion, she daringly interrogates the priests, the philosophers, the psychoanalysts whose theories rationalize the subjection of women (Irigaray 1985). She listens to what male thinkers have said; she mimics their tone, she questions, she amplifies what is only hinted at, filling in the blanks and significant silences. She listens between the lines for what is not said, spins out the meaning of what has been said. She attempts to understand not only what the male thinker wants her to understand, but probes the deeper motivations of his metaphysical pronouncements. Here rational discourse functions in a new way, not as an ordered system of thought in which opponents may catch each other out in inconsistencies, but as a medium of exchange. When Irigaray teases out the incoherences, the sleights of hand, the ambivalence inherent in a text, it is not (as in Derridean deconstruction) the essential pluralism and disorder of the constitution of any linguistic meaning that is in question, but rather the complex ways that we deal with the tangle of emotions and thoughts and relationships that bind us to others. The point is not to illustrate a philosophical theory about language or to prove an opponent wrong, but to find the place where thought leaves itself open for the answer that might provide the exit to a new shared perspective.

This requires a new view of and use of language. Language is not a neutral instrument that is used to state a variety of facts and arguments nor is style an embellishment that must be avoided in fact-stating language. What passes for factual objectivity often amounts to obsessive repetition. In a description that could easily be applied to much contemporary analytic philosophy, she describes the dangers:

> If we continue to speak the same language, we are going to reproduce the
> same story. Begin again the same stories . . . same discussions, same
> disputes, same dramas. Same attraction, same ruptures. Same difficulties,
> impossible to repair. Same . . . Same . . . Always the same (1977, 205).

Such a language, Irigaray continues, passes over our bodies, our heads,
loses itself and loses us. The same problems repeat themselves—other
minds, reference, truth. Philosophy as a "theoretical discipline" becomes a skirmishing according to established rules (or in some recent
formulations, a "play") that has no direct bearing on the struggle
between rich and poor, colonist and colonized, men and women.[16]
Turning back again and again on itself, philosophical theorization
becomes increasingly complex and arcane until it is closed to everyone
but a few intellectually adroit practitioners who are sufficiently insu-
lated from reality to follow. Irigaray's style, on the other hand, is likely
to shock this orthodoxy. She comes to her subject as a feminist partisan,
with a passionate interest in and complaint about the positions she
discusses. She writes with a particular hearer or reader in mind. She
pays attention to metaphor. She weaves elements from psychoanalysis,
literature, and myth, producing a complexity bewildering to readers
used to sequential linear argument. What she institutes is not a debate
but a dialogue. Although the participants in a dialogue may remain
hostile, the point is not to declare a winner. Irigarary does not attempt
to defeat or kill off the other's point of view, but to reason with it,
mirror it, cajole, and seduce it from its obdurate, self-interested rigidity.

Again, however, there are some differences between Irigaray and
the serpent. The serpent wastes no time in dialogue with Yahweh. It
addresses itself directly to the woman, Eve. It is not interested in
persuading or seducing the Father. The serpent communicates the truth
to Eve, a truth no less communicable because it is forbidden. Cixous and
Irigaray had to recover from their poststructuralist fathers not only the
possibility of the expression of desire, but also the possibility of
communication in language. For Lacan, what passes for communication
is an acceptance of the symbolic patriarchal authority that makes
meaning possible; for Derrida, it is the license to spin out the text of
another. In neither case do we penetrate to the thought or feeling of
others through words or speak to them directly. At the same time, it is
the possibility of such a communication and such an answering that
both Irigaray and Cixous place as crucial for women's liberation.

Cixous, for example, begins with the desperation of a woman
trapped in a language that dictates a certain constellation of meaning
based on hierarchical family relations. Her struggle, however, is not

always only to get beyond language to a mystical union between words and things. It is also to get past a "meta-language dominated by men, to a way of writing and speaking in which there can be an 'endless circulation of desire.'" Language can be a way to establish "a rapport with another so I pass in the other without trying to bring all to me" (1976, 15). The significant breakthrough of the woman in *Illa* comes when she reads these words written by the novelist Lispector: "I will write to you all that comes to my spirit with the least surveillance possible" (1980, 178). With this invitation to a free, frank communication, Cixous can now begin to speak. She can speak because there is someone to speak to, someone who will listen and understand. The mystical communion with things themselves has become the possibility of active listening and openness to another.

Irigaray also sees the answer for women in an abandonment of sterile repetitive discourse for a *"parler-entre-elles."* The "merchandise" will begin to speak to each other.[17] This will cause a revolution in a cultural economy dominated by the exchange of women. The language that women will speak among themselves, however, must be different from the language theorized by philosophers of language. It will not be centered around rigid semantic structures. Instead the anchor points will be exactly those linguistic elements that semanticists and logicians neglect: the pronominal system of I's, yous, hes, shes, and its that are the skeleton of linguistic interaction. In *Passions Elémentaires*, Irigaray constructs dialogue in which "I's" and "yous" are put into moving relation. No longer is there one "I" whose suppression of any "you" is elided in anonymous assertion. Irigaray's "yous" and "I's" are the shifting positions between which a dialogic communication can move.

Her coupling of tu/je points out the distinctive and crucial linguistic functioning of "you." To say "you" is to establish a complex relation with an "I," a relationship that implies a degree of complicity and identity as well as difference. The license of this relationship allows one to speak for another, to say for a "you" what she (or he) cannot say for herself. The result is a plurality of meanings that cannot be reduced to unity. Instead, language serves as a medium of exchange that implies a common project of understanding and works to bring positions into relationship. The speaker may then escape from the sterile catgories an authoritarian "I" must presuppose as the basis for an illusory understanding.

There are similarities between this *"parler-entre-elles"* and the communication of the serpent. There is no fusional intimacy between the serpent and Eve in which each flows into the other; instead they both stay quite intact, speaking from different positions in the drama that unfolds. At the same time, the serpent's tone implies that it will only say what Eve must already know although she may not be willing to admit it: Surely you realize that the Fathers threat is empty, that to act without his authority is not to die? In speaking to Eve, the serpent expresses her desire: And why not taste of the apple? Yahweh knows when you eat it your eyes will be open and he is jealous of that knowledge. Having listened to the serpent, Eve is now able to speak as well as to gratify and share her desire: "So when the woman saw that the tree was good for food, a delight for the eyes, and truly to be desired to make one wise, she ate of the tree, and gave it to Adam to eat" (Genesis 3,6). She and Adam are no longer automatons blindly repeating Yahweh's law. Their eyes are opened and they see where and who they are. For this communication the serpent does not become Eve, it finds her where she is. Cixous almost expresses it when she says we must pass into the other without destroying her. Irigaray almost expresses it when she returns to the nominal system in place of the magisterial "I" that masks itself in objective truth. Lacan's "I" arranges objects around its own center, but Irigaray's "I" is a "you" that an "I" can speak, an "I" that is already a "me" for "you" to understand.

Nevertheless, some of Irigaray's and Cixous's poststructuralist inheritance has stood in the way of the full development of those promising new possibilities in theory of language. The tendency to criticize language itself (instead of the structuralist theories of language that claim, even by their own admission, only to present a theoretical ideal) has forced French feminists into the project of discovering *another* feminine language. This has in turn necessitated a removal from concrete confrontations (with oppressive orders conducted in "rational" language) and provoked the charge that Irigaray's and Cixous's approaches lead to feminist marginality and impotence. It has also hindered the development of an account of language adequate to the facts of linguistic expression and communication. Related is the concern that this "other" language of Cixous and Irigaray is a mystic "women's" language ratifying the sterotypic feminine characteristics of irrationality and emotionality. If, however, a feminist linguistics took as its project the attempt to encourage uses of language in which one could speak to and for another, that language need not constitute a marginalized women's speech.

Cixous and Irigaray also inherit from Lacan and Derrida a confinement in the "prison house" of western culture. They often share in the idealistic tendency of structuralist thought to ignore the historical/social specificity of language structures. Hellenic/Christian metaphysical and mythic categories, expressed in IndoEuropean grammars, become the structure of all possible thought. Once this is accepted, the only alternative is to return to preculture, to what is animal, bodily, hysterical, or even psychotic. If, however, not only the Law of the Father but also the mirroring substitutive functions described by both Lacan and Derrida are linked to the history and development of a historically specific way of life and thought, then other more promising and civilized alternatives may be available.

Working through and beyond these problems must occupy the next generation of femininst theorists. What they will discover about speakers and about the role language plays in both the maintenance and the overcoming of oppressive social structures must involve a new understanding of the interrelations between power, desire, and language. When philosophy of language and linguistics occlude these questions in the very theoretical foundations of their disciplines, the intentional force and power of language are hidden; cognitive science, the mechanization of institutional judgements, conservative educational practices that a logical approach to language supports, operate unchecked by any critical evaluation.

What might be the prolegomena for a future feminist linguistics that would reopen questions of desire and power? First, such a linguistics would have to focus on the language we all speak to each other. There could be no question of carving out from the body of speech an artificial formal object of scientific research. For the description and analysis of the diversity of language, formalization would be a temporary but never totally adequate tool that must always give way before the facts of how we speak. This is not to say that linguistics should not take as its object technical languages, but it would study them as language, as human communication that is passionate and intentionally motivated, and that establishes certain kinds of relations between speakers. Technical language, just as informal speech, would not be understood apart from personal and political concerns. Those concerns would not be reduced to mere bodily sensations that incidently prefigure or traverse language, but would be validated as desire embodied in language and giving to language its force and meaning.

Second, a feminist linguistics must at the same time accommodate the fact that we are sometimes "imprisoned" in ways of thinking and speaking that are alien and not of our making. This is only an insolvable problem when desire is seen as solipsistic, when private "pulsions" or drives are seen to press hopelessly against the necessarily alienated Other of language. But this is to ignore the fact that desire, like language, has objects, objects that are not privately constructed but are framed out of our life together. This is not to say, however, that the objects of our desires are constructed by language. Instead they are constantly reworked by us, in each conversation between communicating speakers. As we speak to someone, the objects of our desire are remade for another. The point is not to attempt the impossible expression of a private inner self, but to speak to express what others can understand. This is not to restore Lacan's anonymous Other that is language, but to establish an understanding with the other people with whom we work, live, and love. In these relationships, the symbolic structures that imprison us can be reformed.

The expression of such reformed desires implies a power different from Yahweh's. It is not a power to ordain what people say or do, a power which must always be limited as long as subjects are in any way allowed the freedom to speak for themselves. Instead it is the power of another that comes when we succeed in speaking for her, in saying what she means. "So this is what you really mean," said the serpent to Yahweh. "So this is what you understood," said the serpent to Eve. Eve may no longer be able to continue to be obedient when her legitimate desires are put into words. Even Yahweh, after the serpents resaying of his law, may be ashamed to continue to be a petty tyrannt.

Third, a feminist linguistics must not remove itself from the political power of language. Whether language is seen as "structure" or as the expression of private sensations, in both cases political action becomes problematic and a revolutionary language impossible to theorize. The grammatical and semantic structures that constitute Lacan's Law of the Father impose a conservatism that despairs of deep change in sexist or racist categories. Saussure makes clear that in his structuralist view of language individuals cannot wilfully change grammar; grammatical structures do evolve, but according to linguistic laws (Saussure 1966, 74). Alternately, if language is seen as expressing private sensation with the power to disrupt structures of meaning, this disruption cannot be constructive. It may break apart old truths, old hierarchies, but it cannot substitute any new values or forms of life. Julia Kristeva, also a prominent French language theorist, in her latest book (*The Powers of Horror*) is resigned to the fact that the symbolic order of the Father and the abjection of the Woman/Mother must always be reinstituted. This despair, however, is the result of a linguistics that recognizes only alienated structures and its underside, private physiological sensation. In such a linguistics, either speech is the exercise of an absolute power against which only diversionary tactics may be used, or the expression of an objectless libido that can never be satisfied.

If, instead, language is seen as the constantly reworked shape of desires whose reworking constitutes our mutual power over each other—especially the power to understand each other—then language is the very substance of political action. Each time we speak, as long as we do not numbly repeat the words of those who legislate what is to be believed and said, as Eve seems inclined to do at the beginning of her talk with the serpent, then we must, as we speak, remake the terms on which we live with each other. It can't be any other way. It is only in Yahweh's mythic constitution of his godly power that the subject speaks only for himself. Even Yahweh always speaks, as we all do, for others, and his power over us is absolute only as long as we are silent. Even as Eve obediently repeats Yahweh's orders, there is already in her repetition a new tone that indicates that the meaning of that order has changed. Even as she mouths his words, his laws begin to seem not an absolute theocracy, but a shallow admonition directed against the legitimate desires of his subjects for health, wisdom, and happiness.

Fourth, a feminist linguistics would have to be focused on changing usage and not "timeless" structures. Language cannot be studied outside its social, economic, familial context. It cannot be separated from the historically situated desires and motivations that give it meaning. As part of its initial project, structuralism imposes on the researcher a distance from those desires; the linguist will study patterns that might be discernible if he and the object of his study were without desire, motivation, or location in space and time. In this ideal of scientific objectivity, all that is left of language is a kind of fossil, the meaningless remains of actual living speech studied for formal patterns rather than as a clue to the life that once gave it shape.

A feminist linguistics would point the way to a new kind of textual practice, in which the point is not to map the licit or illicit tracing of signifiers. Historic texts such as *Genesis* would be studied in context, situated in the desires of the Hebrew women for the comforts of Asherah worship, and in the intent of the priests to enforce fidelity to their imagined treaty with the war god Yahweh. Linguistics itself would have to be understood as a discourse rooted in desire.[18] No pretension to the status of an objective metalanguage can elevate any meaningful account of language beyond intention and passion. Even a theory of language must admit to the intentions that make it understandable.

The account of language currently popular among American philosophers, which is based on a semantics borrowed from mathematical logic and a cognitive science that assumes that the human brain is functionally equivalent to a computer, might be so questioned. Beneath the supposed founding question of this semantics—how can we devise a formal system that duplicates rational thought?—might be found another question: how can we mechanize thought so that no personal intervention is necessary. The political advantages of such an achievement are obvious. Power to speak for others is asserted finally in a way that makes response impossible. It is no longer Yahweh who speaks by fiat, but the computer who tells us what we may and may not do. It would be the business of a feminist linguistics to uncover such desires and motivations in this and other philosophies of language. At the same time, accepting the paradoxes of reflexivity that have constantly marred the machinery of a logical analysis, it would have to remain conscious of and critical of its own motivations and desires.

If part of that motivation could be tentatively stated as the desire to remove the constraints on our talk that keep in place unjust institutions, and to encourage a freedom of speech that can institute new kinds of relations between women and men, this is not to say that any language can have absolute power. Silencing is always possible by force; repetition is often imposed by sanctions that we have no power to resist. The serpent, I am sure you are ready to remind me, *was* ground into the dust, *was* ordained as the enemy of women. Adam and Eve *were* condemned to their present roles as laborer and childbearer. But here is where the serpent might whisper again, "Didn't you realize? Didn't you understand that this was not a history?" *Genesis* is not a simple statement of fact. It is a cautionary tale. Yahweh does not have the absolute power he boasts of. The story itself shows it. There is another power in words that is not the power to legislate and threaten. What power? The power to bring people to their and our desire. The power to enter into a resolute circle of mutual understanding against which repression must be blunted. The power to seduce our enemies. The power to reveal a simple obvious truth buried beneath layers of rationalization and technical jargon. It is this power that a feminist linguistics might try to describe and in describing make possible.

NOTES

1. See: Aristotle's *Politics* I:3–7, where the conceptual symmetry between man/woman, master/slave, mind/body, reason/emotion is used to support both natural slavery and the subjection of women to men; Thomas Aquinas, "On the First Man." where Thomas adapts this Aristotelian scheme to Christian doctrine and uses the connection between man and rationality to justify the separate creation of woman, Eve's pre-fall subjection to the male head of the family, and the restriction of women to the work of generation; more recently, a semantics based on hierarchical oppositions for which the paradigm is male-female. See my "Inequalities of Semantic Structure," for an account of the ways in which such a semantics supports and does not support the view that the deep structures of linguistic meaning are sexist.

2. See, for example, the argument of Christine Fauré in "The Twilight of the Goddesses"; Catherine Clément's criticism of Hélène Cixous's feminist practice in *"The Newly Born Woman"*; Julia Kirsteva's indictment of women's writing in *"La révolution du langage poétique,"* 614.

3. Frege's term was the "Farbung," or coloring that had to be stripped off words to exhibit logical form.

4. This is the distinction that defines the subject matter of structural linguistics as laid down by its founder Ferdinand Saussure in his *Course in*

General Linguistics. Speech, or *"parole,"* Saussure argued, is "many sided and heterogeneous; straddling several areas simultaneously—physical, physiological, psychological—it belongs both to the individual and to society; we cannot put it into any category of human facts, because we can't discover its unity" (9). Instead the linguist will study *"la langue,"* language as a "self-contained whole and a principle of classification." This structure is not the function of speakers, but is "passively assimilated" (14). With this move, linguistics casts out of the province of its study the personal, passionate, and intentional sources of linguistic expression.

5. This is the innovation of recent speech act theory that grafts onto a logically structured propositional core, a system of rules for the accomplishment of various speech acts. We may assert, propose, promise, command, etc., a proposition. John Searle, in his *Speech Acts*, faithfully repeats the logician Frege's account of propositional meaning, but adds constitutive rules by which we do things with words. In this way propositional truth remains cordoned off from use and even use is mapped out in rules that allow no room for personal expression or commitment.

6. This is the position of Julia Kristeva in her monumental study of *The Revolution in Poetic Language*. Kristeva distinguished symbolic language structures from semiotics, a prewriting of physiological drives that both prepares the way for language and remains as an energizing and disruptive force. See my critique of her linguistic dualism in "The Woman Clothed in the Sun: Julia Kristeva and the Escape to/from Language."

7. Noam Chomsky was the innovator here, combining Saussurian linguistic methods with a rationalistic view of geometric competence. Transformational grammar derives rules by which a plurality of grammatical sentence forms can be generated from a propositional core, thus reconciling the variability of speech with the invariability of logical form.

8. There is no easy introduction to the very difficult often hermetic work of Jacques Lacan. Selections from his *Écrits* have been translated (1977), and a selection from his writings on sexuality and love (including his seminar on love, *Encore*) is available in *Feminine Sexuality* (1982). Otherwise, summaries can be found in Alice Jardine's recent *Gynesis* or in my *Feminist Theory and the Philosophies of Man,*" Chapter 5, "The Limits of the Thinkable: Lacan's Symbolic." Although Lacan never makes very clear the sense in which the symbolic phallus and the Name of the Father are the basis for linguistic meaning, it seems to be related to the necessity for plus (phallic presence) and minus (phallic absence) features in semantics, and to patrilineality.

9. The foundational text for Derrida's view of language and textual practice is his *Of Grammatology* (1976).

10. "There is only woman as excluded by the nature of things which is the nature of words, and it is necessary to say that if there is something of which they themselves complain at the moment it's very much that—simply they don't know what they say, that is all the difference between them and me" (Lacan 1976, 68).

11. See Lacan's discussion of women's mysticism in *Encore* (1975), especially "Dieu et la Jouissance de la Femme," (61ff).

12. See Derrida: "it remains then, for us to speak, to make our voices

resonate throughout the corridors in order to make up for the break-up of presence" (1973, 104).

13. Cixous 1975, 115–6. Further evidence can be found in the fact that semanticists almost invariably illustrate component analysis of meaning with the example of family relations. Words like "mother," "father," "sister," "brother," are taken as the model of the relations between component and word meaning as the constitutive components—male, female, parent, sibling—are factored out. A particular kind of family life becomes the model for the structure of linguistic meaning.

14. The manifesto for this project is "The Laugh of the Medusa" (1976), where Cixous urges an "*écriture féminine.*"

15. An example of such knowledge in the field of science might be the work of biologist Barbara McClintock as interpreted recently by the philosopher of science, Evelyn Fox Keller (1983).

16. See Richard Rorty's 1985 speech, "From Language to Logic to Play," to the International Congress of Philosophy in Mexico. Answering charges brought by Central American and South American philosophers that North American philosophy exercises a cultural imperialism, Rorty argued that philosophy should not be seen as a foundation for politics or be judged by its political implications, but should be engaged in as a kind of "experimental self-creation," a kind of play that we should not expect to "rescue and redeem us" (Rorty 1985, 753). For an expansion of this view see his *Mirror of Nature*.

17. See Irigaray's "Des Marchandises Entre Elles" in *This Sex* (1981).

18. See Julia Kristeva's interesting account of the "The Ethics of Linguistics," in *Desire in Language* (1980, 23–35).

REFERENCES

Aristotle. 1941. *Complete Works.* Edited by Richard McKeon. New York: Random House.

Austin, John. 1962. *How to Do Things with Words.* Cambridge: Harvard University Press.

Clément, Catherine, and Hélène Cixous. 1975. *La Jeune Née.* Paris: Union Generale d'Editions. (English version: 1987. *Newly Born Woman.* Translated by B. Wing. Miami: University of Miami Press.)

Cixous, Hélène. 1976. "The Laugh of the Medusa." Translated by K. Cohen and P Cohen. *Signs* 7(4):875–93.

———. 1980. *Illa.* Paris: des Femmes.

Davidson, Donald. 1984. *Inquiries into Truth and Interpretation.* Oxford: Clarendon Press.

Derrida, Jacques. 1973. *Speech and Phenomena.* Translated by D. B. Allison and N. Garner. Evanston, Ill.: Northwestern University Press.

———. 1976. *Of Grammatology.* Translated by G. C. Spivak. Baltimore, Md.: Johns Hopkins University Press.

Fauré, Christine. 1981. "The Twilight of the Goddesses or the Intellectual Crisis of French Feminisms." *Signs* 7 (1):81–86.

Irigaray, Luce. 1981. *This Sex which is Not One.* Translated by C. Porter with C. Burke. Ithaca, N.Y.: Cornell University Press.

——. 1982. *Passions élementaires.* Paris: Minuit.

——. 1985. *Speculum of the Other Woman.* Translated by G. Gill. Ithaca, N.Y.: Cornell University Press.

Jardine, Alice. 1985. *Gynesis.* Ithaca, N.Y.: Cornell University Press.

Keller, Evelyn Fox. 1983. *A Feeling for the Organism: The Life and Work of Barbara McClintock.* New York: Freeman.

Kristeva, Julia. 1974. *La révolution du langage poétique.* Paris: du Seuil. (English version translated by M. Waller. *Revolution in Poetic Language.* New York: Columbia University Press.)

——. 1980. *Desire in Language.* Oxford: Basil Blackwell.

Lacan, Jacques. 1975. *Encore, Le Séminaire de Jacques Lacan, Livre XV.* Paris: du Seuil.

——. 1977. *Écrits: A Selection.* Translated by A. Sheridan. London: Tavistock.

——. 1982. *Feminine Sexuality.* Edited by J. Mitchell and J. Rose. Translated by J. Rose. Beaconsfield, Eng.: Pitman Press.

Nye, Andrea. 1987a. "The Woman Clothed in the Sun: Julia Kristeva and the Escape to/from Language." *Signs* 12 (4):664–686.

——. 1987b. "The Inequalities of Semantic Structure." *Metaphilosophy* 18 (3–4):222–240.

——. 1987c. "The Unity of Language." *Hypatia* 2 (2):95–109.

——. 1988. *Feminist Theory and the Philosophies of Man.* London: Croom-Helm.

Quine, Willard von O. 1960. *Word and Object.* Cambridge, Mass: MIT Press.

Rorty, Richard. 1979. *Philosophy and the Mirror of Nature.* Princeton: Princeton University Press.

——. 1985. "From Language to Logic to Play." *Proceedings and Addresses of the American Philosophical Association* 59 (5):749–759.

Saussure, Ferdinand. 1959. *Course in General Linguistics.* Translated by Wade Baskin. New York: McGraw Hill.

Thomas Aquinas. 1973. "On the First Man." In *Basic Works of Saint Thomas Aquinas.* Edited by A. Pegis. New York: Random House.

Tarski, Alfred. 1944. "The Semantic Conception of Truth and the Foundation of Semantics." *Journal of Philosophy and Phenomenological Research* 4:341–375.

Wittgenstein, Ludwig. 1953. *Philosophical Investigations.* Translated by G. E. M. Anscombe. Oxford: Basil Blackwell.

——. 1961. *Tractatus Logico-Philosophicus.* Translated by D. Pears and B. F. McGuinness. London: Routledge & Kegan Paul.

Part VI

Philosophy of Mind

Philosophy of mind traditionally has centered around a cluster of problems within metaphysics and theory of knowledge. Some philosophers discuss the nature of a person, personal identity, the concepts of mind/body, the problem of "other minds," or analyses of emotions. Others have focused on consciousness, mental phenomena, and lived experience. Throughout traditional discussions of the topics there has been a tendency to posit hierarchical categories, giving higher value to mind than to body. Even calling the field "philosophy of mind" indicates the predominance given to the mental; feminists often prefer to call it philosophical psychology. Since philosophers give greater value to mind and at the same time identify mind with man, and body with woman, women are once again devalued.

Feminist thinkers approach philosophy of mind in ways that value women and focus on women's experience in the formulations of the problems themselves. We offer alternative pictures of personhood, ways of conceptualizing and knowing persons that do not split off the mind from the body, or the person from her body. We also consider the implications that differences among women have for theories of personhood or personal identity. In addition, feminists prioritize the analysis of consciousness, perhaps because of the consciousness-raising that women engaged in at the outset of the present women's movement.

Exploring some of Simone de Beauvoir's valuable contributions to feminist philosophy, Judith Butler discusses Beauvoir's philosophical views about the body. She considers the notion that the natural body assumes meaning within an historical context, the way in which, specifically, the human body takes on a gendered form. Examining the dictum that one is not born, but rather becomes, a woman, Butler shows some of the ways that we construct ourselves as women.

Elizabeth Spelman discusses the relationship between theories of the emotions and the logic of anger. She uses a cognitivist approach that holds that anger is always about something we perceive as unfair. Because the dominant male culture does not wish to be judged as unfair, women are therefore deflected from their anger. Spelman would like a politics of the emotions that would enable women to assert our own agency.

María Lugones relates the theory of personal identity to the problem of difference among women. Expressed as "world"-traveling, she writes of understanding another woman's world through loving perception instead of with an arrogant eye. A "world" according to Lugones is a real inhabited place—a life, not a utopia. As an outsider, she shifts from being one person to being another when she travels into the mainstream world. "Being at ease" in a world is being a fluent speaker, happy, bonded, with a shared history in that "world." The shift in her person when she is at ease in a world explains why she can have characteristics such as playfulness in one world but not in another where she is an outsider.

Chapter 15

Gendering the Body: Beauvoir's Philosophical Contribution

Judith Butler

Simone de Beauvoir's *The Second Sex* is foundational to contemporary feminist philosophy in at least two senses. As a founding or original work that argued the case that women are, indeed, oppressed, *The Second Sex* made oppression visible through a cross-disciplinary methodology, appealing to literary images, biological and psychological theories, and historical and anthropological evidence. But Beauvoir's text also offers a foundation for an explicitly feminist account of bodily experience and so provides a distinct philosophical contribution to feminist theory. Although Beauvoir claims that she is writing an "existentialist ethics," it is not immediately clear how that philosophical program is to be reconciled with the various other kinds of analyses present in the work. She has said that she is no philosopher, though Sartre maintained she was a better philosopher than he was. So where are we to find philosophy in *The Second Sex*, and what are the signs of its presence? I would like to suggest that the philosophical content of the work is to be found precisely amidst the various concrete and cross-disciplinary analyses that she offers. In this sense, *The Second Sex* exemplifies and enacts *a philosophy in situation*. Beauvoir's distinctive manner of infusing the philosophical into the details of mundane life is the source both of her philosophical invisibility and of her largely unexamined philosophical significance.

Like Sartre and Merleau-Ponty, Beauvoir works to reveal the structures of lived experience, especially the structures of *embodiment*. But whereas for Sartre and Merleau-Ponty we hear only about "the body" in its abstract and ostensibly universal form, Beauvoir warns us that the universal is often equated with the masculine, that bodies for the most part come in gendered pairs, and that a concrete analysis of the body requires an answer to the question, "How is it that the human body takes on a gendered form?" Although some consider Beauvoir's *The Second Sex* to be exclusively concerned with documenting the facts of women's oppression, the text also offers an underacknowledged theory of gender identity and gender acquisition. It is this latter theory that characterizes the text as foundational in the second sense mentioned above: Beauvoir provides a few key formulations that suggest a distinction between the natural body and the body as an historical construct or signifier—this is the distinction between *sex* and *gender*. In addition, she provides a way of understanding how the natural body becomes transformed into an historical construct—in short, how it is that we become our genders, how we acquire them, and indeed embody them. Although some contemporary French and American feminist theorists claim to transcend Beauvoir even as they acknowledge their indebtedness to her, I would like to argue that her theory of gender identity has yet to be fully appreciated, and that Beauvoir's intellectual career, which has not ended with her recent death, is a philosophical enterprise only tentatively begun.

I do not mean to simplify her work by identifying its main philosophical preoccupation, for I am not prepared to claim that there is one. I would like to suggest, however, that Beauvoir makes two significant claims in *The Second Sex* that require closer scrutiny: (1) the body is not a natural fact but an historical idea[1] and (2) one is not born, but rather becomes, a woman.[2] The first claim is not as fanciful as it might first appear. Taken from Merleau-Ponty's *Phenomenology of Perception*, the notion of the body as an historical idea suggests only that for the body to have meaning for us, for the body to appear within a field of intelligibility, it must first be signified within an historically specific discourse of meaning. Applied to the gendered body, this formulation suggests that the gender is an historical idea or construct that the body assumes as if it were its natural form. The formulation does not dispute the biological or physiological facticity of the body, but is concerned, rather, with the meaning that the body—in all its facticity—comes to assume within the context of historical experience. The second claim, that one is not born, but rather becomes, a woman, follows from the first. How does a body come to signify an historical idea? By what mechanism or modality does a natural body become an historical construct and, in the case of gender, how is it that a natural body becomes historically constructed as a gendered body, which subsequently disguises itself as a natural fact? At its most basic level, the second formulation argues that one is perhaps born a given sex with a biological facticity, but that one becomes one's gender; that is, one acquires a given set of cultural and historical significations, and so comes to embody an historical idea called "woman." Thus, it is one thing to be born a female, but quite another to undergo proper acculturation as a woman; the first is, it seems, a natural fact, but the second is the embodiment of an historical idea.

But what does it mean to embody an historical idea, and how are we to understand Beauvoir's usage of the verb "become?" The phrase appears problematic on at least two counts: first, who is the "I," the subject, who is said to execute this process of becoming, who embodies the historical idea of gender, and who acquires gender as its cultural signification? Is this an "I" that precedes gender, that is the Subject, the Person, or some other pregendered universal agency? If it is the case that the body is always already gendered, if personhood is coextensive with gender itself, then what sense does it make to appeal to a subject who maintains an ontological status prior to gender itself? If we are to understand this becoming a gender as a kind of agency or volition, then a second and related problem emerges: what sense does becoming a gender have in a world where gender relations appear to be firmly established and deeply entrenched? What kind of freedom is this?

In what follows, I would like to meditate on the meaning of the verb "to become" in Beauvoir's formulation both to answer the question just posed, and to explicate the transition from the natural to the historical body. Finally, I would like to consider some of the radical cultural consequences of her provocative distinction between sex and gender.

So what does it mean that some of us are not born women, but *become* women? Note that Beauvoir does not say that one is not born, but rather made into, a woman. Gender is not passively received, and the process of acculturation cannot be likened to the passive process of being molded or inscribed by cultural conventions that are not only external but potent with agency. Although feminist theorists very often describe acculturation in terms of passive verbs—women are culturally constructed; gender is received—such formulations fail to account for the precise mechanism by which acculturation is enacted. For Beauvoir, acculturation is not a fact or even a precondition, but a peculiar kind of achievement, the culturally mediated relationship of an embodied agency to itself.

It would be mistaken to think that one becomes a woman only finally to "be" one. For Beauvoir, one never "is" a woman, for the act of becoming is never really completed. To "become" a woman means freely to realize a set of cultural possibilities, but this realization is never finished; on the contrary, it is an activity incessantly renewed. We can of course posture, as if we have achieved the teleological closure of our genders, as if we have become a given gender and now quite smugly inhabit that self-identical place, but even that posture must be maintained through a constant and tacit effort of freedom. Of course, one may well choose to embody a reified concept of womanhood or manhood, but in choosing the reification, one chooses also to sustain it. The constant presence and pressure of this effort, however, attests to the arbitrary ground of that construction, the illusory character of its substantial and self-identical reality. Just as Sartre's famous waiter *is* a waiter, so can we *be* our gender in a similarly false way. Indeed we might well call such being the bad faith of gender.

If one becomes a woman, according to Beauvoir, then one is always in the process of becoming a gender, and the process itself has no teleological end. In this sense, then, gender is a project, a skill, a pursuit, an enterprise, even an industry, the aim of which is to compel the body to signify one historical idea rather than another. Instead of claiming that one is a man or is a woman, it is necessary to substitute a vocabulary of action and effort for the reified vocabulary of self-identical nouns. Hence, one does one's womanhood, one executes it, institutes, produces and reproduces it, wears it, flaunts it, hides it, but always stylizes it in one way or another. For gender is a corporeal style, a way of acting the body, a way of wearing one's own flesh as a cultural sign. This is perhaps most clear in the various skills that advertisements encourage in order to approximate most closely the historical idea of a given gender: one puts on one's face, one puts in one's eyes; indeed, one does one's hair.

But surely it is not possible to become any gender we please at a moment's notice. Well, perhaps on stage, if we are very skilled; but such improvisation carries strict penalties when acted out on the gender stage of everyday life. One does not become a gender through a free and unconstrained act of choice, for gender identity is governed by a set of stringent taboos, conventions, and laws. There are punishments for not doing gender right: a man in Maine walks down the street in a dress, walking the way that women are supposed to walk; next day his body is found dead in a ravine. And though we may not have experienced his punishment directly (although much of childrearing is involved in inculcating the rules of gender through the fear of punishment), we nevertheless know something of the terror and shame of being told that we are somehow doing our gender wrong, that we have failed in some way to measure up to the cultural norm and expectation.

In the case of women, cultural norms constrain us to become, to choose, that which is the very opposite of choice. In other words, we are compelled to become the Other, the opposite of the Subject. As Other, women are not devoid of choice; rather, they are constrained to choose against their own sense of agency, and so to distort and undermine the very meaning of choice. While man is understood to be a cognitive and choosing subject, woman is culturally obligated to become a pure body, an instrument of his desire, a reflector or medium for his agency. Here we immediately confront a contradiction. How can women be a process of becoming, the realization of culturally constrained possibilities, and yet also be the Other, the opposite of possibilities, the fixity of the always already realized? For Beauvoir, it seems, we must understand the gender of woman as that particular modality of choice that is culturally constrained to choose against itself.

And though Beauvoir maintains that gender has been for women a project of self-defeat, she is also clear that that posture is in no sense either naturally or historically necessary. But what conditions Beauvoir's view of change? Does she posit an abstract freedom that can have no concrete meaning for women, or is there perhaps another way to read her theory so that gender hierarchy and reified gender identity might be subverted from within the very terms of culture? If one becomes one's gender, one does it within a network of gender rules and relations. From the moment of birth, the body is culturally signified by a language and a set of institutions that immediately classify the infant as either male or female before even the bestowal of a proper name. Hence, the question to consider is what it might mean to become one's gender within a cultural context in which one is not, really, free to become much of anything else. Is becoming one's gender a redundancy in a world in which gender marks the infant from the moment of its birth? If we are always already gendered, inasmuch as we are bodies in culture, then what sense does it make to say that we become what we have always been?

There is a sense to this circularity, for to say that we are marked by gender is not to say that we are marked in a permanent and irrevocable way, the mark to end all marks. If the body is named and classified, if it is upon its inception in the world institutionalized and governed by historically entrenched gender norms, that self-same body must take up that mark and reproduce it in and through its own corporeal style. In other words, bodies are not only marked, but must live their marks, and it is in the possibility of living one's gender mark differently that cultural variation and indeed, transformation, exist. When does the mark of gender become truly effective? When it is taken up and taken on, when the norm is internalized and then dramatized in the very project of the person. The strength of Beauvoir's analysis is that it shows us the contingency at the foundation of gender, the uneasy but exhilarating fact that *it is not necessary* that we become the genders that we have in fact become.

As Sartre once claimed that human beings *exist* their bodies, using "exist" as a transitive verb, so Beauvoir seems to be claiming that one becomes one's gender, where "become" is similarly transitive. One embodies gender, but one has been embodying it all along, since embodied life is from the outset governed by specific gender norms. Hence, there is no beginning to this becoming, nor is there an end. In a sense, gender is a mode of becoming that by definition can have no inception and no closure. Hence, the body is a field of cultural possibilities that are enacted and modalized in various ways, and we might think of the body as the theatre of gender, the sites of received cultural meanings, and yet also the place of their reproduction and variation. If the body is a modality for realizing possibility, and if possibilities governing the gendered body are culturally constrained, then it would seem that the body is a site for the constant production and reproduction of cultural possibilities.

But how exactly would this notion be made clear? In the first place, since woman is no longer a noun, no longer a self-identical substance, then there is much that requires reconceptualization. When Aretha Franklin sings, "you make me feel like a natural woman,"[3] the senti-ment of substantial gender identity there makes itself felt. For if "woman" denotes an essence, a soul, a core, a substance, then her various acts and pleasures, desires and dreams are taken to be the necessary attributes of that essential gender substance. And certainly there has been a great deal of popular and scientific thinking that has tacitly subscribed to gender as a kind of being. We speak quite often of someone being a real or true man or woman, being "manly" or "womanly" as if participating in an ideal Form of man or woman, and here we tend to assume that man and woman are substances that not only exist but are causally responsible for certain kinds of behavior. This is nowhere more present, de Beauvoir suggests, than when we explain that someone's action can be understood "because she is a woman." We tend to assume that if one is of a given sex, then it follows that one is a given gender, and it follows also that sexual desire will be directed toward the opposite sex. It seems to be a kind of unity of experience—one's biological facticity, one's cultural identity, and one's sexual desire, as if cultural identity were a necessary reflection of sex, and sexual desire an expression of both cultural identity and biological facticity. When Aretha claims to feel like a natural woman, her pleasure is understood to be a natural expression of her sex, and that pleasure has a certain gender-specific quality that she takes to be natural. On the one hand, we might wonder why Aretha wants to feel natural, and why this is clearly a compliment she is paying to her presumably male lover, and there we might speculate that feeling natural makes her feel right, makes her feel that she fits in, and fits together, and that her existence somehow feels justified. But note that Aretha says that she is made to feel *like* a natural woman. She uses a simile that suggests that she knows the natural woman to be a figure and a fiction. Her claim, then, seems to translate into the following: "you allow me a fantasy for a moment, the experience of a unity of my sex, gender, and desire that I know to be false but wish were true." Aretha, then, doesn't dispute Beauvoir, but gives us some understanding of the emotional pull of the illusion of a natural and substantial gender identity.

How might Beauvoir explain Aretha's unsung theory of substantial gender identity? Remember that according to that opposing belief, sex is a substance expressed not only in the various expressions of femininity or masculinity that govern the cultural appearance of the sexed body, but also in the various modalities of desire and pleasure. There is here a kind of causality or, better yet, a theory, that desire and gender are attributes of sex, that they are expressions of sex, and essential ones at that, ones that make sex known. Sex itself is secretive, as Michel Foucault suggests, for we only know sex through gender and desire, but they in turn everywhere point back to this core, this essence, this substantial self—the most elusive of noumenal beings. But what if this substantial sex does not exist, and our experience of gender, pleasure, and desire are nothing other than the set of acts, broadly construed, that *constitute* an identity rather than reflect one. In other words, what if, in existentialist fashion, gender is nothing other than the acts that realize it, so that gendered behavior and desire are the modes through which gender is regularly constituted? In other words, perhaps Beauvoir criticizes the notion of gender as a natural substance in much the same way that Sartre disputed the reality of the substantial self. Let us consider further the radical cultural consequences of her view.

Let us imagine there is a man—note the faulty use of the noun—and that something he does, something he wears, strikes us as feminine. For the moment, let's not question whether we all agree on what such a characterization might mean or where such notions come from, but let us indulge our most sorry of cultural intuitions and begrudgingly assent to the fact that we have some notion of what I am suggesting. The tendency might be to claim that this is a man, but he is acting in a feminine way, and that the attribute that we ascribe to him does not quite adhere to the natural substance that he is. In such a case, we might conclude that he is acting unnaturally, that his action does not suit a man; i.e., that this attribute does not rightly express the sex that he is. There may even be situations in which one might argue, on behalf of oneself or others, that one's gender does not suit one's sex, but there again, invariably, sex is understood already to have an intrinsic meaning and reality. In making the claim that sex and gender are dissonant, we don't regard sex as a simple facticity, but as a natural dictate to which certain forms of cultural identity, action, and feeling are said properly to adhere. The possibility of claiming that a sex is right or wrong with respect to a given gender, that a gender is right or wrong given a certain sex, or that a desire is right or wrong given a certain sex, presupposes that there is a natural causality linking sex, gender, and desire, and that the latter two ought properly to reflect the former and be its natural expressions.

If we reject this notion of substantial sex, sex as a being, if we call its bluff and claim that it was a fictitious unity from the start, how then do we understand the man who takes on a feminine attribute? Can we say, "But, oh, he is really a man, and he is just taking on the attribute of a woman," or does he constitute the kind of man he is by taking on the attribute? Indeed, by taking on the attribute, he is amplifying the very notion of what it is to be a man. If gender is nothing other than the continuous presence of actualizing certain cultural possibilities, this actualization must be conceived apart from the existence of any interior essence or teleology to be actualized; indeed, what is actualized is an *external* cultural possibility. Importantly, gender is the enactment of cultural possibilities already established. Hence, if a man does something we call feminine, then the femininity of the act reconceptualizes what it means to be a man. And if a woman acts in a masculine way, then it is no longer possible to claim, "Oh, she is acting that way, but really she is a woman, and we all know what that is," as if the substance is there, lurking but latent. The acting is itself the constituting, and in acting in a masculine way, she changes the very meaning of what it is to be a woman; indeed, she expands the meaning of what it means to be a woman to include a cultural possibility that it previously excluded.

But note that the retroactive reconceptualization of gender through the mixing of conventional attributes involves a fundamental confusion of terms. The very meanings of "masculine" and "feminine" become fluid, interchangeable, and indeterminate, and their repeated usage in dissonant contexts erodes their descriptive power. Indeed, we might imagine a carnival of gender confusion that not only confuses fatally the sorry cultural intuitions that we originally accepted at the outset of this discussion, but institutes a new gender vocabulary, a proliferation of genders freed from the substantializing nomenclature of "woman" and "man." Such a vocabulary is occasionally found in homosexual cultural contexts where a proliferation of fluid categories like "butch" and "femme" are already operative. The effect of this carnival can be conceptualized in one of two ways, either as an internal expansion of existing gender categories or as a proliferation of gender itself beyond the usual two. But this is a matter for a different discussion altogether.[4]

If gender is released from the ontological trappings that the noun form sets for it, then we can understand it as the kind of transitive verb that Beauvoir intended it to be. In the first place, it is no longer possible to discriminate between right and wrong genders, right and wrong sexes, or right and wrong directionalities for sexual desire, for there would be no natural model against which to judge any of their myriad expressions. Gender is revealed as a thoroughly cultural innovation, a constant activity whereby the body comes to signify any number of cultural possibilities. When we think closely about Beauvoir's formulation, that one becomes one's gender and that, equivalently, gender is a form of becoming, we realize that there is no necessary relation between sex and gender. If sex is the anatomical facticity of binary difference among human bodies, and if gender is the cultural significance that sex comes to assume, then gender is in no way causally dependent on sex, and we might well ask whether there cannot be a number of different genders that each sex permits, or even a number of genders that might equally well be attributed to either biological sex, or both. Not only is there no causal relation between sex and gender, but more recent readers of Simone de Beauvoir have suggested that "sex" itself is a misnomer, and that the ostensibly biological reality that we designate as sex is itself an historical construct and, indeed, a political category.[5]

By refusing a naturalistic vocabulary that reifies gender and, specifically, the gender of women, Beauvoir occasions an historical understanding not only of gender, but of sex as well. Once gender is no longer causally dependent upon sex, gender itself becomes a principle of cultural innovation, an "act," a daily performance that constitutes identity. As a result, the various gendered acts and attributes, now freed from the burden of reflecting a natural sex that was always a fiction, become key moments in the cultural reproduction and invention of gender. No one can be said to have a gender anymore; it's not a possession, nor is it something that one simply *is*. Gender is a mundane drama specifically corporeal, constrained by possibilities specifically cultural. But this constraint is not without some moments of contingency, of possibility, of unprecedented cultural confusion that will invariably work to destroy the illusion that gender constraint is a dictate from nature.

In closing, I would like to consider Beauvoir's general reasons for refusing the human body as natural. At the close of *A Very Easy Death*, Beauvoir's reflections on the death of her mother, she refers to the unnaturalness of death. Yes, she knows that everyone does die, and she needed no lessons in biology to understand the necessity of human mortality. But death, as regular and sure as it is, is never part of human experience, and for Beauvoir the body that does not live, that does not dramatize its possibilities, is no longer part of the human realm. At her mother's bedside she tells us, "It was there that I saw Death, the Death of the dance of death, with its bantering grin, the Death of fireside tales that knocks on the door, a scythe in its hand, the Death that comes from elsewhere, strange and inhuman: it had the very face of Maman when she showed her gums in a wide smile of unknowingness."[6]

Beauvoir goes on to say, "You do not die from being born, nor from having lived, nor from old age. You die from *something*."[7] For

Beauvoir death is a perpetual scandal and offense because it is the body deprived of its project, it is the cessation of all becoming. She reflects that the experience of her mother's death was "a dress rehearsal for [her] own burial."[8] But what did she there rehearse? Her final reflection in that essay on finality advises us how to think about her own recent death. In her words, "There is no such thing as a natural death: nothing that happens to a [human being] is ever natural, since a [human] presence calls the world into question. [Everyone] must die, but for [every person] [one's] death is an accident and, even if [one] knows it and consents to it, an unjustifiable violation."[9]

NOTES

1. Simone de Beauvoir, *The Second Sex*, tr. H. M. Parshley (New York: Bantam Books, 1974), 30.

2. Simone de Beauvoir, *The Second Sex*, 249.

3. The song is originally Carole King's.

4. See Esther Newton, "The Misunderstanding: Toward a More Precise Sexual Vocabulary," in *Pleasure and Danger: Exploring Female Sexuality*, ed. Carole S. Vance (Boston: Routledge & Kegan Paul, 1984), 242–250.

5. See Monique Wittig, "One is Not Born a Woman," *Feminist Issues* 1:2; and "The Category of Sex," *Feminist Issues* 2:2. For a more comprehensive comparison of de Beauvoir and Wittig, see my "Variations on Sex and Gender: Beauvoir, Wittig, and Foucault," *Praxis International* 5:4.

6. Simone de Beauvoir, *A Very Easy Death*, tr. Patrick O'Brian (New York: Pantheon, 1965), 105.

7. *A Very Easy Death*, 105.

8. *A Very Easy Death*, 100.

9. *A Very Easy Death*, 106, my pronomial replacements.

Chapter 16 —————————————————————

Anger and Insubordination

Elizabeth V. Spelman

[anyone] who does not get angry when there is reason to be angry, or does not get angry in the right way at the right time and with the right people, is a dolt.

Despite appearances to the contrary, this uncompromising remark about the propriety of anger is not from a late twentieth century self-help book on the importance of "getting in touch with your feelings." Its source is Aristotle, and it is found in one of his best known and most highly regarded works, the *Nicomachean Ethics*.[1] For Aristotle, thinking about the appropriateness of anger and other emotions was part of thinking about how we ought to conduct our lives. In this brief essay I hope to begin to make clear a few of the ways in which assumptions about the appropriateness and inappropriateness of our emotions are intimately tied to the moral and political dimensions of our relations to each other. In particular I want to reflect on what Aristotle's comment tells us about the nature of anger, and think about how the idea that there are right, and wrong, reasons for becoming angry is played out in our lives.

But first of all I have to say that I fudged a bit in supplying the quotation to you. Aristotle actually said that the *man* who does not get angry when he has reason to be angry, or does not get angry in the right way at the right time with the right people is a dolt. And when Aristotle said "man," he meant *man* (in fact, only certain men—for example, not men who were slaves), not woman. Aristotle thought that women were deformed men,[2] and that the virtues of men were different from those of women: a man's courage, for example, is shown in commanding, while a woman's courage is seen in her obeying.[3] So we cannot assume that Aristotle meant those remarks about anger to be about or addressed to women, slave or free.[4]

Secondly, we find elsewhere in Aristotle, as we find most everywhere in Plato and in the history of western philosophy in general, considerable anxiety about the emotions:[5] for the emotions typically are seen as interfering with the smooth and successful functioning of

263

reason, and hence as lessening the prospects of good philosophy (which requires that reason be in control) and good government (which requires that people with a high degree of rationality be in command). As Plato more or less put it in the metaphor of the cave,[6] a day without reason is like a day without sunshine.

Indeed, over the centuries there have been special stakes involved in the question of how the emotions are related to reason, and the case of anger has revealed these stakes in telling ways. In western cultures there has long been an association of reason with members of groups that are dominant politically, socially, and culturally, and of emotion with members of subordinate groups. (R. S. Peters, who is established in the firmament of Anglo-American philosophy of education, told us not long ago: "we speak of emotional outbursts, reactions, upheavals, and women."[7]) It has been argued again and again, in one form or another, that just in virtue of this association, rational types ought to dominate emotional types.

But there is a striking exception to this assignment: while members of subordinate groups are expected to be emotional, indeed to have their emotions run their lives, their anger will not be tolerated: the possibility of their being angry will be excluded by the dominant group's profile of them. Women are expected to be easily given to sadness, say, or to jealousy—indeed, women who don't cry or don't get jealous may have their credentials as "real women" challenged; but anger is not appropriate in women, and anything resembling anger is likely to be redescribed as hysteria or rage instead. In the United States, whites aren't surprised that Blacks should sing the blues; whether depicted as very sad, or as very happy, Blacks have been typically depicted by whites as in any case full of emotion—but *not* full of anger. In fact, the emotion of anger seems positively to be excluded by the image of the shuffling step-and-fetchit or the field hand ecstatic to be working under a friendly sun.[8]

(This apparent anomaly about anger can be illustrated in quite another way too: in the third century A.D., the theologian Tertullian insisted that surely anger was a part of the rational element of the soul, not the irrational; otherwise, in rightly attributing anger to God, one would wrongly and blasphemously be charging God with irrationality.)[9]

Why has anger been appropriated by and for dominant groups or beings when in so many other ways emotions are thought to be the province of subordinate groups? What did Shakespeare tell us about anger when he had Lear cry out,

> touch me with noble anger,
> And let not women's weapons, water drops,
> Stain my man's cheeks![10]

Some theories of the emotions do a better job than others of enabling us to understand how it is possible for theological, social, and political issues to get so easily attached to what might appear to be a straightforward metaphysical question about what the emotions are and how they are related to reason.

Recently there has been an intense revival of interest in what have been called "cognitivist" theories of the emotions. Cognitivist theories are so called because they insist that judgments or beliefs (or some kind of cognitive state) are constituent of emotions. For example, having fear involves believing that some danger is imminent; being angry involves judging that some wrong or injustice has been done. Cognitivist theories are often contrasted to the view that emotions are like feelings of dizziness or spasms of pain since they do not involve any kind of cognitive state. According to this view emotions are, quite literally, dumb events. (I shall refer to this view without prejudice as the "Dumb View.") Cognitivists insist that any adequate theory of the emotions has to be compatible with familiar ways that emotional states are described and evaluated. When people are sad or angry or jealous or happy, they typically are sad or angry or jealous or happy *about* or *at* someone or something: I'm sad that my friend died; I fear that there will be nuclear war. Moreover, sadness or anger or jealousy or happiness can be regarded as appropriate or inappropriate, reasonable or unreasonable, justified or unjustified, by others or by oneself. (Indeed, our emotions are educated, or miseducated, Aristotle held, through learning what emotional responses are appropriate for which moments.)

According to cognitivists, the Dumb View cannot account for the "aboutness" of emotions, nor for the ways in which they are evaluated and judged. How could the happenings or events or dumb sensations that emotions are supposed to be, be characterized as being *about* anything, and in what sense could they be described as justified or unjustified? According to the Dumb View, emotions are at best arational and at worst irrational: they either can't be judged as rational or irrational (any more than spasms can), or they are by definition irrational. But cognitivists point out that a phrase such as "irrational fear" is not a mere redundancy, nor is "rational fear" a contradiction in terms: we may not only think of fear as a rational response to a particular circumstance, but in fact describe someone as foolhardy for not knowing that a situation is fearful.

I shall not make it my business here to defend any or all versions of the cognitivist view of the emotions. I shall assume that in its general outlines the view is widely taken now to be an eminently defensible one,[11] and that the Dumb View has lost whatever hold it has had in philosophical psychology. What I want to explore here are aspects and implications of the cognitivist view for understanding the significance of emotion in our individual and communal lives. In particular, I want to see what the cognitivist theory tells us about the importance of anger in the lives of those relegated to positions of subordination in and through the political, social, economic, and cultural institutions of their society. I think the cognitivist theory considerably deepens our understanding of the significance of the claim that people in subordinate positions have the right to be angry; moreover, that in conjunction with certain views about the nature of self-knowledge, self-deception, and self-respect, the cognitivist theory enables us to understand why at least in certain circumstances people perhaps *ought* to be angry.

We already noted that according to the cognitivist theory, emotions, anger included, typically have objects:[12] when I am angry I am angry *about* something and/or *at* someone. But it is not just that my attention is directed towards someone or something; part of what makes it correct to say that I am angry at someone is that I am making a negative evaluative judgment about him or her—let's say him—that he's done something not just that I wish he hadn't done, but something I think he should not have done, because it was bad, or wrong, or unfair, or uncalled for, or harmful to me or to others (or perhaps to himself). Moreover, insofar as my anger at him is appropriate, there must be good reason to believe he is responsible for the wrong or hurtful deed: if he didn't do it, or did it in circumstances in which he couldn't be said to be responsible for what he did, my anger would not be justified. My being angry at him means, in addition, not just that I hold him responsible, but that I find him blameworthy, since I think that what he did is the kind of thing he shouldn't have done.

But the regard I have for *myself* when I get angry at him is perhaps even more interesting than what my being angry implies about my regard for him. To be angry at him is to make myself, at least on this occasion, his judge—to have, and to express, a standard against which I assess his conduct. If he is in other ways regarded as my superior, when I get angry at him I at least on that occasion am regarding him as no more and no less than my equal. So my anger is in such a case an act of insubordination: I am acting as if I have as much right to judge him as he assumes he has to judge me. So I not only am taking his actions seriously but by doing so I am taking myself seriously, as a judge of the goodness or badness of his actions.

Given the cognitivist account of the logic of anger—the assumptions about oneself and the object of one's anger that make one's response a case of anger and not some other emotion[13]—we can begin to understand why dominant groups would not want to regard anger as the province of people who otherwise are conceived of as "emotional." The capacity to be angry just doesn't fit in as part of a personality profile designed by dominant people for those they see and wish to maintain as subordinate to them. For it would mean both that the subordinates would have standards of conduct applicable to the dominants, and express and apply those standards; and that dominants would thereby be subject to the judgments of those they've deemed to be beneath them. This undoubtedly would be perceived as threatening to the dominants—not only because the subordinates' anger might be followed up by action, but because it surely signals that subordinates take themselves seriously; they believe they have the capacity as well as the right to be judges of those around them, even of those who are said to be their "superiors." (A man's telling a woman how "cute" she is when she is angry signals his desire to undermine the moral and political agency of the angry woman. He may not take her seriously, but he recognizes that she is taking herself seriously.)

Moreover, the cognitivist theory allows us to make sense of the claim that subordinate groups have the right to be angry—that since they are oppressed, exploited, or otherwise treated unfairly, their anger is a justified response to their situation. In addition, the features of emotions, and of anger in particular (to which the cognitivist theory attends), may help to explain the fear and confusion surrounding the occurrence of anger. It may sometimes be quite rational for subordinates to fear expressing their anger—as opposed, say, to their sadness or most other emotions—just because those who have power over them may be threatened by such expressions and take steps to stifle them. The cognitivist theory also directs us to think about the objects of anger, and finding a clearly defined object may be a source of confusion, especially in the case under consideration, i.e., where a subordinate group is oppressed by a dominant one. For the success of such domination often depends, among other things, on making the mechanism of that subordination invisible—is it your boss? your husband? a parent? the "system"? that is responsible and blameworthy? If I can't be clear about the appropriate object of my anger, it makes having the anger all the more difficult to deal with. It might then appear to be simpler to regard the anger as an unwanted internal event and a "dumb" one at that, something due to a failing on my part.

Finally, the cognitivist theory helps us to make sense of the none-too-accidental ways in which subordinate groups are discouraged from thinking about their situation—whether through the denial of basic education; the erasure of facts about how they've been treated; the availability of drugs, alcohol, and other inducements to placidity or madness. Dominant groups surely know, at some level, that good clear thinking on the part of people in subordinate positions is likely to make such people angry. Once again, as Aristotle so neatly put it centuries ago:

> [anyone] who does not get angry when he has reason to be angry, or does not get angry in the right way at the right time and with the right people, is a dolt.

Some cognitivists have pointed out that one of the strengths of the cognitivist view is that unlike the Dumb View it can make sense of the idea of reason controlling the emotions: since part of having the emotion is judging that such-and-such is the case, coming to see that such-and-such is *not* the case will make one no longer have the emotion. George Pitcher offers this example:

> if I am first angry at someone for having done something, and later learn that what he did was entirely justified, then I shall almost certainly no longer be angry with him.[14]

Although our anger may not always be quite as tidy as Pitcher suggests, his example invites us to think about the variety of ways in which reason and emotion might be related. Unless we think that emotions are embarrassments to our lives—and most cognitivists seem pleased at the implications their theories have for the prospect of our ceasing to think of emotions as undermining human dignity—we will note that this point about reason controlling the emotions can be made in more than one way. "Control" does not necessarily mean "subdue" or "diminish," and to assume that it does is to weaken the import of this aspect of the cognitivist theory. A thermostat "controls" the temperature in the sense that it can result either in the shutting off of the furnace or in its being turned on. Reasoning about a situation may result in one's ceasing to be angry; but it may just as easily result in one's *becoming* angry. Rather than discovering that what someone did was "entirely justified," as in the above example, I may come to realize that what someone did was entirely *unjustified*. And, as Aristotle suggests, if under the circumstances I am *not* angry, then perhaps I am a "dolt," or someone without self-respect, or a bad friend. And, as Aristotle goes on to say in another passage from the *Ethics*, one who doesn't get angry when one ought to "is thought not to feel things nor to be pained by them, and, since he does not get angry, he is thought unlikely to defend himself; and to endure being insulted, and put up with insult to one's friends, is slavish."[15]

If the absence of anger in certain circumstances leads us to describe someone as a dolt, or a bad friend, or as lacking in self-respect, this suggests that in some circumstances people ought to be angry—e.g., when friendship or self-respect calls for it. But the claim that one ought to be angry raises questions not posed by the idea that one has the right to be angry.

It is one thing to say that we can ask whether an emotional reaction that has occurred is justified/unjustified, warranted/unwarranted. It is quite another to say that a particular emotional reaction that has not occurred ought to come into being. And whether we focus on the feeling component typical of many emotions (which the Dumb View tries to do exclusively) or its cognitive component, it may sound very strange to say that someone *ought* to have a particular emotional reaction. For example, "you ought to be angry" would have to be spelled out not just as "you ought to have a particular feeling."[16] If being angry means, as noted above, judging that someone has done a harmful or unjustified act, then enjoining Mary to be angry at John involves enjoining her to believe or judge that John has done a bad or harmful or unjustified act. If it makes sense to say that Mary ought to be angry at John, then Mary's being angry at John must be something within Mary's power to bring about—something she must be able to will, so to speak. And are beliefs or judgments the kinds of things we can be enjoined to have? In what way is what we believe or judge under our control?

A very clear example of a case in which we think of someone as having beliefs under her/his control is when we charge someone with self-deception: to deceive oneself involves avoiding or ignoring, refusing to rehearse or "spell out"[17] evidence one has for a proposition the truth of which one does not wish to face. Suppose I have deceived myself, for example, about whether I actually love someone else: I have managed to avoid spelling out for myself and to myself the evidence that would otherwise be readily available to me that I do not love that person. Self-deception provides a familiar way to exercise or try to exercise control over what we believe, by choosing to pay attention to, or to ignore, relevant evidence.[18] When we think and say that for prudential or moral reasons people ought not to deceive themselves, we seem to be saying that they ought or ought not to believe certain things. In fact, in the case of self-deception we seem to be saying that in some sense they know that what they believe is not true but they are taking steps—quite successfully—to try to convince themselves that it is true.

These comments about self-deception can now take us back to the original question about whether or not people in subordinate positions have the obligation to be angry. For if people are in such positions, and also are capable of understanding the forces that work to keep them there, why *aren't* they angry? The implication here is that either they can see and articulate the situation they are in, but lack the self-esteem or self-respect or respect for their community necessary to make them protest it; or they won't see or articulate the situation they are in, and are deceiving themselves. (As discussed in the conclusion, these alternatives do not exhaust the possibilities.) So it seems that the failure to be angry in the appropriate circumstances is linked in a variety of ways to questions about our capacity to make and to bear moral judgments.

So far, then, I have been trying to give some idea of why analysis of the emotions, and of anger in particular, can be regarded as revelatory of important parts of our lives as moral agents in our social and political relationships with others. I also hope to have shown thereby that insofar as dominant groups wish to place limits on the kinds of emotional responses appropriate to those subordinate to them, they are attempting to exclude those subordinate to them from the category of moral agents. Hence there is a politics of emotion: the systematic denial of anger can be seen as a mechanism of subordination, and the existence and expression of anger as an act of insubordination.

Is this essay, then, a call to members of subordinate groups to get angry? I recall Aristotle again:

> to get angry is easy. To do it to the right person, to the right extent, at the right time, with the right motive, and in the right way—that is hard.[19]

It is important to heed this caution for a number of reasons. First of all, identifying exactly what anger is, is not easy. Neither the Dumb View nor the cognitivist view as I've outlined them answer some of the hard questions about how to distinguish anger from its close relatives. The Dumb View would have us check to see whether a particular event is occurring inside us, but that can't settle the question. For part of what the cognitivist view teaches us is that we typically identify the feeling we are having by way of the judgment involved. For example, anger typically involves the judgment that one has been wronged or insulted; fear typically involves the judgment that one is in danger. Furthermore, one fear—e.g., my fear about nuclear war—is differentiated from another—e.g., my fear about being in a plane crash—not, obviously, by reference to some inner feeling but by reference to what my fear is about. However, the cognitivist view as I've described it so far still leaves me unclear and uneasy about what anger is. What does it mean to say that one ought to get *angry*? Merely that one ought to make a particular judgment about the world (i.e., that an injustice has been done)? It cannot be merely that, for one surely could make that judgment without being angry; some people, after all, are pleased by injustice. If there is a "right way" to be angry, as Aristotle suggests, what is it?

We have words for the close relatives of anger, from which we ought to distinguish it. Anger is different from rage, along all the dimensions typical of emotional states: whatever felt physiological or mental state is involved seems more pronounced in rage than in anger. A person in a rage tends to fixate on the object of his rage to the exclusion of all else, which is not so in many ordinary cases of anger (recall that we speak of rage as blind); we expect different behavior from a person who is raging than a person who is angry (in fact, to refer to someone as raging is to refer to their behavior in a way that is not so clear in the case of anger). However, since one of the ways subordinate groups in particular have been discouraged from looking positively or clearly at their anger has been through the conflation of rage and anger (with the connotation of hysteria or insanity), it has not always been easy for us to mark and rely on the distinction between the two. And if we are given to self-deception, we may ignore the facts to which anger, though not rage, would be an appropriate response. The general point—as Aristotle noted—is that anger is not only distinguishable from its excess, rage, but from its defect, which perhaps has no particular name but which nonetheless, as we know, can be handily arranged.

When I have spoken above about anger (as opposed to its "excess" or its "deficiency") as being justified, or about one being in some sense obliged to be angry, I have in mind an example such as the following: a woman from Spokane, Washington, who in an article in *off our backs*[20] described herself as having been "angry for 5 or 6 years" about the nursing care provided for elderly women. If she had merely been in a rage, she would have lacked the clarity of vision fully compatible with anger; if she had not been angered by what she saw, she may not have been motivated to act.

But there are other difficulties with the occurrence of anger than those mentioned by Aristotle, and these difficulties derive in part from the entrenched social and political relations that Aristotle helped to foster. To the extent that people in dominant positions wish to maintain their power and authority, then, because anger means what it does, expressions of anger by people in subordinate positions are much more likely to bring on violent reactions than expressions of other emotions. So encouraging persons in subordinate positions to recognize why they have the right to or why they ought to be angry must be done with concern for the consequences of their acting on that anger (though always with a view to Audre Lorde's stunning question: what are you paid for your silence?).[21] Moreover, there may be cases in which the evil of self-deception—as a means of forestalling anger—may seem easier to endure than the evils attendant upon knowing just how awful something is and being angered and moved to do something about it. What I have in mind here is the overweening importance to some prisoners in Nazi concentration camps of "not noticing"[22] the unconscionable treatment by the guards of the other prisoners. It wasn't just that if the guards noticed you noticing, you might be punished; it was that if you *did* notice, and quite rightly were angered or otherwise moved by what you saw, the frustration of not being able to act without almost certain severe penalty may have seemed unendurable. And so the only alternative may have appeared to become a "musselman"—a walking corpse, who no longer *felt* anything because you no longer *saw* anything.

My remarks about anger don't answer any of the mercilessly difficult questions about how any particular group of oppressed people ought to have acted. But such questions could not even arise unless we thought that certain situations not only justify but cry out for anger and other emotions in response. And we can be sure that those who unjustly wield power and authority over others will be pleased if those they oppress find some way to censor their anger.

And that returns me to one last note about the access the cognitivist theory provides to the politics of anger. If we recognize that judgments about wrong-doing are in some sense constitutive of anger, then we can begin to see that the censorship of anger is a way of short-circuiting, of censoring, judgments about wrong-doing. As Peter Lyman has recently pointed out,[23] anger is the "essential political emotion," and to silence anger may be to repress political speech.

NOTES

1. *Nicomachean Ethics*, 1126a4 ff.
2. *On the Generation of Animals*, 728a, 766a, 767b, 775a.
3. *Politics*, 1260a23.
4. Aristotle almost invariably uses "woman" in reference to women who were not slaves, though of course the slave population of his time included both males and females.
5. See for example, in Aristotle, *Nicomachean Ethics* 1150b9 ff. (". . . some men after deliberating fail, owing to their emotion, to stand by the conclusions of their deliberation . . . [others] are not defeated by their emotion . . ."); *Politics* 1254b5 ff. (". . . it is clear that the rule of the soul over the body, and of the mind and the rational element over the passionate, is natural and expedient; whereas the equality of the two or the rule of the inferior is always hurtful"). See also my "Aristotle and the Politicization of the Soul," in *Discovering Reality: Feminist Perspectives on Epistemology, Metaphysics, Methodology, and the Philosophy of Science*, ed. Sandra Harding and Merrill Hintikka (Dordrecht: Reidel, 1983). Among the reasons Plato gives in Book X of the *Republic* for his distrust of

poetry is this: "after feeding fat the emotion of pity there, it is not easy to restrain it in our own sufferings" (606b). See also my "Woman as Body: Ancient and Contemporary Views," *Feminist Studies*, vol. 8, no. 1 (Spring 1982): 109–131.

6. See the *Republic*, Book VII.

7. *Proceedings of the Aristotelian Society*, New Series, vol. 62 (1962), 119.

8. See Cecil Brown's "Blues for Blacks in Hollywood," *Mother Jones*, January 1981. Among other things, Brown points out that if Blacks ever *are* portrayed as angry, their anger will be quieted by other Blacks in the film or television show.

9. *De Anima*, ch. 16.

10. *King Lear*, II. iv, 279.

11. See for example Robert Solomon, *The Passions* (New York: Doubleday, 1976); *Explaining Emotions*, ed. Amelie O. Rorty (Berkeley: University of California Press, 1980).

12. There may be a subset of emotions for which this is not true; seeing this is part of the growing realization among philosophers of how many different kinds of states the coverall term "emotion" includes.

13. We have a rich and complicated vocabulary of the emotions, of which we could make neither head nor tail unless there were generally agreed-upon ways of telling when it was appropriate to say someone felt love instead of hate, anger instead of contempt, fear instead of envy, etc. See Solomon, *The Passions*, ch. 11.

14. George Pitcher, "Emotion," in *Education and the Development of Reason*, ed. R. F. Deardon, Paul H. Hirst and Richard S. Peters (London: Routledge & Kegan Paul, 1972), 236.

15. *Nicomachean Ethics*, 1126a6–8.

16. Though in fact, cognitivists don't hold that having a feeling is even a necessary condition of having an emotion. And they note how difficult it is to specify what feeling it is one is having without a specification of the judgment that goes with it.

17. Herbert Fingarette, *Self-Deception* (London: Routledge & Kegan Paul, 1969), 39 ff.

18. For a thoughtful discussion of the meaning of one's changing relationship to her own anger, see Naomi Scheman, "Anger and the Politics of Naming," in *Women and Language in Literature and Society*, ed. Sally McConnell-Ginet, Ruth Borker, and Nelly Furman (New York: Praeger, 1980) 174–187.

19. Paraphrase from *Nicomachean Ethics*, 1109a26 ff.

20. *Off our backs*, October 1981.

21. I first heard Audre Lorde raise this question in a talk at Mt. Holyoke College years ago. It is echoed in much of her work, e.g., "The Transformation of Silence into Language and Action," in *Sister Outsider* (Trumansburg, NY: The Crossing Press, 1984).

22. Bruno Bettelheim, *The Informed Heart* (New York: Avon, 1971), 153 ff. Bettelheim's views about various aspects of prisoners' and survivors' behavior have been sharply challenged: see for example Terrence Des Pres, *The Survivor* (New York: Oxford University Press, 1976; and Pocket Books).

23. Peter Lyman, "The Politics of Anger," *Socialist Review*, vol. 11, no. 3, 1981.

Chapter 17

Playfulness, "World"-Traveling, and Loving Perception

María Lugones

*T*his paper weaves two aspects of life together. My coming to consciousness as a daughter and my coming to consciousness as a woman of color have made this weaving possible. This weaving reveals the possibility and complexity of a pluralistic feminism, a feminism that affirms the plurality in each of us and among us as richness and as central to feminist ontology and epistemology.

The paper describes the experience of "outsiders" to the mainstream of, for example, white/Anglo organization of life in the U.S. and stresses a particular feature of the outsider's existence: the outsider has necessarily acquired flexibility in shifting from the mainstream construction of life where she is constructed as an outsider to other constructions of life where she is more or less "at home." This flexibility is necessary for the outsider but it can also be willfully exercised by the outsider or by those who are at ease in the mainstream. I recommend this willful exercise, which I call "world"-traveling, and I also recommend that the willful exercise be animated by an attitude that I describe as playful.

As outsiders to the mainstream, women of color in the U.S. practice "world"-traveling, mostly out of necessity. I affirm this practice as skillful, creative, rich, enriching and, given certain circumstances, as a loving way of being and living. I recognize that much of our traveling is done unwillfully to hostile white/Anglo "worlds." The hostility of these "worlds" and the compulsory nature of the "traveling" have obscured for us the enormous value of this aspect of our living and its connection to loving. Racism has a vested interest in obscuring and devaluing the complex skills involved in it. I recommend that we affirm this traveling across "worlds" as partly constitutive of cross-cultural and cross-racial

Source: First published in *Hypatia* 2, 2 (Summer 1987): 3–19. Copyright © 1987 by María Lugones. Reprinted with permission.

loving. Thus I recommend to women of color in the U.S. that we learn to love each other by learning to travel to each other's "worlds."

On the other hand, the paper makes a connection between what Marilyn Frye has named "arrogant perception" and the failure to identify with persons that one views arrogantly or has come to see as the products of arrogant perception. A further connection is made between this failure of identification and a failure of love, and thus between loving and identifying with another person. The sense of love is not the one Frye has identified as both consistent with arrogant perception and as promoting unconditional servitude. "We can be taken in by this equation of servitude with love," Frye (1983, 73) says, "because we make two mistakes at once: we think, of both servitude and love, that they are selfless or unselfish." Rather, the identification of which I speak is constituted by what I come to characterize as playful "world"-traveling. To the extent that we learn to perceive others arrogantly or come to see them only as products of arrogant perception and continue to perceive them that way, we fail to identify with them—fail to love them—in this particularly deep way.

IDENTIFICATION AND LOVE

As a child, I was taught to perceive arrogantly. I have also been the object of arrogant perception. Though I am not a white/Anglo woman, it is clear to me that I can understand both my childhood training as an arrogant perceiver and my having been the object of arrogant perception without any reference to white/Anglo men, which is some indication that the concept of arrogant perception can be used cross-culturally and that white/Anglo men are not the only arrogant perceivers. I was brought up in Argentina watching men and women of moderate and of considerable means graft the substance[1] of their servants to themselves. I also learned to graft my mother's substance to my own. It was clear to me that both men and women were the victims of arrogant perception and that arrogant perception was systematically organized to break the spirit of all women and of most men. I valued my rural "gaucho" ancestry because its ethos has always been one of independence in poverty through enormous loneliness, courage, and self-reliance. I found inspiration in this ethos and committed myself never to be broken by arrogant perception. I can say all of this in this way only because I have learned from Frye's "In and Out of Harm's Way: Arrogance and Love." She has given me a way of understanding and articulating something important in my own life.

Frye is not particularly concerned with women as arrogant perceivers but as the objects of arrogant perception. Her concern is, in part, to enhance our understanding of women "untouched by phallocratic machinations" (Frye 1983, 53) by understanding the harm done to women through such machinations. In this case she proposes that we could understand women untouched by arrogant perception through an understanding of what arrogant perception does to women. She also proposes an understanding of what it is to love women that is inspired by a vision of women unharmed by arrogant perception. To love women is, at least in part, to perceive them with loving eyes. "The loving eye is a contrary of the arrogant eye" (Frye 1983, 75).

I am concerned with women as arrogant perceivers because I want to explore further what it is to love women. I want to explore two failures of love: my failure to love my mother and white/Anglo women's failure to love women across racial and cultural boundaries in the U.S. As a consequence of exploring these failures I will offer a loving solution to them. My solution modifies Frye's account of loving perception by adding what I call playful "world"-travel.

It is clear to me that at least in the U.S. and Argentina women are taught to perceive many other women arrogantly. Being taught to perceive arrogantly is part of being taught to be a woman of a certain class in both the U.S. and Argentina, it is part of being taught to be a white/Anglo woman in the U.S and it is part of being taught to be a woman in both places: to be both the agent and the object of arrogant perception. My love for my mother seemed to me thoroughly imperfect as I was growing up because I was unwilling to become what I had been taught to see my mother as being. I thought that to love her was consistent with my abusing her (using, taking for granted, and demanding her services in a far reaching way that, since four other people engaged in the same grafting of her substance onto themselves, left her little of herself to herself) and was to be in part constituted by my identifying with her, my seeing myself in her: to love her was supposed to be of a piece with both my abusing her and with my being open to being abused. It is clear to me that I was not supposed to love servants: I could abuse them without identifying with them, without seeing myself in them. When I came to the U.S. I learned that part of racism is the internalization of the propriety of abuse without identification: I learned that I could be seen as a being to be used by white/Anglo men and women without the possibility of identification, i.e., without their act of attempting to graft my substance onto theirs, rubbing off on them at all. They could remain untouched, without any sense of loss.

So, women who are perceived arrogantly can perceive other women arrogantly in their turn. To what extent those women are responsible for their arrogant perceptions of other women is certainly open to question, but I do not have any doubt that many women have been taught to abuse women in this particular way. I am not interested in assigning responsibility. I am interested in understanding the phenomenon so as to understand a loving way out of it.

There is something obviously wrong with the love that I was taught and something right with my failure to love my mother in this way. But I do not think that what is wrong is my profound desire to identify with her, to see myself in her; what is wrong is that I was taught to identify with a victim of enslavement. What is wrong is that I was taught to practice enslavement of my mother and to learn to become a slave through this practice. There is something obviously wrong with my having been taught that love is consistent with abuse, consistent with arrogant perception. Notice that the love I was taught is the love that Frye (1983, 73) speaks of when she says "We can be taken in by this equation of servitude with love." Even though I could both abuse and love my mother, I was not supposed to love servants. This is because in the case of servants one is and is supposed to be clear about their servitude and the "equation of servitude with love" is never to be thought clearly in those terms. So, I was not supposed to love and could not love servants. But I could love my mother because deception (in particular, self-deception) is part of this "loving." Servitude is called abnegation and abnegation is not anlayzed any further. Abnegation is not instilled in us through an analysis of its nature but rather through a heralding of it as beautiful and noble. We are coaxed, seduced into abnegation not through analysis but through emotive persuasion. Frye makes the connection between deception and this sense of "loving" clear. When I say that there is something obviously wrong with the loving that I was taught, I do not mean to say that the connection between this loving and abuse is obvious. Rather I mean that once the connection between this loving and abuse has been unveiled, there is something obviously wrong with the loving given that it is obvious that it is wrong to abuse others.

I am glad that I did not learn my lessons well, but it is clear that part of the mechanism that permitted my not learning well involved a separation from my mother: I saw us as beings of quite a different sort. It involved an abandoning of my mother while I longed not to abandon her. I wanted to love my mother, though, given what I was taught, "love" could not be the right word for what I longed for.

I was disturbed by my not wanting to be what she was. I had a sense of not being quite integrated, my self was missing because I could not identify with her, I could not see myself in her. I could not welcome her world. I saw myself as separate from her, a different sort of being, not quite of the same species. This separation, this lack of love, I saw, and I think that I saw correctly as a lack in myself (not a fault, but a lack). I also see that if this was a lack of love, love cannot be what I was taught. Love has to be rethought, made anew.

There is something in common between the relation between myself and my mother as someone I did not used to be able to love and the relation between myself or other women of color in the U.S. and white/Anglo women: there is a failure of love. I want to suggest here that Frye has helped me understand one of the aspects of this failure, the directly abusive aspect. But I also think that there is a complex failure of love in the failure to identify with another woman, the failure to see oneself in other women who are quite different from oneself. I want to begin to analyze this complex failure.

Notice that Frye's emphasis on independence in her analysis of loving perception is not particularly helpful in explaining this failure. She says that in loving perception, "the object of the seeing is another being whose existence and character are logically independent of the seer and who may be practically or empirically independent in any particular respect at any particular time" (Frye 1983, 77). But this is not helpful in allowing me to understand how my failure of love toward my mother (when I ceased to be her parasite) left me not quite whole. It is not helpful since I saw her as logically independent from me. It also does not help me to understand why the racist or ethnocentric failure of love of white/Anglo women—in particular of those white/Anglo women who are not pained by their failure—should leave me not quite substantive among them. Here I am not particularly interested in cases of white women's parasitism onto women of color but more pointedly in cases where the failure of identification is the manifestation of the "relation." I am particularly interested here in those many cases in which white/Anglo women do one or more of the following to women of color: they ignore us, ostracize us, render us invisible, stereotype us, leave us completely alone, interpret us as crazy. All of this *while we are in their midst.* The more independent I am, the more independent I am left to be. Their world and their integrity do not require me at all. There is no sense of self-loss in them for my own lack of solidity. But they rob me of my solidity through indifference, an indifference they can afford and that seems sometimes studied. (All of this points of course toward separatism in communities where our substance is seen and celebrated, where we become substantive through this celebration. But many of us have to work among white/Anglo folk and our best shot at recognition has seemed to be among white/Anglo women because many of them have expressed a *general* sense of being pained at their failure of love.)

Many times white/Anglo women want us out of their field of vision. Their lack of concern is a harmful failure of love that leaves me independent from them in a way similar to the way in which, once I ceased to be my mother's parasite, she became, though not independent from all others, certainly independent from me. But of course, because my mother and I wanted to love each other well, we were not whole in this independence. White/Anglo women are independent from me, I am independent from them, I am independent from my mother, she is independent from me, and none of us loves each other in this independence.

I am incomplete and unreal without other women. I am profoundly dependent on others without having to be their subordinate, their slave, their servant.

Frye (1983, 75) also says that the loving eye is "the eye of one who knows that to know the seen, one must consult something other than one's own will and interests and fears and imagination." This is much more helpful to me so long as I do not understand Frye to mean that I should not consult my own interests nor that I should exclude the possibility that my self and the self of the one I love may be importantly tied to each other in many complicated ways. Since I am emphasizing here that the failure of love lies in part in the failure to identify and since I agree with Frye that one "must consult something other than one's own will and interests and fears and imagination," I will proceed to try to explain what I think needs to be consulted. To love my mother was not possible for me while I retained a sense that it was fine for me and others to see her arrogantly. Loving my mother also required that I see with her eyes, that I go into my mother's world, that I see both of us as we are constructed in her world, that I witness her own sense of herself from within her world. Only through this traveling to her "world" could I identity with her because only then could I cease to ignore her and to be excluded and separate from her. Only then could I see her as a subject even if one subjected and only then could I see at all how meaning could arise fully between us. We are fully dependent on each other for the possibility of being understood and without this understanding we are not intelligible, we do not make sense, we are not solid, visible, integrated; we are lacking. So traveling to each other's "worlds" would enable us to *be* through *loving* each other.

Hopefully the sense of identification I have in mind is becoming clear. But if it is to become clearer, I need to explain what I mean by a "world" and by "traveling" to another "world."

In explaining what I mean by a "world" I will not appeal to traveling to other women's worlds. Rather I will lead you to see what I mean by a "world" the way I came to propose the concept to myself: through the kind of ontological confusion about myself that we, women of color, refer to half-jokingly as "schizophrenia" (we feel schizophrenic in our goings back and forth between different "communities") and through my effort to make some sense of this ontological confusion.

"WORLDS" AND "WORLD" TRAVELING

Some time ago I came to be in a state of profound confusion as I experienced myself as both having and not having a particular attribute. I was sure I had the attribute in question and, on the other hand, I was sure that I did not have it. I remain convinced that I both have and do not have this attribute. The attribute is playfulness. I am sure that I am a playful person. On the other hand, I can say, painfully, that I am not a playful person. I am not a playful person in certain worlds. One of the things I did as I became confused was to call my friends, far away people who knew me well, to see whether or not I was playful. Maybe they could help me out of my confusion. They said to me, "Of course you are playful" and they said it with the same conviction that I had about it. Of course I am playful. Those people who were around me said to me, "No, you are not playful. You are a serious woman. You just take everything seriously." They were just as sure about what they said to me and could offer me every bit of evidence that one could need to conclude that they were right. So I said to myself: "Okay, maybe what's happening here is that there is an attribute that I do have but there are certain worlds in which I am not at ease and it is because I'm not at ease in those worlds that I don't have that attribute in those worlds. But what does that mean?" I was worried both about what I meant by "worlds" when I said "in some worlds I do not have the attribute" and what I meant by saying that lack of ease was what led me not to be playful in those worlds. Because you see, if it was just a matter of lack of ease, I could work on it.

I can explain some of what I mean by a "world." I do not want the fixity of a definition at this point, because I think the term is suggestive and I do not want to close the suggestiveness of it too soon. I can offer some characteristics that serve to distinguish between a "world," a utopia, a possible world in the philosophical sense, and a world view. By a "world" I do not mean a utopia at all. A utopia does not count as a world in my sense. The "worlds" that I am talking about are possible. But a possible world is not what I mean by a "world" and I do not mean a world-view, though something like a world-view is involved here.

For something to be a "world" in my sense it has to be inhabited at present by some flesh and blood people. That is why it cannot be a utopia. It may also be inhabited by some imaginary people. It may be inhabited by people who are dead or people that the inhabitants of this "world" met in some other "world" and now have in this "world" in imagination.

A "world" in my sense may be an actual society given its dominant culture's description and construction of life, including a construction of the relationships of production, of gender, race, etc. But a "world" can also be such a society given a nondominant construction, or it can be such a society or a society given an idiosyncratic construction. As we will see it is problematic to say that these are all constructions of the same society. But they are different "worlds."

A "world" need not be a construction of a whole society. It may be a construction of a tiny portion of a particular society. It may be inhabited by just a few people. Some "worlds" are bigger than others.

A "world" may be incomplete in that things in it may not be altogether constructed or some things may be constructed negatively (they are not what "they" are in some other "world.") Or the "world" may be incomplete because it may have references to things that do not quite exist in it, references to things like Brazil, where Brazil is not quite part of that "world." Given lesbian feminism, the construction of "lesbian" is purposefully and healthily still up in the air, in the process of becoming. What it is to be a Hispanic in this country is, in a dominant Anglo construction purposefully incomplete. Thus one cannot really answer questions of the sort "What is a Hispanic?", "Who counts as a Hispanic?", "Are Latinos, Chicanos, Hispanos, Black Dominicans, white Cubans, Korean-Colombians, Italian-Argentinians, Hispanic?" What it is to be a "Hispanic" in the varied so-called Hispanic communities in the U.S. is also yet up in the air. We have not yet decided whether there is something like a "Hispanic" in our varied "worlds." So, a "world" may be an incomplete visionary nonutopian construction of life or it may be a traditional construction of life. A traditional Hispano construction of Northern New Mexican life is a "world." Such a traditional construction, in the face of a racist, ethnocentrist, money-centered anglo construction of Northern New Mexican life is highly unstable because Anglo have the means for imperialist destruction of traditional Hispano "worlds."

In a "world" some of the inhabitants may not understand or hold the particular construction of them that constructs them in that "world." So, there may be "worlds" that construct me in ways that I do not even understand. Or it may be that I understand the construction, but do not hold it of myself. I may not accept it as an account of myself, a construction of myself. And yet, I may be *animating* such a construction.

One can "travel" between these "worlds" and one can inhabit more than one of these "worlds" at the very same time. I think that most of us who are outside the mainstream of, for example, the U.S. dominant construction or organization of life, are "world travelers" as a matter of necessity and of survival. It seems to me that inhabiting more than one "world" at the same time and "traveling" between "worlds" is part and parcel of our experience and our situation. One can be at the same time in a "world" that constructs one as stereotypically Latin, for example, and in a "world" that constructs one as Latin. Being stereotypically

Latin and being simply Latin are different simultaneous constructions of persons that are part of different "worlds." One animates one or the other or both at the same time without necessarily confusing them, though simultaneous enactment can be confusing if one is not on one's guard.

In describing my sense of a "world," I mean to be offering a description of experience, something that is true to experience even if it is ontologically problematic. Though I would think that any account of identity that could not be true to this experience of outsiders to the mainstream would be faulty even if ontologically unproblematic. Its ease would constrain, erase, or deem aberrant experience that has within it significant insights into nonimperialistic understanding between people.

Those of us who are "world"-travelers have the distinct experience of being different in different "worlds" and of having the capacity to remember other "worlds" and ourselves in them. We can say "That is me there, and I am happy in that "world." So, the experience is of being a different person in different "worlds" and yet of having memory of oneself as different without quite having the sense of there being any underlying "I." So I can say "that is me there and I am so playful in that "world." I say "That is *me* in that "world" not because I recognize myself in that person; rather, the first-person statement is noninferential. I may well recognize that that person has abilities that I do not have and yet the having or not having of the abilities is always an "I have . . ." and "I do not have . . ."; i.e., it is always experienced in the first person.

The shift from being one person to being a different person is what I call "travel." This shift may not be willful or even conscious, and one may be completely unaware of being different than one is in a different "world," and may not recognize that one is in a different "world." Even though the shift can be done willfully, it is not a matter of acting. One does not pose as someone else, one does not pretend to be, for example, someone of a different personality or character or someone who uses space or language differently than the other person. Rather one is someone who has that personality or character or uses space and language in that particular way. The "one" here does not refer to some underlying "I." One does not *experience* any underlying "I."

BEING AT EASE IN A "WORLD"

In investigating what I mean by "being at ease in a world," I will describe different ways of being at ease. One may be at ease in one or in all of these ways. There is a maximal way of being at ease, viz. being at ease in all of these ways. I take this maximal way of being at ease to be somewhat dangerous because it tends to produce people who have no inclination to travel across "worlds" or have no experience of "world"-traveling.

The first way of being at ease in a particular "world" is by being a fluent speaker in that "world." I know all the norms that there are to be followed. I know all the words that there are to be spoken. I know all the moves. I am confident.

Another way of being at ease is by being normatively happy. I agree with all the norms, I could not love any norms better. I am asked to do just what I want to do or what I think I should do. At ease.

Another way of being at ease in a "world" is by being humanly bonded. I am with those I love and they love me too. It should be noticed that I may be with those I love and they love me too. It should be noticed that I may be with those I love and be at ease because of them in a "world" that is otherwise as hostile to me as "worlds" get.

Finally one may be at ease because one has a history with others that is shared, especially daily history, the kind of shared history that one sees exemplified by the response to the "Do you remember poodle skirts?" question. There you are, with people you do not know at all. The question is posed and then they all begin talking about their poodle skirt stories. I have been in such situations without knowing what poodle skirts, for example, were and I felt so ill at ease because it was not *my* history. The other people did not particularly know each other. It is not that they were humanly bonded. Probably they did not have much politically in common either. But poodle skirts were in their shared history.

One may be at ease in one of these ways or in all of them. Notice that when one says meaningfully "This is *my* world," one may not be at ease in it. Or one may be at ease in it only in some of these respects and not in others. To say of some "world" that is is "*my* world" is to make an evaluation. One may privilege one or more "worlds" in this way for a variety of reasons: for example because one experiences oneself as an agent in a fuller sense than one experiences "oneself" in other "worlds." One may disown a "world" because one has first person memories of a person who is so thoroughly dominated that she has no sense of exercising her own will or has a sense of having serious difficulties in performing actions that are willed by herself and no difficulty in performing actions willed by others. One may say of a "world" that it is "my world" because one is at ease in it; i.e., being at ease in a "world" may be the basis for the evaluation.

Given the clarification of what I mean by a "world," "world"-travel, and being at ease in a "world," we are in a position to return to my problematic attribute, playfulness. It may be that in this "world" in which I am so unplayful, I am a different person than in the "world" in which I am playful. Or it may be that the "world" in which I am unplayful is constructed in such a way that I could be playful in it. I could practice, even though that "world" is constructed in such a way that my being playful in it is kind of hard. In describing what I take a "world" to be, I emphasized the first possibility as both the one that is truest to the experience of "outsiders" to the mainstream and as ontologically problematic because the "I" is identified in some sense as one and in some sense as a plurality. I identify myself as myself through memory and I retain myself as different in memory. When I travel from one "world" to another, I have this image, this memory of myself as playful in this other "world." I can then be in a particular "world" and have a double image of myself as, for example, playful and as not playful. But this is a very familiar and recognizable phenomenon to the outsider to the mainstream in some central cases: when in one "world" I animate, for example, that "world's" caricature of the person I am in the other "world." I can have both images of myself and to the extent that I can materialize or animate both images at the same time I become an ambiguous being. This is very much a part of trickery and foolery. It is worth remembering that the trickster and the fool are significant characters in many nondominant or outsider cultures. One then sees any particular "world" with these double edges and sees absurdity in them and so inhabits oneself differently. Given that Latins are constructed in Anglo "worlds" as stereotypically intense—intensity being a central characteristic of at least one of the Anglo stereotypes of Latins—and given that many Latins, myself included, are genuinely intense, I can say to myself "I am intense" and take a hold of the double meaning. And furthermore, I can be stereotypically intense or be the real thing and, if you are Anglo, you do not know when I am which *because* I am Latin-American. As Latin-American I am an ambiguous being, a two-imaged self: I can see that gringos see me as stereotypically intense because I am, as a Latin-American, constructed that way but I may or may not *intentionally* animate the stereotype or the real thing knowing that you may not see it in anything other than in the stereotypical construction. This ambiguity is funny and is not just funny, it is survival-rich. We can also make the picture of those who dominate us funny precisely because we can see the double edge, we can see them doubly constructed, we can see the plurality in them. So we know truths that only the fool can speak and only the trickster can play out without harm. We inhabit "worlds" and travel across them and keep all the memories.

Sometimes the "world"-traveler has a double image of herself and each self includes as important ingredients of itself one or more attributes that are *incompatible* with one or more of the attributes of the other self: for example being playful and being unplayful. To the extent that the attribute is an important ingredient of the self she is in that "world"; i.e., to the extent that there is a particularly good fit between that "world" and her having that attribute in it and to the extent that the attribute is personality or character central, that "world" would have to be changed if she is to be playful in it. It is not the case that if she could come to be at ease in it, she would be her own playful self. Because the attribute is personality or character central and there is such a good fit between that "world" and her being constructed with that attribute as central, *she* cannot become playful, she is unplayful. To become playful would be for her to become a contradictory being. So I am suggesting that the lack of ease solution cannot be a solution to my problematic case. My problem is not one of lack of ease. I am suggesting that I can understand my confusion about whether I am or am not playful by saying that I am both and that I am different persons in different "worlds" and can remember myself in both as I am in the other. I am a plurality of selves. This is to understand my confusion because *it is to come to see it as a piece* with much of the rest of my experience as an outsider in some of the "worlds" that I inhabit and of a piece with significant aspects of the experience of nondominant people in the "worlds" of their dominators.

So, though I may not be at ease in the "worlds" in which I am not constructed playful, it is not that I am not playful *because* I am not at ease. The two are compatible. But lack of playfulness is not caused by lack of ease. Lack of playfulness is not symptomatic of lack of ease but of lack of health. I am not a healthy being in the "worlds" that construct me unplayful.

PLAYFULNESS

I had a very personal stake in investigating this topic. Playfulness is not only the attribute that was the source of my confusion and the attitude that I recommend as the loving attitude in traveling across "worlds," I am also scared of ending up a serious human being, someone with no multi-dimensionality, with no fun in life, someone who is just someone who has had the fun constructed out of her. I am seriously scared of getting stuck in a "world" that constructs me that way. A world that I have no escape from and in which I cannot be playful.

I thought about what it is to be playful and what it is to play and I did this thinking in a "world" in which I only remember myself as playful and in which all of those who know me as playful are imaginary beings. A "world" in which I am scared of losing my memories of myself as playful or have them erased from me. Because I live in such a "world," after I formulated my own sense of what it is to be playful and to play I decided that I needed to "go to the literature." I read two classics on the subject: Johan Huizinga's *Homo Ludens* and Hans-Georg Gadamer's chapter on the concept of play in his *Truth and Method*. I discovered, to my amazement, that what I thought about play and playfulness, if they were right, was absolutely wrong. Though I will not provide the arguments for this interpretation of Gadamer and Huizinga here, I understood that both of them have an agonistic sense of "play." Play and playfulness have, ultimately, to do with contest, with winning, losing, battling. The sense of playfulness that I have in mind has nothing to do with those things. So, I tried to elucidate both senses of play and playfulness by contrasting them to each other. The contrast helped me see the attitude that I have in mind as the loving attitude in traveling across "worlds" more clearly.

An agonistic sense of playfulness is one in which *competence* is supreme. You'd better know the rules of the game. In agonistic play there is risk, there is *uncertainty*, but the uncertainty is about who is going to win and who is going to lose. There are rules that inspire hostility. The attitude of *playfulness is conceived as secondary to or derivative from play*. Since play is agon, then the only conceivable playful attitude is an agonistic one (the attitude does not turn an activity into play, but rather presupposes an activity that is play). One of the paradigmatic ways of playing for both Gadamer and Huizinga is role-playing. In role-playing, the person who is a participant in the game has a *fixed conception of him or herself*. I also think that the players are imbued with *self-importance* in agonistic play since they are so keen on winning given their own merits, their very own competence.

When considering the value of "world"-traveling and whether playfulness is the loving attitude to have while traveling, I recognized the agonistic attitude as inimical to traveling across "worlds." The agonistic traveler is a conqueror, an imperialist. Huizinga, in his classic book on play, interprets western civilization as play. That is an interesting thing for Third World people to think about. Western civilization has been interpreted by a white western man as play in the agonistic sense of play. Huizinga reviews western law, art, and many other aspects of western culture and sees agon in all of them. Agonistic playfulness leads those who attempt to travel to another "world" with this attitude to failure. Agonistic travelers fail consistently in their attempt to travel because what they do is to try to conquer the other "world." The attempt is not an attempt to try to erase the other "world." That is what assimilation is all about. Assimilation is the destruction of other people's "worlds." So, the agonistic attitude, the playful attitude given western man's construction of playfulness, is not a healthy, loving attitude to have in traveling across "worlds." Notice that given the agonistic attitude one *cannot* travel across "worlds," though one can kill other "worlds" with it. So for people who are interested in crossing racial and ethnic boundaries, an arrogant western man's construction of playfulness is deadly. One cannot cross the boundaries with it. One needs to give up such an attitude if one wants to travel.

So then, what is the loving playfulness that I have in mind? Let me begin with one example: We are by the river bank. The river is very, very low. Almost dry. Bits of water here and there. Little pools with a few trout hiding under the rocks. But mostly it is wet stones, grey on the outside. We walk on the stones for a while. You pick up a stone and crash it onto the others. As it breaks, it is quite wet inside and it is very colorful, very pretty. I pick up a stone and break it and run toward the pieces to see the colors. They are beautiful. I laugh and bring the pieces back to you and you are doing the same with your pieces. We keep on crashing stones for hours, anxious to see the beautiful new colors. We are playing. The playfulness of our activity does not presuppose that there is something like "crashing stones" that is a particular form of play with its own rules. Rather *the attitude that carries us through the activity, a playful attitude, turns the activity into play.* Our activity has no rules, though it is certainly intentional activity and we both understand what we are doing. The playfulness that gives meaning to our activity includes uncertainty, but in this case the uncertainty is an *openness to surprise.* This is a particular metaphysical attitude that does not expect the world to be neatly packaged, ruly. Rules may fail to explain what we are doing. We are not self-important, we are not fixed in particular constructions of ourselves, which is part of saying that we are *open to self-construction.* We may not have rules, and when we do have rules, *there are no rules that are to us sacred.* We are not worried about competence. We are not wedded to a particular way of doing things. While playful we have not abandoned ourselves to, nor are we stuck in, any particular "world." We *are there creatively.* We are not passive.

Playfulness is, in part, an openness to being a fool, which is a combination of not worrying about competence, not being self-important, not taking norms as sacred and finding ambiguity and double edges a source of wisdom and delight.

So, positively, the playful attitude involves openness to surprise, openness to being a fool, openness to self-construction or reconstruction and to construction or reconstruction of the "worlds" we inhabit playfully. Negatively, playfulness is characterized by uncertainty, lack of self-importance, absence of rules or a not taking rules as sacred, a not worrying about competence, and a lack of abandonment to a particular construction of oneself, others, and one's relation to them. In attempting to take a hold of oneself and of one's relation to others in a particular "world," one may study, examine, and come to understand oneself. One may then see what the possibilities for play are for the being one is in that "world." One may even decide to inhabit that self fully in order to understand it better and find its creative possibilities. All of this is just self-reflection and it is quite different from resigning or abandoning oneself to the particular construction of oneself that one is attempting to take a hold of.

CONCLUSION

There are "worlds" we enter at our own risk, "worlds" that have agon, conquest, and arrogance as the main ingredients in their ethos. These are "worlds" that we enter out of necessity and that would be foolish to enter playfully in either the agonistic sense or in my sense. In such "worlds" we are not playful.

But there are "worlds" that we can travel to lovingly and traveling to them is part of loving at least some of their inhabitants. The reason why I think that traveling to someone's "world" is a way of identifying with them is because by traveling to their "world" we can understand *what it is to be them and what it is to be ourselves in their eyes*. Only when we have traveled to each other's "worlds" are we fully subjects to each other (I agree with Hegel that self-recognition requires other subjects, but I disagree with his claim that it requires tension or hostility).

Knowing other women's "worlds" is part of knowing them and knowing them is part of loving them. Notice that the knowing can be done in greater or lesser depth, as can the loving. Also notice that traveling to another's "world" is not the same as becoming intimate with another. Intimacy is constituted in part by a very deep knowledge of the other self and "world" traveling is only part of having this knowledge. Also notice that some people, in particular those who are outsiders to the mainstream, can be known only to the extent that they are known in several "worlds" and as "world"-travelers.

Without knowing the other's "world," one does not know the other, and without knowing the other one is really alone in the other's presence because the other is only dimly present to one.

Through traveling to other people's "worlds" we discover that there are "worlds" in which those who are the victims of arrogant perception are really subjects, lively beings, resistors, constructors of visions, even though in the mainstream construction they are animated only by the arrogant perceiver and are pliable, foldable, file-awayable, classifiable. I always imagine the Aristotelian slave as pliable and foldable at night or after he or she cannot work anymore (when he or she dies as a tool). Aristotle tells us nothing about the slave *apart from the master*. We know the slave only through the master. The slave is a tool of the master. After working hours he or she is folded and placed in a drawer till the next morning. My mother was apparent to me mostly as a victim of arrogant perception. I was loyal to the arrogant perceiver's construction of her and thus disloyal to her in assuming that she was exhausted by that construction. I was unwilling to be like her and thought that identifying with her, seeing myself in her necessitated that I become like her. I was wrong both in assuming that she was exhausted by the arrogant perceiver's construction of her and in my understanding of identification, though I was not wrong in thinking that identification was part of loving and that it involved in part my seeing myself in her. I came to realize through traveling to her "world" that she is not foldable and pliable, that she is not exhausted by the mainstream Argentinian patriarchal construction of her. I came to realize that there are "worlds" in which she shines as a creative being. Seeing myself in her through traveling to her "world" has meant seeing how different from her I am in her "world."

So, in recommending "world"-traveling and identification through "world"-traveling as part of loving other women, I am suggesting disloyalty to arrogant perceivers, including the arrogant perceiver in ourselves, and to their constructions of women. In revealing agonistic playfulness as incompatible with "world"-traveling, I am revealing both its affinity with imperialism and arrogant perception and its incompatibility with loving and loving perception.

NOTES

1. Grafting the substance of another to oneself is partly constitutive of arrogant perception. See M. Frye (1983, 66).

REFERENCES

Frye, Marilyn. 1983. *The Politics of Reality: Essays in Feminist Theory*. Trumansburg, N.Y.: Crossing Press.

Gadamer, Hans-Georg. 1975. *Truth and Method*. New York: Seabury Press.

Huizinga, Johan. 1968. *Homo Ludens*. Buenos Aires, Argentina: Emecé Editores.

Part VII —————————————————————

Philosophy of Religion

R eligion has been a powerful institutional force in the marginalization and devaluation of women, not only in its rituals but more profoundly in its underlying myths, dogmas, and conceptual schemes. The religious enterprise has served to bulwark and sanction male domination and female subordination. The male God (or gods) as object of worship is, of course, the most obvious as well as most central example.

Philosophy of religion explores issues and concepts included in and presupposed by religious practice. Traditionally, these include arguments for the existence of God, the nature, origin, function, and meaning of the concept of God, as well as the practices and discourses that use this concept as their fundamental ground. Philosophy of religion also deals with the nature of religious belief, the problem of evil, human suffering, and so on.

Feminist philosophers are questioning the ways that the concepts and practices of patriarchal religions and the sanctions to them specifically negate women and effectively disempower them. Feminist religious discourses and practices are emerging that celebrate women's spirituality and connect with women's experiences and power. One of the underlying purposes of feminist philosophy of religion is to open up liberating possibilities of thinking, knowing, and being. In the 1970s, for example, Mary Daly called for women to reject the notion of God the Father in order to seek our own transcendence;[1] and Carol Christ explored reasons for women to adopt the concept of the Goddess and to reclaim our past matriarchal heritage.[2]

In this part, Hilde Hein points out that we may question whether women can be spiritual at all in a patriarchal world that has designated us as body/matter—that which is opposed to spirit. At the same time, woman has also been cast by patriarchy as the maker of spiritual values or "the angel in the house." Hein scrutinizes these contrasting views of women's spirituality. She posits in their place a feminist notion of spirituality as a source of liberation.

Toinette Eugene explores the relationship of Black spirituality to Black sexuality. She defines spirituality as "the human capacity to be self-transcending, relational and freely connected, [which] encompasses all of life, including our human sexuality." Eugene focuses on the quest for mutuality and community among Black women and men, in spite of the conditions of racism and sexism. She finds in the wholistic African-Christian heritage a world-view and life experience that encourages the integration of sexuality and spirituality.

According to Gail Stenstad patriarchal religious institutions have kept women divided; past theory-building, such as patriarchal monotheism, has kept us from creating our own community. She argues that we should practice "anarchic thinking," which she characterizes as breaking rules, being open to a multiplicity of meanings and possibilities, and basing our beliefs on the deep concerns of women. Citing Susan Griffin and Luce Irigaray, Stenstad urges us to push boundaries, decenter past male thinking, and find the strange in the familiar in order to create a women's space.

NOTES

1. Mary Daly, "The Qualitative Leap Beyond Patriarchal Religion," *Quest* 1, 4 (Spring 1975): 20–40.

2 Carol P. Christ, "Why Women Need the Goddess: Phenomenological, Psychological, and Political Reflections," in *Womanspirit Rising*, ed. Carol P. Christ and Judith Plaskow (San Francisco: Harper & Row, 1979): 273–286.

Chapter 18

Liberating Philosophy: An End to the Dichotomy of Spirit and Matter

Hilde Hein

*T*he concept of spirituality is amply interpretable. It has been identified with the transcendent and supernatural, but also with the immanent and natural. It has been associated with the mental and intellectual, but also with bodily feeling and passion. It has been considered the "besouling" or animating principle, but also to be other-worldly or beyond life. It is often regarded as of positive moral value, but it can be perverted to evil ends. It is most commonly opposed to the material. But even this claim is problematic, for some theories regard matter and spirit as continuous or even as merely aspectival. Matter becomes spirit as it flows from the indefinite infinite into the "utterly subtle." The notion that matter complexified or rarefied becomes spirit has been one of the classic alternatives to philosophical dualism.

The ascription of spirituality to women has also been problematic. Women are sometimes understood as fundamentally incompatible with the spiritual, but at other times as its primary human representation. If one looks for patterns of intelligibility in these attributions, they are hard to discern. One thing seems clear: women have had little to do with making the assignments and associations. Furthermore, the associations have not been coordinated with any particular changes in the lives of women. Throughout western civilization, women's lives have been predominantly devoted to and defined in terms of procreation, including preparation for reproduction and its aftermath of nurturance, homemaking, and child care. Yet despite this historic sameness of women's experience, their alleged relation to spirituality has fluctuated wildly.

The affirmations and denials of spirituality to women have generally been made by men, and so we must look to men's philosophical

Source: From *Beyond Domination: New Perspectives on Women and Philosophy,* ed. Carol Gould (Totowa, NJ: Rowman & Allanheld, 1984), 123–141. Copyright © 1984 by Rowman & Allanheld. Reprinted by permission of the author and of the publisher.

preconceptions to make sense of the apparently random vacillations. I have argued elsewhere that male-generated philosophy, and specifically the western mainstream that descends from Greek philosophy, tends to regard the universe in terms of dichotomies—light and dark, permanence and change, finite and infinite, dry and moist, even and odd, male and female, day and night, intelligence and emotion.[1] The extremes are then opposed to one another upon a hierarchical value scale and so grouped that, with few exceptions, the positive ends of each pair are assimilated and so are the negative poles. Thus the female is associated with the cluster including the moist, the dark, the odd, night, and other negative qualities, while the male lines up with the positive attributes at the opposite pole. I have discussed some of the philosophical and practical implications of this polarizing and hierarchicalizing tendency, pointing out its irrelevance to women's experience as it systematically devalues it.

Spirit and matter, however, do not appear on this scale as primary oppositions. Sometimes they are held to be compatible and sometimes not. I suggest that they should nevertheless be understood as secondary oppositions, at least insofar as differentially applicable to men and women. Where male and female are opposed, spirituality is derivatively affirmed of the one and denied of the other. Whatever state of spirituality (or its absence) men claim for themselves within the western tradition, they automatically declare the opposite for women. However men see themselves with regard to spirituality at any given moment, and whatever the logic or rational justification for that representation, women are automatically relegated to its antipode. Thus, their identification of women as spiritual or not has relatively little to do with men's actual perception of women, much less with that which women might have of themselves, but only with an historic male self-perception.

I suggest that this mechanical designation of spirituality or its opposite to women, depending upon the primary and orthogonal status of men, accounts for its apparent arbitrariness and lack of conformity to either reason or experience. I will here consider four distinct analyses of the association between women and spirituality. The first three, all argued by men, are radically incompatible with one another. Yet they reveal no significant differences in the actual traits and functions they ascribe to women, apart from the specific involvement with or incompatibility with spirituality. These analyses may best be understood as reflecting shifts in the sociohistoric self-representation of men. The fourth view of women's spirituality, currently held by some women, is largely reactive and therefore follows the pattern of understanding women as defined by men, i.e., as their opposite. Hence the attribution of spirituality to women continues to be consequent upon their gender, and that, in turn, is represented by negation, although it is positively evaluated.

I. THE ARISTOTELIAN/CHRISTIAN VIEW:
SPIRIT IS TO MATTER AS MAN IS TO WOMAN

Aristotle is clear, especially with respect to procreative functions, that woman plays an essentially material role, while the male parent is the source of "besoulment."[2] Women, he says, do have vegetative and locomotive souls and even some degree of rationality, but it is "without authority."[3] Women lack the combustible soul-making element, the entelechy, which is the male contribution to reproduction—transmitted by means of the notably material semen. While women are obviously not altogether devoid of the animating principle or spirit, Aristotle depicts them as primarily receptive to it. Women are passive receptacles who nurture life. Spirit is active agency; only spirit, the male principle, generates life.[4]

On this account, the female parent has little influence on the positive character of her offspring. The mother's intrinsic defectiveness limits the child's possible perfection, but its actual identity is fixed and imparted by paternal agency. It is merely temporarily domiciled in her nurturant womb.*

Women's preeminent materiality also renders her morally deficient. Aristotle does not follow Plato's belief that the possession of virtue is ultimately a consequence of knowledge of the Good. But he does regard virtue as a kind of knowledge, following from an intellectual, hence spiritual, capacity. The practice of virtue is the result of a state of character acquired by habitual action and good judgment.[5] The recognition of the appropriate action to perform is a cognitive act of syllogistic reasoning. One who lacks intellect is incapable of such judgments, and the virtue appropriate to persons who are constitutionally so deprived is therefore obedience. Whereas men are fit to rule, thanks to their rational souls, Aristotle affirms that obedience is the virtue appropriate to woman. Thus woman's lack of spirituality, her lack of a full-fledged active intelligence, justifies her social subordination as it rationalizes her moral inferiority. Biologically and metaphysically deficient, she lives at the level of matter, where her moral and social aspirations are accordingly fixed.

Aristotle, who never believed that all human beings are created equal, did not perceive women's consignment to inferior status as

---

*No wonder the notion of "renting" a womb for purposes of artificial insemination seems plausible and so attractive to so many.

either a punishment or an injustice. It was simply a matter of observable fact that, happily, supported the existing social order. His doctrine was carried over with some modifications into Christian doctrine. The notion of the woman's body as nurturant host to the paternally provided embryo persists to this day, despite the 16th-century discovery of the reproductive role of the ovum and the modern understanding of genetic dimorphism. But rhetoric and "common" sense agree that men have children "by" (i.e., through the instrumentality of) women, just as race horses are "sired by" male stallions "out of" mares.

Women's material nature (carnality) was much discussed by the Fathers of the early Church, who held it in horror as much for its inherent depravity as for its capacity to evoke the uncontrollable lust of men.[6] St. Augustine, for example, clearly indicates that the Fall of Man brought in its wake not sexual intercourse, which must have existed prior to that event, but its accompaniment with concupiscence.[7] Women's lack of spirituality is thus no mere deprivation, nor is materiality a neutral, if deficient, state relative to a high mode of being. Matter, insofar as it is a privation of Spirit (God), is a positive evil. Hence woman as matter is evil and, furthermore, threatens to unleash the potential for evil in man.

Thomas Aquinas actually expresses a view closer to that of Aristotle in describing female materiality as essentially passive. But it is ironic that, in his view, in consequence Eve as mere passive vehicle is responsible neither for the commission nor for the transmission of original sin.[8]

> It has been stated that original sin is transmitted by the first parent in so far as he is the mover in the begetting of his children. And so it has been said that if anyone were begotten only materially of human flesh, they would not contract original sin. Now it is evident that, in the opinion of philosophers, the active principle of generation is from the father, while the mother provides the matter. Therefore original sin is contracted, not from the mother, but from the Father; so that if Eve and not Adam had sinned, their children would not contract original sin. Whereas if Adam, and not Eve, had sinned, they would contract it [Summa Theologica, Q 81, Art V].

It does not follow, of course, that Eve is *good*, but only that she lacks responsibility for evil. The commission of sin presupposes active agency, i.e., a soul; if Eve is sheer material potency, then she is no more capable of sin than she is of doing good. She is the occasion of sin; but not the performer of it. Neither does she transmit it to the next generation.

Strictly speaking, Eve's materiality ought to render her morally neutral, or amoral—a being to whom ethical attributes are inapplicable.

In fact, we do speak in morally neutral terms of inanimate objects that, however offensive they may be to us, are not taken to act deliberately.* In the case of such nonresponsible beings, we assign their supervision to a higher authority, and that is exactly what Aristotle had in mind. But the Christian Fathers did not equate Eve's lack of spirituality simply with lack of intellect, although they undoubtedly regarded her as benighted in that dimension as well. They considered the defect of Eve's nature to be more sinister. As nature abhors a vacuum, so does spiritual deficiency invite the seduction of the Evil one. Pure spirit is not properly opposed to the absence of spirit, pure indeterminate matter, but to its diametric opposite, the depraved and corrupted spirit—Satan. Eve is subject to the beguilement of the fallen spirit, the serpent, and she, in turn, passes its seduction on to her imperfect companion, Adam.

Woman's capacity to elicit reprehensible thoughts (and deeds) in men can hardly be a postlapsarian fault, since Adam succumbed unprotestingly to her blandishments when Eve offered him the apple. Yet this ability to tempt and seduce, preeminently associated with her materiality, has caused woman to be most despised.† Evidently the contagion of her spiritual weakness is to be feared, for if men were spiritually perfect beings, they would be unmoved and unaffected by women's attraction.

Ultimately, then, men detest the dark forces within themselves on consideration of women's lack of spirituality. Yet in all cultures the reasoning is the same, regardless of what women are or do. They must be covered, shaved, disfigured, maimed and locked away—not as a corrective for their own spiritual lack, for which they are in a sense blameless, but as a protection against men's spiritual fallibility. The point is not that women must be protected against men. Rather, the denunciation of women's materiality is a means devised by men for deflecting attention from their own spiritual fallibility (as they understand it.) It is odd that little effort has been made to correct that fallibility. Instead, moral and spiritual weakness is projected upon woman as "the weaker vessel," and she is incarcerated and mummified to forestall the greater temptations of men.

On this view, matter and spirit are opposed to one another and are attributed, respectively, to the female and male principles. Spirit is

---

*The National Rifle Association has capitalized on that distinction, declaring that "Guns do not kill: People do." Guns, however, are designed by people exclusively for the purpose of killing.

†This horror of woman's charm is certainly not unique to Christianity. It is the heart of Hesiod's fable of Pandora's box, and of countless fairy tales and popular stories in which woman, the enchantress, is also reviled as "troublemaker." It is the familiar notion "cherchez la femme" whenever things go wrong.

furthermore associated with the rational, the principled, and the ethically sound, as well as with the generative and divine. Spirit is in all respects superior to matter and is rightfully destined to dominate it. Yet matter, the passive female potency, has its dark powers that must be curbed and suppressed. Thus it is that whenever it appears in women, in the physical world of nature, and not least in man himself, material nature must be ruthlessly surveyed and controlled. The presumption is, of course, that the universe is well served by such hierarchic domination.

II. WOMEN AS NATURE: SPIRIT AS IMMANENT

Woman's materiality may be affirmed without denying her spirituality. An alternative conception of spirituality assimilates it to the natural forces that animate the physical universe, rather than to the intellect or to a word-reifying deity.

Some archeological evidence supports the argument that regions of the Mediterranean and Middle East were once inhabited by matriarchal societies that worshipped a Mother-Goddess.[9] Perhaps, as feminist scholars have claimed, the scant evidence of these societies has been further invalidated and discredited by patriarchal scholarship,[10] not to mention the ruthless extermination of the societies in the first place. There are some indications even in patriarchal history and literature that alternative cultures might have existed with different social structures, different values, and different patterns of thought and feeling. I am concerned here only to explore the concept of spirituality that might have been derived from such prehistoric societies and that surely has been a persistent mythological strand of patriarchal culture. I am not arguing in defense of the actual existence of prehistoric matriarchal societies.

It is plausible that there once was a time when men were ignorant of their own role in procreation and were aware only that women had a miraculous, life-giving capacity. It is not unlikely that this ability would be regarded with reverential awe, and that women might be esteemed as goddesses and exercise considerable power. One may imagine that matrilineal descent would be the norm in such a society and that kin groups would be matrilocal. It does not follow that there would be matriarchy, a pattern of domination that seems dictated only by analogy to later patriarchal power structure. One can speculate, however, that once men discovered their part in the drama of birth, they might wish to aggrandize that role.

The agricultural model would surely be available to them, and could reasonably be extended to human generation. It allows men to claim preeminence as planters of seeds and producers of crops, harvesting women as women harvest nature. The assimilation of the fecundity of women to the fecundity of nature then seems justified and warrants similar rituals and practices. Thus woman as nature becomes the object of religious ceremony—not as transcendent being, but as the incarnation of natural processes whose rhythms must be respected and whose rites observed.

Natural processes, however, as Simone de Beauvoir has pointed out,[11] are not highly valued in our patriarchal culture. Only such activities as are deliberate, intentional, and represent the project of a self transcendent over nature qualify as truly human acts. Sheer process is perceived as unreflective and passive. The woman in childbirth is taken to be an acquiescent medium. She is impregnated: the child comes to fruition within her body and is expelled. She participates as in a dream, but she is not responsible for the event. Few women who have undergone the experience of pregnancy could subscribe to this description of their uninvolvement, but that is how it appears from the vantage point of patriarchy. By contrast, the deliberate taking of life is a transcendent act. To impose death (as distinct from suffering it) is to declare oneself a Self. Thus men have glorified death, awarded themselves authority over it, and mystified it where their power to control it was lacking. Meanwhile, they have devalued the capacity to engender life, treating it as a force to be reckoned with and even feared, but above all to be husbanded and controlled like any natural resource, such as water power or electricity. Women thus become a repository within which that force resides, a garrison of nature that must be held hostage for the sake of life.

On this account spirituality is not denied of woman and is indeed equated with her materiality. But it is not an individuating, intellectualizing, or morally elevating property. It is rather an elemental and undifferentiated force that "passes through" and occupies a woman as heat may be conducted through a metal or an electrical impulse through a wire. Woman's spirituality is in no way incompatible with her passivity or with her lack of moral authority.

This very neutrality or omnipotence of spirituality renders it suspect from a male perspective. Since women have no preordained commitment to patriarchy nor investment in it save the habit of subservience, their fidelity to it is not to be counted upon. That is why women are easily enlisted in conspiracy. (Witness again the guile of the serpent. Why did he not approach Adam directly?) That is why women's "gift" is precariously placed and may as readily be "perversely" applied as used to the benefit of patriarchy. Viewed from the standpoint of patriarchy, spirituality as so conceived is clearly a mixed blessing.

Nowhere is this ambivalence more clearly reflected than in the rich literature of Lilith, Eve's predecessor as Adam's consort.[12] Banished from Adam's side because she refused to submit to his importunings, Lilith is said to have wandered throughout Asia Minor, consorting and coupling with a variety of quasi-human creatures. A menace to men, she was an aide to women, presiding over childbirth and bringing them mid-wifely comfort. The legend of her autonomy, her bad reputation, her ostracism from civilized society, and the particular arts that she is alleged to have practiced certainly suggests the uneasy grafting of a patriarchal mythology and value system upon some more ancient and more female-oriented trunk.

No claims of superiority may be drawn either from the priority of the older system or the victory of patriarchalism. Neither antiquity nor power are measures of value, nor are they indices of greater or lesser spirituality. But patriarchy has continued to pay a grudging and ambivalent respect to the subterranean forces of life and passion that are viewed as woman's spirituality. Benevolently represented, these forces empower women as healers and comforters. Women are herbalists, alchemists, nurturers, and bringers of solace and repose. Malevolently feared, the same forces reflect women's trafficking with diabolical agents as witches and enchantresses, with dangerous hands as murderous as they are seductive.

Spirituality as thus depicted is a natural force attendant upon woman's materiality and closeness to nature. Intrinsically, it is neither good nor evil, but instrumentally it may be a means to the production of either. The control and domination of women who harbor this spirituality are therefore essential to the survival of patriarchy. Whether through witch burnings or the apotheosis of maternity and the "eternal feminine," women are culturally and politically collectivized, used as a resource, and "contained" as a potential hazard.

III. SPIRITUALITY DOMESTICATED

Still another representation of spirituality distinguishes it from both matter and the realm of intellect and places it in a pseudo-morally refined dimension of sentiment. This view arose with the advent of modern science, which treats nature as an abstraction and matter as inanimate and inert. Neither invested with spirit nor viewed as a menacing evil, no longer the repository of secret forces and powers, nature is neutrally objectified. Its conquest and control are rationally achieved and methodically maintained. Reason is the instrument of control, and its function is largely utilitarian.

Far removed from the Nous or Logos of the Hellenic-Christian tradition, modern reason adjudicates means to ends that it neither originates nor justifies. It will take us to outer space and to the moon, but it is essentially pedestrian. It is not the crowning glory of humanity, but is perhaps better exhibited in such machines as are unimpaired by human flaws and fallibilities. Little spirituality is left in this conception of reason, which has been denounced by mystics and romantics as the preserve of small-minded shopkeepers. Yet the power of this reason is not to be underestimated, for it is capable of building empires and destroying nations. Indeed, it may destroy the world altogether if it is not opposed by something other than reason. Scientific reason adjusts human destinies and may, with genetic engineering, redesign human potentialities. Thus it is a powerful manipulator of values, but it does not ground or preserve value. It has ceased to be the link between mankind and the divine.

Matter too has been demoted to an inert status. It is transformable into energy and is fluid and volatile, but it is not besouled. Unreceptive to spirit, it is a dead mechanism. Whatever spirit inspirits the world is not immanent in matter or its nature, but alights upon it as from another sphere and is held captive or enshrined.

Women, or rather "the Feminine," are the hostage to this transcendent spirit. Intuitive and feeling, they are nonrational: nurturant, and caring, and not purely material. Identified by default with spirituality, they are required to satisfy the dimension of affect and sensitivity that both reason and matter ignore. This spirituality gives meaning to life and makes it worthwhile. It imbues action with value and suffuses character with worth. But it is not to be confused with moral righteousness, which is lawful and derives from reason. Love, not morality, is the realm of the spirit, and love is the domain of women.

The home is also the domain of women, and there spirituality is enshrined. According to the doctrine of "separate spheres," which came to particular prominence in the 19th century and is still deeply embedded in patriarchal mythology, the home is the sanctuary of the spirit, and there the woman presides. From her pedestal she relieves the harsh reality of the lives of men (a reality from which she herself is supposedly protected), and indirectly she dispenses an inspiriting influence upon the public sphere by softening the hearts of the men to whom she ministers.[13]

Men are governed by reason and occupied with material concerns from which women have been largely excluded, but men are also the chief beneficiaries of women's spirituality. The solace and comfort that women purvey, not to mention their unpaid labor, are no doubt renewing both to men who are themselves oppressed and to those who oppress them. The spiritualizing role of women is thus a socially stabilizing force, and it has been harnessed to politically and economically conservative causes. We see again in this instance how the attribution (by men) of spirituality to women works to subjugate and to imprison women while it uses that spiritual capacity as a device for the maintenance of social order.

While from a woman's perspective the comparative social esteem of being regarded as a font of spirituality may be preferable to (and certainly safer than) being burned at the stake as a witch, the caliber of spirituality involved is somewhat truncated and ultimately degrading. Far from the romanticized "at-oneness" with a transcendent spirit from which it is alleged to stem, this hearth-bound spirituality is miniaturized and manicured. The little mother is all sweetness and tenderness, as depicted in countless sentimental works of literature and art, and the same slightly eroticized affection is displayed toward her errant man. No sign is apparent of the ferocity and bitter calculation that often mark genuine maternal concern. Nor are violent tremors of sensual passion allowed to mar the serene face of spirituality that romantic patriarchy ascribes to women. Above the crass materialism and rationalism of the world of men, the sentimentally spiritualized woman is removed from the rough traffic of life. But woe unto her if she descend, for she is instantly transformed into her mirror image—cold, hard, unnatural, and desexed. The compromise of her spirituality denatures her feminity, though not necessarily her sexuality. Hence the distinction, ridiculed by both feminists and their abusers, between the lady and the woman. The spiritualized lady is "pure" in her wifely dedication and motherhood: the despirited woman is depraved, either as sexually wanton (the whore) or as sexually neutralized and frigid.

As a heuristic paradigm for living, such tender spirituality must be deeply dispiriting. The survival of such a fragile artifact as the "spiritual" woman, or even the perpetuation of her illusion, is possible only through the beneficence and organized protection of men. The very special femininity that makes the hot-house flower vulnerable and dependent evokes in men a sense of power and sometimes responsibility. Male protectiveness is the obverse of male aggression, and both are linked to the ideal of manhood and virile self-esteem. That is why rape is the inevitable and salacious underside of male protection, the ultimate degradation, and the greatest tribute to male power.

Though woman's spirituality is alleged to arise from her communion with a transcendent being, she is in fact cut off by the social arrangements that protect her from actual communication with those resources that would empower her. These constraints, experienced from infancy, prohibit the female child from acquiring those kinesthetic and calculative aptitudes later denied of her as a "natural" deficiency.

Women continue to be discouraged from following the pursuits or entering the professions that have been denominated as belonging in the male domain. But long before these choices are articulated, the gender roles are cast, dictating conventional fears and expectations, rewarding patience and docility in girls and aggressive probing of limits in boys. The wonder is not that so many are turned away from the "male" activities, but that so many girls apply themselves to their achievement. It is clear that the societal rewards, including the esteem awarded to occupants of the male sphere, are higher than those of the female sphere. Yet women are rewarded as women, if not necessarily as people, for remaining in their "proper" sphere.

Lest this account of woman's spirituality and the "proper" sphere of womanhood appear quaintly archaic and absurdly out of date, I suggest that with only small modifications of language, it is still very much with us in the form of such contemporary doctrines as sociobiology. As its preeminent promulgators, E. O. Wilson and his associates, have maintained, the nurturant, maternal inclinations of the female are inherent expressions of the genetic drive for replication.[14] Male dominance and aggressiveness are similar genetic manifestations. Given the difference of their biological roles, the male is motivated to impregnate as many females as possible, a hit-and-run tactic calculated to preserve a widely distributed genetic progeny. The female, on the other hand, since her destiny includes the care and nurturance of her young, is motivated to associate sexual affiliation with long-term protection. She seeks a provider as well as a mate and so distributes her favors less casually. She evaluates a potential partner qualitatively as well as quantitatively and thus preserves a higher, less promiscuous standard of behavior. These patterns of conduct are described as "naturally" fixed in gender identity, and therefore the efforts of individuals to extricate themselves from their tyranny are ill-fated and ultimately deleterious to one's own genetic heritage, not to mention the established social order.

It might be observed that there is no glorification of the female sphere in this account, no rhapsodizing over woman's spirituality. Indeed, the very notion of any kind of spirituality or even moral worth has become debased. Altruism is reduced in significance to the status of a device for the perpetuation of a kindred gene pool. Where egoistic self-preservation is precluded, it is a shrewd alternative.

Strictly speaking, even the dubious merits of egoism are superseded by sociobiology. This is no philosophy of a transcendent spirit any more than it is of an immanent one. The apparently conscious and deliberate intentions of individuals, now represented as gene bearers, are all but immaterial in view of the exigencies of biological destiny. It is the genes that exhibit a rather demented if not demonic "purposiveness without a purpose." This presumed triumph of evolutionary selection assures the personal characteristics and social arrangements by means of which the relentless perpetuation of homologous genes is achieved. Not even the survival of the individual is at stake; nor that of the species, which some varieties of ethical humanism have promoted as a naturalistic version of spiritualism. According to sociobiology, the end and order of all things, that to which all human and biological endeavor is ordained, is the indefinite replication of ordered sequences of DNA. Sic transit gloria mundi!

In characterizing sociobiology as a reformulation of the 19th-century sentimentalized view of women, I do not mean to suggest that it is a theory of spiritualism. On the contrary, it renders the very notion of spirituality insignificant and even makes nonsense of the concept of significance. But it is a very effective and highly persuasive modern "scientific" defense of traditional beliefs regarding the ultimacy of gender dichotomy. And insofar as these beliefs embody previously established dogma linking sex identity with spirituality, that dogma is automatically and uncritically reinforced. It is in fact subtly incorporated into the rhetoric of the scientific theory itself. The popularized language of the "selfish" and "sneaky" gene capitalizes on prior prejudice and conveys a classic image of the war between the sexes in which the wily, intelligent, and adventurous male impregnates the dumb and passively receptive female.

Perhaps any defense of radical gender differentiation would, in the wake of the history I have described, carry the associative burden of making polarized attributions of spirituality. Clearly, differences between male and female do exist. The most obvious difference is physical, but it is not evident what further differences of a moral, intellectual, or spiritual nature might follow from these. Assuming that the material and functional differences lead to gender-specific experience, one might expect some social accommodations that would enlarge the original difference. The converse is also possible. One might make social arrangements that would minimize the effect of the natural disparity. Thus, nothing follows with necessity, even granted the fact of an initial material difference between the sexes. There is certainly no self-evident basis for drawing conclusions about comparative spirituality. I have tried to show that the dissociation between matter and spirit is not constant. But the polarization of male and female is constant, and therefore whatever qualities are taken to be essential to the one are promptly denied of the other.

This gender opposition has pervaded the mainstream of western philosophy as it has been transmitted under male domination, but there are indications of its presence even in some forms of feminist philosophy. And where the polarization persists there is a similar tendency to preserve the unnecessary and irrelevant orthogonal assign-

ment of spirituality to the sexes. I will consider one example of such a
theory.

IV. WOMAN'S SPIRITUAL SUPREMACY:
THE FEMINIST CLAIM

Among the most ardent opponents of patriarchy are some feminists
who insist not only upon the existence of gender differences, but upon
the spiritual superiority of the female. Some of these advocate the
repudiation of patriarchal religion and the return to a reconstructed
form of the Goddess religion described in Section II. It must be
emphasized that this is not a recommendation of matriarchy as a
replacement for patriarchy. The notion of matriarchy is in fact a male
invention conceived as a parallel counterpart to existing forms of
governance, including their mode of hierarchy and domination. But
there is no particular reason to believe in the historicity of such forms.

The Goddess religion as represented by its contemporary proponents stresses female symbolism and immanence. The Goddess animates all of nature and is especially evident as female power. Power in
this context does not refer to control or mastery over others, but to
creative self-engenderment. S. Budapest calls it "self-blessing" and
invites the worshippers of the Goddess to personal rituals and communal celebrations.[15] To honor the Goddess is to honor and elevate,
rather than denigrate, the "traditional" female attributes—closeness to
nature, nurturance, sensuality, and receptiveness. Adherents of the
Goddess religion do not deny the role ascribed to women by patriarchy,
but they reverse the patriarchal estimation of its value. Where patriarchy sees weakness, incompetence, and dependency, they see strength,
wisdom, and freedom. Proponents of this religion, while they do not
invariably exclude or reject men, tend to regard the established,
male-contrived religions as immature in their rigidity, excessively
formalistic, and defective in their inhumanity and lack of universality.
The Goddess religion denies transcendence and stresses community. It
emphasizes the continuity of natural phenomena, including human life,
and their interdependence. It encourages mutual aid, while not exclud-
ing the affirmation of individual will and purpose. It rejects formal
subordination and servility and a mechanical system of reward and
punishment. It is clearly based upon a compassionate analysis of
women's cultural experience and thus offers an historic alternative to
"the religion of the fathers." In this respect it is an attractive rectifica-
tion.

But while the exaltation of the Womanspirit is producing a ground-
swell of women's communities and some collaborative political and

social action, I believe that its ultimate effect is both politically and theoretically regressive.[16] However vitalizing to women's self-esteem, and however truly meritorious are the spiritual values that it extols, the Goddess religion, like sociobiology, tends to reaffirm existing prejudices. Here again, the polarities are overstated and are presumed to entail unrelated distinctions whose gender-specificity has not been established. Even when men are invited to take part in the rituals of the Goddess religion and to learn from women's experience, the old pathways of the male-supremacist tradition are not abandoned. They are a constant beckoning presence, inasmuch as they are allowed to define the terrain of human experience. Given the profound maldistribution and misdefinition of power that has emerged so far, its mere realignment is not a sufficient corrective. It will not do to glorify as virtue what men have labeled vice, or to denounce what they have celebrated. Such transvaluations are hardly new. But the very notions of virtue and vice must be called into question and the polarities themselves discredited.

Women theologians (or thealogians, as they sometimes call themselves)[17] have rightly noted that the so-called primal sins of pride, lust, greed, and avarice, and the corresponding virtues of humility, modesty, and generosity are male-identified.[18] They are not unheard of in women, but not notably common. Women are more prone to such offenses as trivialty and self-wastefulness. But this is not to indicate that a standard of female merits and demerits should be set alongside of, separate but equal to, that of males. Instead, it implies that we must reappraise the entire system of cataloguing so fundamental to male reflection. Perhaps the whole contextless abstraction of virtue and vice, good and evil, along with their attendant praise and blame, punishment and reward, damnation and redemption, are mere instances of simplistic patriarchal dichotimization. Little would be gained by a duplication of the list of simplifications.

The affirmation of a female ascendant theology, although its symbols be pleasing, its rituals satisfying, and its doctrines benevolent, nevertheless seems to perpetuate just those metaphysical and epistemological errors of traditional male philosophy that ought to be corrected. Furthermore, the political and psychological edge that male-generated polarizations already possess admonish us to cautiousness in the construction (or reconstruction) of yet another bipolar religion. At the same time, we must avoid insensitivity to the psychological and political fortification that the enunciation of such a religion might provide to women. The role of symbol and ritual in the establishment of beliefs and attitudes cannot be underestimated, especially in this instance where the entire counterweight of masculine culture must be offset.

But counterweapons will not serve where disarmament must be our end and wars of opposition rendered meaningless. My point is not simply that the Goddess is likely to be out-gunned and defeated, but that even her triumph would be a form of defeat where victory is to become an outmoded concept. In my view, the very notion of religion, though not devoid of features that may be gratifying to women as well as to men, must be so contaminated with patriarchal structures and residual associations of polarized values, hierarchy, and transcendence that even the most scrupulous feminist expurgation could not disinfect it. Something more radical than the resurrected Goddess is required.

I will end by sketching the beginnings of a possible reconceptualization of spirituality. I have indicated several historic analyses of spirituality and suggested that neither the opposition of spirit and matter nor the positive value of spirituality has been invariant. The more fundamental dichotomy between male and female has been determinative. However patriarchy has defined the nature of man, it has accorded the opposite qualities to women. But suppose we take an altogether different approach, and examine spirituality not as an adherent to this or that type of being, but rather as an end in and of oneself. One feature that is commonly ascribed to spirituality and that may be an essential condition of its possibility is freedom, which concept we will next explore.

V. BEGINNINGS OF A PROPOSED NEW ANALYSIS OF SPIRITUALITY

The spirit can be bound by ignorance or dogmatism, by false consciousness, or by tyrannical oppression. Nonetheless, it is of the spirit that freedom is quintessentially predicated. A free-falling body acts according to law, but the spirit unencumbered is truly free. Philosophers have for centuries exhorted us to be mindful that even where the body is enchained, the spirit can be free, and some have urged the cultivation of spiritual freedom. Indeed, where that freedom is lacking, the uncoerced body is hardly significant. What would a spiritless freedom mean?

Assuming this inherent integration of freedom and spirit, an analysis of spirituality in its relationship to freedom and especially as pertinent to a philosophy of women's liberation seems appropriate.

In patriarchal philosophy, freedom is classically defined in relation to constraint. It does not usually mean the absence of constraint. Most philosophers reject the absence of constraint as formlessness, lawlessness, anomie, anarchy, disorder, and chaos. Hence it is not only morally and politically undesirable, but ultimately conceptually absurd. We could not describe a condition of lawlessness, we could only react to it, for without definition as given by law and hence constraint, things have no identity. They cannot be objectively experienced. A world without law is a nullity, and so cannot be said to be free.

It is noteworthy that women are frequently taken to be just such nullities. Lacking ego boundaries, they are not defined as selves. They do not extricate themselves from their environment as transcendent beings, but remain contextually integrated. Consequently, the attribute of freedom is misapplied, though not falsely applied, to women. In other words, women are neither free nor unfree, just as success and failure have not been appropriate female characterizations until recently.

If freedom is not the absolute lack of constraint, it may be more fruitfully and is more commonly understood as self-imposed limitation or autonomy. The subject is not independent of all law, but only of that imposed by sources other than itself.[19] It is acknowledged that constraint is not only inevitable but essential to the very possibility of freedom, indeterminacy being the opposite of freedom. By this definition the meaning of freedom does not exclude lawful constraint, but the reality of freedom excludes heteronomy. One who is subject to the law of another is unfree, and, *a fortiori*, one whose very being is defined by the perception of another is unfree. According to this representation of freedom, women are thus irretrievably unfree. They live in a world whose laws are contingently dictated by men, and they exist as creatures categorically designed by and for men. If spirituality has to do with self-legislation, then women are clearly without spirit—but so also are most men.

Yet another view of freedom defines it as the recognition and acquiescence in necessity.[20] Here there is no question of self-determination, much less the absence of determination. Instead, the harmonious subordination of self to the necessary order of things is taken to be the intellectual and moral equivalent of freedom. This is not meant as a passive surrender, but as an act of comprehension in which the understanding self is in voluntary attunement with the ultimate (and usually rational) order of things. Because of the emphasis on the active, the voluntary, and the intellectual, the capacity for such attunement is usually denied to women. Though they too are bound by necessity, it is as object that is unfree, not as freely willing subject.

It seems then that by all the classic definitions of freedom, women are unfree and the very notion of women's liberation is a contradiction in terms. Yet I have argued that spirituality that is quintessentially associated with freedom is not incompatible with women and has sometimes been regarded as their specific domain. A redefinition of some key concepts is clearly called for.

I suggest that spirit be defined as an active, generative, and generous source—its materiality is irrelevant—whose fulfillment is the exercise of freedom. While the presence or absence of constraint is pertinent to the full realization of freedom, it is not included in its definition. Bondage is a restriction of freedom, as may be bodily conditions, such as illness or physical impairment. But inasmuch as human beings are corporeal, their spirituality as well as their freedom is expressed in and through bodies present in a physical world. This is as true of men as it is of women and does not represent a difference between them.

Furthermore, the freedom of such beings is not manifested in their coping with constraints, but in their enablement and accomplishment. Freedom is an impetus from within, not a reaction to what is without the agent. It expresses the nature of a being rather than defining its limits. Just as one's lived space moves as one moves, so does one's spiritual freedom expand as one expands. To the extent that spirituality entails freedom, it is because the spirit is the theater of freedom, not its legislator. And the spirit is neither self-contained by self-made law nor uncontained by license.

The freedom of spirit is expressed and evidenced in the capacity to formulate purposes and act in accordance with them. It does not follow that these purposes are always successfully accomplished. Their achievement may be concretely obstructed or variously frustrated, but freedom is not thereby, or not necessarily, denied. One is not unfree because one has failed in an attempt, but the inability to try is a failure of freedom. It is also a failure of spirit, for spirit is the purposing agent.

There is no reason to deny spirituality of beings other than women and men. Perhaps it is appropriately ascribed even to collective bodies and communities whose purposes are emergent from and irreducible to the aims of constituent members.

While spirituality may be characterized by intelligence, it is not reducible to it, nor is it a tributary of some irrational cosmic force. Spirituality is surely not antithetical to matter but, as we have seen, may well be found there. And since the only certain distinction between men and women is a physical one, it is most improbable that spirituality is a gender-linked capacity. In all likelihood it is found throughout nature. We know it best through those objects that human beings make as a consequence of its presence, such objects as works of art and science, but also through other human beings and human relationships.

I suggest that children, the offspring of joint parenthood and like their parents a complex of physical, mental, and moral being, are a paradigm spiritual product. Controversy over the disposition of credit seems absurd. Whether we look at the child from the patriarchal perspective as "ensouled seed" implanted in a passive vessel, or alternatively as a "dead seed' quickened and animated by the maternal environment, both contributors seem to carry considerable responsibility. Furthermore, both parents as parents are products of one another's history and one another's interactions. Neither conceives or is conceivable without the other. Their offspring is a commingling of both, not drawn from mutually exclusive segments of each.

I cite children as obviously of bisexual origin, but cultural artifacts more generally are the spiritual products of communal enterprise, though not necessarily of gendered pairs. Here, too, the description of formed matter or embodied spirit as applied, say, to a code of laws, a work of art, or an institutionalized ritual practice seems hopelessly inadequate. Such descriptions invariably mystify both matter and spirit while failing to grasp the rich integrity of the objects they purport to describe.

I conclude, then, that the best way to understand spirituality is to consider those objects that are its acknowledged products. Such reflection reveals that matter and spirit are not exclusive, that intellect and spirit are not identical, that neither men nor women have a monopoly on spirituality, but that an analysis of the relationship of woman to spirituality is warranted in order to rectify the philosophical biases of the past.

NOTES

1. Hilde Hein, from "Half a Mind: Philosophy from a Woman's Perspective" (unpublished manuscript, 1979).

2. Aristotle, *On Generation and Corruption* (1930) Vol. II in *The Works of Aristotle*, ed. W. D. Ross (London: Oxford Univ. Press, 1962).

3. Ibid., Vol. X.

4. Ibid., Vol. III.

5. Ibid., Vol. IX.

6. Tertullian, "De cultu feminarum" (The Apparel of Women) in *Disciplinary, Moral and Ascetical Works*, translated by R. Arbesmann et al. (New York: Fathers of the Church, Inc., 1959); Clement of Alexandria, *Paedogogus* (Christ the Educator), translated by Simon P. Wood, C. P. (New York: Fathers of the Church, Inc., 1954).

7. St. Augustine, *Treatises on Marriage and Other Subjects*, ed. Roy J. Deferrari (New York: Fathers of the Church, Inc., 1959).

8. St. Thomas Aquinas, *Summa Theologica*, translated by Fathers of the English Dominican Province (New York: Benziger Brothers, 1947).

9. Merlin Stone, *When God Was a Woman* (New York: Harcourt Brace Jovanovich, 1976); Carol Ochs, *Behind the Sex of God* (Boston: Beacon Press, 1977).

10. Mary Daly, *Gyn/Ecology: The Metaethics of Radical Feminism* (Boston: Beacon Press, 1978).

11. Simone de Beauvoir, *The Second Sex* (1940) (New York: Bantam, 1970).

12. Robert Graves and Raphael Patai, "Adam's Helpmeets," *Hebrew Myths: The Book of Genesis* (New York: McGraw-Hill, 1966); Lilian Rivlin, "Lilith," *Ms,* December 1972.

13. Barbara Walter, "The Cult of True Womanhood: 1820–1860" *American Quarterly* 12 (Summer 1966).

14. E. O. Wilson, *Sociobiology* (Cambridge: Harvard Univ. Press); Richard Dawkins, *The Selfish Gene* (New York: Oxford Univ. Press, 1976); David Barash, *Sociobiology and Behavior* (New York: Elsevier, 1977).

15. S. Budapest, "Self-Blessing Ritual," in *Womanspirit Rising,* ed. Carol P. Christ and J. Plaskow (San Francisco: Harper & Row, 1980); Starhawk, "Witchcraft and Women's Culture," in Christ and Plaskow, eds., *Womanspirit Rising.*

16. Judith Christ, "Why Women Need the Goddess: Phenomenological, Psychological, and Political Reflections," in Christ and Plaskow, eds., *Womanspirit Rising.*

17. Naomi R. Goldenberg, *Changing of the Gods* (Boston: Beacon Press, 1979).

18. Valerie Saiving, "The Human Situation: A Feminine View," *The Journal of Religion,* April 1960.

19. Immanuel Kant, *Foundations of the Metaphysics of Morals,* translated by L. W. Beck (Indianapolis: Bobbs-Merrill Co., 1969).

20. Benedict De Spinoza, *Ethics,* ed. James Gutmann (New York: Hafner Publishing Co., 1949).

Chapter 19 ————————————————————————

While Love is Unfashionable: Ethical Implications of Black Spirituality and Sexuality

Toinette M. Eugene

> For you there shall be no longing, for you
>   shall be fulfillment to each other;
> For you there shall be no harm, for you
>   shall be a shield for each other;
> For you there shall be no falling, for you
>   shall be support to each other;
> For you there shall be no sorrow, for you
>   shall be comfort to each other;
> For you there shall be no loneliness, for you
>   shall be company to each other;
> For you there shall be no discord, for you
>   shall be peace to each other;
> And for you there shall be no searching,
>   for you shall be an end to each other.
>   —Kawaida Marriage Commitment

INTRODUCTION

*B*lack spirituality and Black sexuality, properly understood as aspects of the holistic life-style of Afro-American women and men, are a closer fit than hand and glove. Nonetheless, taken together these issues also represent two of the most serious ethical challenges that the contemporary Black church must address. While we may affirm the covenantal poetry above, which is based on an African worldview and value system, we must also acknowledge another Afro-American

Source: From *Women's Consciousness, Women's Conscience* by Barbara Hilkut Andolsen et al. (eds). Copyright © 1985 by Barbara Hilkut Andolsen, Christine E. Gudorf, and Mary D. Pellauer. Reprinted by permission of the author and of Harper & Row, Publishers Inc.

313

reality that sorely lacks the spiritual and sexual fidelity expressed in the poem.

One of the most neglected ministries in the Black church has been the holistic integration of sexuality and life. Although the Black church has been one of the key supportive institutions for upbuilding family life and values,[1] the need to address issues and attitudes dealing with sexuality, with mutuality in male/female relationships, and with the more recent impact of Black feminism has never been greater than today.

This essay investigates the relationships between Black spirituality and sexuality in the quest for mutuality among Black women and Black men. I will examine these issues with particular reference to the unifying factor of Black love. The focus is holistic, that is, it illuminates Black spirituality and sexuality as they are experientially related. The assumptions of this approach are incarnational. Consequently, a theology of Black male/female friendship that is mutual, community seeking, as well as other-directed, is a central, incarnational, and liberational premise for this work in an era in which any effort at committed love appears unfashionable.

SPIRITUALITY AND SEXUALITY AS RELIGIOUS ASPECTS OF THE CONTEMPORARY BLACK EXPERIENCE

We must acknowledge at the outset a widespread and well-known experience within the Black community. Michelle Wallace, among others, agrees that experience of distrust has driven a wedge between Black women and Black men:

> For perhaps the last fifty years there has been a growing distrust, even hatred between black men and black women. It has been nursed along, not only by racism on the part of whites, but by an almost deliberate ignorance on the part of blacks about the sexual politics of their experience in this country.[2]

This basic distrust between Black women and Black men accounts for the inability of the Black community to mobilize as it once could and did. The religious aspect of *Black sexuality*, by which I mean the basic dimension of our self-understanding and way of being in the world as Black male and female persons, has been distorted into a form of Black sexism. Because of this basic distrust, the beauty of Black sexuality, which also includes our sex-role understandings, our affectional orientations, physiological arousal and genital activity, and our capacity for sensuousness, has become debilitated. The power of Black sexuality to contribute to our liberating mission to change our oppressive condition has been weakened. This basic distrust disables and distracts us as we strive to bring about the reign of God, which is a theological as well as a political reality, for Black women and Black men.[3]

Theologian Jacquelyn Grant adds another significant aspect of the nexus between Black spirituality and Black sexuality: the effects of sexism on the kerygmatic and proclamatory mission of the Black church. She insists:

> If the liberation of women is not proclaimed, the church's proclamation cannot be about divine liberation. If the church does not share in the liberation struggle of Black women, its liberation struggle is not authentic. If women are oppressed, the church cannot possibly be "a visible manifestation that the gospel is a reality"—for the gospel cannot be real in that context. One can see contradictions between the church's language or proclamation of liberation and its action by looking both at the status of Black women in the church as laity and Black women in the ordained ministry of the church.[4]

The holistic expression of Black spirituality is a central part of what is at stake in liberating relationships between Black women and men in the church and society.

Spirituality is no longer identified simply with asceticism, mysticism, the practice of virtue, and methods of prayer. Spirituality, i.e., the human capacity to be self-transcending, relational and freely committed, encompasses all of life, including our human sexuality.

Specifically, Christian spirtuality involves the actualization of this human transcendence through the experience of God, in Jesus the Christ, through the gift of the Spirit. Because God, Jesus, and the Spirit are experienced through body-community-history, a Black Christian spirituality includes every dimension of Black life. We must begin to re-employ the power of Black spirituality as a personal and collective response of Black women and Black men to the gracious presence of the God who lives and loves within us, calling us to liberating relationships with one another and with all people on Earth.

BLACK LOVE AS FOUNDATIONAL FOR THE EXPRESSION OF BLACK SPIRITUALITY AND SEXUALITY

A Black liberating love must serve as the linchpin to link Black spirituality and sexuality. Black love is the agent of gospel liberation as well as the strongest asset of the Black and believing community. Black love, expressed through the faithful witness of our spirituality and sexuality, creates awareness of the living God who is in every place. Black love sustains our own ability to choose and to discern, and nurtures the sense of the bonding and *esprit d'corps* that allows Black women and men to be distinctive in the style of our self-acceptance. Black love confirms and affirms our affection for God, self, and others, especially those who have also been oppressed.

Historically, Black love enabled the incredibly crushed spirits of enslaved Black women and men to look beyond their immediate, undeserved suffering to a God who would never forsake them in their hour of anguish and despair. Historically, it has been the religious aspect of Black love that enabled Black Christians to believe always in the worth of each human life: born and unborn; legitimate and "illegitimate"; single and several-times married; young and old; unemployed and inexperienced.

Any major misunderstandings or doubt about the ability of Black love to link and liberate the power of spirituality and sexuality can be traced to the effects of our enslavement experiences. Historically, it was criminal for Blacks to express extended love for one another or to establish lasting relationships of social interdependence and care. Blacks were wrenched from our African societies in which sexual behavior was orderly and under firm family and community controls. Under the system of slavery Black people were bred like animals; white men were allowed to sexually coerce and abuse Black women; Black families were frequently broken up and legal marriage was often prohibited. Sexual instability was forced upon the Afro-American community.[5]

Racist myths and stereotypes perpetuated these distortions to this day, falsely detailing Black hypersexual activity and an inability to maintain and nurture marital commitments. Racists also repeat ubiquitous rumors about violent relationships among Black men and their women or wives. It is impossible for the many white Americans reared on this pathological mythology to think, speak, or write with historical accuracy or ethical understanding about the integrity of Black love and relationships.

Despite these assaults, Black love has continuously flowed between Black people, almost like breath (the *nepesh*, the *ruah*, or the *pneuma*, which scriptural studies tell us is like the breath of God), breathing life into dead or desperate situations. This death-defying capacity of Black women and men to go on giving and receiving love has been incredibly preserved within a hostile and rascist American environment. Such tenacious Black love had its spiritual genesis in African soil where it developed unencumbered, at least in its beginnings, by the prejudices of American puritanical Christianity. We must hold on to this strong inheritance from our African past if there is to be any hope for nurturance, growth, and fruitfulness, in Black male/female relationships in our Black church and society.

Racist assumptions and myths perpetuate the lie of a "Black love deficiency." Black persons educated in the Black religious experience have recognized that if Black people today are to be liberated, we must continue to conceive of and model ourselves as a morally creative and spiritually generative race of women and men who choose to act out of our own positive *ethos*. We must continue to create and articulate our own positive expressions and standards of excellence rather than continue to be confined and defined by the negative images of a dominant social, sexual, cultural, and political system that does not value Blackness as inherently good.

Black love ought always to serve as an essential normative and descriptive referent for the relationship found in Black spirituality and sexuality. I arrive at this ethical "ought" or injunction for our future based on results that are verifiable in our brutal and painful past history as a people in this country. It may be historicaly demonstrated that in times past whenever Black women and men consciously and consistently dared to express Black love through an integration of their spirituality and sexuality, they became a source for liberating social transformation in both the Black community and in the white world around them. The abolitionist and feminist Sojourner Truth, through her involvement in redressing the racist and sexist oppression of her times, is an excellent example of the way in which the integration of personal spirituality and sexuality may come to fruition in a prophetic paradigm for the sake of the reign of God. (I shall return to examine the religious experience of Sojourner Truth as a model for our theme.)

In the days gone by, Black love expressed between Black women and men was at worst illegal or at least highly unprofitable in every way for those trying to survive in impossible situations. Nonetheless deliberate choices were made by our foreparents which: (1) enabled Afro-American peoples to create and perform under great duress their own wedding rituals such as the slave marriage custom of "jumping the broomstick" or the practice of "marrying in blankets";[6] (2) promoted an internal sexual ethic in the slave communities that safeguarded marriages, secured the welfare of children, and forbade indiscriminate or irresponsible sexual relations; (3) prompted hundreds of former slaves to search endlessly for a reunion with their spouses, children, and relatives after the Emancipation Proclamation of Lincoln.

These realities are foundational for an understanding that Black love expresses a sacramental statement about the relationship of Black spirituality to sexuality. Without a realistic assessment of the innumerable ways Black women and men have endeavored to hold fast to each other, and to cherish one another, it is easy to generate theological premises and sociological strategies based on false foundations. For example, it is true that urban lifestyles and escalating unemployment have contributed greatly to the breakdown of many Black marriages and families. However, it is equally critical to assert the historical fact that until the third decade of the twentieth century, the majority of Black marriages and families were thriving and stable.[7]

This practical understanding of Black integrity, fidelity, as well as familial stability, enables a clearer assessment of the pathologies of racism and sexism that affect Black male/female relationships in church and society. Racism and sexism continue to hinder us from expressing the depths of Black spirituality and sexuality as epitomized in Black love.

RACISM AND SEXISM AS CRITICAL FACTORS AFFECTING THE BLACK QUEST FOR MUTUALITY

Racism and sexism, operative in our midst, are the two primary negative factors that affect Black male/female relationships. Any ethical reflection on the issue of sexism in relation to racism requires a coming to terms with the suffering and oppression that have marked past pathological relationships between Black women and Black men. Honest reflection on the issue of sexism in relation to racism may also highlight positive aspects of the challenge and conversion available to Black and believing women and men who want to deal with their own spirituality and sexuality as a means of coming to terms with a new life in God.

Jacquelyn Grant explains the effects of sexual dualism on the self-image of Black people. "Racism and sexism are interrelated," she says, "just as all forms of oppression are interrelated."[8] Racism and sexism have provided a theological problem within the Christian community composed of both Black women and men who theoretically are *equally* concerned about the presence of freedom and justice for all. "Sexism, however, has a reality and significance of its own because it represents that peculiar form of oppression suffered by Black women at the hands of Black men. It is important to examine this reality of sexism as it operated in both the Black Community and the Black Church."[9]

A careful diagnosis of the sickness and the sin of sexism within the Black church calls forth a challenge to ministers and laity alike. The failure of the Black church and of Black theology itself to proclaim explicitly the liberation of Black women indicates, according to this assessment, that neither theology nor the church can claim to be agents of divine liberation or of the God whom the evangelist describes as the Author and Exemplar of Black love. If Black theology, like the Black church, has no word for Black women, then its conception of liberation is inauthentic and dysfunctional.

There are two basic forms that such sexism takes in Black male/ female relationships: sexist and spiritualistic splits or divisions within reality.

Sexist dualism refers to the systematic subordination of women in church and society, within interpersonal relationships between males and females, as well as within linguistic patterns and thought formulations by which women are dominated.[10] Hence the term "patriarchal dualism" may be also appropriate, or more simply, the contemporary designation of "sexism" may be used. *Spiritualistic dualism* has its roots in the body-spirit dichotomy abounding in white western philosophy and culture introduced at the beginning of the Christian era. Hence, the term "Hellenistic dualism" may also be appropriate. It must be noted in offering these descriptive distinctions about sexual and spiritual dualisms that African philosophy and culture was and still is significantly different from these white western conceptualizations.[11] It is this African worldview that has given rise to the holistic potentiality residing in authentic expressions of Afro-American spirituality and sexuality today.

Sexist dualism has pathologically scarred not only the white community from which it originated by has also had its negative effect within the Black religious community.[12] Sexist dualism, which has been organized along racial lines, refers to "schizophrenic" male attitudes toward women in general, who are imaged as either the virgin or the whore—the polemical Mary or Eve archetype represented by the female gender. The prevailing model of beauty in the white, male-dominated American society has been the "long-haired blond" with all that accompanies this mystique. Because of this worldview, Black women have had an additional problem with this pseudo-ideal as they encounter Black men who have appropriated this norm as their own.

Sexist as well as racist dualism have elevated the image of the white woman in accordance with the requirements of a white world-view into becoming the respected symbol of femininity and purity, while the Black woman must represent an animality which can be ruthlessly exploited for both sex and labor. Similarly the sexist dualism present within pseudo-biblical teaching argues that *woman* is responsible for the fall of "*man*kind," and is, consequently the source of sexual evil. This dualistic doctrine has had its double detrimental effect in the experience of many Black women.[13]

The self-image and self-respect of many Black women is dealt a double blow by both Black religion and Black society. Thus, Black women are made to believe or at least accept on the surface that they are evil, ugly, insignificant, and the underlying source of trouble, especially when the sense of intimacy begins to break down in Black love relationships.

This dualistic doctrine has nurtured a kind of compensatory Black male chauvinism (as evidenced in typical Black church patterns and Black nationalism movements) in order to restore the "manliness" of the one who had traditionally been humiliated by being deprived (according to a white patriarchal model) of being the primary protector for his family. In such manner, sexist dualism has been a central limitation in the development of a Black love that at its zenith is the most authentic expression we have of the unity of Black spirituality and sexuality.

A disembodied spirituality has also been a central limitation in the development of Black love. Spiritualistic dualism has been a central factor in persistent efforts to portray faithful Black love as an unfashionable and hoplessly anachronistic way of establishing Black liberation and Black material success and achievement. Eldridge Cleaver obviously recognized the racism and sexism in this spiritualistic form of dualism. Cleaver readily identified bodily scapegoating as an aspect of the sickness within racist/sexist relationships: "Only when the white man comes to respect his own body, to accept it as part of himself will he be able to accept the Black man's mind and treat him as something other than the living symbol of what he has rejected in himself."[14] Bodily scapegoating implies a discomfort with our own bodies that leads us to discredit any human body-person that differs too much in appearance and similarity from our own. This scapegoating is particularly evident in racist, white-Black relationships. But it is equally obvious in the revealing and discrediting attitudes of some men, white and Black, about the assumed menstrual "uncleanliness" of women, or the intrinsic "repulsiveness" of the pregnant female form.

Because Blackness has long been understood as a symbol for filth as well as evil, a spiritualistic dualism prevalent in the worldview of many white persons has allowed them the racist option of projecting onto Black persons any dirty or disgusting bodily feelings that they may harbor within themselves. Because of the fertility potential symbolized by the female menstrual and pregnancy cycles, a spiritualistic and sexist dualism has also been created and sustained by white and Black males, which has allowed them to act out their own latent anxieties and hostilities by sexually depreciating the value and worth of the Black female person.

As long as we feel insecure as human beings about our bodies, we will very likely be anxious or hostile about other body-persons obviously racially or sexually different from our own embodied selves. Thus, the most dehumanizing spoken expressions of hostility or overt violence within racist and/or sexist experiences are often linked with depreciating the body or body functions of someone else. Worse yet, though, the greatest dehumanization or violence that actually can occur in racist and/or sexist situations happens when persons of the rejected racial- or gender-specific group begin to internalize the judgments made by others and become convinced of their own personal inferiority. Obviously, the most affected and thus dehumanized victims of this experience are Black women.

Racism and sexism diminish the ability of Black women and men to establish relationships of mutuality, integrity, and trust. Racism and sexism undermine the Black communities in which we live, pray, and work out our salvation in the sight of God and one another. However, in coming to terms with racism and sexism as oppressions affecting us all, the Black church does have access to the Black community in ways that many other institutions do not. The Black church has a greater potential to achieve both liberation and reconciliation by attending carefully to the relationships that have been weakened between Black males and females.

Because the Black church has access, and is often indeed the presiding and official agent in the process of sexual socialization, it has a potentially unlimited opportunity to restore the ancient covenant of Scripture and tradition that upholds the beauty of Black love in its most profound meaning. Wherever Black love is discouraged or disparaged as an unfashionable or unattainable expression between Black women and Black men, the Black church has an unparalleled option to model these gospel values of love and unconditional acceptance. By offering from its storehouse an authentic understanding of Black spirituality and sexuality, the Black church becomes paradigmatic of the reign of God materializing and entering into our midst.

I have referred to spirituality as a commitment and lifestyle, as the growth and response of the human personality to the beauty and benevolence of a liberating God. For Black Christians in particular, the praxis of spirituality is a conscious response to the call for discipleship by Jesus. It is intimately related to the moral and ethical conviction that moves us from the private, prayerful posture of bowed head and bent knee to the public, prophetic position of proclaiming before oppressor and oppressed alike: "Thus saith the Lord of Justice. . . ."

For Black Christian women and men, the importance of the spiritual life cannot be overplayed. It is what unites those of African ancestry in the possession of a distinctive *ethos*. For Black Christians, our African heritage allows us to comprehend spirituality as a *Lebenswelt*—as a life-experience—as well as a world-view. Our African heritage allows us to share in a collective mindset that recognizes yet does not rigidly separate the sacred from the secular, or insist negative, polemic (i.e.,

Hellenistic) distinctions about the relative merits of the ideal and actual, the body and the spirit, or the profane and the pristine.[15]

Dualisms, sexist or spiritualistic, have no place within the seamless garment of authentic Black religious experience. It is this integrative understanding implicit and inherent in the Afro-American religious *Lebenswelt* that allows spirituality and sexuality to be considered together and as aspects of a holistic religious experience for Black women and men in the church and society. Whatever one decides in the historical debate surrounding the actual degree of African retentions in the New World, it is certain that the Black church in America has thrived on the dynamic qualities of an African spirituality. History has evidenced a faith affirmation among Black religionists that indicates "both the individual and community have a continuous involvement with the spirit world in the practical affairs of daily life."[16]

A striking description of African Christian spirituality provides in summary format a Black perspective:

> [African Christian] spirituality is a dynamic and outgoing concept. . . . There is nothing cerebral or esoteric about spirituality; it is the core of the Christian experience, the encounter with God in real life and action. Spirituality is the same thing as continuous or experiential prayer—prayer as a living communion with God who is experienced as being personally present in the relationships of humanity. It is the mode of living, the essential disposition of the believer, and it imparts a new dimension to the believer's life. In other words, it is not only a new way of looking at human life, but a new way of living it. It is unnecessary, perhaps, to draw any sharp dividing line between theology and spirituality. Theology should be spiritual theology . . . it should not be merely speculative, but should encourage active commitment.[17]

Because of this overarching emphasis in Black spirituality on human persons, relationships, and values, the Black church is in a prime position to invite and reestablish in creative ways a dialogue between Black women and Black men. Because the Black church is seen to be the driving force of the movement toward the recovery of a meaningful value system for the Black community, it has tremendous potential for fostering constructive, instructive, and reconciling discussion on issues of mutuality, sexuality and spirituality for Black women and men. It is obvious that the foundational theory and the theology are all in place to accomplish this dialogue, yet the praxis is still limited or lacking if we are at all honest in our reflection upon our lived experience. The recovery of a meaningful value system enriching the relationships between Black women and men still remains underdeveloped, or at best only moderately achieved.

The tendency to opt for a spirituality that is unrelated to our Black bodily existence or the temptation to become too heavily fixated at the level of the physical, material, or genital expressions of Black love keeps us off balance and unintegrated in religiously real ways. Thus, relationships between Black women and men in the Black church and community still struggle to reveal that *imago Dei* of which Scripture speaks:

> Then God said, "Let us make man in our image, after *our likeness*" . . . so God created . . . Male *and* female . . . (Gen 1:26f.)

> For as many of you as were baptised into Christ have put in Christ. There is neither slave nor free, there is neither male or female; for you are all one in Christ Jesus. (Gal 3:27f.)

It is impossible to adequately establish any Christian perspective on human sexuality without first returning to and affirming the value that God has forever made human flesh and "body-persons" the privileged place of the divine encounter with us. Perhaps, as we are able to deepen our understanding of Black spirituality as an embodied, incarnational, holistic, and earthy reality and gift given to us by the God who became enfleshed to dwell with us as a "body-person," we may become better at the praxis that this implies.

If God has so trusted and honored the human body by taking on a human form and accepting human sexuality as a way of entering into relationship with all humanity, how much more must we strive to imitate the model of spirituality and sexuality offered to us by the Word-Made-Flesh. God freely chose to become a body-person as we are. I am persuaded to think that many of us are simply too afraid to take ourselves that seriously and act "freely mature with the fullness of Christ himself" (Eph 4:13).

In the process of exploring theologically how this ontological Blackness points to the *imago Dei* in Black humanity we are immediately referred back to the context of the feminist challenge. To theologically explore ontological Blackness requires us to engage in open and nondefensive dialogue with others about creative use of sexually inclusive *language* for God as well as sexually inclusive *images* that serve to symbolize God. Although we may take great pride and satisfaction in the language and image of the phrase "God is Black," there is still a Black feminist question that is appropriately raised for our consideration: "Have we simply shifted from imaging and thinking of God in white male terminology into conceiving and speaking of God as a Black male figure?"

James Evans offers a straightforward reply to this concern in his article on "Black Theology and Black Feminism."

> If blackness is an ontological symbol [pointing out the *imago Dei* in humanity] then it means more than physical blackness and also more than maleness. . . . Blackness must mean the racism and liberation from it experienced by black men. It must also mean the racism/sexism and the liberation from them experienced by black women. If blackness as an ontological symbol refers to authentic humanity, then it cannot become simply a "living testament" to failure in white male/female relationships, but must point to new relationships.[18]

This consideration of new relationships between Black women and Black men and with a God whom we choose to image as Black and as androgynous within our contemplation and conversation necessarily urges us onward in the ethical task of reintegrating and restoring the fullness of meaning to Black spirituality and sexuality. The search for ways of expressing and experiencing an inclusive vision of God calls us to the task of offering and receiving Black love that joins and sustains our spiritual and sexual lives in appropriate ways.

Through a deepening trust and mutuality in our relationships with God, self, and others, the expressions of Black love that may seem so unfashionable or unsophisticated to the world may serve to bond Black women and men even more closely together in our worst periods of trial and tribulation as well as in our best moments of joy and achievement.

FEMINISM AND FRIENDSHIP AS EMBODIED EXAMPLES OF BLACK LOVE

There are hopeful signs on the horizon pointing to an increasing sense of mutuality and deepening of understanding in Black male/female relationships. Black women who are feminists do want to deepen their exchange of experiences with Black men, and to make plans together for a future full of hope. As Jeanne Noble puts it: "Black women want to be involved. . . . Black women want to be partners, allies, sisters [with black men]! Before there is partnering and sharing with someone, however, there is the becoming of oneself. And the search and discovery of authentic selfhood on the part of Black women has begun."[19] Black feminism as a concept is *not* meant to describe militant, man-hating females who are strict separatists without sensitivity for anyone but themselves—a sort of chauvinism in reverse. Black feminism is defined as a self-acceptance, satisfaction, and security of Black women within themselves. Similarly, in the case of Black men who understand themselves as feminists, Black feminism for them is an attitude of acceptance of Black women as peers—an attitude that is verifiable in their behavior and efforts on behalf of and in solidarity with Black women. Black feminism proceeds from the understanding, acceptance, and affirmation of Black women as equal and mutual in relation to Black men, to an increasing openness of mind and heart to be in solidarity with and in self-sacrificing compassion and action for others who have also been oppressed or marginal in society. This solidarity includes being in communion and consultation with all Third World peoples, and implies dialogue and discussion with White women's liberation actions as well as with gay liberation movements in this country.

As Black men and women come to understand and to express this kind of Black feminist perspective in relation to one another and for the sake of bringing about the reign of God into our world, this kind of Black love is not always going to be fashionable or acceptable to everyone. However, by accepting the divine demand to struggle against both sexism and racism, Black feminists (both men and women) can experience and express a Black love that is both redemptive and refreshing. There are those who have been there in the struggle before us and can show us the way. A renowned example of Black Christian feminism, and a model of the quest for mutuality between Black women and men and all oppressed others, was the emancipated slave and celebrated mystic, Sojourner Truth.

Born into slavery in upstate New York at the end of the eighteenth century, Isabelle Bomefree received a call to begin a new life in 1843. At the age of forty-six she took a new name that summed up her vocation and conviction to be a sojourner or pilgrim of the Truth. She suddenly felt called to leave her employment in New York City and set out to do God's work in the world. For the next forty years she moved about the country, lecturing, singing, and helping the cause of abolition of slavery. After the Civil War she worked tirelessly and selflessly for the betterment of the lot of freed slaves as well as for all women's rights. She knew well that Black love expressed in Black spirituality and sexuality was not always welcomed warmly as a means of liberation or reconciliation in the places where she was called to minister. As a Black Christian feminist on a quest for mutuality among all peoples, she offers an embodied example for our consideration.

A tall, forceful woman with a booming voice, we are told she spoke plainly about prayer to God. In the autobiographical account of her life, which she dictated since she was unable to write, she recounted in *The Narrative of Sojourner Truth* this religious experience that she had when she was still a slave:

> . . . (Sojourner) told Mrs Van Wagener that her old Master Dumont would come that day, and that she should go home with him on his return . . .

... before night, Mr Dumont made his appearance. She informed him of her intention to accompany him home. He answered with a smile, "I shall not take you back again; you ran away from me." Thinking his manner contradicted his words, she did not feel repulsed, but made herself and child ready . . . [to] go with him. . . .

... But ere she reached the vehicle, she says that God revealed himself to her, with all the suddenness of a flash of lightning, showing her "in the twinkling of an eye, that he was *all over*"—that he pervaded the universe—"and that there was no place God was not." She became instantly conscious of her great sin of forgetting her Almighty Friend and "ever present help in time of trouble."

... She plainly saw that there was no place, not even in hell where he was not; and where could she flee? Another such "a look" as she expressed it, and she felt that she must be extinguished forever, even as one, with the breath of his mouth "blows out a lamp," so that no spark remains.

... When at last the second look came not, and her attention was once more called to outward things, she observed that her master had left, and exclaiming aloud, "Oh God, I did not know you were so big," [she] walked into the house.[20]

The rest of Sojourner's life was a long conversation with her "Almighty Friend," God. All who met her would always be struck by the calm self-possession of this stately Black woman. The most characteristic aspect of her spirituality was the vivid sense of God's presence everywhere (a distinctively African world-view), and her simple manner of praying everywhere.

Sojourner's suffering was as direct a result of her Blackness as it was a result of her ministry, and it was a significant element in her spiritual development. And, "because of this humility," according to Heb 5:7–8, "this prayer was heard." Daughter though she was, she learned obedience in the school of suffering, and once transformed, she became a model of liberation and of the quest for mutuality for us and for the encouragement of all who will learn from her example.

Through her intimate relationship with God, Sojourner Truth offers us a model for a theology of friendship which may serve to further our understanding of the quest for mutuality between Black women and men as well as with all other persons. Sojourner Truth understood and related to God consistently and continuously as her dear and "Almighty Friend." The narrative of her life declares that, "she talked to God as familiarly as if he had been a creature like herself; and a thousand times more so, than if she had been in the presence of some earthly potentate."[21]

Relationships that are mutual, community-seeking, and other-directed are critical in the encouragement of any lasting commitments between Black women and men. They are also critical for the development of friendships or intimacy between couples or groups who wish to embody the meaning of what has been defined as Black love. It is these characteristics of mutuality, communality, and disinterestedness (in the best sense of its meaning as an unbiased personal interest or advantage in a relationship) that have the most potential to transform our culture and to create the preconditions necessary for the reign of God to take root and to grow in our midst.

Such a theology of friendship seems much more adequate than just a theology of sexuality standing alone, or just a simple rendition of spirituality offered for application in our times. A theology of friendship is more adequate and appropriate for us because it acknowledges that it is not sexuality or spirituality *per se*, but friendship that determines what the quality of a relational life can be with God and others.

When we can accept and relate to God as our "Almighty Friend," we are no longer left only with the limiting notions of God available to a patriarchal system—i.e., Father, Lord, and King. Nor are we stuck with the alternate prevailing terms of Mother Hen, or the recently reclaimed feminine Holy Spirit or Holy Wisdom that are often rolled out to balance the gender images of God. With Sojourner Truth as a witness we may discover the androgynous, unfettered notion of God as Friend—a notion that can serve to strengthen and encourage the quality of all of our intimate and personal relationships as well as our broader social connectedness.

Some characteristics that may prove useful for understanding God as Friend are mutuality, the urge toward community, and disinterestedness. Mutuality has been suggested by theologians and others who are concerned with how God is affected by humankind and vice versa. One feminist theologian describes it in this way:

> Mutuality is that quality of the otherness of God which is really God's oneness with us. To characterize otherness as mutuality is to say that God can only be understood in human terms, but that very understanding is affected by our belief in God. In short, mutuality means that our relationship with God is freely chosen on both sides (unlike family or government images like Father and Lord in which the relationships are not necessarily intentional and gratuitous).[22]

A related characteristic of mature friendships, i.e., a sense of and need for communality, is an essential quality of the Christian and triune God. The idea of the reign of God, the gathering of all that is into a harmonious community, is another way of describing the God-human cooperation that results in salvation and liberation. Jesus is the Force in Christianity, the Friend whose relationship with us is manifested in our being part of the Christian community of God. Our membership is authenticated, as it was in Sojourner Truth's case, by the works of love and justice that we embrace. This is not the pietistic, "What a friend I have in Jesus." Rather, it is the lived experience we have of a historical group of friends. Jesus's friendships with his immediate community of women and men disciples are a model for our contemporary Christian life. This is the community that derives its identity from the laying down of life for friends. We can conclude that the missionary vocation that springs forth from Christianity is in fact a call and an invitation for Black women and men in particular to go forth in ministry and mutuality together to make friends with all people all over the world.

The sexist and spiritualistic dualisms previously discussed would have us believe that "the world, the flesh, and the devil" are a collective evil that militates against our enjoyment of any meaningful relationships. However, when we begin to recognize and respect one another as embodied persons with a body-soul unity, and when we begin to see the world not as some grimy abstraction but as the clean and earthly clay from which we were created, then a final characteristic of a theology of friendship can come into play. Other-centeredness, disinterestedness, or a willingness and desire to place others ahead of our own personal ambition, is the quality of relationality that is essential to making the love expressed between Black women and men a reflection of God's love for us and others. In this world when a philosophy of "make way for me first" is so prevalent, other-directedness as an aspect of the theology of friendship can help us to see how the world is really oriented not just for our individual pleasure but for our collective future. The pleasure of a few cannot be allowed to determine the future of everyone, or it will soon become no future for anyone. While self-centeredness and narcissism remain the fashionable norm regulating the self and larger society (including our governmental policies and positions on nuclear disarmament and over-involvement in Third World nations' political liberation decisions), we must work at expressing a currently unfashionable praxis of Black love.

> While love is unfashionable
> let us live
> unfashionably.
> Seeing the world
> a complex ball
> in small hands;
> love our blackest garment.

Let us be poor
in all but truth, and courage
handed down
by the old
Spirits.
Let us be intimate with
ancestral ghosts
and music
of the undead.
While love is dangerous
let us walk bareheaded
beside the Great River.
let us gather blossoms
under fire.[23]

NOTES

1. For an excellent theological treatment of the unique relationship between the two institutions of the Black family and the Black church, see J. Deotis Roberts, *Roots of a Black Future: Family and Church* (Philadelphia: Westminster Press, 1980). See also Andrew Billingsley, *Black Families in White America* (Englewood Cliffs, NJ: Prentice-Hall, 1968) and Herbert G. Gutman, *The Black Family in Slavery and Freedom, 1750–1925* (New York: Pantheon, 1976) for extensive documentary examinations of this issue.

2. Michelle Wallace, *Black Macho and The Myth of Superwoman* (New York: Dial Press, 1979), 13.

3. See J. Deotis Roberts, *A Black Political Theology* (Philadelphia: Westminster Press, 1974), for further explanation of the reign of God as both a theological and political reality.

4. Jacquelyn Grant, "Black Theology and the Black Woman," in *Black Theology: A Documentary History, 1966–1979,* ed. Gayraud Wilmore and James Cone (Maryknoll: Orbis, 1979), 423.

5. See Wade Nobles's "African–American Family Life," in *Black Families,* ed. Harriet Pipes McAdoo (Beverly Hills, CA: Sage Publications, 1981), 77–86.

6. See Gutman's *The Black Family in Slavery and Freedom, 1750–1925,* 273–84 for fuller discussion of Black slave marriage rituals. "Jumping the broomstick" served as the most common practice to transform a "free" slave union into a legitimate and respected slave marriage. "Marrying in blankets" referred to the ritual by which a slave woman brought her blanket or bedroll to place beside that of her intended husband to signify their intent to share life and love together as a committed couple. In a note Gutman records that this simply symbolic action so disturbed Yankee missionaries that they even imposed "severe strictures" on South Carolina slaves "marrying in blankets."

7. See Herbert G. Gutman as cited in Edward P. Wimberly, *Pastoral Counseling and Spiritual Values: A Black Point of View* (Nashville: Abingdon, 1982), 62.

8. Grant, "Black Theology and The Black Woman," 422.

9. Grant, "Black Theology and The Black Woman," 422.

10. James B. Nelson has made extensive use of the concepts of "sexist and spiritualistic dualism" in *Embodiment: An Approach to Sexuality and Christian Theology* (New York: Pilgrim Press, 1976). See especially Chapter Three. I have attempted to turn his categories into explicit reflection on Black sexual experience.

11. See John Mbiti, *The Prayers of African Religion* (New York: Orbis, 1975) and *Concepts of God in Africa* (London: SPCK, 1970) for further connections made on the nexus between Black spirituality and an integral world-view.

12. See Rosemary Radford Ruether, *New Women, New Earth: Sexist Ideologies and Human Liberation* (New York: Seabury, 1975), Chapter Five.

13. Grant, "Black Theology and The Black Woman," 422.

14. Eldridge Cleaver, as quoted by Robert Bellah in *The Broken Covenant: American Civil Religion in Time of Trial* (New York: Seabury, 1975), 105.

15. See John Mbiti, *African Religion and Philosophy* (Garden City, NY: Anchor Press, 1969), for additional emphasis on the integration of African lifestyles and value systems: epistemology and axiology.

16. Gayraud S. Wilmore, *Black Religion and Black Racialism* (Garden City, NY; Anchor Press, 1973), 197.

17. Aylward Shorter, ed., *African Christian Spirituality* (Maryknoll: Orbis, 1978), 47.

18. James H. Evans Jr., "Black Theology and Black Feminism," *The Journal of Religious Thought* 38 (Spring–Summer, 1982), 52.

19. Jeanne Noble, *Beautiful Are The Souls of My Black Sisters* (New York: Prentice-Hall, 1978), 343.

20. Sojourner Truth, as quoted by Olive Gilbert in *Narrative of Sojourner Truth* (Chicago: Johnson Publishing Company, 1970), 46–48.

21. Gilbert, *Narrative of Sojourner Truth*, 43. The *Narrative* also relates Sojourner's affection for her friend Jesus in detail, 48–52, 119–22, and elsewhere.

22. Mary E. Hunt, ". . . A Feminist Theology of Friendship," in *A Challenge to Love*, ed. Robert Nugent (New York: Crossroads, 1983), 153.

23. Alice Walker, "While Love is Unfashionable," in *Revolutionary Petunias and Other Poems* (New York: Harcourt, Brace, Jovanovich, 1972), 68. In an interview the author indicates that this poem was written during the period of her marriage to a white man and while they lived in a southern state with laws against miscegenation. I have used the same poem to encapsulate the difficulties and devotion entailed in the love expressed by Black women and men for each other. Although the applications of the poem may differ, the larger context in which Walker explains her Black feminist freedom to love in her own fashion and with whom she chooses does not appear to be violated.

Chapter 20

Anarchic Thinking: Breaking the Hold of Monotheistic Ideology on Feminist Philosophy

Gail Stenstad

Historically, the institutions of domination have established themselves by destroying community. . . . We must be intimately concerned with preserving and creating community (Starhawk, 97).

The constant calls for unity and homogenization in the Western world derive from our long-standing ideology of monotheism . . . monotheism is a political and psychological ideology as well as a religious one (Adler, 24).

*A*nd, I would add, monotheism is also a philosophical ideology. I want to begin by taking the words of two pagans seriously and to suggest that they have important implications for feminist philosophy. What happens if we hold monotheistic ideology in question not only in regard to religion, but in regard to our doing of philosophy in other areas as well?

We have become well aware of the ways in which patriarchal institutions and practices have isolated women and kept them divided from one another. Feminists are not likely to fall into the trap of viewing other women as competitors for men. We are trying to bridge the barriers of race and class. The notion of community among women *as women* has become thinkable. But we may have fallen into another trap: that of confusing unity and homogenization with community.

Feminist philosophy has, over the years, been primarily concerned with theory-building. The practice of theory-building presupposes some philosophical notions that serve to validate the contents of theories: truth, reality and objectivity. A theory seeks to give an objectively true account of the domain of reality with which it is concerned. The best theory is that which most closely approximates the

Source: Part of the material in this chapter first appeared in *Hypatia* 3, 2 (Summer 1988): 87–100. Copyright © 1988 by Gail Stenstad. Reprinted with permission.

true and the real. The root assumption is that there really *is* one truth, one reality, and that it is the business of philosophy to give an account of it. The rider is that it is our responsibility to conform our lives to it. The true. Goodness as conformity to the true. Conformity: sameness. God the father. God the son and his priests. All the same. Women: those who are defined in terms of privation (lack of a penis). Difference as lack. Lacking: truth, reality, goodness. Now, we do not feel our difference from men as a lack. But what about our differences from each other? I would suggest that if we persist in theory-building, we risk doing to each other what the patriarchs have tried to do to us.

It has been pointed out by feminists who are women of color that the prominent feminist theories (whether liberal, radical, or socialist) speak primarily from and to the experience of white, middle-class women. If, in our quite understandable desire for a viable political strategy, we fall for the assumption that such strategy requires *a* theoretical base, we silence the voices of and trivialize the experiences of the majority of our sisters. Also, with the exception of some of the radical theorists (such as Mary Daly), theorists tend to either ignore the women's spirituality movement, or castigate it as an escapist diversion from (political) realities. And what about cleaning women, waitresses, and farm laborers: where do they find a voice within any of our theories? Adherence to theory results in the creation of in-groups and out-groups (those who "see the truth" and those who do not). Then the divisions and lack of community become issues in themselves, and we think, "if only we could devise the ultimate feminist theory, the one on which we could all agree." Which amounts to saying, "if only we were all the same." I would suggest that the root of the problem is our adherence to the assumptions that underly theory-building. Feminists in the 1980s have begun to question such assumptions. For example, feminists working in science and the philosophy of science have begun to call the assumption of pure objectivity in research into question. I would suggest that we need to question these assumptions even more radically.

We need to do much more than confront patriarchal thinking in its own terms and by its own rules. We also need to think in ways that deliberately break the rules, ways that deny to patriarchy the right to set a standard for feminist thinking. Why should we, in our resistance to patriarchy and our attempt to create something different from it, continue to echo some of its most fundamental presuppositions (that there is *a* truth, *a* reality, *the* good, etc.)? One of the most subversive things feminists can do is to think anarchically and then to speak and act from this thinking. Anarchic, unruled, thinking is atheoretical thinking; that is, it is thinking that does not work from, posit, or yield objective distance, supra-historical truth, hierarchical orderings, or a unitary reality. It is thinking that has "renounced the claim to a binding doctrine," accepting no one ultimate referent on which such a doctrine could be based (Heidegger 1971, 185). Thus it is open to a multiplicity of meanings, interpretations, styles and possibilities.

In some ways the difference between theoretical thinking and anarchic thinking is analogous to the difference between monotheism and polytheism. Theoretical thinking and monotheism both tend toward "the one." Monotheism, obviously, is oriented toward one god; historically, many monotheistic religions have also been very concerned with one-ness in doctrine, with arriving at doctrine that can be taken to be the only true or correct one. "One lord, one faith, one baptism." This sort of focus creates an in-group and an out-group: the saved and the damned. While none but the most rigid theorists would go so far in demarcating an in-group and an out-group, accusations of "incorrectness" have been used to silence disagreement. Further, in its very structure, any claim to possess *the* truth, or *the* correct account of reality or the good, creates an out-group, whether we like it or not. The out-group is all those whose truth or reality or values are different from those posited in the theory. As Margot Adler has pointed out, polytheism has room to include a monotheistic perspective (though the reverse is not the case). A belief in many gods, or in many possibilities of sacred manifestation, can allow for an individual's preference for any one (or more) of those manifestations (Adler, viii). Likewise, anarchic thinking does not abandon or exclude or negate the insights achieved by theoretical thinking, but rather demotes "the theory" to a situational analysis, useful and accurate within limits clearly demarcated in each case. Other, very different analyses, based on other women's situations and experiences, are not ruled out.

How can we think anarchically? What sets anarchic thinking in motion, and what keeps it moving? What are some of the important elements of the actual practice of anarchic thinking? These are the questions I need to address next.

What sets anarchic thinking in motion? There are no limiting rules for what is worthy of thought. The traditional distinction between passion and reason, with only the latter assigned to the realm of "real thinking", is not operative here.

> Let's never give ourselves orders, commands, or prohibitions. Let our imperatives be only appeals to move, to be moved, together (Irigaray 1985b, 217).

Anything that deeply concerns us, touches us in mind and heart, sparks thinking. It might be something as particular as one sentence heard or read, or as general as wonder in the face of life. It might be the bruises on the face of a battered woman, or the nearly incomprehensible prospect of nuclear annihilation. It could be some oppressive situation calling for action, or the success of an act of resistance to oppression. It might be the touch of a hand or the sound of a voice.

Then what? Once we get underway in anarchic thinking, what moves it along? One of the main things that keeps thinking moving is the play of unresolved tension. The important elements or moments of anarchic thinking all seem to act to maintain such tension, and thus to keep anarchic thinking fluid, always in motion, always on the way. Such fluidity serves as well to maintain openness to possibilities that would otherwise remain closed. Persistence in questioning, working and playing with ambiguities, being alert for the presence of the strange within the familiar, and allowing for concealment or unclarity in the midst of disclosure are four elements of anarchic thinking that stand out as particularly significant in this respect.

Persistence in questioning keeps anarchic thinking moving. As feminists, we are questioning the authority of patriarchal structures, institutions and practices. The tidiest and most comprehensive theories, the most self-evident presuppositions, solid truths, and hard facts become questionable. Hairline cracks open up into which we can insert our questions. These questions and our thoughtful responses engender further questions. That is, there is a great deal of caution about letting any of our own "answers" stand unquestioned. Since we are not looking for a theoretical resolution of this question-and-response tension, thinking remains in motion.

We might ask ourselves: how do we view the language we think about and with?

> Words are not terms, and thus are not like buckets and kegs from which we can scoop a content that is there. Words are wellsprings that are found and dug up in the telling (Heidegger 1968, 130).

Anarchic thinking welcomes the ambiguities, the multiplicity of meanings, of the words we encounter and use. Anarchic thinking embraces multiple interpretations of texts. The tensions that arise from such ambiguity and multiplicity serve to keep thinking moving.

Another of the tensions that keeps anarchic thinking moving and opens up new possibilities is the tension between the familiar and the strange or uncanny. Theory-building seeks, in a sense, to make the strange familiar, to tame it and place it in its proper slot in the totality. Anarchic thinking, on the other hand, takes note of the previously unnoticed or unheeded strangeness in what is familiar. Feminists are already acquainted with this making-strange in the works of, for example, Mary Daly, Luce Irigaray, and Susan Griffin. Daly has made some of the most familiar, taken-for-granted presuppositions and activities of patriarchy appear to us as something strange or even bizarre. I will discuss Griffin and Irigaray in more detail below.

The effect of this making-strange is to decenter the familiar, the taken-for-granted, the true, the real, etc. The boundaries set for our thinking by familiarity are transgressed. The prevously unthinkable becomes thinkable. Anarchic thinking is boundary thinking, pushing at the very boundaries of the thinkable, stretching them, rearranging them, breaking them. The practice of thinking at the boundary transforms our thinking; it transforms *us*. When a boundary or limit is seen for what it is, it is loosened; its power to limit is subverted. The transformative experience of anarchic thinking is perhaps one of its most subversive effects. It is a powerful way to clear out lingering internalizations of patriarchal presuppositions. This clears the way, as well, for us to think creatively.

Susan Griffin's *Woman and Nature* serves as a powerful example of this transformative boundary-thinking. *Woman and Nature* is not a theoretical work. Some of the key movements in the text, the movement from dis-membering to re-membering and the closely intertwined movement from silence to speech, serve as a powerful demonstration of the practice of anarchic thinking and the transformative experience which accompanies it.

The book begins by quoting or paraphrasing the voices of the philosophers, the theologians, the scientists, the engineers, the technicians. These voices (the voices of patriarchy, echoing and re-echoing each other) are all very, very familiar. Plato, Aristotle, Aquinas, Bacon, Descartes, Kant, and Schopenhauer. Copernicus, Kepler, Newton, Boyle, and Bohr. The *Malleus Malleficarum*. Pavlov and Freud. The foresters, dairymen, and doctors. All speaking from an ever-increasing objective distance, analyzing, ordering, establishing hierarchies (in which we again and again find ourselves at the bottom), proclaiming the truth, defining reality, dividing the real into useful layers and manageable bits. Listen to Griffin:

> Separation. The clean from the unclean . . . The changing from the sacred. Death from the city. Wilderness from the city. The cemetery. The Garden. The Zoological Garden. The ghetto. The ghetto of Jews. The ghetto of moors. The quarter of prostitutes. The ghetto of blacks. The neighborhood of lesbians. The prison. The witchhouse. The underworld. The underground. The sewer. Space divided. The inch. The foot. The mile. The boundary. The skin of the sea otter . . . from the sea otter . . . the tusk of the elephant . . . from the elephant . . . the pelt of the fox . . . from the fox . . . the weed from the flower, the metal from the mountains, uranium from the metal, plutonium from uranium, the electron from the atom . . . energy splitting, the chromosome split, spirit burned from flesh, desire devastated from the earth. (95–8)

As we experience the violence of the tradition with which we are familiar, as we experience the numbing into fearful silence of women's voices down through time, the familiar becomes very, very strange.

We open our mouths. We try to speak. We try to remember (44).

We question and question and question. We notice ambiguities. We ponder alternate interpretations of the familiar words. We begin to speak with each other.

. . . what is buried emerges . . . What is unearthed is stunning, the one we were seeking . . . is ourselves (160).
We are flesh, we breathe. . . . We speak (46). The time of our silence is over . . . we do not deny our voices (174–5).

The transformative experience of reading and thinking along with Susan Griffin does not yield some one thought or way of thinking or voice but rather, as she said, *voices*, many voices, all of our voices, however similar or different they may be. Since this thinking is atheoretical, it will not fall into the trap of replacing patriarchal truth and reality with some unitary truth or reality of our own. Anarchic thinking, on the contrary, empowers a multiplicity of strong feminist voices. The speaking (or writing) that is empowered by anarchic thinking gives voice to the movement of the thinking and not the new possibilities that arise along the way. Our own transformative experience in reading (or hearing) and thinking along with such a voice provokes us to continue the movement of thinking *in our own ways* and to give voice to the new possibilities we encounter and create.

Thus far I have characterized the practice of anarchic thinking as calling for persistence in questioning, openness to ambiguity and multiple interpretations, and attentiveness to the strange-within-the-familiar. As exemplified in Griffin's work, such thinking decenters the familiar, the taken-for-granted, the "true" and the "real." It stretches, rearranges and breaks the boundaries of the thinkable—the thinkable as delimited by the kinds of thinking to which patriarchal institutions give their seal of approval. In so doing, it clears the way for the possibility of creative thinking, of thinking something genuinely different. Those who attempt to think differently, creatively, and to communicate this thinking to others, however, encounter another boundary or barrier: our expectations of language itself. We expect language to disclose something clearly. When we encounter language (whether our own or another's) that seems unclear, that seems to conceal as much as it discloses, we tend to resist or even reject it. It may be helpful here to consider that such expectations of language are linked to traditional, rule-bound thinking. Analysis wants to divide, define, clarify, and master its material. Instrumental rationality takes this further, using such analysis for the purpose of control, of power-over.

In creative feminist thinking, this traditional, rule-bound thinking may run up against something that is opaque to it, something resistant to its penetration, something incalculable and elusive. For example, the possibility of "speaking as (a) woman," as it is explored by Irigaray, is *deliberately* presented as something opaque to traditional modes of thinking. If we are bound to such modes of thinking, we would see Irigaray's "woman's voice" as something irrational, to be rejected out of hand, or as an obstacle to be overcome, to be forcibly penetrated and made clear and mastered. I would suggest that anarchic thinking instead allows for opacity and for language that conceals as it reveals. One thing that the self-concealing quality of such language creates is a shelter from patriarchal and/or instrumental and/or analytic violation. But this somewhat defensive move is only one (and perhaps a lesser) thing that occurs. The other is the way in which its elusiveness actually makes a place for, and *makes way* for the opening up of creative possibilities.

To see how anarchic thinking can help us think these creative possibilities, let us take a closer (though necessarily very brief) look at what Irigaray is trying to accomplish.

> [Whatever we attempt to say], in order to be interpreted, [has] to pass through the master discourse: the one that prescribes ... [i.e.,] the discourse on discourses, philosophical discourse. . . . But this philosophical mastery . . . cannot simply be approached head-on, nor simply within the realm of the philosophical. Thus it was necessary to deploy other languages . . . so that something of the feminine as the limit of the philosophical might be heard (Irigaray 1985b, 149–150).

We cannot simply use the logical and analytical tools of philosophy to break the limits of philosophical discourse, the master discourse. So Irigaray has deployed two other strategies. The first, which places us *at* the limit, is transformative mimesis, a repetition of the master discourse that evokes the oppressiveness of what is said (and has been said, over and over and over); the familiar discourse becomes strange, alienating, and perhaps optional. We have already encounterd a similar transformative move in Griffin. To attempt to go *beyond* the limit, Irigaray explores the possibility of "speaking as (a) woman".

The first question that arises in this attempt is: what is this (word) "woman"? We know what "woman" has been in the master discourse and we know as well how far it is from what we might say of ourselves. But what shall we say of ourselves? To say "woman is _____" (fill in the blank) is to acquiesce to the syntax and presuppositions of the master discourse. This syntax allows us to fill in the blank with: a being, entity, subject, object, proper name, concept, formal identity, or intelligible ideality, i.e., something formulated, formed, fixed, finished, complete. In the master discourse, if "woman" is none of these things, then "she" is simply . . . a blank, a nothing. We know we are not simply nothing. Yet we cannot, according to Irigaray, "fill in the blank" in the master discourse.

> One woman + one woman + one woman will never add up to some generic entity: woman (1985a, 230).

Neither blank, nor definite and finished, "woman" is multiple, ambiguous, indefinite, unfinished, something not fixable within the master grid (1985b, 156; 1985a 229–230).

When we then go on to explore the creative possibility of *"speaking as (a) woman"*, we are thus already speaking from a place of multiplicity and indefiniteness. Therefore, says Irigaray,

> . . . there is simply no way I can give an account of "speaking (as) woman"; it is spoken, but not in metalanguage (1985b 134).

No metalanguage, no rules of syntax: no *proper* meanings, *proper* names, *proper* attribution, etc. Yet, it is spoken. We have all heard it, if only seldom, in the words of some of our poets (Piercy, Rich, Shange and others). Most philosophers would ask, here, can a speaking for which there is no metalanguage be thinkable? The hidden agenda in this question is that (1) "thinkable" means philosophically thinkable, in the traditional manner, and that (2) something that is not "thinkable" in this sense should not be used in doing philosophy. I would reject the notion that thinking is restricted to what the tradition has allowed it to be, and suggest that *to hear*, in this context, is *to think*. It is, as Mary Daly put it, to "hear forth new words" (Daly, 414).

> [These words are] inaudible for whoever listens to them with ready-made grids, with a fully elaborated code in hand. . . . One would have to listen with another ear, as if hearing another meaning always in the process of weaving itself, of embracing itself with words, but also getting rid of words in order not to become fixed, congealed in them. For if "she" says something, it is not, it is already no longer identical with what she means. What she says is no longer identical with anything, moreover; rather, it is contiguous. It touches (upon) (Irigaray 1985b, 29).

As the words are woven together, arising to disclose something, they are also, at once, withdrawing. There is no self-identity, no pure disclosure. The demand for a pure disclosure is a demand of the master discourse.

Anarchic thinking allows us to hear/think words that are not identical with but are, rather, contiguous with their meaning, words that touch (upon) their meaning, fluidly. In this context, "I hear" is not "I see" but "I am touched". I hear words that draw near and slip away, intimately, yielding only intimations. These intimations spark my desire to draw nearer, to listen . . . to listen not only to the reticence of what is held back, but also for what might arise. I listen for the words of she who attempts to "speak as (a) woman", whoever she may be. . . .

Breaking the hold of monotheistic ideology on feminist philosophy, anarchic thinking shapes a sheltering place for attentiveness and response to the elusiveness of voices other than those allowed for within the master discourse. It makes the master discourse's demand for a pure and conceptually analyzable disclosure optional. Anarchic thinking opens up a space for an *other* thinking, and an *other* speaking, where what has not been sayable can be said . . . and thought, without violation.

REFERENCES

Adler, Margot. 1986. *Drawing Down the Moon*. Boston: Beacon Press.

Daly, Mary. 1978. *Gyn/Ecology*. Boston: Beacon Press.

Griffin, Susan. 1978. *Woman and Nature: The Roaring Inside Her*. New York: Harper & Row.

Heidegger, Martin. 1971. *Poetry, Language, Thought*. Translated by Albert Hofstadter. New York: Harper Colophon Books.

———. 1968. *What Is Called Thinking?* Translated by J. Glenn Gray. New York: Harper Colophon Books.

Irigaray, Luce. 1985a. *Speculum of the Other Woman*. Translated by Gillian C. Gill. Ithaca: Cornell University Press.

———. 1985b. *This Sex Which Is Not One*. Translated by Catherine Porter. Ithaca: Cornell University Press.

McWhorter, LaDelle. 1987. "Thinking Through the Metaphysics of the Real." Unpublished paper.

Starhawk. 1982. *Dreaming the Dark*. Boston: Beacon Press.

List of Contributors

Jeffner Allen is associate professor of philosophy at SUNY Binghamton. She is co-editor of *The Thinking Muse: Feminism and Recent French Philosophy*, editor of *Lesbian Philosophies and Cultures*, and author of *Lesbian Philosophy: Explorations*. She is active in the Society for Women in Philosophy and Editor of the SUNY Press Series in Feminist Philosophy.

Judith Butler teaches philosophy at George Washington University. She is the author of *Subjects of Desire: Hegelian Reflections in Twentieth Century France* (1987) and is completing a manuscript on the politics of gender identity theory to be published in 1989. She has written articles in continental philosophy, French feminism, and poststructuralist theory.

Lorraine Code is a Canada Research Fellow with the Department of Philosophy and the Women's Studies Research Group at York University. In addition to numerous articles in philosophy and in feminist theory, she is the author of *Epistemic Responsibility* (1987) and co-editor of *Feminist Perspectives: Philosophical Essays on Minds and Morals* (1988) and of *Changing Patterns: Women in Canada* (1988). Her manuscript on knowledge and gender is scheduled for completion in 1989.

Toinette M. Eugene is provost and associate professor of education, society, and Black church studies at Colgate Rochester Divinity School-Bexley Hall-Crozer Theological Seminary in Rochester, NY. She has published a variety of articles in educational and theological journals, and is currently completing *Sometimes I Feel Like a Motherless Child: A Black Feminist Ethic of Care*.

Ann Ferguson is a feminist, lesbian, and leftist philosopher whose book *Blood at the Root: Motherhood, Sexuality, and Male Dominance* (1989: Unwin Hyman/Pandora Press) grounds male dominance in historical modes of sex/affective reproduction. She is also working on a book of essays on androgyny, racism, sexism and sexuality, and lesbian culture. Ferguson is professor of philosophy and women's studies at the University of Massachusetts, Amherst.

Marilyn Frye teaches women's studies and philosophy at Michigan State University. She is the author of *The Politics of Reality* and numerous papers in feminist philosophy. She works and writes to further lesbian feminist community, culture and politics.

Ann Garry is professor of philosophy at California State University, Los Angeles. Her publications are in feminist philosophy, philosophical method, philosophy of mind, and applied ethics. She is an associate editor of *Hypatia: A Journal of Feminist Philosophy* and has long been active in the Society for Women in Philosophy.

Sandra Harding is professor of philosophy and director of women's studies at the University of Delaware. She is the author of many articles and of *The Science Question in Feminism* (1986), which won the 1987 Jessie Bernard Award of the American Sociological Association. She is the editor of *Can Theories be Refuted* (1976) and *Feminism and Methodology: Social Science Issues* (1987), and co-editor with Merrill Hintikka of *Discovering Reality: Feminist Perspectives on Epistemology, Metaphysics, Methodology, and Philosophy of Science* (1983), and with Jean O'Barr of *Sex and Scientific Inquiry* (1987).

Hilde Hein is associate professor of philosophy at Holy Cross College in Worcester, MA. Her book, *Exploring the Exploratorium*, is an analytical history and museum study. She teaches aesthetics and philosophy of biology, as well as feminist theory.

Alison M. Jaggar is Obed J. Wilson Professor of Ethics and professor of philosophy at the University of Cincinnati. Her books include: *Feminist Frameworks*, co-edited with Paula Rothenberg (1974), *Feminist Politics and Human Nature* (1983) and *Gender/Body/ Knowledge: Feminist Reconstructions of Being and Knowing*, co-edited with Susan R. Bordo (1989). Jaggar was a founding member of the Society for Women in Philosophy, serves on the editorial board of several journals, and chairs the American Philosophical Association Committee on the Status of Women.

Evelyn Fox Keller is professor of rhetoric, women's studies, and the history of science at University of California, Berkeley. She has published numerous articles in theoretical physics, molecular biology, mathematical biology, and, more recently, in the history, philosophy, and sociology of science. She is the author of *Reflections on Gender and Science* (1985) and *A Feeling for the Organism: The Life and Work of Barbara McClintock* (1983).

Genevieve Lloyd is professor and head of the School of Philosophy at the University of New South Wales in Sydney, Australia. She is the author of *The Man of Reason: "Male" and "Female" in Western Philosophy* (1984) and of numerous scholarly articles in such journals as *Australasian Journal of Philosophy, Mind, Philosophy, Metaphilosophy*, and *Philosophy and Literature*.

Helen Longino is associate professor of philosophy at Mills College in Oakland, CA. She is the author of the forthcoming *Science as Social Knowledge* and of numerous articles in philosophy of science and feminism and science. She is also the co-editor with Valerie Miner of *Competition: A Feminist Taboo?* (1987), and an associate editor of *Hypatia: A Journal of Feminist Philosophy.*

María C. Lugones identifies herself as a U.S. Latina, a brown woman, Raza. She is a community organizer among Hispanos in the North of Nuevo Mejico and a philosopher who teaches her craft at Carleton College. What moves her in this life is the creation of a feminist theory that is truly pluralistic.

Janice Moulton was a visiting professor of linguistics at Huazhong Shifan University in Wuhan, China in 1986–87. She is a research associate at Smith College, working (with G. M. Robinson) on *Scaling the Dragon*, a tale of their adventures as minorities in the People's Republic of China. She has published *The Guidebook for Publishing Philosophy* (with M. Yudkin), *Ethical Problems in Higher Education* (with G. M. Robinson), and *The Organization of Language* (with G. M. Robinson).

Andrea Nye teaches philosophy at the University of Wisconsin–Whitewater. Her published papers have been in the areas of philosophy of language and French feminism. She is the author of *Feminist Theories and the Philosophies of Man* (1988). She is working on a book of feminist readings in the History of Logic.

Marilyn Pearsall is a lecturer at San Diego State University, where she has taught philosophy and women's studies. She has been on the faculty of San Jose State University, Eastern Michigan University, and Spelman College. She is the editor of *Woman and Values: Readings in Recent Feminist Philosophy* (1986) and the co-editor of *The Female Experience* (1974).

Susan Sherwin teaches philosophy and women's studies at Dalhousie University. Her academic interests are in the area of feminist theory, feminist ethics, and medical ethics and she continues to wrestle with the sense of schizophrenia she finds inherent in being an academic feminist. She is working on a book on feminist medical ethics.

Elizabeth V. Spelman is associate professor of philosophy at Smith College. Among her most recent publications are "Passion for Justice" (with Martha Minow) and *Inessential Woman: Problems of Exclusion in Feminist Thought* (1988).

Gail Stenstad teaches philosophy at Vanderbilt University and is the director of the graduate program in women's studies of the International Institute for Advanced Studies. Her areas of interest are contemporary continental philosophy and environmental ethics.

Caroline Whitbeck is a philosopher of science, technology, and medicine in MIT's Center for Technology and Policy and the Department of Mechanical Engineering. Her current research centers on medical technology, especially technology used in procreation, and engineering ethics. She is completing a book, *Designing a Life, the Ethical Concerns of Engineering Students.*

Index

Abortion, 15–16, 20, 167–8
Abuse
  racism and, 277
Acceptability, criteria of, 28–9
Accountability, in science, 213
Acculturation, 254–5
Activism
  social, 28–9
Activities
  women's, 88, 194–6
  See also "Women's work"
Adam, 206–97, 299–300
Adversary method, 5–20, 29, 30, 170
Adversary paradigm, 2, 9–20
  defects of, 10–11
Affirmative action, 95
Aggression, 2, 29, 54, 97, 182–4
  male, 302–3
  negative connotations of, 5–6
  success and, 5–20
Agon, 54, 289
Altruism, 303
Amazons, 38–40, 42
Ambiguity, 285, 334, 336
  in language, 225
Ambivalence, 43
Analogy
  of self to other, 62–3, 68
Androcentricity, 189, 191–4
  bias in science, 175–8
  of traditional philosophy, xiii, xv
Anger, 145–6, 263–73
  appropriateness of, 266, 270
  in Blacks, 273
  denial of, 270
  logic of, 252, 266–7
  politics of, 272
  v. rage, 271
  women and, 264
Aristotle, 56–7, 87, 246, 265, 268, 270–2, 271, 289
  on anger, 263
  on procreation, 295–7
Aspect Theory, 49, 93–110
Assimilation, 45, 287

Assumptions, 10, 28
  about sex, 86
  criticism of, 198
  emotion and, 138
  examination of, 31–2
  in metaphysics, 14
  sexist, 210
  value-laden, 207
Attention, 91–2
Attraction, 54
Augustine, 25, 112
Authenticity
  of self, 102, 105
Authority, 5, 87, 123
  lack of in women, 295
  of women, 90–1
Autonomy, 100, 119, 121, 300, 308
  objectivity and, 179–80
  psychic, 181

Beauvoir, Simone de, 48, 251–62, 299
Becoming, 255–7, 261
  cessation of, 262
Being at ease, 283–6
Besoulment, 295, 301
Bias, 27–8
  androcentric, 54, 59, 193, 210
  androcentric, in science, 175–8
  masculine, 208
  in philosophy, xiv
  social, 191–4
Black church, 313–23
Black love, 314–21, 324–5, 328
Black sexuality, 313–30
Black spirituality, 313–30
Black theology, 318–19
Body, gendering of, 253–62

Childbirth, 299–300
Childrearing, 72–3, 98, 104, 165
  gender-dichotomous, 101
Choice, 91
Christian doctrine
  women and, 296
Church, Black, 313–23

Cixous, Hélène, 233, 237–8, 240–2
Claims, 10–11, 189
  positive, 28
  programmatic, 11
  universal, 198
Classification, 238
Cognition, 160
  of emotion, 133–4
Cognitivism, 265–73
Collective enterprise, 29–30
Collective learning, 31
Community, 305, 309, 331, 332
  Black, 314, 321–2, 327–8
Competence, 5–7, 181–2, 287–8
  aggression and, 7
Competition, 7, 29, 57, 66, 68
Conceptual scheme, 77–9, 83–4, 91–2
Conclusion, 10–11, 17
Conformity, 332
Confrontation, 10–11
Confusion
  anger and, 267
Conquerors, 38–9
Consciousness, 123, 275
  analysis of, 251
  oppositional, 199
  value of, 183
Consciousness-raising, 21, 96, 251
  methodology of, 26–7
Constraint, 307–9
Construction, dominant, 281–2
Contraception, 176
Contradiction, 43
Control, 181–3
Cooperation, 29
Cooperative activity, 70
Counterexample, 9, 10–11, 15–17, 27–8
Creativity, 53, 70
  women's, 63–4
Criticism, 11, 77
  criteria of, 28–9
  by feminists, 33
  goal of, 30
  liberal, 176
  radical, 176
Culture, 63–4
  androcentric, 47
  authority of, 162
  masculist, 53
  projects of, 86

Daly, Mary, 332, 334, 338
Death, 261–2, 299
Debate, 12–13
Deconstruction, 2
Deduction, 8–9, 13–14, 17, 114–15
Dependency, 181
Derrida, Jacques, 41, 235–7, 242–3

Descartes, René, 17, 26–7, 69, 109–10, 114–18, 122–3
Desire, 233–7, 243–5
  auto-erotic, 236
  expression of, 240
  language of, 238
  sexual, 258–60
Determinism, 14, 17–18
  biological, 97
Development, 56–7
  female v. male, 54
  gender, 93
  human, 58
  mutual, 60
  psychological, 58–9
  of women, 59
Dichotomies, 48, 294
  patriarchal, 32, 306
Dichotomous thinking, 32
Difference, 37, 39, 41–5, 97, 332
  gender, 51, 101
  woman as, 38, 40
  among women, 252
Difference Theory, 49, 96–101, 103
Differentiation, 48, 51, 56, 63
Disciplinary boundaries, 158–9
Discipline, 43, 45
Discovery, 39
Disinterestedness, 327–8
Dispassionate investigation
  myth of, 139–42
Dominant groups
  anger and, 267–8
  limits on emotions, 270
Dominant reality, 87
Domination, 55, 68, 211
  by language, 218, 221
  logic of, xiv
  male, 93, 109
  by males in religion, 291
  of nature, 182–3
  psychological meaning of, 181–3, 186
  science and, 179–80
Dualism, 48, 51–3, 62–3, 69
  mind–body, 62
  normative, xiv
  ontological, 54
  philosophical, 293
  racist, 319
  sexist, 318–20, 322
  sexual, 56
  spiritualistic, 319–20, 322
Dualistic ontology, 68
Dumb View, 133–4, 137–8, 151, 265, 268–70

Economic parity, 96
Ecriture féminine, 233, 237

Education
  feminist, 95
  of women, 113, 116
Egoism, 20, 65, 151, 303
  refutation of, 14
Ego psychology, 59
Elenchus, 12–13
Embodiment, 253
Emotion, 120
  as active engagement, 136–7
  analysis of, 270
  appropriateness of, 146–7, 264
  cognitivist accounts of, 133–4
  concept of, 131–8
  in daily life, 44
  in eighteenth century, 125
  epistemic potential of, 147–9
  feeling v., 132–3
  in feminist epistemology, 129–55
  identification of woman with, 110
  intellect v., 116
  as intentional, 132–4
  object of, 266
  "outlaw," 144–7, 149
  personal, 26–7
  politics of, 270
  reason and, 110, 129–31, 264–5, 268
  repression of, 142, 152
  scientific practice and, 140–1
  as social construct, 134–6, 138, 143
  as stereotype, 141–2
  subordinate groups and, 264
  theories of, 252, 265
  universal, 151
  values and, 137–8
  in western epistemology, 129
  women and, 116–17
Empathy, 146–7
Empiricism, feminist, 174, 191–200
Epistemology, 109–72
  changing assumptions and, 33
  ethics and, 157
  feminist, 110, 129–55
  justificatory strategies and, 189–90
  "malestream," 158, 169
  western, 129–31
Equality, 25, 57, 113–14
  language and, 221
Equal Rights Amendment, 232
Erasure, 89
  of women, 78, 85, 87
Essence, 100, 260
  woman as, 43–4
Estrogens, 209
Ethical values, 17
Ethics, 51, 65–8
  changing assumptions and, 33
  epistemology and, 157

  masculine, 102
  pluralism in, 105
  responsibilities view of, 66–7
  rights view of, 65
Evaluation
  objective criteria for, 24
  of philosophy, 10
  procedures in, 18
Eve, 241–2, 244–6, 296–7, 300
Experience, 18, 42, 283
  Black, 314
  common, 22
  continuity and, 166
  dominant conceptual schemes v., 195
  emotion and, 133
  feminist methodology and, 22
  gender-specific, 47, 304
  knowledge and, 164–8
  in learning, 31
  lived, 253
  moral, 169
  personal, 29
  political significance of, 23–4
  theory and, 167
  transformative, 336
  women's, xv–xvi, 2, 48, 52–3, 69, 110, 157–72
Experimentation, 184
  bias in, 176–8

Fact-value distinction, 8
Family, Black, 318
Fear
  anger and, 267
Feeling
  v. emotion, 132–3
Female
  association with non-rational, 112–14
  irrationality and, 129
Female development, 54
Female thought styles, 124
Feminine
  v. feminist, 38, 40–3, 204
Feminism, 190
  approaches to, 30
  Black, 314, 323–5, 330
  French, and philosophy of language, 233–49
  lesbian, 282
  philosophical aspects of, 111
  pluralistic, 275
  postmodernism and, 40–1
  radical, 99
  science and, 175–88
Feminist
  feminine v., 38, 40–3, 204
Feminist aspect theory, 93–110

Feminist criticism
of philosophy, xiv
of science, 175–9
Feminist empiricism, 174, 191–200
Feminist epistemology
emotion in, 129–55
Feminist movement, xiii
See also Women's movement
Feminist theory, xv, 44, 99, 332–3
outlaw emotions and, 145–9
radical, 97
Feminist view
construction of, 54
Freedom, 32, 120
of speech, 246
spiritual, 307–9
Free will, 14, 17–18, 47, 94
Friendship
theology of, 326–8

Gay liberation, 325
Gender, 210
assumptions about, 222
confusion about, 260
development of, 93
dichotomy in, 304–5
division of activity by, 194
dualistic view of, 71
historical idea of, 255
implications of in science, 173
indifferentiation of, 41
morality and, 164–5
neutrality of, 219–32
scientific inquiry and, 184
sex v., 254–5, 259–61
social construction of, 93
Gender difference, 93, 96, 101
assumptions about, 159
Gender identity, 303
theory of, 254–9
Gender preferences, 95
Gender roles, 303
Gender rules, 256–7
Generalizations, 26, 161–2
Gilligan, Carol, 164–8
Goals
gender-defined, 100
God
androgynous, 324, 327
existence of, 14, 17–18
gender images of, 327
Goddess, 291, 298, 305–7
Grammar
transformational, 247
Griffin, Susan, 334–6

"He"
as neutral term, 219–32

Heterosexuality, 81–2, 101, 105
compulsory, 97
for women, 91
Hierarchical theories, 184–5
Homophobia, 143
Homosexuality, 81
effect of androgens on, 209
Honi phenomenon, 138
Hostility, 10
aggression v., 7
to emotion, 139
to feminists, 33
of nonfeminist philosophers, 23
"Human," 225, 227–8
Humanism, 43
Hysteria, 264, 271
female, 163

Ideas
history of, 40
Identification, 63, 290
failure of, 276, 278
love and, 276–80
Identity
cultural, 258
personal, 96–7, 102
Ideology
male-dominated, 1
masculinist, 186
monotheistic, 331–9
Imagination, 32, 122
Imago Dei, 323–4
Incest, 59
Independence, economic, 104
Indeterminism, 14
Individualism, 51–8, 66, 70–3, 119, 121
Inquiry
feminist-inspired, 189–201
feminist scientific, 205
method of, 203
objective, 190
scientific, 209
value-free, 204
Insanity, 271
Insubordination, 263–73
anger as, 270
Intentionality, 211
of emotion, 132–4, 138
of value judgments, 137
Interactionism, 184–5, 213–15
Intercourse, 80–1
Interdependence, 58
Interdisciplinary scholarship, 27–8
Interpretation
of "neutral" language, 227, 229
Interpretive model, 213
Intuition, 114–16, 126–7
reason and, 122–4

Investigation
  dispassionate, 139–42, 147, 152–3
  theoretical, 148–9
Invisibility, 279
Irigaray, Luce, 233, 237, 239–42, 338
Irony, 19
Isomorphism, 115

Joint action, 70, 72
Justificatory strategies, 189–201

Knowledge, 157–72
  acquisition of, 110, 114
  construction of, 133
  emotion and, 140–1, 147–50
  experience and, 157, 164–8, 194
  love and, 129–55
  reason and, 129
  theories of, xv, 14, 109–72, 251
  theory of, 251

Lacan, Jacques, 235–8, 240, 242–4, 247
Language, 18, 64
  biased use of in science, 177
  communication in, 240
  feminine, 242
  gender–neutral, 217, 219–32
  gender–specific, 220, 222–3, 225, 228–31
  logic and, 235
  new use of, 239
  philosophy of, 11, 13, 217–49
  political power of, 244
  political stands and, 221
  poststructuralist analysis of, 237
  power and, 233–5
  reality and, 83
  role of, 243
  sexism in, 1
  women's, 233, 237
Lesbian, 48, 77–92, 101, 210
  definition of, 78–84
  erasure of, 78
Liberation
  of Black women, 318–19
  of practices, 67–8
  social, 191
Lilith, 300
Linear model, 210–12, 215
Linguistics
  feminist, 217–18, 233–4, 242–6
  patriarchal practices of, 217–18
  structural, 246–7
Logic
  authority of, 233–4
  in feminist scholarship, 28
  language and, 235
  power and, 236

Love
  Black, 314–21, 324–5, 328
  as domain of women, 301
  knowledge and, 129–55
  romantic, 135
Loving
  cross-cultural, 275–7

Male chauvinism
  Black, 320
Male development, 54
Male-dominant society, 94–5
Male priority, 221
"Man," 86
Man
  emotion and, 142
"Man"
  as neutral term, 219–32
Manhood
  ideals of, 111
Manipulation, 84, 96
Man of Reason, 111–28
Margin, romance of, 41–2, 45
Marginality, feminist, 242
Marked terms, 223
Marriage
  Black, 317–18, 329
Masculine
  ideal of, 120
  v. universal, 253
Masculinity
  objectivity and, 179–81
  reason and, 111–28
Masculist theory, 63, 71
Masculist tradition, 37
Master–slave relation, 56
Mastery, 181–3
Materiality, 295–300
Matriarchal heritage, 291, 298
Matter
  conceptions of, 207–8
  v. spirit, 300–1, 304
Maturity
  moral, 164, 167–8
Meaning
  changes in, 229–30
  theory of, 225–7, 231
Metaphysics, 47–107
  assumptions in, 14
  changing assumptions and, 33
  feminist, 51–76
  male-centered, 47
  nature of, 126
Methodology, 1–46, 123–4
  of consciousness-raising, 26–7
  feminist, 21–35
  interdisciplinary, 27–8
  philosophical v. feminist, 21–35

theory and, 185
Mind
  matter *v.*, 116
  philosophy of, 251–90
Miscegenation, 330
Misogyny, 25, 32, 81
  in philosophy, xiv
  science and, 140, 204
Modernism, 37–8, 43–5, 192
Monotheism, 331–3
Moral integrity, 53, 64, 67
Morality, 22, 164–5
  caring *v.* rights/justice, 168
  female, 168
  foundation of, 20
Moral maturity, 167–8
Moral principle, 13–14
Mother
  identification with, 278–80
Mother–child relation, 56
Mother–child relationship, 61
Motherhood, 105
Motivation, 84, 90, 245–6
Mutuality, 324, 326–8
  Black, 318–24
Myth
  of dispassionate investigator, 139–42
  ideological function of, 141–3
  of neutral "man," 219–32
  racist, 316–17
  in religion, 291
Mythology
  patriarchal, 300–1

Narrative, 42
Nature
  mastery over, 182–3
  women as, 298–300
Neopositivism
  emotion and, 139
New Right woman, 103–4
Nurturing, 52, 59, 60, 65, 71, 104–5, 149, 293

Objectivity, 190, 196
  ideology of, 179
  masculinity and, 174, 179–81
  in philosophy, 9
  pure, 332
  in science, 173–4, 178
object relations theory, 59, 180–1
Observation
  emotion and, 138
  feminist, 205
  subversive, 145
Oedipal consolidation, 182–3
Ontology, 47–107
  dualistic, 51, 55–8, 64–5, 68
  feminist, 48, 51–76

masculist, 53–5
  of the person, 63–5
Openness, 288
Opposition, 48, 70
  dualistic, 53, 60, 63, 65
  between male and female, 56–7
  self–other, 51, 55–6, 62, 68, 72
  See also Adversary method; Adversary paradigm
Oppression, 146, 160
  of Blacks, 318
  of a group, 94–5
  linguistic practices and, 217
  racial, xv, xvi
  resistance to, 334
  role of language in, 243
  of women, xiii, 59–60, 92, 253
Orgasm, 80–1
Original sin, 296
Other, 256

Paradigm, 8, 9–10
Parasitic Reference, 230–1
Parasitism, 279
Parler-entre-elles, 233, 237, 241
Passions, 118–21, 125, 130, 136, 236
  v. reason, 333
Patriarchal view, 51–3, 71
Patriarchy, 29, 55–8, 62, 292, 298–9, 332, 335
  dichotomies in, 32, 306
  economic priorities of, 98
  models of, 63
  self-worth and, 96
  victory of, 300
  women's experience and, 27
Pedagogy
  feminist, 31
Peers, 71
  relationships among, 58
Penis, 80–1
Perception, 89–91, 122
  arrogant, 276–8, 280, 289–90
  emotion and, 138
  feminist *v.* dominant, 144
  loving, 275–90
  men's, 87
  stereotypes and, 159
  tolerance of, 119
  women's, 86–7
"Person," 228
Personal identity, 96, 102
  theory of, 252
Perspective
  women's, 27
Phallocentricity, 236–7
Phallocratic scheme, 77–8, 80, 84–8, 90–2
Phallogocentrism, 37
Philogyny, 81

Philosophical methodology, 21–35
 approaches to, 31–2
Philosophy
 analytic, 1, 24
 feminist, 31, 69, 331–9
 feminist critique of, xiv
 history of, 11–13, 25
 of language, 217–49
 of mind, 251–90
 rational methods of, 32
 of religion, 291–339
 of science, 173–216
 in situation, 253
 traditional, xiii
 value-free, 9, 18
Plato, 10, 19, 25, 263–4
Playfulness, 275–90
 agonistic sense of, 287–8, 290
Plurality
 of selves, 286
Politics, 63
 of the classroom, 31
 emotion and, 148–9
 feminist, 37–8, 42, 214
 of reality, 48, 77–92
Polytheism, 333
 See also Religion
Pornography, 93
Positivism, 130–3, 148–9
 emotion and, 139–41, 151
 logical, 206–9
Postmodernism, 2–3, 37–8, 43–6
 feminist, 40–1, 174, 198–200
 reform, 37
Poverty
 feminization of, 104
 independence in, 276
Power, 5–6
 female, 305
 language and, 233–5, 246
 logic and, 236
 to name, 218
 personal, 94, 99, 102
 psychological meaning of, 181
 public, of women, 104–5
 reality and, 79
 reason and, 127
 of representation, 40
 science and, 179–80
Power-minority, 16
Practices, 63–4, 67
 feminist, 72
 social, 101–2
 women's, 69–70
Premises, 12, 17–18
Principle
 feminine, 54–5
Problem selection, 193, 206

Procreation, 293, 295, 298
Programmatic claim, 11
Property rights, 16, 55
Psychology
 ego, 59
 philosophical, 251
Punishment, 233, 256

Quest
 metaphysical, 39

Racism, 275, 277, 282, 292, 314–18
 Black mutuality and, 318–24
 visceral, 143
Radicalism, 24
Rage, 264
 v. anger, 271
Rape, 41, 54
Ratiocination, 122–3
Rational discourse
 phallocentric, 236
Rationalism, 52
Rationality, 17, 49, 109–17, 124, 236
 abstract, 37, 44
 contemporary, 126
 instrumental, 197, 337
 male ideal of, 127, 129
 men and, 54
 modern definition of, 130
 in science, 178
Rational Maximizer theory, 49, 94–6,
 99–101, 103–5
Realism, 160–1, 179
Realist tradition, 209
Reality, 70, 79
 creation of, 88–9
 dominant, 85, 87
 feminist theory of, 48
 patriarchal concept of, 48
 phallocratic, 90–2
 politics of, 48, 77–92
 principles of, 53
 theory of, 47
Realization
 mutual, 48, 52, 57, 60–1, 67
Reason, 111–28, 300–1
 disaffection with, 126
 dominant groups and, 264
 emotion and, 129–31, 264–5, 268
 ideals of, 25
 intuition and, 122–4
 knowledge and, 129
 passion v., 333
 religion and, 125
 role of, 109
 in seventeenth century, 114–17
 women's relationship to, 125

Reasoning
　"bad," 12, 15–17
　deductive, 8, 13–14, 17
　inductive, 207
　moral, 13, 16, 101
　philosophy, 9–10
　practical, 165
　scientific, 7–9, 12
　value-free, 29
Reference, 42, 45
Relation
　self–other, 51, 54
Relationships, 66, 68
　affectional, 67
　lived, 64, 67
　occupational, 67
Relativism, 13, 196–7
　cultural, 178
　feminist, 179
Religion
　disempowering of women by, 291
　Goddess, 291, 298, 305–7
　patriarchal, 291
　philosophy of, 291–339
　reason and, 125
　See also Church; God; Monotheism;
　　Polytheism; Theology
Replicability, 139–40
Research, 8, 191
Responsibility, 68, 117, 157–72
　epistemic, 157–8, 160–3
　interpretation and, 166
　moral, 66–7
　in science, 209
　stereotypes and, 159–63
Right to life, 65
Rights
　human, 66
　moral, 67
　property, 55
Rights/justice orientation, 102–3
Rights view of ethics, 65–7
Role
　feminine, 102
　gender, 103
Role model, 98
Romanticism, 52, 125

Sappho, 82–3
Saussure, Ferdinand, 244, 246–7
Scholarship
　feminist, 29–30
　interdisciplinary, 27–8
Science
　"bad," 191, 203, 205, 208, 212
　feminism and, 175–88
　feminist, 203–16

　gender-free, 212
　"good," 203, 205
　history of, 190
　interactionist, 203–4
　misogynist, 104
　objectivity in, 173–4
　philosophy of, 13, 130, 173–216
　social studies of, 178
　value-free, 7, 173–4, 190–1, 205–12
Scientific method, 28, 192–3, 196, 211
Scientific practice, 177
　emotions and, 140–1
　values and, 140–1
Scientific reasoning, 7–9
Scientist
　feminist, 191–3
Self
　aspect theory of, 101–5
　authenticism of, 100–1
　feminist aspect theory of, 93–110
　sense of, 94, 104–5
　theories of, 48, 94
Self-acceptance
　Black, 316
Self-consciousness, 210–11
Self-deception, 266, 269, 271, 278
Self-determination, 210–11, 308
Self-esteem, 98
　women's, 306
Self-integrity, 94
Self-interest, 67, 94, 121
Self-knowledge, 162–3, 266
Self–other relation, 60–2, 64, 68, 71
Self-perception
　male, 294
　stereotypes, 162
Self-realization, 94
Self-reflection
　critical, 179
Self-respect, 266, 268–70
Self-sacrifice, 52
Self-worth, 94–6, 103, 105
Semantics, 234–8, 241, 248
Semantic theory, 13
Semiotics, 247
Sense-data theories, 11
Sentiment, 300
Separate spheres, 301
Separatism, 97, 279
Serpent, 233–49
Servitude, 276, 278
Sex hormones, 209–11
Sexism, xvi, 93, 95, 189, 191–4, 197
　Black, 314
　Black mutuality and, 318–24
　in language, 1
　language and, 220, 222
Sex research, 177

Sexual harassment, 144
Sexuality, 93
  Black, 292, 313–30
  human, 323
  male, 54
  spirituality *v.*, 302
  theology of, 327
Sexual preference, 91
Sexual relations, 80–1
  between women, 82
Sex *v.* gender, 254–5, 259–61
Slavery, 317
  abolition of, 325
Slaves, 55–7, 289
  marriage customs of, 329
Social activism, 28–9
Social construct
  emotion as, 134–6, 138, 143
  woman as, 43–4
Socialization, 6, 26, 93
  for mothering, 98
  sexual, 321
Social policy
  feminist, 95
Socrates, 19, 26
Socratic Method, 12–13, 30
Speech
  power of, 7
  women's, 6
Speech act theory, 235, 247
Spinoza, 118–22, 125
Spirit
  dichotomy of, 293–311
  as immanent, 298–300
  matter and, 294, 297–8, 304
Spirituality
  African, 322
  attribution to women, 294, 302
  Black, 292, 313–30
  domesticated, 300–4
  reconceptualization of, 307–10
  of women, 291–3
Standpoint theory, 194–200, 205
Stereotypes, 110
  emotion and, 141–2
  of morality, 164–5
  racist, 316
  rejection of, 169
  responsibility and, 159–63
  of science, 184
  sex-role, 6
  sexual, 127
  tyranny of, 168
  of women of color, 282–3, 285
  of women's nature, 170
Strategies
  justificatory, 189–201
Structuralism, 245

Structures
  authoritarian, in teaching, 31
Subject, 256
  woman as, 41, 218
Subjectivity, 41, 181
Subordination, xv, 94, 182, 291
Substance, 258
Success, 2
  aggression and, 5–20
Survival, 181–2
Syllogism, 227–8

Teaching, feminist, 30–1
Theologians
  women, 306
Theology
  Black, 318–19
  of friendship, 326–8
  See also Religion
Theory
  difference, 96–9
  feminist, xv, 44, 97, 99, 145–9, 332–3
  feminist aspect, 93–110
  hierarchical, 184–5
  masculist, 71
  of meaning, 225–7, 231
  method and, 185
  moral, 157, 169
  of personhood, 251
  psychoanalytic, 59, 97, 99
  psychological, 53–5
  rational maximizer, 96
  of reality, 47
  reflexivity of, 148
  social difference, 99
  speech act, 235, 247
  standpoint, 194–200, 205
Theory-building, 331–4
Thinking
  anarchic, 292, 331–9
  contradiction in, 102
  epistemological and moral, 166–7
  maternal, 60
Training, 95–6
Truth, Sojourner, 317, 325–8

Underdetermination thesis, 206
Universality, 27–8
Unmarked terms, 223–5, 232

Value
  of feminine skills, 104
  of reason, 130
  of women, xiv
Value-free philosophy, 18
Value-free reasoning, 29
Value-hierarchical thinking, xiv

Values, xv
  constitutive, 206, 212
  contextual, 206–8, 211–12
  emotion and, 137–8
  feminist, 28, 30
  oppressive, 147
  predominant, 143–4
  science and, 7–8, 140–1, 173–4
  women-centered, 97
Violence, 39, 321, 336
Virtue, 53, 113, 306
  as knowledge, 295
Voice
  feminist, xvi
  moral, 98
  passive, 209
  woman's, xvi, 337
  women's, 164, 167

Wedding rituals
  Black, 317, 329
White/Anglo "world," 275–80
Wollstonecraft, Mary, 117
Woman
  acculturation as, 254–5
  inferiority of, 295–6
Woman-identified-woman, 77–8
Woman-loving-woman, 81
Woman's nature, 157, 159

Women
  anger in, 264
  of color, 142, 275–6, 279–80, 332
  as deformed men, 263
  erasure of, 87
  histories of, 40
  marginalization of, 291
  nature of, 170
  as nature, 298–300
  New Right, 103–4
  spirituality and, 293–311
Women's liberation, 325
  philosophy of, 307
Women's movement, 21, 93, 100, 103, 192,
    195
  See also Feminist movement
Women's practices, 52, 68, 69
  liberation of, 53
Women's studies, xv
"Women's work," 58, 95, 194
  value of, 105
Work, men's, 194–5
"World"-traveling, 275–90
World-view, 281
  African, 313, 319, 321, 326
Writing
  feminist, 42–3
  women's, 233, 237–8

Yahweh, 233–46